# CO

# ENCYCLOPEDIA

The Diagram Group

HarperCollins*Publishers*

HarperCollins Publishers
P O Box, Glasgow G4 0NB

A Diagram Book first created by Diagram Visual Information
Limited of 195 Kentish Town Road, London NW5 8SY

With special thanks to Christopher Riches for his tireless
efforts in bringing this book to fruition

First published 1993

Reprint 10 9 8 7 6 5 4 3 2 1

© Diagram Visual Information Limited 1993

ISBN 0 00 470371 5

Printed in Italy by Amadeus S.p.A., Rome

The *Collins Gem Encyclopedia* follows in the tradition
of the Collins Gem series by providing a wealth of
information presented in a concise and innovative
manner within a truly pocket-sized book.

The *Collins Gem Encyclopedia* is a digest of the basic
subjects traditionally contained within a single-volume
encyclopedia. The style of presentation is thematic,
allowing all the topics included to be examined in
context rather than with the fragmented viewpoint
typical of an alphabetically organized encyclopedia.
The contents pages (pages 6–11) show how the
*Encyclopedia* has been structured with six major parts,
each of which is divided into a series of sections and
groups of self-contained pages and two-page units.
Wherever possible within these units, the information
is further subdivided into headed paragraphs, captions,
charts, tables and structured diagrams.

The information in each of the sections is presented in
a way that is appropriate for the subject concerned – for
example: a tabular style has been used for 'Countries of
the World'; 'History' is displayed as a series of
timecharts; and explanatory text and labelled diagrams
illustrate the intricacies of machinery and technology in
'How Things Work'.

As information can be much more clearly presented
with the aid of diagrams and charts, much of the
*Encyclopedia* has been extensively illustrated with
simple line drawings. They readily reveal the pattern of

information, whether it relates to the world distribution of religious faiths, the groups of chemical elements, the orders of classical architecture or an explanation of how an aeroplane flies.

A second colour has also been employed to facilitate access to information. It is used in the text to highlight

---

# HOW TO USE THE *ENCYCLOPEDIA*

The *Collins Gem Encyclopedia* is organized so that information can be found in a number of ways. The three methods by which you can find the information that you need are given here.

**1 The contents pages**
These pages (pages 6–11) list all the parts, sections and major subsections of the book. The six main parts are listed below.
**The World** (pages 12–133) covers the physical structure of the Earth, the weather, the environment, world population and religions of the world.
**Countries of the World** (pages 134–83) gives basic statistical information for countries and locates them on maps.
**History** (pages 184–259) details key events within timecharts of specific periods in world history.
**Science** (pages 260–541) contains major sections on astronomy, mathematics, physics, chemistry, biology, and the human body, including explanations of key principles. In addition, there is a chronology of inventions and a section explaining how things work.

keywords, dates and headings, and in diagrams to help
clarify the subject.

By adopting a visual approach to the presentation of
information the *Collins Gem Encyclopedia* offers a
stimulating and refreshing approach to understanding
key information on all the major areas of study.

**The Arts** (pages 542–91) combines timecharts of
the major developments in the visual arts, music,
theatre and literature, with illustrated explanations of
particular aspects of these topics.
**The British Isles** (pages 592–623) gives political,
geographical and historical information about the
United Kingdom, its dependencies and the Republic
of Ireland.

By using the contents pages you will be able to find
any subject area in the *Encyclopedia* with ease.

**2 The top of each page**
You can quickly locate information by glancing at
the top of each page. The part titles appear on
the left-hand pages, and the subject titles appear on
the right-hand ones.

**3 The index**
There is a standard alphabetical index of the subject
areas covered at the back of the *Encyclopedia*.

# PART ONE: THE WORLD

## SECTION 1: THE EARTH

## SECTION 2: MAPPING

## SECTION 3: THE WEATHER

## SECTION 4: THE ENVIRONMENT

## SECTION 5: WORLD POPULATION

# PART THREE: HISTORY

# PART FOUR: SCIENCE

## SECTION 1: THE UNIVERSE

## SECTION 2: MATHEMATICS

## SECTION 3: PHYSICS

## SECTION 4: CHEMISTRY

# 10 CONTENTS

## SECTION 8: HOW THINGS WORK

# PART FIVE:  THE ARTS
## SECTION 1:  CHRONOLOGIES

## SECTION 2:  VISUAL ARTS

## SECTION 3:  PERFORMING ARTS

# PART SIX:  THE BRITISH ISLES

# 1

# THE WORLD

# ORIGINS

### How the Earth formed

The Earth began to form about 4600 million years ago from particles of dust, swirling gases and tiny forming planets. The force of gravity compressed or tightly squeezed these elements together. This created intense heat and pressure inside the swirling mass.

At the same time, the pull of gravity was drawing the heavier elements in this mass towards the centre. Lighter elements and compounds, including gases, gathered near the surface. The young Earth was surrounded by poisonous gases which were eventually replaced by air. The outer layer of the Earth cooled and hardened, although the centre remained liquid.

**1** A cloud of moving dust particles, gases and chemical compounds
**2** The heavier particles were drawn towards the centre of the cloud
**3** The earliest form of Earth, with a metal core (**a**) and meteorite-like matter around the core (**b**)
**4** Outer rocks melted, forming the mantle (**c**) and the crust (**d**), and chemicals from the Earth's interior rose to form the oceans (**e**) and the early atmosphere (**f**)

**Evolving continents**
**200 million years ago** the Earth had only one large landmass called Pangaea. This mass was just beginning to break up, the start of continental drift.

**135 million years ago** the pieces of Pangaea broke into a northern landmass called Laurasia. India formed a separate, unattached area. A southern landmass was called Gondwanaland.

**65 million years ago** the landmasses began forming today's continents with their recognizable shapes. They were moving towards their present positions. India had not yet joined Asia.

**Today** the Earth's continents are Asia, Africa, North America, South America, Australia, Europe and Antarctica.

# GEOLOGICAL TIMESCALE

The Earth's history is recorded in the rocks of the Earth's crust. Rocks have been forming, eroding and re-forming from the beginning of the Earth's existence. Pieces of rocks which have worn away are called sediments. They accumulate in layers or strata, forming new rock. Strata hold clues about the Earth's history as they contain varied elements and settle in different ways.

## Earth's ancient history

Geologists explain the clues in rocks by looking at the processes shaping the Earth's surface today. They believe these processes have always been the same. Many rocks contain fossils revealing the history of life on Earth. Fossils help geologists discover the age of rock strata and when a plant or animal lived. However, rocks do not provide a complete history of the Earth, as many rocks are destroyed by weathering and erosion or changed by heat and pressure deep in the Earth's crust. Geological clues in rocks only give a picture of Earth at the time the rock was formed. Geologists have pieced together clues from rocks of different ages but the complete history of the Earth will never be known.

## Dividing geological time

The known history of the world is divided into four periods of time called eras: Precambrian, Palaeozoic, Mesozoic and Cenozoic. Eras are divided into periods, which in turn are divided into epochs. These divisions are based on various stages in the development of life shown by fossils. The lengths of eras, periods and epochs are not equal. A chart showing the Earth's history by using the different time divisions is called a geological timescale. The Earth's earliest history is shown at the bottom and the most recent at the top. This pattern resembles how rock strata are formed, with the youngest uppermost.

| Era<br>millions of<br>years ago | Period | Epoch |
|---|---|---|
| Cenozoic<br>65–present | Quaternary<br>2–present | Holocene<br>0.01–present |
| | | Pleistocene 2–0.01 |
| | Tertiary<br>65–2 | Pliocene 7–2 |
| | | Miocene 26–7 |
| | | Oligocene 38–26 |
| | | Eocene 54–38 |
| | | Palaeocene 65–54 |
| Mesozoic<br>248–65 | Cretaceous 136–65 | |
| | Jurassic 193–136 | |
| | Triassic 225–193 | |
| Palaeozoic<br>590–248 | Permian 280–225 | |
| | *Carboniferous 345–280 | |
| | Devonian 395–345 | |
| | Silurian 440–395 | |
| | Ordovician 500–440 | |
| | Cambrian 590–500 | |
| Precambrian<br>before 590 | | |

\* Mississippian and Pennsylvanian periods in N. America

# EARTH'S STRUCTURE

The Earth consists of four layers. The crust (**1**) is the outermost layer. It is made of rock and it carries the land and the oceans. The mantle (**2**) lies under the crust and consists of liquid rock. The outer core (**3**) is liquid iron and the inner core (**4**) is solid iron.

**Earth's measurements**
**Mass** 5976 million million million tonnes
**Surface area** 510 066 million sq km (196 935 million sq mi)
**Polar circumference** 40 008 km (24 859.7 mi)
**Equatorial circumference** 40 075 km (24 901.5 mi)

**Distance from Earth's crust**
**a** 21 km (13 mi)          **c** 4935 km (3065 mi)
**b** 2935 km (1823 mi)      **d** 6291 km (3906 mi)

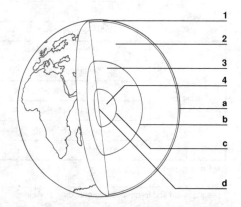

# EARTH'S COMPOSITION

The Earth is made up of elements and minerals. There are 93 naturally occurring elements. Nine of these make up 99 per cent of the mass of the Earth's crust. Two nonmetals, oxygen and silicon, make up three-quarters of the mass. The rest consists of seven metals: aluminium, iron, calcium, sodium, potassium, magnesium and titanium.

Inside the crust, most elements are present as minerals, of which there are around 2000 types. Some, like gold, exist as just one element. However, a majority consist of two or more elements joined together to form compounds. The most abundant minerals are silicates. These are minerals which contain silicon and oxygen. They make up four-fifths of our planet's volume.

Oxygen 46.5%

Silicon 27.72%

Aluminium 8.13%

Iron 5%

Calcium 3.63%

Sodium 2.83%

Potassium 2.59%

Magnesium 2.09%

Titanium 0.4%

Other elements 1.01%

# MINERALS

Minerals are the most common solid materials found on the Earth. They are the compounds which make up the Earth's rocks. Some minerals are composed of a single element but most are composed of two or more elements. About 2000 minerals have been identified but fewer than 100 are commonly found.

## Composition and structure

Minerals are nonliving and inorganic. They are found in nature but they are not made of substances which were alive, such as plants. A mineral has the same chemical make-up wherever it is found in the world. Its atoms are arranged in a regular pattern and form solid units called crystals.

## Appearance and hardness

Minerals can be identified by features such as colour, hardness, the amount of light that can pass through them, their density and their crystal formation. The appearance and feel of minerals varies greatly. Some, such as quartz, have a glass-like surface. Others look metal-like, such as pyrite, or dull and greasy, such as graphite. Some minerals, such as talc, are so soft that they can be scratched with a fingernail. Diamond is the hardest mineral. It is used for cutting other materials.

## CRYSTALS

In the Earth's crust most elements occur as minerals. Most minerals contain two or more elements joined together as compounds. For example, silicates contain the elements silicon and oxygen.

Many minerals exist in the form of crystals. The reason for this is that most minerals are made when hot. Liquid rocks cool down to form solids. When this happens crystals are formed.

The diagrams show some common crystal shapes, and gives examples of minerals that are made of them.

**1** Cubic, e.g. halite (rock salt)
**2** Tetragonal, e.g. copper sulphide
**3** Orthorhombic, e.g. topaz (fluorine and aluminium silicate)
**4** Hexagonal, e.g.quartz
**5** Monoclinic, e.g. augite (iron and magnesium silicate)
**6** Triclinic, e.g. copper sulphate

# ROCK CYCLE

The rock cycle is a continuous round of erosion, deposition and heat.

**1** Igneous (volcanic) rocks are formed when magma (liquid rock) is forced to the surface under pressure and erupts through a volcano. As the magma reaches the surface it solidifies and becomes igneous rock.

**2** The rock is now exposed to the elements, and over a long period of time begins to be eroded and weathered. The rock particles are carried by rivers, wind and rain to the oceans and seas. The particles build up into layers which over many thousands of years are buried deeper and deeper. The weight of layers presses the lowest layers into a solid; this is called sedimentary rock.

**3** The constant pressure pushes the sedimentary rock further and further down, where it begins to be affected by heat from the Earth's core. This heat causes the structure of the rock to change or metamorphose, and it now becomes known as metamorphic rock. If it remains under high pressure and constant heat, the rock will eventually become magma, which may rise to the surface under pressure and erupt again as a volcano.

# ROCK TYPES

**Igneous rocks** are formed when magma or molten rock from the inside of the Earth rises to the surface and cools down to harden. The size of the crystals in the rock shows the speed at which the magma cooled. Granite and basalt are igneous rocks.

**1 Pumice** is made by gases bubbling through lava. It is very light.

**2 Basalt** hardens quickly above the surface. The rock crystals are small because they have not had much time to form and grow.

**3 Granite** hardens slowly below the surface and so the crystals in the rock are large.

**Sedimentary rocks** are mainly made from the remains, or sediments, of older rocks which have been worn away. These are washed into rivers and out to sea.

Fragments settle near the shore forming sandstone (**1**). Further offshore rock deposits collect to form shale (**2**), and in warm seas deposits collect to form limestone (**3**). On the sea-bed the sediments are squeezed together, eventually becoming solid rock.

**1** Sandstone

**2** Shale

**3** Limestone

**Metamorphic rocks** are formed from other rocks which have been heated or placed under pressure. These factors change the rock. Metamorphic rocks such as marble or slate tend to have crystals in bands, or layers.

**1** Magma heats (**a**) limestone

**2** Heated limestone is compressed (**b**)

**3** Erosion reveals marble

# PHYSICAL FORCES

Forces that produce changes to the Earth's physical appearance are of two types. Those that operate on the Earth's surface (external forces) and those that operate within the Earth's crust (internal forces).

**External forces**
**1 Denudation** The erosion of rock layers, exposing rock below
**2 Deposition** The accumulation of sediment, especially mud and sand carried by rivers
**Internal forces**
**3 Earth movement** Faults that produce changes in the elevation of rocks, e.g. horsts (**a**), escarpments (**b**) and basins (**c**). Movements sideways causing folding or fractures to the surface, e.g. rift valleys (**d**)
**4 Volcanic eruptions** The external features produced by lava flow and geysers, e.g. volcanic cones (**e**), lava plains (**f**), geyser ponds (**g**). The internal pressures from volcanoes produce dykes, sills, batholiths and laccoliths

4

**External forces**

**Denudation**
**1 Weathering** Caused by alternate changes of temperature, chemical actions or living organisms (e.g. screes (**a**)).
**2 Erosion** Rocks breaking up owing to the friction of water, wind and ice (e.g. cliffs).
**3 Transport** The movement of rock particles by water, wind and ice (e.g. soil erosion).

**Deposition**

**4 By water** The movement by seas or rivers (e.g spits).

**5 Ice** The movement of particles by ice flows (e.g. glaciers).

**6 Wind** The transportation of particles by wind (e.g. sand dunes).

**7 Living particles** Atolls formed by coral (e.g. lagoon).

**8 Evaporation and precipitation** Heat drying up sea water to leave salt deposits (e.g. salt marsh).

**9 Organic Matter** Fossil fuel deposits formed from plants and marine creatures (e.g. coal).

**Internal forces**
**Folds**
Folds are the buckling of once horizontal rock strata, frequently caused by rocks being crumpled at plate boundaries (see page 32).

**Anticline fold** Pressure from beneath forces the Earth's surface upwards.

**Syncline fold** Activities within sedimentary layers allow the surface to sink.

**Over fold** Sideways pressures force the surface to buckle and fold over itself.

**Nappe fold** Extreme overfolding shears rocks which ride over subterranean layers.

### Faults

Faults are fractures in the Earth's crust either side of which rocks have been moved relative to each other.

**Normal Fault** Stretching surfaces cause rocks to move upwards and downwards to reveal an escarpment (exposed new surface).

**Reverse fault** Compression of an area causes rocks to ride up over others to produce an overhang.

**Tear fault** Sideways-moving plates which produce earthquakes.

**Graben** A long narrow area which sinks between two parallel faults.

**Horst** A horizontal block raised between two normal faults.

# PLATE TECTONICS

The Earth's surface consists of large pieces, or plates, which fit together rather like a jigsaw. They form the lithosphere, or the Earth's outer shell. The plates are constantly moving. Plate tectonics is the study of how they move. When plates slide past each other, they cause fractures or faults. If the rock bends instead of breaking, it creates folds.

**1 Spreading**
Two plates spreading apart form ocean floors and underwater volcanoes

**2 Subduction**
Plates which push against each other and bend downwards are called subduction zones

**Lithospheric plates**

| | |
|---|---|
| **1** African plate | **7** Nazca plate |
| **2** Antarctic plate | **8** North American plate |
| **3** Arabian plate | **9** Pacific plate |
| **4** Caribbean plate | **10** Philippines plate |
| **5** Eurasian plate | **11** South American plate |
| **6** Indo-Australian plate | |

Lithospheric plates

Subduction zones

Spreading

# EARTHQUAKES

Earthquakes are sudden movements in the ground which occur when parts of the Earth's crust move or fracture. Most earthquakes happen when the plates forming the Earth's crust push against each other or when one plate moves under another. Some earthquakes occur when molten rock rises from beneath the Earth's crust, pushing the plates apart.

## Magnitude

The size and extent of an earthquake is measured in units on the Richter Scale. This scale, from 0 to over 8, measures the amount of energy released. Every year there are more than 300 000 Earth tremors which have a magnitude of 2 to 2.9. However, earthquakes measuring 8.5 or higher happen only every five to ten years.

## Intensity

The extreme force of an earthquake and its effects are measured on the Mercalli Scale. This measures the intensity of an earthquake at particular locations on the Earth's surface. Below are listed the numbers on the Mercalli Scale and the physical characteristics of earthquakes.

## Mercalli Scale

| No. | Intensity | Effects |
|-----|-----------|---------|
| 1 | Instrumental | Animals sense tremors; tremors recorded on seismograph |
| 2 | Weak | Noticed by people resting |
| 3 | Slight | Tremors similar to truck vibrations |
| 4 | Moderate | Felt indoors; parked cars shake |
| 5 | Fairly strong | Tremors felt generally and waken sleepers |
| 6 | Strong | Trees shaken; furniture falls over |
| 7 | Very strong | Plaster falls and walls crack |
| 8 | Destructive | Weak walls, columns and chimneys fall |
| 9 | Ruinous | Some houses collapse; ground cracks |
| 10 | Disastrous | Destruction of many buildings; railway lines bend |
| 11 | Very disastrous | Floods, landslides; few buildings left standing |
| 12 | Catastrophic | Ground forms waves; overall destruction |

## Most powerful earthquakes

| | | | | |
|---|---|---|---|---|
| **1** | Gansu | China | 1920 | 8.6 |
| **2** | Nan-shan | China | 1927 | 8.3 |
| **3** | Kwanto | Japan | 1923 | 8.3 |
| **4** | Tangshan | China | 1976 | 8.2 |
| **5** | Shensi | China | 1556 | * |
| **6** | Calcutta | India | 1737 | * |
| **7** | Antioch | Turkey | 526 | * |
| **8** | Hokkaido | Japan | 1730 | * |

* denotes too early to be recorded on Richter Scale

## Deaths from earthquakes

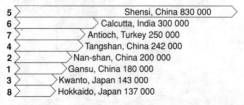

5  Shensi, China 830 000
6  Calcutta, India 300 000
7  Antioch, Turkey 250 000
4  Tangshan, China 242 000
2  Nan-shan, China 200 000
1  Gansu, China 180 000
3  Kwanto, Japan 143 000
8  Hokkaido, Japan 137 000

# VOLCANOES

Sometimes holes and cracks appear in the Earth's crust.
These release hot liquid rock, called magma, ash, gases and
other matter. As the magma and ash cool, they harden to
form rock. Generally, volcanoes erupt when the Earth's
plates move apart or when one plate is forced beneath
another. Throughout the world there are 500 to 800 active
volcanoes. However, during a year only 30 might erupt on
land. An inactive, or dormant, volcano is still capable of
erupting. An extinct volcano is dead and cannot erupt.

**Most active volcanoes**

| Volcano | Country | Major periods of eruption |
|---|---|---|
| 1 Kilauea | Hawaii | 1823–1987 |
| 2 Stromboli | Italy | 1768–1952 |
| 3 Santorini/Thira | Greece | 1470 BC–1870 |
| 4 St Helens, Mt | USA | 1800–87, 1980s |
| 5 Vulcano | Italy | antiquity–1890 |
| 6 Krakatoa | Sumatra | 1680–1969 |
| 7 Mauna Loa | Hawaii | 1859–1950 |
| 8 Mayon | Philippines | 1616–1984 |
| 9 Vesuvius | Italy | AD 79–1906 |
| 10 Hekla | Iceland | 1693–1970 |

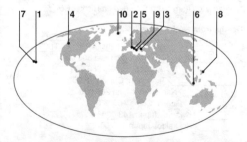

### Anatomy of a volcano

Vent
Cone
Side vent
Subsidiary cone
Pipe
Magma chamber

3
2
1

Gases in the magma escape and form expanding bubbles (1, 2, 3). These gases push magma out of the volcano.

### Major volcanic areas

## MOUNTAINS
**Highest mountains in the world**

| Mountain | Range | m | ft |
|---|---|---|---|
| A Everest | Himalayas | 8848 | 29 029 |
| B K2 (Godwin Austen) | Himalayas | 8611 | 28 251 |
| C Kanchenjunga | Himalayas | 8598 | 28 208 |
| D Lhotse | Himalayas | 8511 | 27 923 |
| E Yalung Kang | Himalayas | 8502 | 27 893 |
| F Makalu | Himalayas | 8481 | 27 824 |
| G Dhaulagiri | Himalayas | 8172 | 26 811 |
| H Manaslu | Himalayas | 8156 | 26 758 |
| I Cho Oyu | Himalayas | 8153 | 26 748 |
| J Nanga Parbat | Himalayas | 8126 | 26 660 |

**Highest mountains by continent**

| Mountain | Continent | m | ft |
|---|---|---|---|
| 1 Everest | Asia | 8848 | 29 029 |
| 2 Aconcagua | S. America | 6906 | 22 834 |
| 3 McKinley | N. America | 6194 | 20 320 |
| 4 Kilimanjaro | Africa | 5895 | 19 340 |
| 5 Elbrus | Europe | 5633 | 18 481 |
| 6 Vinson Massif | Antarctica | 5140 | 16 863 |
| 7 Kosciusko | Australia | 2230 | 7 316 |

**Major mountain ranges**
 **1 Adamawa Highlands** Central West Africa
 **2 Alps** Central Europe
 **3 Altai** Siberia
 **4 Andes** West South America
 **5 Apennines** South Europe
 **6 Appalachians** East North America
 **7 Atlas** North-west Africa
 **8 Carpathians** East Europe
 **9 Caucasus** South-west Russia
 **10 Drakensberg** South Africa
 **11 Ethiopian Highlands** East Africa
 **12 Great Dividing Range** East Australia
 **13 Himalayas** South Central Asia
 **14 Hindu Kush** South Central Asia
 **15 Maoke/Central Range** New Guinea
 **16 Pyrenees** West Europe
 **17 Rockies** West North America
 **18 Sierra Madre** Central America
 **19 Sierra Nevada** West North America
 **20 Taurus** Asia Minor

## LONGEST RIVERS

| River | Continent | km | mi |
|---|---|---|---|
| **1** Nile | Africa | 6670 | 4145 |
| **2** Amazon | South America | 6448 | 4007 |
| **3** Mississippi-Missouri-Red Rock | North America | 5970 | 3710 |
| **4** Yenisey-Angara-Selenga | Asia | 5540 | 3442 |
| **5** Yangtze | Asia | 5530 | 3436 |
| **6** Ob-Irtysh | Asia | 5410 | 3362 |
| **7** Huang He | Asia | 4830 | 3000 |
| **8** Zaïre | Africa | 4700 | 2920 |

1 6670 km
2 6448 km
3 5970 km
4 5540 km
5 5530 km
6 5410 km
7 4830 km
8 4700 km

# LARGEST WATERFALLS

**By height**

| Waterfall | Country | m | ft |
|---|---|---|---|
| A Angel | Venezuela | 979 | 3212 |
| B Tugela | South Africa | 948 | 3110 |
| C Utigård | Norway | 800 | 2625 |
| D Mongefossen | Norway | 774 | 2540 |
| E Yosemite | USA | 739 | 2425 |
| F Østre Mardøla Foss | Norway | 657 | 2154 |
| G Tyssestrengane | Norway | 646 | 2120 |
| H Kukenaom | Venezuela | 610 | 2000 |

**By volume**

| Waterfall | Country | cu m/s | cu ft/s |
|---|---|---|---|
| 1 Boyoma (Stanley) | Zaïre | 16 980 | 600 000 |
| 2 Guaíra | Brazil/Paraguay | 13 300 | 470 000 |
| 3 Khône | Laos | 11 605 | 410 000 |
| 4 Niagara | Canada/USA | 6 000 | 212 000 |
| 5 Paulo Afonso | Brazil | 2 830 | 100 000 |
| 6 Urubu-pungá | Brazil | 2 745 | 97 000 |
| 7 Cataratas del Iguazú | Brazil/Argentina | 1 745 | 61 660 |
| 8 Patos-Maribondo | Brazil | 1 500 | 53 000 |

# LARGEST OCEANS AND SEAS

| Ocean/sea | sq km | sq mi |
|-----------|------:|------:|
| **1** Pacific | 165 760 000 | 64 000 000 |
| **2** Atlantic | 81 585 000 | 31 500 000 |
| **3** Indian | 73 556 000 | 28 400 000 |
| **4** Arctic | 14 100 000 | 5 440 000 |
| **5** South China Sea | 2 975 000 | 1 063 000 |
| **6** Caribbean | 2 718 200 | 1 049 500 |
| **7** Mediterranean | 2 512 300 | 970 000 |
| **8** Bering Sea | 2 275 000 | 878 000 |
| **9** Gulf of Mexico | 1 800 000 | 695 000 |
| **10** Sea of Okhotsk | 1 589 840 | 613 838 |

# LARGEST ISLANDS

| Island | sq km | sq mi |
|---|---|---|
| **1** Greenland | 2 176 000 | 840 000 |
| **2** New Guinea | 820 657 | 316 856 |
| **3** Borneo | 743 254 | 286 967 |
| **4** Madagascar | 587 930 | 227 000 |
| **5** Baffin (Canada) | 476 068 | 183 810 |
| **6** Sumatra | 473 623 | 182 866 |
| **7** Honshu (Japan) | 230 329 | 88 930 |
| **8** Great Britain | 229 878 | 88 756 |
| **9** Victoria (Canada) | 212 688 | 82 119 |
| **10** Ellesmere (Canada) | 212 199 | 81 930 |

## LARGEST DESERTS

| Desert | Continent | sq km | sq mi |
|---|---|---|---|
| **1** Sahara | Africa | 8 397 000 | 3 242 000 |
| **2** Australian | Australia | 1 549 000 | 598 000 |
| **3** Arabian | Asia | 1 300 000 | 502 000 |
| **4** Gobi | Asia | 1 039 000 | 401 000 |
| **5** Kalahari | Africa | 521 000 | 201 000 |
| **6** Turkestan | Asia | 360 000 | 139 000 |
| **7** Takla Makan | Asia | 321 000 | 124 000 |
| **8** Sonoran | N. America | 311 000 | 120 000 |
| **9** Namib | Africa | 311 000 | 120 000 |
| **10** Thar | Asia | 259 000 | 100 000 |

# FORESTS

## Tropical

Tropical forests grow near the Equator, where the climate is warm and wet all year round. They have the greatest variety of trees of any type of forest. Tropical seasonal forests grow in parts of the tropics and subtropics. These areas have a wet and a dry season and are cooler than tropical rainforests.

## Coniferous and broadleaf

Coniferous forests consist of trees that have long narrow needle-like leaves and that are cone-bearing. Broadleaf forests have trees with broad flat leaves and are found in temperate areas of the world wth mild climates. Most broadleaf trees shed their leaves in autumn.

## OCEAN CURRENTS

Ocean currents are the movements of the surface water of an ocean. The most important causes of these movements are the prevailing winds and differences in water density due to temperature or salinity. The shape of the continents and the rotation of the Earth can also influence the direction of currents. Ocean currents caused by prevailing winds are called drift currents, the best known being the Gulf stream. Between the Equator and the temperate regions in the northern hemisphere (1), the circulation of ocean currents is clockwise, whereas in the southern hemisphere (2) it is anticlockwise.

In Equatorial regions, the currents move in opposite directions, those in the north moving left to right, and those in the south from right to left (3). Currents moving north and south from Equatorial regions carry warm water and those moving south and north from Polar regions carry cold water.

**Major cold currents**

1 California
2 Humboldt
3 Labrador
4 Canaries
5 Benguela
6 Falkland
7 West Australian
8 Okhotsk

**Major warm currents**

1 North Atlantic
2 South Atlantic
3 South Indian Ocean
4 South Pacific
5 North Pacific
6 Monsoons

# LONGITUDE AND LATITUDE

## Longitude

On a map or a globe, longitude is marked by vertical lines which run from north to south (**1**). Lines of longitude are also called meridians. Longitude is measured east or west of the prime meridian, which lies at 0 degrees longitude (0°) and passes through Greenwich, England. Each degree (°) of longitude is divided into 60 minutes ('). Each minute is divided into 60 seconds (").

## Latitude

Latitude is a position on a map or globe shown by a horizontal line (**2**). This marks a position north (N) or south (S) of the Equator, the imaginary line around the middle of the Earth (**a**). The Equator is at 0° latitude. Lines of latitude are sometimes called parallels because they run parallel to each other and they are evenly spaced from the Equator to the poles. Latitudes are also given in degrees, minutes and seconds.

## Key latitudes

Key lines of latitude (**3**) are the Equator at 0° (**a**), the Arctic Circle at 66° 30'N (**b**), the tropic of Cancer at 23° 27'N (**c**), the tropic of Capricorn at 23° 27'S (**d**) and the Antarctic Circle at 66° 30'S (**e**).

**Locating a point on a globe**

Locating a spot on a map or a globe, for example Washington DC, is done by finding the latitude and longitude of a position. Globes and maps do not show every line of latitude or longitude. They usually only show lines spaced 15° apart. If the longitude lines are combined with the latitude lines they form a grid pattern which can be used to find a location (**1**).

The co-ordinates of a particular place will tell you how far north or south the place is and whether it is east or west of the prime meridian. The exact location of Washington DC is 38° 55'N and 77°W. To find it, first measure 38° 55' north of the equator to find the latitude (**2**).

To find the longitude, locate the position 77° west of the prime meridian (**3**).

**The Earth's axis** is an imaginary line that runs from the North Pole to the South Pole. It is tilted, as the Earth lies at an angle. This is called the angle of inclination and is 23.5 degrees (**4**).

1

2

3

4

23.5°

# MAP PROJECTIONS

A globe is a scale model of the Earth showing land shape and distance in their true proportions. There are many ways to project, or transfer, the shapes on a round globe onto flat paper. Each projection gives a map which shows a particular view of the world. Each projection distorts size or shape.

### The azimuthal projection

This shows either the whole of the northern or southern hemispheres. It shows areas in their proper proportions but distorts the shapes of countries.

### The cylindrical projection

This is made as if a sheet of paper were wrapped around a globe to produce a cylinder or tube shape. This projection is best for navigating at sea because it gives the best compass readings. Areas close to the Equator have land shapes accurately shown but land sizes are badly distorted the nearer they are to the poles. The Mercator projection is a well-known example.

**The conic projection**

This is made as if a cone of paper were wrapped around a globe so that one or two lines of latitude touched the paper. This projection is used mainly to show parts of the world in the middle latitudes which run east to west. This map shows the shape of limited areas accurately but distorts size from one area to another.

**The mathematical projection**

This is called an Interrupted-Homolosine map. Oceans and continents are shown with little distortion in shape or size. In order to show this, each continent or ocean is centred on its own central meridian. This may involve interruption, or breaks, in the projection.

## MAP SYMBOLS

**How to read a relief map**

Most relief maps are provided with keys to show meanings of symbols. Shown below are examples of the types of symbol used on maps.

> **Colour key**
> red (r)
> blue on white (b on w)
> green (g)
> blue (b)
>
> green on white (g on w)
> pink (p)

**Roads**

Primary road (r)

Secondary road (r)

Other road, surfaced

Unsurfaced road

**Relief**

Index contour

Supplementary contour

.8463
Spot elevation

Intermediate contour

**Railways**

Main-line track

Single track

Cutting

Embankment

**Boundaries**

National boundary

State boundary

County/Parish boundary

## Geographical features

Perennial streams (b)

Seasonal streams (b)

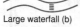

Large waterfall (b)

Small waterfall (b)

Large rapids (b)

Small rapids (b)

Water well (b)

Spring (b)

Temporary lake (b)

Dry lake bed (b)

Glacier (b on w) (b)

## Vegetation

Marsh or swamp (b on p)

Woods (g)

Vineyard (g)

Orchard (g on w)

Scrubland (g on w)

## Other features

Urban area (p)

Viewpoint

Quarry

Landmark

# THE ATMOSPHERE

The atmosphere is a layer of mixed gases surrounding the Earth. It stretches from the Earth's surface into outer space (about 160 km from the surface). The atmosphere exerts pressure on us all the time. This is caused by the weight of the air at the top of the atmosphere pressing down on air below. The atmosphere is divided into layers which merge. The temperature, composition and properties of each layer vary.

The atmosphere of the Earth is concentrated in the troposphere (**1**). Its composition is given below.

| Gas | % by volume |
| --- | --- |
| nitrogen | 78.08 |
| oxygen | 20.95 |
| argon | 0.93 |
| carbon dioxide | 0.03 |
| neon | 0.0018 |
| helium | 0.0005 |
| methane | 0.0002 |
| krypton | 0.0001 |

In addition there are smaller traces of hydrogen, ozone and zenon. The atmosphere also contains variable quantities of water vapour, and particles such as dust and industrial pollutants.

### The layers of the atmosphere

**The troposphere (1)** A shallow layer extending up to 8 km
at the poles and 15 km at the Equator. It is the first layer of
the atmosphere around the Earth. It contains 80% of the total
mass of the atmosphere, all the Earth's weather, and all life
on Earth. Temperature falls with height at a rate of about
6° C for every kilometre.

**The stratosphere (2)** This extends from 8 km to 50 km.
Concorde and military aircraft fly in it. The temperature is
fairly constant in the lower stratosphere and then increases to
around 0° C at the stratopause, its outer limit. The
stratosphere contains the ozone layer (see page 78), between
approximately 25 km and 40 km.

**The mesosphere (3)** This extends from 50 km to 80 km. The
highest weather balloons reach the mesosphere. The
temperature becomes colder, reaching around –100° C at the
mesopause, its outer limit. Trails of hot gases left by meteors
can be seen in this layer.

**The thermosphere (4)** This extends from 80 km to around
500 km. The density of the atmosphere at the thermopause,
its outer limit, averages less than a billionth of that at sea
level. It contains the ionosphere layers, which reflect radio
waves back to Earth. Meteors and aurorae appear in the
thermosphere.

**The exosphere (5)** This extends from around 500 km to
outer space. Molecules of atmospheric gases are so rare they
hardly ever collide.

## GLOBAL WEATHER PATTERNS

The weather we experience is made up of three elements: the Sun, air and water. The energy needed to create weather movement over the face of the Earth comes from the Sun. The surface of the Earth is curved. This means the Sun's rays are concentrated near the Equator and are more spread out over the poles. This uneven heating effect creates energy, like a machine, to drive the weather. Warm air, which is lighter than cool air, rises and cold air flows beneath it, making a low pressure zone. Air moving like this creates

North Pole

**1** Polar currents
**2** Westerlies
**3** Trade winds
**4** Trade winds

wind. North and south of the Equator, air cools and sinks again. Air pressing down on the surface produces zones of high pressure. At about 30° north and south of the Equator, this air creates no wind in areas called the horse latitudes. Wind always blows from high pressure areas to low pressure areas. Air flows back to the Equator in the trade winds and into the temperate regions in the westerlies. Polar easterlies blow from the polar high pressure areas. These main winds carry our weather around the world.

### Air circulation around the Earth

**1** Polar easterlies       **5** Polar high pressure
**2** Mid-latitude westerlies   **6** Temperate low pressure
**3** NE trade winds       **7** Horse latitudes
**4** SE trade winds       **8** Doldrums

# AIR PRESSURE

Atmospheric pressure influences the wind directions which in turn create precipitation (rainfall) patterns. The Earth's air pressure is primarily the result of four factors. The altitude (the height of the air above sea level); the temperature; the Earth's rotation; and whether the air is over land or sea.

**January high pressure areas**

**January low pressure areas**

**Winter patterns** have high pressure over northern hemisphere land areas

**Summer patterns** have high pressure over southern oceans

**July high pressure areas**

**July low pressure areas**

# WIND

Prevailing winds create patterns which are very different in January and July.

**North America and Asia** High pressure in winter causes out-blowing winds. Low pressure in summer causes in-blowing winds.

**Westerly winds** blow more persistently in January in the northern hemisphere. They blow constantly in the southern hemisphere.

**Monsoon winds** blow south from Asia in January and north from Australia in July.

**Doldrums** are regions in the equatorial areas of the Pacific, Atlantic and Indian oceans.

**January monsoons**          **July monsoons**

 High pressure ☐ Low pressure ➤ Monsoon winds

**January wind pattern**

**July wind pattern**

# CYCLONES

**Cyclones** (**1**) are low pressure systems and anticyclones (**2**) are high pressure systems. In cyclones the air moves towards the centre. In anticyclones the air moves outwards in divergent directions.

Cyclones in the northern hemisphere move in an anticlockwise direction (**3**) and in the southern hemisphere they move in a clockwise direction (**4**). They bring disturbed weather.

**Anticyclones** in the northern hemisphere move in a clockwise direction (**5**) and in the southern hemisphere they move in an anticlockwise direction (**6**). They bring settled weather.

### Cyclonic paths

As well as revolving and circulating warm and cold air, cyclones move over the surface of the Earth carrying cold or warm fronts. They follow fairly predictable paths caused by the influences of the seasons, the changing wind currents and the landmasses over which they pass. In America, cyclones are called hurricanes, and in the Far East, typhoons.

### Major tropical cyclone paths

### Tornadoes

Tornadoes are small, intense cyclones in which the air is spiralling inwards and upwards at a very high speed.

# CLOUD TYPES

Clouds form when water vapour turns into droplets, snowflakes or ice crystals which stick together. There are four main cloud types: cirrus (wispy); stratus (layered); cumulus (heaped); nimbus (rain-bearing).

**1 Cirrus** White or grey.

**2 Cirrostratus** High, nearly transparent layer.

**3 Cirrocumulus** Thin white ribbed layer.

**4 Altocumulus** White or grey heaped cloud.

**5 Cumulonimbus** Towering cloud with anvil head that brings thunderstorms.

**6 Altostratus** White or grey sheets, less dense than stratus.

**7 Nimbostratus** Dark thick layer that brings rain or snow.

**8 Cumulus** Individual clouds with dark even bases and white fluffy tops that bring rain.

**9 Stratocumulus** White layers with wave-like patterns.

**10 Stratus** Low layer that brings rain or snow.

Metres (000s)
14
12
9
6
3
0

# WEATHER FRONTS

The weather in the temperate regions of the world is controlled by lows, or depressions. These are swirling wheels of air hundreds of kilometres across. They form where cold polar air meets warm moist subtropical air. The boundary between them is called the polar front. Lows bring both warm and cold fronts.

**Warm fronts** occur when warm moist air rises above cold air, forming a blanket-like layer of cloud which brings light rain or snow.

**Cold fronts** occur after a warm front. Cold air cuts under the warm air, moving in from behind. This can result in towering cumulonimbus clouds which give heavy showers of rain or snow.

# RAINFALL

Rainfall is unevenly distributed over the surface of the Earth. Westerly winds carry abundant rain to the western parts of Europe and North America and trade winds carry rain to the Amazon rainforest.

**Annual rainfall**

**Less than 200 mm**

**200–500 mm**

Deserts receive little or no rain as they often lie downwind of mountain ranges and by the time the air has reached them it has lost all its moisture crossing the high ground.

500–1500 mm

**More than 1500 mm**

## TEMPERATURE

The Earth's atmosphere is warmed indirectly by heat radiated from the Sun. This radiation passes through the air and strikes the Earth, warming its surface. Heat is then radiated back from the surface.

The temperature of any place is influenced by

**1** Latitude and longitude – the position on the globe
**2** Altitude – the height above sea level

**January: very hot regions over 29° C (85° F)**

**January: very cold regions below –9.4° C (15° F)**

**3** Regional location – distance from the sea
**4** Aspect – whether the Earth's surface is facing or oblique to the Sun's rays
**5** Sky cover – cloud, smoke or dust
**6** Ocean currents – which bring cold or warm water to a region
**7** Prevailing winds – which circulate the air
**8** The season of the year

**July: very hot regions over 29° C (85° F)**

**July: cool regions below 10° C (50° F)**

## CLIMATE

The climate of a region is primarily the result of location (latitude and longitude); altitude (height above sea level); the air pressure; the wind patterns; and the rainfall.

**1** Polar climate zone
**2** Temperate climate zone
**3** Tropical climate zone

▝ = Rainfall (mm)

/\ = Temperature (°C)

**A Polar**
Thule (Greenland)

**B Cold temperate (continental)**
Peace River (Canada)

**C Cool temperate (marine)**
London (UK)

**D Warm temperate**
Athens (Greece)

**E Tropical (desert)**
Cairo (Egypt)

**F Tropical (monsoon)**
Yangon (Myanmar)

## WEATHER MAP SYMBOLS

**Wind direction and speed**

| | |
|---|---|
| Weather station | 3–7 knots |
| Wind direction | 8–12 knots |
| Calm | 13–17 knots |
| | 18–22 knots |
| Wind speed 1–2 knots | 23–27 knots |

**Cloud types**

| | | | |
|---|---|---|---|
| | Thick altostratus | | Partial cirrus cover |
| | Thin altostratus | | Complete cirrus cover |
| | Bands of thin altostratus | | Fair weather cumulus |
|  | Patches of thin altostratus | | Fair weather stratus |
|  | Scattered cirrus | | Stratocumulus |
| | Patches of dense cirrus | | |

## Cloud cover

| | | | |
|---|---|---|---|
| ◯ | Clear sky | ◖ | Cloudy |
| ◔ | Fair | ◑ | Mainly overcast |
| ◕ | Some cloud | ⬤ | Completely overcast |

## Precipitation

| | | | |
|---|---|---|---|
| ● | Rain | ▲ | Hail |
| ❜ | Drizzle | ✳ | Snow |
| ▽ | Showers | ＝ | Fog |
| ↯ | Thunderstorms | | |

## Fronts and pressure systems

Cold front

Warm front

Occluded front

Stationary front

**H**   High pressure centre

**L**   Low pressure centre

# THE BEAUFORT SCALE

The speed of wind is measured by using the Beaufort Scale, based on easily observable factors such as tree movement, smoke behaviour and damage incurred. It was devised by a 19th-century British admiral, Sir Francis Beaufort.

| Number | Description | Speed range km/h | mph |
|--------|-------------|------------------|-----|
| Force 0 | Calm | Below 1 | Below 1 |
| Force 1 | Light air | 1–5 | 1–3 |
| Force 2 | Light breeze | 6–12 | 4–7 |
| Force 3 | Gentle breeze | 13–20 | 8–12 |
| Force 4 | Moderate breeze | 21–29 | 13–18 |
| Force 5 | Fresh breeze | 30–39 | 19–24 |
| Force 6 | Strong breeze | 40–50 | 25–31 |
| Force 7 | Moderate gale | 51–61 | 32–38 |
| Force 8 | Fresh gale | 62–74 | 39–46 |
| Force 9 | Strong gale | 75–87 | 47–54 |
| Force 10 | Whole gale | 88–102 | 55–63 |
| Force 11 | Storm | 103–120 | 64–75 |
| Force 12 | Hurricane | Over 120 | Over 75 |

As air moves across the surface of the Earth, its direction is determined by such factors as the Earth's rotation, variations in temperature, air pressure, and land features such as mountains. Listed below are examples showing the effects of wind as measured on the Beaufort Scale, the variety of winds that are measured and the range of speeds to which they apply.

| Number | Characteristics |
|---|---|
| Force 0 | Smoke rises straight up |
| Force 1 | Smoke shows wind direction |
| Force 2 | Wind felt on face |
| Force 3 | Flag extends |
| Force 4 | Dust and paper blow in wind |
| Force 5 | Small trees sway in wind |
| Force 6 | Umbrellas are difficult to use |
| Force 7 | Difficult to stand up in wind |
| Force 8 | Twigs break off trees |
| Force 9 | Chimneypots and tiles are dislodged |
| Force 10 | Trees are uprooted |
| Force 11 | Extensive damage |
| Force 12 | Extremely violent |

# AIR POLLUTION

Air pollutants from sources including road vehicles, power stations, industry and domestic activity now affect Europe, the USA and South America, and many parts of Asia. Air pollution is especially bad in the cities, causing a dramatic rise in the incidence of respiratory problems among inhabitants.

## Air pollutants and sources
### Pollutant gases

$CO_2$ = carbon dioxide
CFCs = chlorofluorocarbons
$CH_4$ = methane

NOx = nitrogen oxides
$SO_2$ = sulphur dioxide

### Acid rain

**1 Source** Acid rain is produced by smoke and gases from factories, power stations and cars. They all emit sulphur dioxide and nitrogen oxides which mix with water in the air to form clouds, making acid.

**2 Transportation** The acid clouds are blown across the sky by winds and are sometimes carried far from the source of pollution.

**3 Rain** When rain falls from the sky, the acid falls to the ground. This is acid rain.

**4 Seepage** The rain falls on lakes and rivers, killing the fish. The rain is also absorbed into the ground and seeps into lakes and rivers. The acid kills trees, plants and fish.

# CLIMATIC CHANGES
## The greenhouse effect
Heat from the Sun (**1**) enters the atmosphere and heats the Earth (**2**). The heat is reflected by the Earth's surface (**3**) and some heat escapes into space (**4**). In large quantities, certain gases, such as carbon dioxide, build up in the atmosphere and trap some of the heat (**5**). If this happened some of the polar icecaps would melt and sea levels would rise, flooding some land. Scientists do not know if these temperature rises will happen. Limits are now being placed on carbon dioxide emissions. In the mid-21st century temperatures could rise as shown opposite.

## The ozone layer
The ozone layer (**6**) contains ozone, a form of oxygen, in the stratospheric layer of the Earth's atmosphere. It filters out the Sun's harmful ultraviolet rays (**7**) which can cause skin cancer. At present the ozone layer is being depleted as a result of chemical reactions started by chlorofluorocarbons (CFCs). Since the mid-1980s the use of CFCs in aerosols and refrigerators has been reduced.

**Possible rises in temperature by 2050**

8–10° C    4–8° C    2–4° C

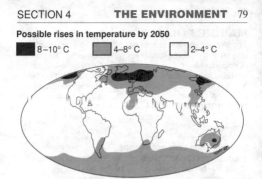

**Growth in the size of the ozone hole over Antarctica**

1982

1985

1987

1989

# MARINE POLLUTION

The world's seas and oceans have always been regarded as legitimate dumping grounds for waste. However, the volume of pollutants is now so great that harmful pollution, once confined to coastal waters, is spreading to the open oceans. Sources of marine pollution include dumping, pollution from rivers, contamination from air pollution and shipping activities. The table (opposite) lists the pollution sources for each of the affected seas and oceans marked on the map below.

## Contaminated seas and oceans

1 South-east Pacific Ocean
2 North American areas
3 Caribbean Sea
4 South-west Atlantic Ocean
5 West African areas
6 North Sea
7 Baltic Sea
8 Mediterranean Sea
9 South African areas
10 Persian Gulf
11 Indian Ocean
12 South-east Asian areas
13 Japanese areas
14 Australian areas
15 New Zealand areas

**Sources of pollution**

# DEFORESTATION

Since 1940 the vast tropical rainforests around the world have been greatly reduced in size. Large areas of forest have been destroyed. Most of the trees have been cut for timber and to clear land for farming and ranching.

**Tropical forests destroyed since 1940**

**Tropical forests under threat in 1990**

# DESERTIFICATION

Deforestation, overgrazing and intensive farming cause desertification. If the soil is dry, it is left exposed to the wind and rain, which strip away the topsoil. Agricultural lands which were once productive become infertile and lose their vegetation. The desert then extends and takes over the land.

**Areas of land threatened by desertification**

| | | |
|---|---|---|
| **1** Africa | 739 million hectares |
| **2** Asia | 365 million hectares |
| **3** China and Mongolia | 216 million hectares |
| **4** South America and Mexico | 206 million hectares |
| **5** Former USSR (in Asia) | 164 million hectares |
| **6** North America | 163 million hectares |
| **7** Australia | 111 million hectares |
| **8** Mediterranean Europe | 22 million hectares |

# POPULATION STRUCTURE

The population pyramid for Equatorial Guinea (**1**), a developing country, has a wide base (many births), reducing steadily to a narrow point (few old people). In contrast, the pyramid for France (**2**), a developed country, has a narrow base and a wide middle, denoting a low birth rate and many middle-aged people.

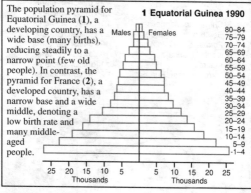

**1 Equatorial Guinea 1990**

## Future patterns

In 1985, 22% of the developed world's population was under 13 and 11% was 65 years or over (**1**). In the developing world (**2**), the number of children under 15 years of age was almost double that for the developed world, and only a small number of people lived to old age. By 2025, the developed world will have a larger proportion of older people than young people and the developing world will see population numbers stabilize.

**1 Developed countries**

Projection
— 2025
— 1985

Male   Female

65+

15–64

0–14

50  0  50
Millions

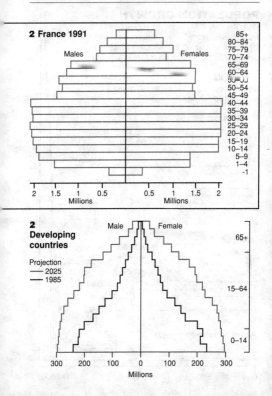

**2 France 1991**

Males    Females

85+
80–84
75–79
70–74
65–69
60–64
55–59
50–54
45–49
40–44
35–39
30–34
25–29
20–24
15–19
10–14
5–9
1–4
-1

2  1.5  1  0.5      0.5  1  1.5  2
Millions        Millions

**2 Developing countries**

Male    Female

Projection
—— 2025
—— 1985

65+

15–64

0–14

300  200  100  0  100  200  300
Millions

## POPULATION GROWTH

Over the past 2000 years the population of the
world has increased thirtyfold. At the time of
Christ there were 65 385 hectares of space per
person. The rapid increase in world population
over the past 150 years has been due to
improvements in medical care, food resources and
production, longer life expectancy and a lower
infant mortality rate.

**Hectares per person**

AD 1
65 385

**2000**
6.25 billion

**1975**
4 billion

AD 1000
34 413

AD 2000
2093

**1930**
2 billion

AD 2100
934

**1850**
1 billion

**World population growth**

**1650**
500 million

0 year      500      1000      1500      2000

# POPULATION DISTRIBUTION

Between 1988 and 2025 it is estimated that the world's population will increase by a third. At present, 58% of the world's population live in Asia. This is expected to increase by the year 2025. The largest growth in population will occur in Africa. It is thought the populations of Europe and North America will decline during this period.

**Population distribution (%)**

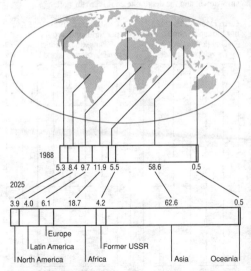

| | | | | | | |
|---|---|---|---|---|---|---|
| 1988 | 5.3 | 8.4 | 9.7 | 11.9 | 5.5 | 58.6 | 0.5 |

| | | | | | | |
|---|---|---|---|---|---|---|
| 2025 | 3.9 | 4.0 | 6.1 | 18.7 | 4.2 | 62.6 | 0.5 |

North America   Latin America   Europe   Africa   Former USSR   Asia   Oceania

# BIRTHS AND DEATHS

Birth rates are affected by such factors as nutrition, the availability of contraception and, to a certain extent, culture. Death rates tend to fall with improved healthcare and nutrition. There is a significant difference in the birth and death rates between the developed and the developing worlds. The graphs below show that birth and death rates for developing countries look set to continue rising into the 21st century. In developed countries, the rise in birth rate should slow down, and the death rate could remain static.

**Birth rates 1955–2025**
per thousand population
— Developing world
— Developed world

**Death rates 1955–2025**
per thousand population
— Developing world
— Developed world

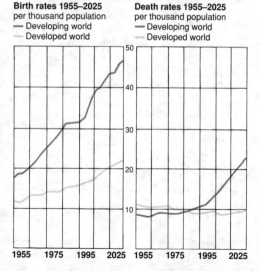

1955   1975   1995   2025        1955   1975   1995   2025

## LIFE EXPECTANCY

People in developed countries have a longer life expectancy on average, with women living longer than men. In the developing world people have a shorter life expectancy.

|   | | Men 1980s | Women 1980s |
|---|---|---|---|
| **1** | Sweden | 72 | 72 |
| **2** | Japan | 72 | 77 |
| **3** | USA | 70 | 78 |
| **4** | UK | 68 | 74 |
| **5** | Former USSR | 64 | 74 |
| **6** | Bolivia | 47 | 51 |
| **7** | India | 46 | 45 |
| **8** | Burkina-Faso | 32 | 31 |

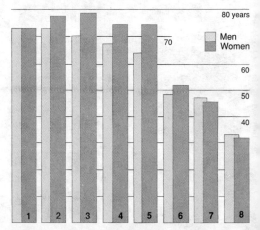

# URBAN AND RURAL POPULATIONS

In many parts of the world, people are packed into cities.
Growing urban populations bring problems, including poor
sanitation, poverty and lack of health care. Growing cities
also mean encroachment on land previously used for
agriculture. While the trend is towards living in cities, there
is still a significant proportion of the population living in the
countryside, especially in the less-developed countries.

|  |  | Rural |  | Urban |
|---|---|---|---|---|
|  | North America | 26% | 🧍🧍🧍🧍🧍🧍🧍🧍🧍🧍 | 74% |
|  | Europe | 28% | 🧍🧍🧍🧍🧍🧍🧍🧍🧍🧍 | 72% |
|  | Australasia | 29% | 🧍🧍🧍🧍🧍🧍🧍🧍🧍🧍 | 71% |
|  | South America | 31% | 🧍🧍🧍🧍🧍🧍🧍🧍🧍🧍 | 69% |
|  | Former USSR | 34% | 🧍🧍🧍🧍🧍🧍🧍🧍🧍🧍 | 66% |
|  | Africa | 69% | 🧍🧍🧍🧍🧍🧍🧍🧍🧍🧍 | 31% |
|  | Asia | 72% | 🧍🧍🧍🧍🧍🧍🧍🧍🧍🧍 | 28% |

**Cities with more than 5 million inhabitants**

**Population (in millions)**

| | | |
|---|---|---|
| London | 1970 | 10.4 |
| | 1980 | 10 |
| | 2000 | 10.2 |

| | | |
|---|---|---|
| New York | 1970 | 16.2 |
| | 1980 | 15.7 |
| | 2000 | 15.8 |

| | | |
|---|---|---|
| São Paolo | 1970 | 8 |
| | 1980 | 16 |
| | 2000 | 24 |

| | | |
|---|---|---|
| Mexico City | 1970 | 9 |
| | 1980 | 17.5 |
| | 2000 | 26 |

Since 1970 cities in the developed world have seen a fall in population. By comparison, cities in the developing world are expanding at a fast rate.

## LANGUAGES

Chinese is spoken by the largest number of people in the world. English, however, is more widespread as it is spoken in several countries (up to 600 million people speak English as a second language). Most languages can be grouped into families. Each covers a range of languages native to one area.

**Main languages spoken**

| | | | | | |
|---|---|---|---|---|---|
| **1** | Chinese | 740 million | **6** | German | 120 million |
| **2** | English | 320 million | **7** | Japanese | 110 million |
| **3** | Hindi | 145 million | **8** | Arabic | 100 million |
| **4** | Russian | 130 million | **9** | Bengali | 100 million |
| **5** | Spanish | 125 million | **10** | Portuguese | 90 million |

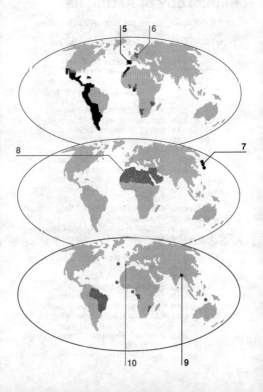

# CHRONOLOGY OF RELIGIONS

| | |
|---|---|
| c. 2000–1400 BC | Jewish patriarchs Abraham, Isaac, Jacob, Joseph and Moses |
| 1500–1200 | Composition of the *Vedas*, earliest scriptures of Hinduism |
| c. 1275 | Jewish exodus from Egypt |
| c. 1050–1020 | Reign of Jewish King Saul |
| c. 700–500 | Composition of Hindu *Upanishads* |
| 751 | Prophet Amos predicts the destruction of Israel |
| c. 660 | Accepted start-date for Shinto |
| c. 628–c. 551 | Zoroaster, founder of Zoroastrianism |
| c. 604–c. 531 | Lao Zi, founder of Taoism |
| 599–527 | Vardhamana Mahavira, founder of Jainism |
| c. 551–479 | Kongzi, founder of Confucianism |
| c. 528 | Siddhartha Gautama becomes the Buddha, founding of Buddhism |
| c. 270 | Emperor Asoka of India converts to Buddhism |
| c. 200 | Composition of Hindu *Bhagavadgita* |
| c. 4 BC–AD 30 | Jesus Christ |
| c. AD 1 | Buddhism introduced into China |
| 50–150 | Composition of Christian New Testament |
| 380 | Christianity the official religion of the Roman Empire |
| c. 380 | Hinduism in SE Asia |
| c. 550 | Buddhism in Japan |
| c. 570–632 | Mohammed, prophet of Islam |
| c. 610 | Koran revealed to Mohammed |
| 622 | The Hegira, Mohammed's flight to Medina, official start of Islam |
| 632 | Abu Bakr succeeds Mohammed as first caliph |
| 685–7 | Beginning of Islamic Shi'ite movement |

| | |
|---|---|
| 691 | Dome of the Rock built in Jerusalem by Muslims |
| 700 | First Buddhist monastery in Tibet |
| 1054 | Great schism between Christian churches of Rome and Constantinople |
| 1096–1215 | First persecution of Jews in Europe |
| 1135–1204 | Moses Maimonides, Jewish religious philosopher |
| 1469–1539 | Nanak, founder of Sikhism |
| 1492 | Jews expelled from Spain |
| 1517 | Martin Luther issues his 95 theses against Papal indulgences, beginning of Reformation |
| 1534 | Church of England established, with Monarch as head |
| 1541 | Calvinism in Geneva |
| 1604 | Sikh *Guru Granth Sahib* completed |
| 1606 | Completion of Sikh Golden Temple at Amritsar |
| 1609 | Baptist Church founded |
| 1647 | First unitarian tract published |
| 1648 | Society of Friends (Quakers) founded |
| 1654 | First Jews arrive in America |
| 1699 | Founding of Sikh Khalsa Path |
| 1703–91 | John Wesley, founder of Methodism |
| 1805–1844 | Joseph Smith, founder of Mormons |
| 1863 | Bahaism founded |
| 1865 | Salvation Army established by William Booth |
| 1866 | Christian Science founded |
| 1897 | First Zionist Congress |
| c. 1920 | Rastafarianism established in Jamaica |
| 1948 | Israel becomes Jewish national home |
| 1954 | Unification Church founded by Sun Myung Moon |
| 1962–5 | Second Vatican Council leads to reform of Roman Catholic Church |

# BAHAISM

**Founded** 1863 in Persia (present-day Iran) by Mirza Hosein Ali (1817–92), known as Baha'ullah or 'Glory of God'.

**Traditions** Bahaism is not apocalyptic; there are no predictions about the end of the world and no direct intervention by God. But change in man and society is inevitable.

**Organization** There are no clergy or sacraments and no formal organization. There are ceremonies for marriage, naming babies and funerals, and some shrines and temples.

---

**Beliefs**

1 Absolute oneness of God
2 The unification of all faiths
3 Harmony of all people
4 Equality of the sexes
5 Universal education
6 Obedience to government

---

**Practices**

1 Membership open to all who profess faith in Baha'ullah and his teachings.
2 Obligation to pray daily and to fast 19 days a year.
3 Abstention from narcotics and alcohol.
4 To practise monogamy.
5 To attend 19th Day Feast each month.

**Sacred texts**

1 *Kitab al-Aqdas* (*The Most Holy Book*) – Baha'ullah's laws.
2 *Ketab e Iqan* (*The Book of Certitude*) – teachings on the nature of God and religion.
3 *The Seven Valleys* – mystic treatise.

**1** Shrine of Baha'ullah
**2** Bahai house of worship, New Delhi

**Calendar of events**
The Bahai year is divided into 19 months of 19 days each.

| | |
|---|---|
| **21 March** | New Year; a holy day |
| **21, 29 April** | Baha'ullah's declaration of his mission |
| **12 November** | Birth of Baha'ullah |
| **29 May** | Passing of Baha'ullah |

**Major Bahaist centres**

# BUDDHISM

**Founded** c. 528 BC in India by Prince Siddhartha Gautama (c. 563–c. 483 BC), known as Buddha ('the enlightened').

**Two traditions**

**1 Theravada Buddhism.** Close to Buddha's original teachings. Believes that the only road to salvation is one of strict discipline and effort.

**2 Mahayana Buddhism.** Later tradition. Teaches salvation is possible for all. Introduced doctrine of Bodhisattva ('enlightened being'). Zen Buddhism, a Japanese branch.

**Organization** Monastic system, involving meditation, personal discipline, and spiritual exercises. Pilgrimages also of spiritual value.

| Buddha's four noble truths | Eightfold Path |
|---|---|
| 1 Suffering is always present in life | 1 Right understanding |
| 2 Desire causes suffering | 2 Right thought |
| 3 Suffering ends when desire is overcome | 3 Right speech |
| 4 Freedom from life achieved by nirvana (release from cycle of birth, death, rebirth). Eightfold Path leads to nirvana | 4 Right action |
| | 5 Right livelihood |
| | 6 Right effort |
| | 7 Right awareness |
| | 8 Right concentration |

**Sacred texts**

*Pali Canon* or *Tripitaka*, comprising:

**1** *Vinaya Pitaka* – rules governing way of life of Buddhist monks and nuns.

**2** *Sutta Pitaka* – oldest teachings given by Buddha.

**3** *Abhidamma Pitaka* – higher teachings or philosophy.

**Mahayana Buddhists** also recognize:

**1** *Prajnaparamita Sutras* – guide to perfect wisdom.

**2** *Saddharmapundarika* – Lotus of Good Law.

**3** *Lankavatara* – revelation of teaching in Lanka

## Objects associated with prayer and meditation

**1** Mandala – symbolic diagram
**2** Wheel of Law symbol (depicting Eightfold Path)
**3** Mantra – meditation chant
**4** Chorten or bell of wisdom
**5** Tibetan hand prayer wheel
**6** Prayer beads (27 beads)

### Calendar of events

| | | |
|---|---|---|
| **April** | Japan | Hana Matsuri (birth of Buddha) |
| **April–May** | Tibet | Saga dawa (Buddha's first sermon) |
| **May–June** | Thailand | Festival of Wesak (celebrating Buddha's birth and enlightenment) |
| **July** | China | Summer Retreat (time of prayer and study) |
| **Dec–Jan** | Sri Lanka | Anniversary of arrival of Sanghamitta |

## Major Buddhist populations

# CHRISTIANITY

**Founded** 1st century AD by Jesus Christ, the 'Messiah' (c. 4 BC–c. AD 30). 12 disciples (Peter, Andrew, James, John, Philip, Bartholomew, Thomas, Matthew, James son of Alphaeus, Simon the Canaanite or 'Zealot', Thaddeus/Judas or James, and Judas Iscariot) became defined body, the Church, which quickly spread through the evangelism of the Apostles and their successors. By AD 380, Christianity was the official religion of the Roman Empire, and became the basis of European civilization in the Middle Ages.

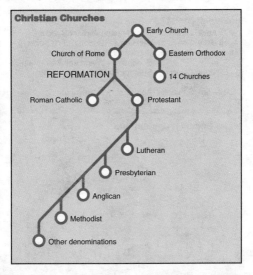

**Christian Churches**

- Early Church
- Church of Rome
- Eastern Orthodox
- REFORMATION
- 14 Churches
- Roman Catholic
- Protestant
- Lutheran
- Presbyterian
- Anglican
- Methodist
- Other denominations

## Main teachings

1 Love of God and of one's neighbour, unselfishness and compassion
2 Divinity of Jesus, and his resurrection (coming to life again) after his death from crucifixion
3 That Christ (Messiah or Saviour) will return to inaugurate 'Kingdom of God'
4 Concept of Trinity, according to which God is made known as Father (in Heaven), Son (Jesus) and Holy Spirit (God's continuing presence in the world)

## Objects associated with prayer

1 Icon (religious painting) of Christ or Mary (Orthodox)
2 Crucifix; statuette of Christ crucified on a cross
3 Rosary beads (one for each prayer) with crucifix and Mary medallion (Roman Catholic)

## Calendar of events

| | |
|---|---|
| **December** | Advent |
| **December/January** | Christmastide (celebration of the birth of Jesus) |
| **January/February** | Epiphany |
| **February/March** | Lent (40 days) |
| **March/April** | Holy Week |
| **April/May** | Eastertide |
| **May** | Ascension |
| **May/June** | Pentecost |

**Sacred texts**

*Holy Bible*, consisting of:

**1 Old Testament** 39 books: Genesis, Exodus, Leviticus, Numbers, Deuteronomy, Joshua, Judges, Ruth, 1 Samuel, 2 Samuel, 1 Kings, 2 Kings, 1 Chronicles, 2 Chronicles, Ezra, Nehemiah, Esther, Job, Psalms, Proverbs, Ecclesiastes, Song of Solomon, Isaiah, Jeremiah, Lamentations, Ezekiel, Daniel, Hosea, Joel, Amos, Obadiah, Jonah, Micah, Nahum, Habakkuk, Zephaniah, Haggai, Zechariah, Malachi.

**2 New Testament** 27 books: Matthew, Mark, Luke, John, Acts of the Apostles, Romans, 1 Corinthians, 2 Corinthians, Galatians, Ephesians, Philippians, Colossians, 1 Thessalonians, 2 Thessalonians, 1 Timothy, 2 Timothy, Titus, Philemon, Hebrews, James, 1 Peter, 2 Peter, 1 John, 2 John, 3 John, Jude, Revelation.

**3 Apocrypha** 15 books: 1 Esdras, 2 Esdras, Tobit, Judith, Additions to Esther, Wisdom of Solomon, Ecclesiasticus, Baruch, Letter of Jeremiah, Prayer of Azariah and the Song of the Three Young Men, Susanna, Bel and the Dragon, Prayer of Manasseh, 1 Maccabees, 2 Maccabees.

## Major Christian populations

Christianity includes many denominations and styles of worship. Some of the most important are described below.

### Orthodox Churches

**Founded** As a result of the schism of 1054, when the Pope excommunicated the Patriarch of Constantinople.

**Traditions** As the name implies, Orthodox Churches regard themselves as maintaining the truth of Christianity. While Roman Catholics focus mainly on the sacrifice of the crucifixion, Orthodox Churches concentrate on the miracle of the resurrection. Priests may marry, but bishops may not.

**Organization** There are 14 self-governing Churches, each under its Patriarch. Each Church is divided into dioceses and parishes. Parishes are led by priests, with deacons to assist.

### Roman Catholic Church

**Founded** Traditionally founded by St Peter, a disciple of Jesus. He arrived in Rome c. AD 50.

**Traditions** Doctrine of the Church set out in Apostles' Creed and Nicene Creed. The Bible is accepted as the word of God, as are all the teachings of Christ. The Pope is recognized as infallible in spiritual matters and is regarded as the supreme head of the Church. Seven sacraments: anointing the sick, baptism, holy orders, confirmation, marriage, holy eucharist, and penance. Veneration of Mary as the Mother of Christ. Celibacy of priesthood.

**Organization** The Pope is the head of the Church, the College of Cardinals elects him. Priests are not allowed to marry. There are many monastic orders. It is the most widespread Christian Church.

### Protestant Churches

#### Baptists

**Founded** In Amsterdam in 1609 by John Smythe and in London in 1612 by Thomas Helwys.

**Traditions** Baptists believe that the Bible is the highest authority, and that everyone can find personal salvation.

Baptism takes place in adulthood. Complete immersion at baptism symbolizes the washing away of sin.

**Organization** Each church is autonomous and functions in a highly democratic way in governing its own affairs.

### Church of England (C of E)

**Founded** 1534 as a result of Henry VIII's break with Rome.

**Traditions** Doctrines are set out in the 39 Articles, its forms of service in the *Book of Common Prayer* and the *Alternative Service Book*. Some sections of the Church of England emphasize the Catholic tradition while others stress Protestantism (High and Low Church).

**Organization** The C of E comprises two provinces, Canterbury and York, with the Archbishop of Canterbury the Primate of All England. The reigning monarch is the official head. Dioceses are governed by bishops, parishes are under the care of clergy. The church parliament is the General Synod, made up of bishops, clergy and lay people. The Anglican Communion is the name given to all Churches that adhere to the basic teaching of the C of E. Each Church is independent but recognizes the Archbishop of Canterbury as its leader.

### Churches of Christ

**Founded** In the USA in the 19th century by Thomas Campbell, his son Alexander and Barton Stone.

**Traditions** Stress on restoring New Testament Christianity, recognizing Christ as the founder, head and saviour of the Church. The New Testament is the sole source of doctrine and practice. Baptism and confession are keys to salvation.

**Organization** There are around 20 000 separate groups, mostly in the USA, governed by a system of elders.

### Episcopal Church

**Founded** In Jamestown, USA, in 1789, as successor to the Church of England in America; the Episcopal Church is also the name of the Anglican Church in Scotland.

**Traditions** Doctrine is similar to that of the C of E.
**Organization** Parishes and missions are grouped into
dioceses, governed by bishops.

## Lutheran Church

**Founded** 1530 by Martin Luther and Philipp Melanchthon,
after split with Rome.

**Traditions** Lutherans believe that death is overcome by the
forgiveness and mercy of God. Individuals are responsible to
God for their conduct. There are two sacraments, baptism
and Holy Communion. Great stress is laid on the importance
of education.

**Organization** Services are conducted by a pastor, churches
are grouped into synods or districts.

## Methodism

**Founded** In England in 1729 by John Wesley, originally as
an evangelical movement within the Church of England,
after 1791 as a separate church. The name derives from the
systematic approach which characterizes the Church.

**Traditions** Direct personal experience of salvation through
Christ is stressed. The scriptures are recognized as the
supreme authority. Members make public declarations of
their faith. Salvation is achieved through faith and good
works, especially evangelism.

**Organization** Congregations select their own minister and
encourage ministry by lay preachers. They are organized
into 'circuits' under the supervision of a Superintending
Minister.

## Pentecostal Churches (Charismatic Renewal)

**Founded** In the USA in the early years of the 20th century.

**Traditions** Pentecostalism is inspired by the visitation of the
Holy Spirit to the Apostles at the first Pentecost (Whit
Sunday), which enabled them to speak in tongues. The core
belief is that the Holy Spirit can come into the life of
anyone, and that healing, speaking in tongues and making

prophecies bear witness to this. The Bible is taken as the literal word of God.

**Organization** Worship is informal, with strong emphasis on singing and spontaneous exclamations of praise.

### Presbyterian Churches

**Founded** 1530s in Geneva by John Calvin.

**Traditions** Doctrine of predestination and irresistible Grace of God. Good works cannot 'earn' salvation, which is pre-determined. Success in the world may be a 'sign' of being elected by God. The two sacraments are baptism and the Lord's Supper.

**Organization** Elected board of elders and ministers govern each church. The General Assembly is made up of equal numbers of ministers and laity. The Church of Scotland is a Presbyterian Church.

### Salvation Army

**Founded** In 1865 by William Booth, a former Methodist minister.

**Traditions** Sacraments are not essential. The Army's chief aim is to rehabilitate the poor and needy. Holiness of life, discipline and loyalty are the key virtues. Music plays an important part. Alcohol and smoking are prohibited.

**Organization** A military-type hierarchy, with elected Generals, and Soldiers who sign 'articles of war'.

### Society of Friends (Quakers)

**Founded** George Fox in England in the 17th century. The name was originally intended to be insulting, after Fox instructed his followers to 'quake' at the word of God.

**Traditions** The faith is built on a belief in immediate contact with the divinity (the 'inner light'). There are no sacraments because the whole of life is considered sacramental.

**Organization** At meetings, the Friends sit in silence until moved by the Spirit to speak. Alternatively, there may be led prayers and discussion. At community business meetings, a 'clerk' leads the discussion.

### Churches with Christian-derived beliefs

### Christian Science

**Founded** 1866 by Mary Baker Eddy.

**Traditions** Adherents believe that evil and disease can be overcome by the individual's awareness of spiritual truth. Emphasizes spiritual healing and the unreality of matter.

**Organization** Headquarters in Boston, USA, is known as the 'Mother Church'. Its affairs are ordered by a five-member board of directors.

### Jehovah's Witnesses

**Founded** 19th century in the USA by Charles Taze Russell.

**Traditions** The Bible is interpreted literally and the Holy Trinity rejected. Witnesses believe that Armageddon is imminent and that after the final battle they will rule with Christ. All other Churches are rejected and only God's war will rid the earth of evil.

**Organization** Witnesses must live plainly and simply. They reject blood transfusions and all stimulants, refuse military service, and do not recognize earthly institutions. Members are actively evangelical.

### Unitarianism

**Founded** First tract published in 1647. Church founded in 1770s as secession from Church of England.

**Traditions** God is one. Rejects the deity of Jesus Christ and the Holy Trinity. Christ was a religious teacher. Denial of everlasting hell, believing that all people can be saved. Emphasis on brotherhood.

**Organization** Self-governing congregations. Use of Christian sacraments of baptism and Lord's Supper, and of preaching and lecture groups.

# CONFUCIANISM

**Founded** 6th century BC in China by Kongzi (Confucius) (c. 551–479 BC).

**Two traditions**

**1** Associated with Confucius and Hsun Tzu (c. 298–238 BC) which says: follow traditional codes of behaviour for their own sake.

**2** Associated with Mencius (Mengzi, c. 372–289 BC) which says: we ought to do as our moral natures dictate.

**Organization** No church or clergy; it is not an institution. No teaching on the worship of God or gods, or life after death. Confucianism in its broadest sense can be seen more as a philosophy of ideas which influenced Chinese government, education and attitudes towards correct personal behaviour and the individual's duty to society. Social life is ritualized, and weddings and funerals follow a tradition handed down by scholars. The colour and patterns of clothes have a sacred meaning.

---

**Some Confucian truths**

**1** Sincerity in public and private conduct

**2** Orderly social life

**3** Moral character

**4** Respect for elders and ancestors

**5** Respect for the ruler

**6** Study and practise self-examination

**7** Become 'superior man' through learning and devotion to moral ideals

**8** Importance of the family

---

**Sacred texts**

**1** The *Analects*, the teachings of Confucius – basic scriptures.

**2** *I Ching*, the book of changes.

**3** *Meng Tzu*, book of second sage Mencius.

**Objects associated with prayer and meditation**

**1** Confucius studied patterns such as this symbolizing good and evil
**2** The Temple of Heaven in Beijing is the largest temple ever built for ancestral worship
**3** The Temple of Confucius, 12th century
**4** An ancestral tablet

**Major Confucianist populations**

# HINDUISM

**Founded** c. 1500 BC by Aryan invaders of India.

**Traditions** Hinduism stresses the right way of living (dharma). There are diverse beliefs and practices. There are many gods and many sects. Important beliefs are the samsara cycle of birth and re-birth, and karma, the law by which the consequences of our actions in this life are carried over into the next.

**Organization** Hinduism varies in nature from region to region. Complex rituals supervised by Brahman priest or teacher.

**Practices** Temple, domestic and congregational worship. The most performed ceremony is prayer (puja).

## Sacred texts

1 *Vedas* – revealed scriptures including songs, hymns, sayings and teachings.

2 *Smriti* – traditional scriptures including the *Ramayana*, *Mahabharata* and the *Bhagavadgita*.

## Symbols associated with prayer and meditation

1 Brahma, the Hindu creator god

2 Vishnu, the god of love, appears in 10 forms, or incarnations

3 Om or Aum – sacred symbol of spiritual goodness

4 Swastika – equilateral cross symbolizing good luck

5 Shri Yantra – symbolizes wholeness

**Calendar of events**

The 12 Hindu months overlap months in the Julian calendar, e.g. Magha runs mid-January to mid-February, and so on.

| Month | Festival |
|---|---|
| Magha | winter solstice and time for peacemaking |
| Phalguna | great Shiva night and spring dedication to goddess of music, Saraswati |
| Chaitra | spring festival; regional new year festivals |
| Vaisakha | Ram Navami – birthday of god Rama, an incarnation of Vishnu |
| Ashadha | Ratha Yatra celebration of Krishna, Lord of the Universe |
| Bhadrapada | Raksha Bandhan holiday for brothers and sisters |
| Asvina | Navaratri Dussehra Durga Puja, marks Rama's victory over his enemy Ravana |
| Karttika | Diwali new year festival and festival of lights |

**Major Hindu populations**

## ISLAM

**Founded** 7th century AD as a result of revelation to Mohammed (c. 570–632) the Prophet.

**Three traditions**

**1** The Sunni form the majority and more orthodox group. They recognize the succession from Mohammed to Abu Bakr to the next three caliphs (rulers of the Islamic world).

**2** The Shi'ites, followers of Ali, Mohammed's nephew and son-in-law. They believe in 12 imams (teachers) who guide the faithful to paradise.

**3** Three other subsects exist: the Sufis, the Ismailis and the Wahhabis.

**Organization** No one priesthood, though great respect is given to descendants of Mohammed, holy men, scholars and teachers (mullahs and ayatollahs). Sharia, Islamic law, applies to every aspect of life and conduct. Religious life centres on the mosque and the family.

### Central beliefs

1 God is creator of the whole universe
2 Absolute unity and power resides in God
3 God is just and merciful
4 Mohammed was last of the great prophets. Jewish prophets and Jesus were his predecessors
5 The *Koran* forbids representation of human and animal figures. It denounces usury, games of chance, the consumption of alcohol and pork
6 Life on earth is a test and only a preparation for the life to come
7 The good and obedient will go to heaven
8 Pride is a cardinal sin

### Sacred texts

**1** The *Koran* – the word of God as revealed to Mohammed.
**2** The *Hadith* – what Mohammed the Prophet said and did.
**3** The *Sunnah* – rules and regulations of Muslim life.

**Five pillars of faith**

1 Profession of faith – there is no God but Allah and Mohammed is his prophet.
2 Prayer – five prayers a day.
3 Zakat – giving a proportion of one's wealth to the needy.
4 Fasting – between dawn and dusk during Ramadan.
5 The Hajj – pilgrimage to Mecca.

---

**Calendar of events**

Muslim calendar based on lunar calendar, which is shorter than the Julian, so festivals fall earlier each year.

| Month | Festival |
| --- | --- |
| 1 Muharram | Mohammed's departure from Mecca |
| 12 Rabi I | Birthday of Mohammed the Prophet |
| 27 Rajab | Night Mohammed ascended to heaven |
| 1 Ramadan | Month of fasting |
| 27 Ramadan | Revelation of *Koran* to Mohammed |
| 1 Shawwal | Festival of breaking the fast (Id al-Fitr) |
| 8–13 Dhu-i-Hijja | Month of great pilgrimage |
| 10 Dhu-i-Hijja | Feast of sacrifice (Id al-Adha) |

---

**Major Islamic populations**

# JAINISM

**Founded** 6th century BC in India by Vardhamana Mahavira (599–527 BC), sometimes considered an offshoot of Hinduism.

**Two traditions**

**1** The Svetambara ('white-robed') follow a canon of scripture containing the sermons and dialogues of Mahavira.

**2** The Digambara ('sky-clad' or 'naked') believe original teachings have been lost but the original message is preserved. Monks and nuns vow nudity.

**Organization** Monastic system, followers dedicated to life of the ascetic. Some temple rituals. There are a series of vows and religious practices for lay people to follow. No creator

## Vows of Jainist monk

**1** No harming any living thing (ahimsa)
**2** No stealing
**3** No lying
**4** No sexual activity
**5** No possession of property
**6** Devotion of whole life to task (Moksha)

## Objects associated with prayer

**1** Offerings of flowers, fruit, perfumes and lamps to idols
**2** Pillars surmounted by elephants
**3** Wheel of law

**Sacred texts**

1 *Agama* – believed by the Svetambara to be the dialogues and discourses of Mahavira written down and collected together by his disciples. There are a total of 45 texts, 11 parts.

2 *Cheda-sutras* – the rules of asceticism.

3 *Chika-sutras* – texts concentrating on the nature of the mind and knowledge.

| Calendar of events | |
|---|---|
| **Month** | **Festival** |
| **August–September** | Pajjusana – a period of forgiving, giving to the poor and confession of sins |
| **March–April** | Oli – a period of nine days spent fasting |
| **September–October** | Oli – a period of fasting and of mythical celestial worship of Jina images |
| **October–November** | Commemoration of the Nirvana of Mahavira by lighting lamps |

**Major Jainist populations**

# JUDAISM

**Founded** c. 2000 BC, consolidated by Abraham and Moses.

**Three traditions**

1 Orthodox Judaism. Strict adherence to laws and traditions.
2 Conservative Judaism. Recognizes law and tradition but holds that revelation is open to many interpretations.
3 Reform Judaism. Each generation can accept, reject and modify traditions.

**Organization** Synagogue is house of worship and centre of Jewish education and communal affairs. Rabbi is spiritual leader, teacher and interpreter of Jewish law. Each congregation chooses its own rabbi. There is no world leader and no ruling body with authority over practice.

### Central beliefs

1 Faith in one God
2 God created man in his own image
3 Abraham, father of the Jewish people, made a covenant with God
4 Moses superior to all other prophets
5 Believe a Messiah will come one day to redeem mankind

### Sacred texts

1 The Hebrew *Bible* – which includes the Torah, the Prophets and other books (known as the Writings).
2 The *Talmud* – a guide to civil laws, religious laws and the teachings of Judaism.

### Calendar of events and festivals

| Month | Festival |
|---|---|
| March–April | Passover – festival of freedom and exodus from Egypt |
| September | Rosh Hashanah – Jewish New Year |
| October | Yom Kippur – Day of Atonement, the holiest day of the year |
| December | Hanukkah – the Festival of Light |

**Objects associated with prayer and devotion**

**1** Mezuzah – a wood, metal and glass case containing parchments inscribed with 15 verses from the Bible; reminder of God's presence everywhere

**2** Tefillin – containing parchments with four passages from the Bible

**3** Menorah – a candlestick with seven branches. The symbol of Judaism

**Major Jewish populations**

# MOONIES (UNIFICATION CHURCH)

**Founded** 1954 in Korea by Rev. Sun Myung Moon.
**Tradition** Religious sect who believe the Messiah has come
and that he heads the family of perfect children. Jesus
offered spiritual salvation, not physical. Mass wedding
ceremonies are held at intervals with most partners chosen
by the leader.
**Organization** Members are required to spend time raising
money for the organization. They live in community centres,
practise celibacy outside marriage, and follow no other
formal rituals, only a weekly pledge.

**Sacred texts**
1 The *Bible* – Old and New Testaments.
2 *Divine Principle* – additional revelations told to the Rev.
  Sun Myung Moon.

# MORMONS

**Founded** 1830 in USA (Salt Lake City) by Joseph Smith
(1805–44), as the Church of Jesus Christ of Latter-day
Saints.
**Tradition** Souls exist before birth, waiting for a body. The
dead can join the Church through a special posthumous
baptism.
**Organization** No professional clergy, no real distinction
between laymen and officials. All members can participate
through several organizations. The General Authority leads
the Church. Regional and local groups called stakes or
wards. Two orders of priesthood: the Aronic (lesser) order
for youths and the Melchizedek (higher) for men over 20.

**Sacred texts**
1 The *Bible*– regarded as the word of God.
2 *Pearl of Great Price* – the writings of Joseph Smith.
3 The *Book of Mormon* – a history of the early peoples of
  the Western hemisphere; divinely inspired.
4 *Doctrines and Covenants* – revelations made by God to
  Joseph Smith.

# RASTAFARIANISM

**Founded** In Jamaica during the 1920s. Inspired by Marcus Garvey's 'back to Africa' movement.

**Tradition** Named after Ras Tafari, who became Emperor Haile Selassie I of Ethiopia in 1930, and believed to be Jah (God) as prophesied. Strong links with Christianity and Judaism. Guided by the culture and traditions of Ethiopia and unity and pride in African heritage.

**Organization** More a way of life than a religion. Followers meet weekly to discuss community business and spirituality. No church. Song, prayer and music are important.

**Sacred texts**

The *Bible* – All 39 books of Old Testament.

| Calendar of events | |
|---|---|
| **Month** | **Festival** |
| 7 January | Ethiopian Christmas |
| 16 July | Ethiopian Constitution Day |
| 23 July | Haile Selassie's Birthday |
| 17 August | Marcus Garvey's Birthday |

**Origins of Moonies (1), Mormons (2) and Rastafarians (3)**

# SHINTOISM

**Founded** c. 660 BC in Japan.

**Two main traditions**

**1** Shrine Shinto (Jinga). Japanese state cult and national religion until 1945.

**2** Sectarian (Kyoko). Follows the teachings of a particular leader or group.

**Organization** Shinto shrines are visited at a person's convenience, but some may go on the first or 15th of each month. Shinto priests perform ceremonies.

**Sacred texts**

**1** The *Kojiki* – records of ancient masters AD 712.

**2** The *Nihon Shoki* – the chronicles of Japan AD 720.

**Religious objects**

**1** Tori, the sacred gates of shrines

**2** Three sacred treasures – the mirror, sword and jewels.

**3** Grand Shrine of Ise, the most respected shrine

**4** Jino Stone, placed in the garden in a thatched hut to honour Jino, the god who looks after property

**5** The Sakaki, the holy tree

## Calendar of events

| Month | Festival |
|---|---|
| **Spring Festival** | Prayer for good harvest |
| **Autumn Festival** | Shinto thanksgiving |
| **Animal Festival** | Divine Procession – miniature shrines are carried by the faithful |
| **15 November** | Shichi-go-san Festival – children of three, five and seven visit shrines |
| **15 January** | Adults' Day |

**Major Shinto populations**

# SIKHISM

**Founded** 15th century in India by Guru Nanak (1469–1539).
**Tradition** Sikh means 'disciple'. Sikhs are the disciples of
their 10 Gurus (religious teachers). Gurus teach the way to
truth and how to find it. Meditation is a source of Sikh
expression.

**Organization** No priestly caste. Worship is performed in
temples where hymns of praise are sung and morning
prayers said. A guru guides followers to Moksa (release).

## Sacred texts

1 *Guru Granth Sahib* – three versions, 6000 hymns by the
  first five gurus.
2 *Vars* – heroic ballads.
3 *Janam-Sakhis* or 'life stories' written 50 to 80 years after
  Nanak's death.

## Objects associated with worship

1 Chauri – fan
2 *Guru Granth Sahib* – a sacred object of worship
3 Channani – awning
4 Manji sahib – stool
5 Romalla – cloth coverings
6 Takht – platform

**Sikh symbols – the five Ks**

1 Kesa – hair must be retained unshorn
2 Kangha – the 'comb'
3 Kachh – shorts worn under clothes
4 Kirpan – sabre
5 Kara – bracelet of steel worn on the right arm. Boys add Singh (lion) to their surname and girls Kaur (princess)

**Calendar of events**

The 12 Sikh months overlap months in the Julian calendar, e.g. Phagan runs mid-February to mid-March, and so on.

| Month | Festival |
|---|---|
| Phagan | Hola Mohalla (Day of Military Power) |
| Asun | Installation of Guru Granth Nanak. Birthday of Guru Ram |
| Katik | Birthday of Guru Nanak, Diwali (release of Guru Har Gobind) |
| Magar | Martyrdom of Guru Tegh Bahardur |

**Major Sikh populations**

# TAOISM

**Founded** By tradition in the 6th century BC by Lao Zi.
**Traditions** Tao means the way or course of life. It stresses the integral unity of mankind and the natural order.
**1** Spirit Cloud Taoists. Masters of methods or Headed Taoists. Concentrate on meditation not ritual.
**2** Orthodox – Tao masters and Black Headed Taoists. Stress importance of rituals, cosmic renewal and controlling spirits.
**Organization** Priesthood and monastic system. Multitude of sacred texts. Personal and metaphysical preoccupations.

---

### Taoist philosophy

1 All is in flux except Tao
2 Yin balances Yang
3 Belief in meditation and simplicity
4 Te (virtue) and Ch'i (energy) the power of effortless action
5 Quest for immortality
6 Heaven rules earth, earth rules man, Tao rules heaven
7 Tao produces and sustains all things
8 All move in harmony

---

### The Three Pure Ones (San-tsing)

1 Yüan Shih T'ien Tsun (Creator and source of all truth)
2 T'ai Shang Tao-chun (who looks after learning)
3 Lao Zi (who became a god after death)

**Sacred texts**
1 *Dao De Jing* (*Tao te-ching*) – 'the way and its power'.
2 The writings of Zhuang Zi (369 – 286 BC).

**Object associated with prayer and meditation**
Incense burner essential to every rite.

**Symbols and signs**

1 The Tai Chi, the supreme ultimate, which expresses the production of Yin and Yang, complementary and interacting forces of nature – such as male and female, light and dark – to achieve perfect harmony.

2 Lao Zi's divine seal, used in Taoist magic

3 Priest's robe with applied symbols of Tai Chi and the eight mystic trigrams

**Major Taoist populations**

# ZOROASTRIANISM

**Founded** In 6th century BC by Persian prophet Zoroaster.

**Tradition** Before Islam it is thought that Zoroastrianism was the official religion of three major world empires.

**Organization** Priesthood led by Dastûr, a type of bishop, who directs and administers temples. Priesthood is hereditary. Ceremony of initiation in which a child receives a shirt and the Girdle (Kusti) which are worn for life. The Parsis in W. India practise a form of Zoroastrianism.

## Sacred texts

1 *Avesta* – the holy book consisting of prayers, hymns, rituals, instruction, practice and law.

2 *Gathas* – hymns attributed to Zoroaster.

3 *Pahlavi* – literature.

### Zoroastrian beliefs

Two principles – good and evil. Ahura Mazda the supreme deity, creator of all things good. Ahriman the destructive principle of greed, anger and darkness

1 Good will triumph
2 The dead will be resurrected
3 There will be paradise on earth

## Objects associated with prayer and meditation

Fire is sacred and kept burning continuously.

Priests always wear mouth cover while presiding over ceremonies.

### Calendar of events

The 12 Zoroastrian months correspond to those of the Julian calendar.

| Month | Festival |
|---|---|
| Noruz | New Year festival |
| Mehragan | Autumn festival |

# CALENDAR OF WORLD RELIGIONS
## Winter

**Christian** Festival of Christmas
**Jewish** Festival of Light (Hanukkah)
**Sikhs** Celebrate birthday of Guru Gobind Singh
**Hindu** Winter solstice festival (Maker Sankrakanti Lohri)
**Orthodox Christians** celebrate St Basil's Day
**Christian** Epiphany
**Hindu** Spring festival (Saraswati Puja)
**Christian** Ash Wednesday
## Spring

**Orthodox Christian** Annunciation
**Christian** Easter (movable between March and April)
Festival of **Buddha's** birth, enlightenment and death
**Jewish** Passover
**Shinto** Spring festival
## Summer

**Christian** Pentecost
**Sikhs** commemorate martyrdom of Guru Arjan
**Buddhist** Summer retreat (China)
**Hindu** Celebration of Krishna as Lord of the Universe (Ram Navami)
**Rastafarian** celebration of Marcus Garvey's Birthday
**Orthodox Christian** Feast of Transfiguration
## Autumn

**Jewish** New Year (Rosh Hashanah)
**Jewish** Day of Atonement (Yom Kippur)
**Christian** Nativity of Blessed Virgin
**Hindu** and **Sikh** New Year (Diwali)
**Sikhs** celebrate birthday of Guru Nanak
**Christian** All Saints' Day
## Islamic festivals

The **Islamic** calendar is based on cycles of the moon, so the year is shorter. This means that Islamic festivals such as Ramadan occur at a different time each year.

# GODS OF ANCIENT CULTURES

**Egyptian gods**

| God | Influence | God | Influence |
|-----|-----------|-----|-----------|
| **1** Anubis | death | **5** Maat | truth |
| **2** Bastet | pleasure | **6** Osiris | underworld |
| **3** Hathor | love | **7** Ra | sun |
| **4** Horus | light | **8** Thoth | scholarship |

## Norse gods and goddesses

| God | Influence |
|-----|-----------|
| **1** Woden | death, poetry, victory |
| **2** Thor | thunder and war |
| **3** Tyr | war |
| **4** Loki | evil and fire |
| **5** Balder | light or beauty |
| **6** Frey | sun or fertility |
| **7** Idun | eternal youth |

## Greek gods and goddesses

| Gods | Roman equivalent | Position |
|---|---|---|
| **1** Apollo | Apollo | God of sun and youth |
| **2** Ares | Mars | God of war |
| **3** Cronus | Saturn | God of time |
| **4** Dionysus | Bacchus | God of wine |
| **5** Eros | Cupid | God of love |
| **6** Hades | Pluto | God of the underworld |
| **7** Hephaestus | Vulcan | Blacksmith of the gods |
| **8** Hermes | Mercury | Messenger of the Gods |

| | | |
|---|---|---|
| **9** Poseidon | Neptune | God of the sea |
| **10** Zeus | Jupiter | King of the Gods |
| **Goddess** | **Roman equivalent** | **Position** |
| **11** Aphrodite | Venus | Goddess of love |
| **12** Artemis | Diana | Goddess of the moon |
| **13** Athena | Minerva | Goddess of wisdom |
| **14** Demeter | Ceres | Goddess of agriculture |
| **15** Hera | Juno | Queen of the Gods |
| **16** Hestia | Vesta | Goddess of the home |

**Mythical creatures**

| Animals | Appearance |
| --- | --- |
| **1** Basilisk | dragon's body with serpent's tail |
| **2** Cerberus | dog's body with serpent's tail and three heads |
| **3** Dragon | serpent's body, bat's wings, tiger's claws |
| **4** Griffin | lion's body, bird's wings, eagle's head |
| **5** Hippocampus | horse's body with fish's tail |
| **6** Pegasus | horse's body with bird's wings |
| **7** Phoenix | eagle-like bird reborn in fire |
| **8** Unicorn | horse's body with spiral horn on forehead |

| Women | Appearance |
|---|---|
| **9** Harpy | bird with female head |
| **10** Mermaid | female body with fish's tail |
| **11** Siren | female body with bird's legs and wings |
| **12** Sphinx | lion's body with female head |
| **Men** | |
| **13** Centaur | male torso with horse's legs |
| **14** Triton | male sea creature with human head and body, fish's tail and horse's forelegs |

# 2

# COUNTRIES OF THE WORLD

**Largest countries sq km**

| | | | |
|---|---|---|---|
| **1** | The Russian Federation | 17 075 400 | |
| **2** | Canada | 9 922 385 | |
| **3** | China (Mainland) | 9 597 000 | |
| **4** | USA | 9 363 130 | |
| **5** | Brazil | 8 511 965 | |
| **6** | Australia | 7 682 300 | |
| **7** | India | 3 166 830 | |
| **8** | Argentina | 2 777 815 | |
| **9** | Kazakhstan | 2 717 300 | |
| **10** | Sudan | 2 505 815 | |

**Smallest countries sq km**

| | | | |
|---|---|---|---|
| **1** | Vatican City | 0.4 | |
| **2** | Monaco | 1.6 | |
| **3** | Macao | 17 | |
| **4** | Nauru | 21 | |
| **5** | Tuvalu | 25 | |
| **6** | Bermuda | 54 | |
| **7** | San Marino | 61 | |
| **8** | Montserrat | 104 | |
| **9** | British Virgin Islands | 153 | |
| **10** | Liechtenstein | 160 | |

**Largest populations 1990 (000s)**

| | | | | | | |
|---|---|---|---|---|---|---|
| **1** | China | 1 133 696 | **7** | Japan | 123 503 |
| **2** | India | 849 510 | **8** | Nigeria | 117 510 |
| **3** | USA | 250 942 | **9** | Pakistan | 113 687 |
| **4** | Indonesia | 180 580 | **10** | Bangladesh | 113 188 |
| **5** | Brazil | 150 197 | | | |
| **6** | The Russian Federation | 144 000 | | | |

**Smallest populations 1990 (000s)**

| | | | | | | |
|---|---|---|---|---|---|---|
| **1** | Vatican City | 1 | **6** | Montserrat | 12 |
| **2** | Turks & Caicos Is | 7 | **7** | Cayman Islands | 21 |
| **3** | Nauru | 8 | **8** | Liechtenstein | 28 |
| **4** | Tuvalu | 10 | **9** | Monaco | 29 |
| **5** | British Virgin Islands | 12 | **10** | Marshall Islands | 31 |

**Highest per capita GNP (1990 US$)**

| 1 | Switzerland | 32 790 | 6 | Norway | 23 120 |
|---|---|---|---|---|---|
| 2 | Luxembourg | 28 770 | 7 | Germany | 22 730 |
| 3 | Finland | 26 070 | 8 | Denmark | 22 090 |
| 4 | Japan | 25 430 | 9 | USA | 21 700 |
| 5 | Sweden | 23 680 | 10 | Iceland | 21 150 |

**Lowest per capita GNP (1990 US$)**

| 1 | Mozambique | 80 | 6 | Guinea-Bissau | 180 |
|---|---|---|---|---|---|
| 2 | Ethiopia | 120 | 7 | Bhutan | 190 |
| 3 | Tanzania | 120 | 8 | Chad | 190 |
| 4 | Somalia | 150 | 9 | Laos | 200 |
| 5 | Nepal | 170 | 10 | Malawi | 200 |

**Highest population densities per sq km**

| | | | | |
|---|---|---|---|---|
| **1** Macao | 27 000 | **6** Bermuda | 1 074 |
| **2** Monaco | 18 125 | **7** Bangladesh | 786 |
| **3** Hong Kong | 5 442 | **8** Bahrain | 762 |
| **4** Singapore | 4 419 | **9** Maldives | 732 |
| **5** Vatican City | 2 500 | **10** Barbados | 598 |

**Lowest population densities per sq km**

| | | | | |
|---|---|---|---|---|
| **1** Mongolia | 1 | **6** Mauritania | 2 |
| **2** Western Sahara | 1 | **7** Namibia | 2 |
| **3** French Guiana | 1 | **8** Libya | 3 |
| **4** Australia | 2 | **9** Suriname | 3 |
| **5** Botswana | 2 | **10** Gabon | 4 |

## NORTHERN EUROPE

**Countries by size**

| | | sq km |
|---|---|---|
| 1 | Sweden | 449 620 |
| 2 | Finland | 337 030 |
| 3 | Norway | 323 895 |
| 4 | Iceland | 102 820 |
| 5 | Denmark | 43 075 |

### Populations

**1990 (000s)**

| | | | | | |
|---|---|---|---|---|---|
| 1 | Sweden | 8 552 | 4 | Norway | 4 242 |
| 2 | Denmark | 5 139 | 5 | Iceland | 258 |
| 3 | Finland | 4 979 | | | |

**Densities (people per sq km)**

| | | | | | |
|---|---|---|---|---|---|
| 1 | Denmark | 119 | 4 | Norway | 13 |
| 2 | Sweden | 19 | 5 | Iceland | 3 |
| 3 | Finland | 15 | | | |

**Per capita GNP (1990 US$)**

| | | | | | |
|---|---|---|---|---|---|
| 1 | Finland | 26 070 | 4 | Denmark | 22 090 |
| 2 | Sweden | 23 680 | 5 | Iceland | 21 150 |
| 3 | Norway | 23 120 | | | |

| COUNTRY | CAPITAL | LANGUAGE | CURRENCY |
|---|---|---|---|
| **Denmark** | (Kongeriget Danmark) | | |
| | Copenhagen | Danish | Danish krone |
| **Finland** | (Suomen Tasavalta) | | |
| | Helsinki | Finnish | Markka |
| | | Swedish | |
| **Iceland** | (Lydveldid Island) | | |
| | Reykjavik | Icelandic | Krona |
| **Norway** | (Kongeriket Norge) | | |
| | Oslo | Norwegian | Krone |
| **Sweden** | (Konungariket Sverige) | | |
| | Stockholm | Swedish | Krona |

# EASTERN EUROPE

## Populations

**1990 (000s)**

| | | | | | |
|---|---|---|---|---|---|
| **1** Poland | 37 966 | | **5** Lithuania | 3 700 |
| **2** Hungary | 10 554 | | **6** Latvia | 2 600 |
| **3** Czech Republic | 10 032 | | **7** Estonia | 1 500 |
| **4** Slovak Republic | 5 274 | | | |

**Densities (people per sq km)**

| | | | | | |
|---|---|---|---|---|---|
| **1** Czech Republic | 127 | | **5** Lithuania | 57 |
| **2** Poland | 121 | | **6** Latvia | 41 |
| **3** Hungary | 113 | | **7** Estonia | 33 |
| **4** Slovak Republic | 108 | | | |

**Per capita GNP (1990 US$)**

| | | | | |
|---|---|---|---|---|
| **1** Hungary | 2 780 | | Lithuania | NA |
| **2** Poland | 1 700 | | Latvia | NA |
| **3** Czech Republic | 1 461 | | Estonia | NA |
| **4** Slovak Republic | 1 456 | | | |

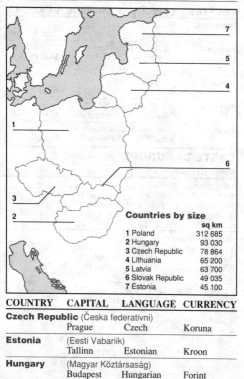

**Countries by size**

| | | sq km |
|---|---|---|
| 1 | Poland | 312 685 |
| 2 | Hungary | 93 030 |
| 3 | Czech Republic | 78 864 |
| 4 | Lithuania | 65 200 |
| 5 | Latvia | 63 700 |
| 6 | Slovak Republic | 49 035 |
| 7 | Estonia | 45 100 |

| COUNTRY | CAPITAL | LANGUAGE | CURRENCY |
|---|---|---|---|
| **Czech Republic** (Česka federativni) | | | |
| | Prague | Czech | Koruna |
| **Estonia** | (Eesti Vabariik) | | |
| | Tallinn | Estonian | Kroon |
| **Hungary** | (Magyar Köztársaság) | | |
| | Budapest | Hungarian | Forint |

| COUNTRY | CAPITAL | LANGUAGE | CURRENCY |
|---|---|---|---|
| **Latvia** | (Latvijas Republika) | | |
| | Riga | Latvian | Latvian rouble |
| **Lithuania** | (Lietuvos Respublika) | | |
| | Vilnius | Lithuanian | Lithuanian rouble |
| **Poland** | (Polska Rzeczpospolita) | | |
| | Warsaw | Polish | Zloty |
| **Slovak Republic** | (Slovenska Federativni) | | |
| | Bratislava | Slovak | Koruna |

# SOUTHERN EUROPE
## Populations

### 1990 (000s)

| | | | |
|---|---|---|---|
| **1** Italy | 57 588 | **7** Greece | 10 048 |
| **2** Turkey | 56 277 | **8** Bulgaria | 8 991 |
| **3** Spain | 39 326 | **9** Albania | 3 255 |
| **4** Yugoslavia | 23 800 | **10** Andorra | 50 |
| **5** Romania | 23 249 | **11** San Marino | 23 |
| **6** Portugal | 10 372 | **12** Vatican City | 1 |

### Densities (people per sq km)

| | | | |
|---|---|---|---|
| **1** Vatican City | 2 500 | **7** Romania | 98 |
| **2** San Marino | 377 | **8** Yugoslavia | 93 |
| **3** Italy | 191 | **9** Bulgaria | 81 |
| **4** Albania | 113 | **10** Spain | 78 |
| **5** Portugal | 113 | **11** Greece | 76 |
| **6** Andorra | 108 | **12** Turkey | 72 |

### Per capita GNP (1990 US$)

| | | | |
|---|---|---|---|
| **1** Italy | 16 850 | **7** Romania | 1 640 |
| **2** Spain | 10 920 | **8** Turkey | 1 630 |
| **3** Greece | 6 000 | **9** Albania | 790 |
| **4** Portugal | 4 890 | Andorra | NA |
| **5** Yugoslavia | 3 060 | San Marino | NA |
| **6** Bulgaria | 2 210 | Vatican City | NA |

**Countries by size**

| | sq km | | | sq km |
|---|---|---|---|---|
| 1 Turkey | 779 500 | | 7 Bulgaria | 110 910 |
| 2 Spain | 504 880 | | 8 Portugal | 91 630 |
| 3 Italy | 301 245 | | 9 Albania | 28 750 |
| 4 Former Yugoslavia | 255 805 | | 10 Andorra | 465 |
| 5 Romania | 237 500 | | 11 San Marino | 61 |
| 6 Greece | 131 985 | | 12 Vatican City | 0.4 |

| COUNTRY | CAPITAL | LANGUAGE | CURRENCY |
|---|---|---|---|
| **Albania** | (Republika e Shqipërisë) | | |
| | Tirana | Albanian | Lek |
| | | Greek | |
| **Andorra** | (Principat d'Andorra) | | |
| | Andorra la Vella | Catalan Spanish French | Spanish peseta French franc |
| **Bulgaria** | (Narodna Republika Bulgaria) | | |
| | Sofia | Bulgarian Turkish | Lev |
| **Greece** | (Elliniki Dimokratia) | | |
| | Athens | Greek | Drachma |

| COUNTRY | CAPITAL | LANGUAGE | CURRENCY |
| --- | --- | --- | --- |
| **Italy** | (Repubblica Italiana) | | |
| | Rome | Italian | Lira |
| **Portugal** | (República Portuguesa) | | |
| | Lisbon | Portuguese | Escudo |
| **Romania** | (Republica Populară Romania) | | |
| | Bucharest | Romanian | Leu |
| **San Marino** | (Repubblica di San Marino) | | |
| | San Marino | Italian | Italian lira |
| **Spain** | (España) | | |
| | Madrid | Spanish | Peseta |
| | | Catalan | |
| | | Basque | |
| | | Galician | |
| **Turkey** | (Türkiye Cumhuriyeti) | | |
| | Ankara | Turkish | Turkish Lira |
| **Vatican City** | (Stato della Città del Vaticano) | | |
| | Vatican City | Italian | Vatican City |
| | | Latin | lira |
| | | | Italian lira |

**(Former Yugoslavia)**

**Bosnia-Herzegovina**

| | CAPITAL | LANGUAGE | CURRENCY |
| --- | --- | --- | --- |
| | Sarajevo | Serbo-Croatian | New dinar |
| **Croatia** | | | |
| | Zagreb | Croatian | New dinar |
| **Macedonia** | | | |
| | Skopje | Macedonian | New dinar |
| **Serbia** | | | |
| | Belgrade | Serbian | New dinar |
| **Slovenia** | | | |
| | Ljubljana | Slovenian | New dinar |

# WESTERN EUROPE
## Populations

### 1990 (000s)

| | | | | | |
|---|---|---:|---|---|---:|
| 1 | Germany | 79 000 | 7 | Switzerland | 6 690 |
| 2 | UK | 57 483 | 8 | Rep. of Ireland | 3 504 |
| 3 | France | 56 453 | 9 | Luxembourg | 378 |
| 4 | Netherlands | 14 931 | 10 | Monaco | 29 |
| 5 | Belgium | 10 016 | 11 | Liechtenstein | 28 |
| 6 | Austria | 7 643 | | | |

### Densities (people per sq km)

| | | | | | |
|---|---|---:|---|---|---:|
| 1 | Monaco | 18 125 | 7 | Switzerland | 162 |
| 2 | Netherlands | 363 | 8 | Luxembourg | 146 |
| 3 | Belgium | 328 | 9 | France | 104 |
| 4 | UK | 235 | 10 | Austria | 91 |
| 5 | Germany | 221 | 11 | Ireland | 51 |
| 6 | Liechtenstein | 175 | | | |

### Per capita GNP (1990 US$)

| | | | | | |
|---|---|---:|---|---|---:|
| 1 | Switzerland | 32 790 | 7 | UK | 16 070 |
| 2 | Luxembourg | 28 770 | 8 | Belgium | 15 440 |
| 3 | Germany | 22 730 | 9 | Ireland | 9 550 |
| 4 | France | 19 480 | | Monaco | NA |
| 5 | Austria | 19 240 | | Liechtenstein | NA |
| 6 | Netherlands | 17 330 | | | |

| COUNTRY | CAPITAL | LANGUAGE | CURRENCY |
|---|---|---|---|
| **Austria** | (Republik Österreich) | | |
| | Vienna | German | Schilling |
| **Belgium** | Koninkrijk België [Flemish]) | | |
| | Royaume de Belgique [French]) | | |
| | Brussels | Flemish | Belgian franc |
| | | French | |
| | | Italian | |
| | | German | |
| **France** | (République Française) | | |
| | Paris | French | Franc |

**Countries by size**

| | sq km | | | sq km |
|---|---|---|---|---|
| **1** France | 543 965 | | **7** Netherlands | 41 160 |
| **2** Germany | 357 048 | | **8** Belgium | 30 520 |
| **3** UK | 244 755 | | **9** Luxembourg | 2 585 |
| **4** Austria | 83 855 | | **10** Liechtenstein | 160 |
| **5** Rep. of Ireland | 66 893 | | **11** Monaco | 1.6 |
| **6** Switzerland | 41 285 | | | |

| COUNTRY | CAPITAL | LANGUAGE | CURRENCY |
|---|---|---|---|
| **Germany** | (Bundesrepublik Deutschland) | | |
| | Berlin | German | Deutschmark |
| **Republic of Ireland** | (Eire) | | |
| | Dublin | English Gaelic | Punt |
| **Liechtenstein** | (Fürstentum Liechtenstein) | | |
| | Vaduz | German | Swiss franc |
| **Luxembourg** | (Grand-Duché de Luxembourg) | | |
| | Luxembourg-Ville | French | Luxembourg franc |
| **Monaco** | (Principality of Monaco) | | |
| | Monaco-Ville | French | French franc Monégasque-franc |
| **Netherlands** | (Koninkrijk der Nederlanden) | | |
| | Amsterdam | Dutch | Guilder |
| **Switzerland** | (Swiss Confederation) | | |
| | Berne | German French Italian | Swiss franc |
| **UK** | (United Kingdom of Great Britain and Northern Ireland) | | |
| | London | English | Sterling |

# CENTRAL ASIA
## Populations

**1990 (000s)**

| | | | |
|---|---|---|---|
| **1** The Russian Federation | 144 000 | **7** Georgia | 5 400 |
| **2** Ukraine | 51 500 | **8** Tajikistan | 5 100 |
| **3** Uzbekistan | 20 700 | **9** Moldova | 4 300 |
| **4** Kazakhstan | 16 700 | Kyrgystan | 4 300 |
| **5** Belarus | 10 200 | **11** Turkmenistan | 3 600 |
| **6** Azerbaijan | 7 100 | **12** Armenia | 3 200 |

**Densities (people per sq km)**

| | | | | | |
|---|---|---|---|---|---|
| 1 | Moldova | 127 | 8 | Tajikistan | 37 |
| 2 | Armenia | 107 | 9 | Kyrgystan | 22 |
| 3 | Ukraine | 86 | 10 | The Russian Federation | 8 |
| 4 | Azerbaijan | 82 | | | |
| 5 | Georgia | 77 | 11 | Turkmenistan | 7 |
| 6 | Belarus | 49 | 12 | Kazakhstan | 6 |
| 7 | Uzbekistan | 40 | | | |

**Per capita GNP (1990 US$)**
No GNP figures available.

**Countries by size**

| | | sq km | | | sq km |
|---|---|---|---|---|---|
| 1 | The Russian Federation | 17 075 400 | 7 | Kyrgystan | 198 495 |
| 2 | Kazakhstan | 2 717 300 | 8 | Tajikistan | 143 100 |
| 3 | Ukraine | 603 700 | 9 | Azerbaijan | 87 000 |
| 4 | Turkmenistan | 488 100 | 10 | Georgia | 69 700 |
| 5 | Uzbekistan | 447 400 | 11 | Moldova | 33 700 |
| 6 | Belarus | 207 600 | 12 | Armenia | 29 800 |

| COUNTRY | CAPITAL | LANGUAGE | CURRENCY |
| --- | --- | --- | --- |
| **Armenia** | (Haikaka Hanrapetoutioun) | | |
| | Yerevan | Armenian | Rouble |
| **Azerbaijan** | (Azerbaijchan Respublikasy) | | |
| | Baku | Azerbaijani | Manat |
| **Belarus** | | | |
| | Minsk | Byelorussian | Rouble |
| | | Russian | Duktat |
| **Georgia** | (Sakartvelos Republica) | | |
| | Tbilisi | Georgian | Rouble |
| | | Russian | |
| **Kazakhstan** | (Kazak Respublikasy) | | |
| | Alma-Ata | Kazakh | Rouble |
| | | Russian | |
| **Moldova** | (Republica Moldoveneasca) | | |
| | Kishinev | Romanian | Rouble |
| | | Ukrainian | |
| **The Russian Federation** | | | |
| | Moscow | Russian | Rouble |
| **Tajikistan** | (Respubliki Tajikistan) | | |
| | Dushanbe | Tajik | Rouble |
| | | Russian | |
| **Turkmenistan** | | | |
| | Ashkhabad | Turkmen | Rouble |
| **Ukraine** | (Ukrayina) | | |
| | Kiev | Ukrainian | Hryvnia |
| **Uzbekistan** | (Ozbekistan Respublikasy) | | |
| | Tashkent | Uzbek | Soum |

# SOUTHERN ASIA
## Populations

### 1990 (000s)

| | | | | |
|---|---|---|---|---|
| **1** India | 849 510 | **5** Sri Lanka | 17 002 |
| **2** Pakistan | 113 687 | **6** Afghanistan | 15 700 |
| **3** Bangladesh | 113 188 | **7** Bhutan | 1 433 |
| **4** Nepal | 19 096 | **8** Maldives | 218 |

### Densities (people per sq km)

| | | | | |
|---|---|---|---|---|
| **1** Bangladesh | 786 | **5** Pakistan | 141 |
| **2** Maldives | 732 | **6** Nepal | 135 |
| **3** India | 268 | **7** Bhutan | 31 |
| **4** Sri Lanka | 259 | **8** Afghanistan | 25 |

### Per capita GNP (1990 US$)

| | | | | |
|---|---|---|---|---|
| **1** Sri Lanka | 470 | **5** Afghanistan | 280 |
| **2** Maldives | 440 | **6** Bangladesh | 200 |
| **3** Pakistan | 380 | **7** Bhutan | 190 |
| **4** India | 350 | **8** Nepal | 170 |

### Countries by size

| | sq km |
|---|---|
| **1** India | 3 166 830 |
| **2** Pakistan | 803 940 |
| **3** Afghanistan | 636 265 |
| **4** Bangladesh | 144 000 |
| **5** Nepal | 141 415 |
| **6** Sri Lanka | 65 610 |
| **7** Bhutan | 46 620 |
| **8** Maldives | 298 |

| COUNTRY | CAPITAL | LANGUAGE | CURRENCY |
|---|---|---|---|
| **Afghanistan** | (De Afghanistan Jamhuriat) | | |
| | Kabul | Pushtu | Afghani |
| | | Dari | |
| **Bangladesh** | (Gama Prajàtantrî Bangladesh) | | |
| | Dhaka | Bengali | Taka |
| **Bhutan** | (Druk-Yul) | | |
| | Thimphu | Dzongkha | Ngultrum |
| **India** | (Bharat) | | |
| | New Delhi | Hindi | Rupee |
| | | English | |
| **Maldives** | (Divehi Jumhuriya) | | |
| | Malé | Divehi | Rufiyaa |
| **Nepal** | (Sri Nepala Sarkar) | | |
| | Kathmandu | Nepali | Nepalese rupee |
| **Pakistan** | (Islam-i Jamhuriya-e Pakistan) | | |
| | Islamabad | Urdu | Pakistani rupee |
| **Sri Lanka** | (Sri Lanka Prajathanthrika Samajavadi Janarajaya) | | |
| | Colombo | Sinhalese | Rupee |
| | | Tamil | |

## SOUTH EASTERN ASIA
### Populations

1990 (000s)

| | | | | |
|---|---|---|---|---|
| 1 | Indonesia | 181 580 | 6 Malaysia | 17 752 |
| 2 | Vietnam | 66 473 | 7 Cambodia | 8 100 |
| 3 | The Philippines | 61 358 | 8 Laos | 4 186 |
| 4 | Thailand | 55 801 | 9 Singapore | 2 722 |
| 5 | Myanmar | 41 609 | 10 Brunei | 397 |

**Densities (people per sq km)**

| | | | | |
|---|---|---|---|---|
| 1 | Singapore | 4 419 | 6 Myanmar | 61 |
| 2 | The Philippines | 205 | 7 Malaysia | 53 |
| 3 | Vietnam | 202 | 8 Cambodia | 45 |
| 4 | Thailand | 109 | 9 Brunei | 44 |
| 5 | Indonesia | 95 | 10 Laos | 17 |

**Per capita GNP (1990 US$)**

| | | | | |
|---|---|---|---|---|
| 1 | Singapore | 12 310 | 6 Indonesia | 560 |
| 2 | Brunei | > 6 000 | 7 Vietnam | < 500 |
| 3 | Malaysia | 2 340 | 8 Cambodia | < 500 |
| 4 | Thailand | 1 420 | 9 Myanmar | < 500 |
| 5 | The Philippines | 730 | 10 Laos | 200 |

**Countries by size**

| | | sq km | | | sq km |
|---|---|---|---|---|---|
| 1 | Indonesia | 1 919 445 | 6 The Philippines | 300 000 |
| 2 | Myanmar | 678 030 | 7 Laos | 236 725 |
| 3 | Thailand | 514 000 | 8 Cambodia | 181 000 |
| 4 | Malaysia | 332 965 | 9 Brunei | 5 765 |
| 5 | Vietnam | 329 565 | 10 Singapore | 616 |

| COUNTRY | CAPITAL | LANGUAGE | CURRENCY |
|---|---|---|---|
| **Brunei** | (Negara Brunei Darussalam) | | |
| | Bandar Seri Begawan | Malay English | Brunei dollar |
| **Cambodia** | (State of Cambodia) | | |
| | Phnom Penh | Khmer | Riel |
| **Indonesia** | (Republik Indonesia) | | |
| | Jakarta | Bahasa Indonesian | Rupiah |
| **Laos** | (Sathalanalat Paxathipatai Paxaxôn Lao) | | |
| | Vientiane | Lao | New kip |
| **Malaysia** | (Federation of Malaysia) | | |
| | Kuala Lumpur | Malay | Ringgit |
| **Myanmar** | (Pyeidaungzu Myanma Naingngandaw) | | |
| | Yangon | Burmese | Kyat |
| **The Philippines** | (Republika ng Pilipinas) | | |
| | Manila | Filipino English | Philippine peso |
| **Singapore** | (Republic of Singapore) | | |
| | Singapore | Malay Chinese English | Singapore dollar |
| **Thailand** | (Muang Thai or Prathet Thai) | | |
| | Bangkok | Thai | Baht |
| **Vietnam** | (Công Hòa Xã Hôi Chu Nghĩa Viêt Nam) | | |
| | Hanoi | Vietnamese | Dong |

# EASTERN ASIA
## Populations

**1990 (000s)**

| | | | | | |
|---|---|---|---|---|---|
| **1** | China | 1 133 696 | **3** | South Korea | 42 789 |
| **2** | Japan | 123 503 | **4** | North Korea | 21 576 |

## Countries by size

| | sq km | | | sq km |
|---|---|---|---|---|
| 1 China | 9 597 000 | 5 South Korea | | 98 445 |
| 2 Mongolia | 1 565 000 | 6 Taiwan | | 35 990 |
| 3 Japan | 369 700 | 7 Hong Kong | | 1 062 |
| 4 North Korea | 122 310 | 8 Macao | | 17 |

### Populations (continued)

| 5 Taiwan | 20 454 | 7 Mongolia | 2 124 |
|---|---|---|---|
| 6 Hong Kong | 5 779 | 8 Macao | 459 |

### Densities (people per sq km)

| 1 Macao | 27 000 | 5 Japan | 334 |
|---|---|---|---|
| 2 Hong Kong | 5 442 | 6 North Korea | 176 |
| 3 Taiwan | 568 | 7 China | 118 |
| 4 South Korea | 435 | 8 Mongolia | 1 |

### Per capita GNP (1990 US$)

| 1 Japan | 25 430 | 5 Macao | 3 499 |
|---|---|---|---|
| 2 Hong Kong | 11 540 | 6 North Korea | 970 |
| 3 Taiwan | 7 510 | 7 Mongolia | 780 |
| 4 South Korea | 5 400 | 8 China | 370 |

| COUNTRY | CAPITAL | LANGUAGE | CURRENCY |
|---|---|---|---|
| **China** | (Zhonghua Renmin Gonghe Guo) | | |
| | Beijing | Mandarin Chinese | Yuan |

| COUNTRY | CAPITAL | LANGUAGE | CURRENCY |
|---------|---------|----------|----------|
| **Hong Kong** | (Crown Colony of Hong Kong) | | |
| | Hong Kong | Cantonese English | Hong Kong dollar |
| **Japan** | (Nippon) | | |
| | Tokyo | Japanese | Yen |
| **North Korea** | (Chosun Minchu-chui Inmin Konghwa-guk) | | |
| | Pyongyang | Korean | North Korean won |
| **South Korea** | (Taehan Min'guk) | | |
| | Seoul | Korean | South Korean won |
| **Macao** | (Macàu) | | |
| | Macao City | Cantonese Portuguese | Pataca |
| **Mongolia** | (Bügd Nayramdakh Mongol Ard Uls) | | |
| | Ulan Bator | Mongolian | Tugrik |
| **Taiwan** | (Chung-hua Min-kuo) | | |
| | Taipei | Mandarin Chinese | New Taiwan dollar |

# AUSTRALASIA
## Populations

**1990 (000s)**

| | | | | |
|---|---|---:|---|---:|
| **1** | Australia | 17 005 | **8** Tonga | 99 |
| **2** | Papua New Guinea | 3 915 | **9** Micronesia | 86 |
| **3** | New Zealand | 3 405 | **10** Kiribati | 70 |
| **4** | Fiji | 749 | **11** Marshall Islands | 40 |
| **5** | Solomon Islands | 324 | **12** Palau | 12 |
| **6** | Western Samoa | 165 | **13** Tuvalu | 10 |
| **7** | Vanuatu | 157 | **14** Nauru | 8 |

### **Countries by size**

| | sq km | | | sq km |
|---|---|---|---|---|
| 1 Australia | 7 682 300 | 8 | Tonga | 699 |
| 2 Papua New Guinea | 462 840 | 9 | Kiribati | 684 |
| 3 New Zealand | 265 150 | 10 | Micronesia | 702 |
| 4 Solomon Islands | 29 790 | 11 | Palau | 365 |
| 5 Fiji | 18 330 | 12 | Marshall Islands | 181 |
| 6 Vanuatu | 14 765 | 13 | Tuvalu | 25 |
| 7 Western Samoa | 2 840 | 14 | Nauru | 21 |

### **Densities (people per sq km)**

| | | | | |
|---|---|---|---|---|
| 1 Tuvalu | 400 | 8 | Fiji | 41 |
| 2 Nauru | 381 | 9 | Palau | 33 |
| 3 Marshall Islands | 221 | 10 | New Zealand | 13 |
| 4 Tonga | 142 | 11 | Solomon Islands | 11 |
| 5 Micronesia | 122 | 12 | Vanuatu | 11 |
| 6 Kiribati | 102 | 13 | Papua New Guinea | 8.5 |
| 7 Western Samoa | 58 | 14 | Australia | 2 |

### **Per capita GNP (1990 US$)**

| | | | | |
|---|---|---|---|---|
| 1 Australia | 17 080 | 3 | Fiji | 1 770 |
| 2 New Zealand | 12 680 | 4 | Vanuatu | 1 060 |

Per capita GNP (1990 US$) (continued)

| | | | |
|---|---|---|---|
| **5** Tonga | 1 010 | Marshall Islands | NA |
| **6** Papua New | | Micronesia | NA |
| Guinea | 860 | Nauru | NA |
| **7** Kiribati | 760 | Palau | NA |
| **8** Western Samoa | 730 | Tuvalu | NA |
| **9** Solomon Islands | 580 | | |

| COUNTRY | CAPITAL | LANGUAGE | CURRENCY |
|---|---|---|---|
| **Australia** | (Commonwealth of Australia) | | |
| | Canberra | English | Australian dollar |
| **Fiji** | (Republic of Fiji) | | |
| | Suva | English | Fiji dollar |
| **Marshall Islands** | (Marshall Islands) | | |
| | Majuro | English | US Dollar |
| **Kiribati** | (Republic of Kiribati) | | |
| | Tarawa | Gilbertese English | Australian dollar |
| **Micronesia** | (Federated States of Micronesia) | | |
| | Palikir | English | US dollar |
| **Nauru** | (Naoero) | | |
| | Yaren | Nauran English | Australian dollar |
| **New Zealand** | (New Zealand) | | |
| | Wellington | English | New Zealand dollar |
| **Palau** | (Republic of Palau) | | |
| | Koror | English | US dollar |
| **Papua New Guinea** | (Papua New Guinea) | | |
| | Port Moresby | English | Kina |

| COUNTRY | CAPITAL | LANGUAGE | CURRENCY |
|---|---|---|---|
| **Solomon Islands** (Solomon Islands) | | | |
| | Honiara | English | Dollar |
| **Tonga** | (Pule 'anga Tonga) | | |
| | Nuku'alofa | Tongan English | Pa'anga |
| **Tuvalu** | (Tuvalu) | | |
| | Funafuti | Tuvaluan English | Australian dollar |
| **Vanuatu** | (Ripablik Blong Vanuatu) | | |
| | Vila | Bislama English French | Australian dollar Vanuatu franc |
| **Western Samoa** (Malotuto'atasi o Samoa i Sisifo) | | | |
| | Apia | Samoan English | Tala |

# NORTH AMERICA
**Populations**

**1990 (000s)**

| | | | | |
|---|---|---|---|---|
| **1** USA | 250 942 | **3** Canada | 26 543 |
| **2** Mexico | 86 161 | | |

**Densities (people per sq km)**

| | | | |
|---|---|---|---|
| **1** Mexico | 44 | **3** Canada | 3 |
| **2** USA | 27 | | |

**Per capita GNP (1990 US$)**

| | | | |
|---|---|---|---|
| **1** USA | 21 700 | **3** Mexico | 2 490 |
| **2** Canada | 20 450 | | |

| COUNTRY | CAPITAL | LANGUAGE | CURRENCY |
|---|---|---|---|
| **Canada** | (Canada) | | |
| | Ottawa | English French | Canadian dollar |

| COUNTRY | CAPITAL | LANGUAGE | CURRENCY |
|---------|---------|----------|----------|
| **Mexico** | (Estados Unidos Mexicanos) | | |
| | Mexico City | Spanish | Mexican peso |
| **USA** | (United States of America) | | |
| | Washington DC | English | US dollar |

**Countries by size**

| | sq km |
|---|---|
| **1** Canada | 9 922 385 |
| **2** USA | 9 363 130 |
| **3** Mexico | 1 972 545 |

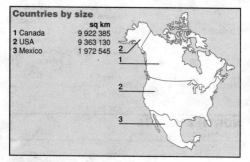

## CENTRAL AMERICA
**Populations**

**1990 (000s)**

| | | | |
|---|---|---|---|
| **1** Guatemala | 9 196 | **5** Costa Rica | 2 801 |
| **2** El Salvador | 5 258 | **6** Panama | 2 418 |
| **3** Honduras | 5 119 | **7** Belize | 189 |
| **4** Nicaragua | 3 853 | | |

**Densities (people per sq km)**

| | | | |
|---|---|---|---|
| **1** El Salvador | 246 | **5** Panama | 31 |
| **2** Guatemala | 84 | **6** Nicaragua | 26 |
| **3** Costa Rica | 55 | **7** Belize | 8 |
| **4** Honduras | 46 | | |

**Per capita GNP (1990 US$)**

| | | | | |
|---|---|---|---|---|
| **1** Belize | 1 970 | | **5** Nicaragua | <1 499 |
| **2** Costa Rica | 1 910 | | **6** Guatemala | 900 |
| **3** Panama | 1 830 | | **7** Honduras | 590 |
| **4** El Salvador | 1 100 | | | |

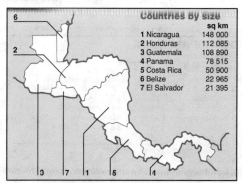

Countries by size

| | | sq km |
|---|---|---|
| **1** | Nicaragua | 148 000 |
| **2** | Honduras | 112 085 |
| **3** | Guatemala | 108 890 |
| **4** | Panama | 78 515 |
| **5** | Costa Rica | 50 900 |
| **6** | Belize | 22 965 |
| **7** | El Salvador | 21 395 |

| COUNTRY | CAPITAL | LANGUAGE | CURRENCY |
|---|---|---|---|
| **Belize** | (Belize) | | |
| | Belmopan | English | Belize dollar |
| **Costa Rica** | (República de Costa Rica) | | |
| | San José | Spanish | Costa Rica colón |
| **El Salvador** | (República de El Salvador) | | |
| | San Salvador | Spanish | El Salvador colón |
| **Guatemala** | (República de Guatemala) | | |
| | Guatemala City | Spanish | Quetzal |

| COUNTRY | CAPITAL | LANGUAGE | CURRENCY |
|---|---|---|---|
| **Honduras** | (República de Honduras) | | |
| | Tegucigalpa | Spanish | Lempira |
| **Nicaragua** | (República de Nicaragua) | | |
| | Managua | Spanish | Córdoba |
| **Panama** | (República de Panamá) | | |
| | Panama City | Spanish | Balboa |

# SOUTH AMERICA
## Populations

### 1990 (000s)

| | | | | |
|---|---|---|---|---|
| **1** Brazil | 150 197 | | **8** Bolivia | 7 310 |
| **2** Colombia | 32 843 | | **9** Paraguay | 4 314 |
| **3** Argentina | 32 293 | | **10** Uruguay | 3 093 |
| **4** Peru | 21 662 | | **11** Guyana | 798 |
| **5** Venezuela | 19 738 | | **12** Suriname | 447 |
| **6** Chile | 13 177 | | **13** French Guiana | 93 |
| **7** Ecuador | 10 559 | | | |

### Densities (people per sq km)

| | | | | |
|---|---|---|---|---|
| **1** Colombia | 25 | | **8** Argentina | 12 |
| **2** Ecuador | 23 | | **9** Paraguay | 11 |
| **3** Venezuela | 22 | | **10** Bolivia | 7 |
| **4** Brazil | 18 | | **11** Guyana | 4 |
| **5** Chile | 18 | | **12** Suriname | 3 |
| **6** Peru | 17 | | **13** French Guiana | 1 |
| **7** Uruguay | 17 | | | |

### Per capita GNP (1990 US$)

| | | | | |
|---|---|---|---|---|
| **1** Suriname | 3 050 | | **8** Colombia | 1 240 |
| **2** Brazil | 2 680 | | **9** Peru | 1 160 |
| **3** Uruguay | 2 560 | | **10** Paraguay | 1 110 |
| **4** Venezuela | 2 560 | | **11** Ecuador | 960 |
| **5** Argentina | 2 370 | | **12** Bolivia | 620 |
| **6** Chile | 1 940 | | **13** Guyana | 370 |
| **7** French Guiana | > 1 500 | | | |

**Countries by size**

| | sq km | | sq km |
|---|---|---|---|
| 1 Brazil | 8 511 965 | 8 Ecuador | 461 475 |
| 2 Argentina | 2 777 815 | 9 Paraguay | 406 750 |
| 3 Peru | 1 285 215 | 10 Guyana | 214 970 |
| 4 Colombia | 1 138 915 | 11 Uruguay | 186 925 |
| 5 Bolivia | 1 098 575 | 12 Suriname | 163 820 |
| 6 Venezuela | 912 045 | 13 French Guiana | 91 000 |
| 7 Chile | 751 625 | | |

| COUNTRY | CAPITAL | LANGUAGE | CURRENCY |
|---|---|---|---|
| **Argentina** | (República de Argentina) | | |
| | Buenos Aires | Spanish | Austral |
| **Bolivia** | (República de Bolivia) | | |
| | La Paz (administrative) | Spanish Aymara | Boliviano |
| | Sucre (legislative, judicial) | Quechua | |
| **Brazil** | (República Federativa do Brasil) | | |
| | Brasilia | Portuguese | Cruzeiro |
| **Chile** | (República de Chile) | | |
| | Santiago | Spanish | Peso |
| **Colombia** | (República de Colombia) | | |
| | Bogotá | Spanish | Peso |
| **Ecuador** | (República del Ecuador) | | |
| | Quito | Spanish | Sucre |
| **French Guiana** | (Département de Guiana) | | |
| | Cayenne | French | French franc |
| **Guyana** | (Cooperative Republic of Guyana) | | |
| | Georgetown | English | Guyana dollar |
| **Paraguay** | (República del Paraguay) | | |
| | Asunción | Spanish | Guarani |
| **Peru** | (República del Perú) | | |
| | Lima | Spanish Quechua | New sol |
| **Suriname** | (Republiek Suriname) | | |
| | Paramaribo | Dutch | Suriname guilder |
| **Uruguay** | (República del Uruguay) | | |
| | Montevideo | Spanish | New peso |

| COUNTRY | CAPITAL | LANGUAGE | CURRENCY |
|---|---|---|---|
| **Venezuela** | (República de Venezuela) | | |
| | Caracas | Spanish | Bolívar |

# CARIBBEAN

**Countries by size**

| | sq km | | | sq km |
|---|---|---|---|---|
| 1 Cuba | 114 525 | | 13 Antigua and Barbuda | 442 |
| 2 Dominican Republic | 48 440 | | 14 Barbados | 430 |
| 3 Haiti | 27 408 | | 15 Turks and Caicos Islands | 430 |
| 4 Bahamas | 13 865 | | 16 St Vincent and the Grenadines | 389 |
| 5 Jamaica | 11 425 | | 17 Grenada | 345 |
| 6 Puerto Rico | 8 960 | | 18 US Virgin Islands | 345 |
| 7 Trinidad and Tobago | 5 130 | | 19 St Kitts and Nevis | 261 |
| 8 Guadeloupe | 1 780 | | 20 Cayman Islands | 259 |
| 9 Martinique | 1 079 | | 21 British Virgin Isles | 153 |
| 10 Netherlands Antilles | 993 | | 22 Montserrat | 104 |
| 11 Dominica | 751 | | 23 Bermuda (not shown) | 54 |
| 12 St Lucia | 616 | | | |

## Populations

### 1990 (000s)

| | | | | | |
|---|---|---|---|---|---|
| **1** Cuba | 10 626 | | **13** St Vincent and | | |
| **2** Dominican | | | the Grenadines | 114 | |
| Republic | 7 140 | | **14** US Virgin Isles | 110 | |
| **3** Haiti | 6 488 | | **15** Grenada | 94 | |
| **4** Puerto Rico | 3 309 | | **16** Dominica | 82 | |
| **5** Jamaica | 2 390 | | **17** Antigua and | | |
| **6** Trinidad and | | | Barbuda | 79 | |
| Tobago | 1 283 | | **18** Bermuda | 58 | |
| **7** Guadeloupe | 343 | | **19** St Kitts and Nevis | 40 | |
| **8** Martinique | 341 | | **20** Cayman Islands | 21 | |
| **9** Barbados | 257 | | **21** British Virgin Isles | 12 | |
| **10** Bahamas | 253 | | **22** Montserrat | 12 | |
| **11** Netherlands | | | **23** Turks and | | |
| Antilles | 191 | | Caicos Islands | 7 | |
| **12** St Lucia | 150 | | | | |

### Densities (people per sq km)

| | | | | | |
|---|---|---|---|---|---|
| **1** Bermuda | 1 074 | | **14** Antigua and | | |
| **2** Barbados | 598 | | Barbuda | 179 | |
| **3** Puerto Rico | 369 | | **15** St Kitts and Nevis | 153 | |
| **4** US Virgin Isles | 319 | | **16** Dominican | | |
| **5** Martinique | 316 | | Republic | 147 | |
| **6** St Vincent and | | | **17** Montserrat | 115 | |
| the Grenadines | 293 | | **18** Dominica | 109 | |
| **7** Grenada | 272 | | **19** Cuba | 93 | |
| **8** Trinidad and | | | **20** Cayman Isles | 81 | |
| Tobago | 250 | | **21** British Virgin Isles | 78 | |
| **9** St Lucia | 243 | | **22** Bahamas | 18 | |
| **10** Haiti | 237 | | **23** Turks and | | |
| **11** Jamaica | 209 | | Caicos Isles | 16 | |
| **12** Guadeloupe | 193 | | | | |
| **13** Netherlands | | | | | |
| Antilles | 192 | | | | |

**Per capita GNP (1990 US$)**

| | | | | |
|---|---|---|---|---|
| 1 | Bahamas | 11 510 | 12 Grenada | 2 120 |
| 2 | Barbados | 6 540 | 13 Dominica | 1 940 |
| 3 | Puerto Rico | 6 470 | 14 St Lucia | 1 900 |
| 4 | Guadaloupe | > 6 000 | 15 St Vincent and | |
| | Netherlands | | the Grenadines | 1 610 |
| | Antilles | > 6 000 | 16 Jamaica | 1 510 |
| | Bermuda | > 6 000 | 17 Dominican | |
| 7 | Martinique | > 5 999 | Republic | 889 |
| 8 | Antigua and | | 18 Haiti | 400 |
| | Barbuda | 4 600 | US Virgin Isles | NA |
| 9 | Trinidad and | | Montsarat | NA |
| | Tobago | 3 470 | Cayman Isles | NA |
| 10 | St Kitts and | | British Virgin Isles | NA |
| | Nevis | 3 330 | Turks and | |
| 11 | Cuba | 2 644 | Caicos Islands | NA |

| COUNTRY | CAPITAL | LANGUAGE | CURRENCY |
|---|---|---|---|
| **Antigua and Barbuda** (Antigua and Barbuda) | | | |
| | St John's | English | East Caribbean dollar |
| **Bahamas** (The Commonwealth of the Bahamas) | | | |
| | Nassau | English | Bahamas dollar |
| **Barbados** (Barbados) | | | |
| | Bridgetown | English | Barbadan dollar |
| **Bermuda** (Bermuda) | | | |
| | Hamilton | English | Bemuda dollar |
| **British Virgin Isles** (British Virgin Isles) | | | |
| | Road Town | English | US dollar |
| **Cayman Isles** (Cayman Islands) | | | |
| | Georgetown | English | Cayman Islands dollar |

| COUNTRY | CAPITAL | LANGUAGE | CURRENCY |
|---|---|---|---|
| **Cuba** | (República De Cuba) | | |
| | Havana | Spanish | Cuban peso |
| **Dominica** | (Commonwealth of Dominica) | | |
| | Roseau | English | East Caribbean dollar |
| **Dominican Republic** | (República Dominicana) | | |
| | Santo Domingo | Spanish | Peso |
| **Grenada** | (Grenada) | | |
| | St George's | English | East Caribbean dollar |
| **Guadeloupe** | (Guadeloupe) | | |
| | Basse-Tenne | French | Franc |
| **Haiti** | (République d'Haiti) | | |
| | Port-au-Prince | French Creole | Gourde |
| **Jamaica** | (Jamaica) | | |
| | Kingston | English | Jamaican dollar |
| **Martinique** | (Martinique) | | |
| | Fort-de-France | French | French franc |
| **Montserrat** | (Montserrat) | | |
| | Plymouth | English | East Caribbean dollar |
| **Netherlands Antilles** | (Nedelandse Antillen) | | |
| | Willemstad | Dutch Spanish | Netherlands Antilles guilder |

| COUNTRY | CAPITAL | LANGUAGE | CURRENCY |
|---|---|---|---|
| **Puerto Rico** (Estado LIbre Asociado de Puerto Rico) | | | |
| | San Juan | Spanish | Dollar |
| **St Kitts and Nevis** (Federation of St Kitts and Nevis) | | | |
| | Basseterre | English | East Caribbean dollar |
| **St Lucia** | (St Lucia) | | |
| | Castries | English | East Caribbean dollar |
| **St Vincent and the Grenadines** | | | |
| | Kingstown | English | East Caribbean dollar |
| **US Virgin Islands** (Virgin Islands of the United States) | | | |
| | Charlotte Amalie | English | US dollar |
| **Trinidad and Tobago** (Republic of Trinidad and Tobago) | | | |
| | Port of Spain | English | Dollar |
| **Turks and Caicos Islands** (Turks and Caicos Islands) | | | |
| | Grand Turk | English | US dollar |

# NORTHERN AFRICA
## Populations

**1990 (000s)**

| | | | |
|---|---|---|---|
| **1** Egypt | 52 061 | **5** Tunisia | 8 175 |
| **2** Sudan | 25 191 | **6** Libya | 4 546 |
| **3** Morocco | 25 091 | **7** Western Sahara | 163 |
| **4** Algeria | 25 056 | | |

**Densities (people per sq km)**

| | | | |
|---|---|---|---|
| **1** Morocco | 57 | **5** Sudan | 10 |
| **2** Egypt | 52 | **6** Libya | 3 |
| **3** Tunisia | 50 | **7** Western Sahara | 1 |
| **4** Algeria | 11 | | |

## Countries by size

| | sq km | | sq km |
|---|---|---|---|
| 1 Sudan | 2 505 815 | 5 Morocco | |
| 2 Algeria | 2 381 745 | (including W. Sahara) | 710 850 |
| 3 Libya | 1 759 540 | (without W. Sahara) | 458 730 |
| 4 Egypt | 1 000 250 | 6 Western Sahara | 252 120 |
| | | 7 Tunisia | 164 150 |

## Per capita GNP (1990 US$)

| | | | |
|---|---|---|---|
| 1 Libya | 5 420 | 5 Egypt | 600 |
| 2 Algeria | 2 060 | 6 Sudan | < 500 |
| 3 Tunisia | 1 420 | 7 Western Sahara | NA |
| 4 Morocco | 950 | | |

| COUNTRY | CAPITAL | LANGUAGE | CURRENCY |
|---|---|---|---|
| **Algeria** | (al-Jumhuriya al-Jazairiya ad-Dimuqratiya Ash-Shabiya) | | |
| | Algiers | Arabic | Algerian dinar |
| **Egypt** | (Jumhuriyah Misr Al-Arabiya) | | |
| | Cairo | Arabic | Egyptian pound |

| COUNTRY | CAPITAL | LANGUAGE | CURRENCY |
|---|---|---|---|
| **Libya** | (al-Jamahiriyah al-Arabiya al-Libya al-Shabiya al-Ishtirakiya) | | |
| | Tripoli | Arabic | Libyan dinar |
| **Morocco** | (al-Mamlaka al-Maghrebia) | | |
| | Rabat | Arabic | Dirham |
| **Sudan** | (Jamhuryat as-Sudan) | | |
| | Khartoum | Arabic | Sudanese pound |
| **Tunisia** | (al-Jumhuriyah at-Tunisiyah) | | |
| | Tunis | Arabic | Tunisian dinar |
| **Western Sahara** | | | |
| | Laâyoune | Arabic | Peseta |

## CENTRAL AFRICA

**Countries by size**

| | | sq km |
|---|---|---|
| 1 | Zaire | 2 345 410 |
| 2 | Angola | 1 246 700 |
| 3 | Zambia | 752 615 |
| 4 | Central African Republic | 624 975 |
| 5 | Congo | 342 000 |
| 6 | Gabon | 267 665 |
| 7 | Equatorial Guinea | 28 050 |
| 8 | São Tomé and Príncipe | 964 |

## Populations

**1990 (000s)**

| | | | | | |
|---|---|---|---|---|---|
| 1 | Zaire | 35 563 | 5 | Congo | 2 277 |
| 2 | Angola | 10 011 | 6 | Gabon | 1 135 |
| 3 | Zambia | 8 122 | 7 | Equatorial Guinea | 417 |
| 4 | Central African Republic | 3 036 | 8 | São Tomé and Príncipe | 123 |

**Densities (people per sq km)**

| | | | | | |
|---|---|---|---|---|---|
| 1 | São Tomé and Príncipe | 128 | 5 | Angola | 8 |
| 2 | Equatorial Guinea | 15 | 6 | Congo | 7 |
| 3 | Zaire | 15 | 7 | Central African Republic | 5 |
| 4 | Zambia | 11 | 8 | Gabon | 4 |

**Per capita GNP (1990 US$)**

| | | | | | |
|---|---|---|---|---|---|
| 1 | Gabon | 3 220 | 6 | São Tomé and Príncipe | 380 |
| 2 | Congo | 1 010 | 7 | Equatorial Guinea | 330 |
| 3 | Angola | 620 | 8 | Zaire | 230 |
| 4 | Zambia | 420 | | | |
| 5 | Central African Republic | 390 | | | |

| COUNTRY | CAPITAL | LANGUAGE | CURRENCY |
|---|---|---|---|
| **Angola** | (República Popular de Angola) | | |
| | Luanda | Portuguese | New kwanza |
| **Central African Republic** | (République Centrafricaine) | | |
| | Bangui | French | CFA franc |
| **Congo** | (République Populaire du Congo) | | |
| | Brazzaville | French | CFA franc |
| **Equatorial Guinea** | (República de Guinea Ecuatorial) | | |
| | Malabo | Spanish | Bipkwele |
| **Gabon** | (République Gabonaise) | | |
| | Libreville | French | CFA franc |

| COUNTRY | CAPITAL | LANGUAGE | CURRENCY |
|---|---|---|---|
| **São Tomé and Príncipe** (República Democrática de São Tomé e Príncipe) | | | |
| | São Tomé | Portuguese | Dobra |
| **Zaïre** (République du Zaïre) | | | |
| | Kinshása | French | Zaïre |
| **Zambia** (Republic of Zambia) | | | |
| | Lusaka | English | Kwacha |

## SOUTHERN AFRICA

**Countries by size**

| | | sq km |
|---|---|---|
| 1 | South Africa | 1 184 825 |
| 2 | Namibia | 824 300 |
| 3 | Mozambique | 784 755 |
| 4 | Madagascar | 594 180 |
| 5 | Botswana | 575 000 |
| 6 | Zimbabwe | 390 310 |
| 7 | Lesotho | 30 345 |
| 8 | Swaziland | 17 365 |
| 9 | Réunion | 2 510 |
| 10 | Mauritius | 1 865 |
| 11 | Comoros | 1 860 |

**Populations**

1990 (000s)

| 1 | South Africa | 35 914 | 7 | Botswana | 1 254 |
|---|---|---|---|---|---|
| 2 | Mozambique | 15 784 | 8 | Mauritius | 1 074 |
| 3 | Madagascar | 11 620 | 9 | Swaziland | 789 |
| 4 | Zimbabwe | 9 809 | 10 | Réunion | 593 |
| 5 | Namibia | 1 780 | 11 | Comoros | 475 |
| 6 | Lesotho | 1 771 | | | |

### Densities (people per sq km)

| | | | | | |
|---|---|---|---|---|---|
| **1** | Mauritius | 576 | **7** | Zimbabwe | 25 |
| **2** | Comoros | 255 | **8** | Madagascar | 20 |
| **3** | Réunion | 236 | **9** | Mozambique | 20 |
| **4** | Lesotho | 58 | **10** | Botswana | 2 |
| **5** | Swaziland | 45 | **11** | Namibia | 2 |
| **6** | South Africa | 30 | | | |

### Per capita GNP (1990 US$)

| | | | | | |
|---|---|---|---|---|---|
| **1** | Réunion | < 5 999 | **7** | Zimbabwe | 640 |
| **2** | South Africa | 2 520 | **8** | Comoros | 480 |
| **3** | Mauritius | 2 250 | **9** | Lesotho | 470 |
| **4** | Botswana | 2 040 | **10** | Madagascar | 230 |
| **5** | Namibia | < 1 499 | **11** | Mozambique | 80 |
| **6** | Swaziland | 820 | | | |

| COUNTRY | CAPITAL | LANGUAGE | CURRENCY |
|---|---|---|---|
| **Botswana** | (Republic of Botswana) | | |
| | Gaborone | English | Pula |
| **Comoros** | (Jumhuriyat al-Qumur al-Itthadiyah al-Islamiyah) | | |
| | Moroni | Arabic | CFA franc |
| **Lesotho** | (Kingdom of Lesotho) | | |
| | Maseru | English Sotho | Maloti |
| **Madagascar** | (Repoblika Demokratika Malagasy) | | |
| | Antananarivo | Malagasy | Malagasy franc |
| **Mauritius** | (State of Mauritius) | | |
| | Port Louis | English | Mauritius rupee |
| **Mozambique** | (República Popular de Moçambique) | | |
| | Maputo | Portuguese | Metical |
| **Namibia** | (Namibia) | | |
| | Windhoek | Afrikaans English | S. African rand |

| COUNTRY | CAPITAL | LANGUAGE | CURRENCY |
|---------|---------|----------|----------|
| **Réunion** | (Département de Réunion) | | |
| | St Denis | French | French franc |
| **South Africa** | | (Republic of South Africa) | |
| | Pretoria | Afrikaans | Rand |
| | (administrative) | English | |
| | Cape Town | | |
| | (legislative) | | |
| | Bloemfontein | | |
| | (judicial) | | |
| **Swaziland** | | (Kingdom of Swaziland) | |
| | Mbabane | Swazi | Lilangeni |
| | | English | |
| **Zimbabwe** | (Republic of Zimbabwe) | | |
| | Harare | English | Zimbabwe dollar |

# EASTERN AFRICA

**Countries by size**

| | | sq km |
|---|---|---|
| 1 | Ethiopia | 1 203 050 |
| 2 | Tanzania | 939 760 |
| 3 | Somalia | 630 000 |
| 4 | Kenya | 582 645 |
| 5 | Uganda | 236 580 |
| 6 | Malawi | 94 080 |
| 7 | Burundi | 27 835 |
| 8 | Rwanda | 26 330 |
| 9 | Djibouti | 23 000 |
| 10 | Seychelles | 404 |

**Populations**

**1990 (000s)**

| | | | | | |
|---|---|---|---|---|---|
| **1** Ethiopia | 51 183 | | **6** Rwanda | 7 113 | |
| **2** Tanzania | 24 518 | | **7** Somalia | 6 284 | |
| **3** Kenya | 24 368 | | **8** Burundi | 5 470 | |
| **4** Uganda | 17 358 | | **9** Djibouti | 427 | |
| **5** Malawi | 8 504 | | **10** Seychelles | 68 | |

**Densities (people per sq km)**

| | | | | | |
|---|---|---|---|---|---|
| **1** Rwanda | 270 | | **6** Ethiopia | 43 | |
| **2** Burundi | 197 | | **7** Kenya | 42 | |
| **3** Seychelles | 168 | | **8** Tanzania | 26 | |
| **4** Malawi | 90 | | **9** Djibouti | 19 | |
| **5** Uganda | 73 | | **10** Somalia | 10 | |

**Per capita GNP (1990 US$)**

| | | | | | |
|---|---|---|---|---|---|
| **1** Seychelles | 4 670 | | **6** Burundi | 210 | |
| **2** Djibouti | < 1 490 | | **7** Malawi | 200 | |
| **3** Kenya | 370 | | **8** Somalia | 150 | |
| **4** Rwanda | 310 | | **9** Ethiopia | 120 | |
| **5** Uganda | 220 | | **10** Tanzania | 120 | |

| COUNTRY | CAPITAL | LANGUAGE | CURRENCY |
|---|---|---|---|
| **Burundi** | (Republika y'Uburundi) | | |
| | Bujumbura | French | Burundi |
| | | Kirundi | franc |
| **Djibouti** | (Jumhouriyya Djibouti) | | |
| | Djibouti | French | Djibouti |
| | | Arabic | franc |
| **Ethiopia** | (Ye Etiyop'iya Hezbawi Dimokrasiyawi Republek) | | |
| | Addis Ababa | Amharic | Birr |
| **Kenya** | (Jamhuriya Kenya) | | |
| | Nairobi | Swahili | Kenyan shilling |

| COUNTRY | CAPITAL | LANGUAGE | CURRENCY |
|---|---|---|---|
| **Malawi** | (Republic of Malawi) | | |
| | Lilongwe | English | Kwacha |
| | | Chewa | |
| **Rwanda** | (Republika y'u Rwanda) | | |
| | Kigali | Kinyarwanda | Rwanda |
| | | French | franc |
| **Seychelles** | (Republic of Seychelles) | | |
| | Victoria | English | Seychelles |
| | | French | rupee |
| **Somalia** | (Jamhuriyadda Dimugradiga Somaliya) | | |
| | Mogadishu | Somali | Somali |
| | | Arabic | shilling |
| **Tanzania** | (Jamhuriya Mwungano wa Tanzania) | | |
| | Dodoma | Swahili | Tanzanian |
| | | English | shilling |
| **Uganda** | (Republic of Uganda) | | |
| | Kampala | English | Ugandan |
| | | | shilling |

# WESTERN AFRICA
**Populations**

**1990 (000s)**

| | | | | | |
|---|---|---|---|---|---|
| **1** | Nigeria | 117 510 | **10** | Chad | 5 679 |
| **2** | Ghana | 14 870 | **11** | Benin | 4 741 |
| **3** | Ivory Coast | 12 233 | **12** | Sierra Leone | 4 137 |
| **4** | Cameroon | 11 941 | **13** | Togo | 3 638 |
| **5** | Burkina Faso | 9 016 | **14** | Liberia | 2 560 |
| **6** | Mali | 8 461 | **15** | Mauritania | 1 969 |
| **7** | Niger | 7 666 | **16** | Guinea-Bissau | 981 |
| **8** | Senegal | 7 428 | **17** | Gambia | 875 |
| **9** | Guinea | 5 718 | **18** | Cape Verde | 371 |

## Densities (people per sq km)

| | | | | | |
|---|---|---|---|---|---|
| **1** Nigeria | 127 | | **10** Burkina Faso | 33 |
| **2** Cape Verde | 92 | | **11** Guinea-Bissau | 27 |
| **3** Gambia | 82 | | **12** Cameroon | 25 |
| **4** Togo | 64 | | **13** Guinea | 23 |
| **5** Ghana | 62 | | **14** Liberia | 23 |
| **6** Sierra Leone | 57 | | **15** Mali | 7 |
| **7** Benin | 42 | | **16** Niger | 6 |
| **8** Ivory Coast | 38 | | **17** Chad | 4 |
| **9** Senegal | 38 | | **18** Mauritania | 2 |

## Per capita GNP (1990 US$)

| | | | | | |
|---|---|---|---|---|---|
| **1** Cameroon | 940 | | **10** Benin | 360 |
| **2** Cape Verde | 890 | | **11** Burkina Faso | 330 |
| **3** Ivory Coast | 730 | | **12** Niger | 310 |
| **4** Senegal | 710 | | **13** Mali | 270 |
| **5** Mauritania | 500 | | **14** Nigeria | 270 |
| **6** Liberia | < 500 | | **15** Gambia | 260 |
| **7** Guinea | 480 | | **16** Sierra Leone | 240 |
| **8** Togo | 410 | | **17** Chad | 190 |
| **9** Ghana | 390 | | **18** Guinea-Bissau | 180 |

| COUNTRY | CAPITAL | LANGUAGE | CURRENCY |
|---|---|---|---|
| **Benin** | (République du Benin) | | |
| | Porto-Novo | French | CFA franc |
| **Burkina Faso** | (République du Burkina Faso) | | |
| | Ouagadougou | French | CFA franc |
| **Cameroon** | (Republic of Cameroon) | | |
| | Yaounde | English French | CFA franc |
| **Cape Verde** | (República de Cabo Verde) | | |
| | Praia | Portuguese | Escudo |
| **Chad** | (République du Tchad) | | |
| | N'djamena | French Arabic | CFA franc |

## Countries by size

| | | sq km |
|---|---|---|
| 1 | Chad | 1 284 000 |
| 2 | Mali | 1 240 140 |
| 3 | Niger | 1 186 410 |
| 4 | Mauritania | 1 030 700 |
| 5 | Nigeria | 923 850 |
| 6 | Cameroon | 475 500 |
| 7 | Ivory Coast | 322 463 |
| 8 | Burkina Faso | 274 122 |
| 9 | Guinea | 245 855 |
| 10 | Ghana | 238 305 |
| 11 | Senegal | 196 720 |
| 12 | Benin | 112 620 |
| 13 | Liberia | 111 370 |
| 14 | Sierra Leone | 72 325 |
| 15 | Togo | 56 785 |
| 16 | Guinea-Bissau | 36 125 |
| 17 | Gambia | 10 690 |
| 18 | Cape Verde | 4 035 |

| COUNTRY | CAPITAL | LANGUAGE | CURRENCY |
|---|---|---|---|
| **Ivory Coast** | (République de Côte d'Ivoire) | | |
| | Abidjan | French | CFA franc |
| **Gambia** | (Republic of the Gambia) | | |
| | Banjul | English | Dalasi |
| **Ghana** | (Republic of Ghana) | | |
| | Accra | English | Cedi |
| **Guinea** | (République de Guinée) | | |
| | Conakry | French | Guinea franc |
| **Guinea-Bissau** | (República da Guiné-Bissau) | | |
| | Bissau | Portuguese | Peso |
| **Liberia** | (Republic of Liberia) | | |
| | Monrovia | English | Liberian dollar |

| COUNTRY | CAPITAL | LANGUAGE | CURRENCY |
|---|---|---|---|
| **Mali** | (République du Mali) | | |
| | Bamako | French | Mali franc |
| **Mauritania** | (République Islamique de Mauritanie) | | |
| | Nouakchott | Arabic | Ouguija |
| | | French | |
| **Niger** | (République du Niger) | | |
| | Niamey | French | CFA franc |
| **Nigeria** | (Federal Republic of Nigeria) | | |
| | Abuja | English | Naira |
| **Senegal** | (République du Sénégal) | | |
| | Dakar | French | CFA franc |
| **Sierra Leone** | (Republic of Sierra Leone) | | |
| | Freetown | English | Leone |
| **Togo** | (République Togolaise) | | |
| | Lomé | French | CFA franc |

# MIDDLE EAST
## Populations

**1990 (000s)**

| | | | | | |
|---|---|---|---|---|---|
| **1** Iran | 56 924 | | **8** Jordan | 3 154 |
| **2** Iraq | 18 914 | | **9** Kuwait | 2 141 |
| **3** Saudi Arabia | 14 902 | | **10** United Arab | |
| **4** Syria | 12 533 | | Emirates | 1 592 |
| **5** Yemen | 11 500 | | **11** Oman | 1 554 |
| **6** Israel | 4 636 | | **12** Bahrain | 504 |
| **7** Lebanon | 3 340 | | **13** Qatar | 439 |

### Densities (people per sq km)

| | | | | | |
|---|---|---|---|---|---|
| **1** Bahrain | 762 | | **8** Qatar | 38 |
| **2** Lebanon | 322 | | **9** Iran | 34 |
| **3** Israel | 223 | | **10** Jordan | 33 |
| **4** Kuwait | 88 | | **11** United Arab | |
| **5** Syria | 67 | | Emirates | 21 |
| **6** Yemen | 60 | | **12** Saudi Arabia | 6 |
| **7** Iraq | 43 | | **13** Oman | 6 |

## Countries by size

| | sq km | | sq km |
|---|---|---|---|
| 1 Saudi Arabia | 2 400 900 | 8 United Arab | 75 150 |
| 2 Iran | 1 648 000 | Emirates | |
| 3 Iraq | 438 445 | 9 Kuwait | 24 280 |
| 4 Oman | 271 950 | 10 Israel | 20 770 |
| 5 Yemen | 189 850 | 11 Qatar | 11 400 |
| 6 Syria | 185 680 | 12 Lebanon | 10 400 |
| 7 Jordan | 96 000 | 13 Bahrain | 661 |

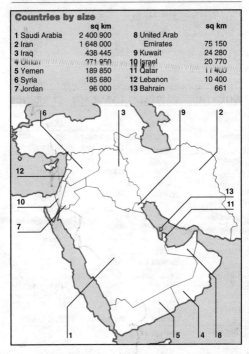

**Per capita GNP (1990 US$)**

| | | | | |
|---|---|---|---|---|
| **1** United Arab Emirates | 19 860 | **7** Jordan | 1 240 |
| **2** Kuwait | 16 380 | **8** Syria | 1 020 |
| **3** Bahrain | 9 994 | **9** Israel | 940 |
| **4** Qatar | 9 920 | **10** Lebanon | 690 |
| **5** Iraq | 1 950 | **11** Yemen | 640 |
| **6** Iran | 1 800 | Oman | NA |
| | | Saudi Arabia | NA |

| COUNTRY | CAPITAL | LANGUAGE | CURRENCY |
|---|---|---|---|
| **Bahrain** | (Dawlat al-Bahrayn) | | |
| | Manama | Arabic | Dinar |
| **Iran** | (Jomhori-e-Islami-e-Iran) | | |
| | Tehran | Farsi | Rial |
| **Iraq** | (Al Jumhouriya Al 'Iraqia) | | |
| | Baghdad | Arabic | Dinar |
| **Israel** | (Medinat Israel) | | |
| | Jerusalem | Hebrew Arabic | Shekel |
| **Jordan** | (al Mamlaka al Urduniya al Hashemiyah) | | |
| | Amman | Arabic | Jordanian dinar |
| **Kuwait** | (Dowlat al-kuwait) | | |
| | Kuwait City | Arabic | Kuwaiti dinar |
| **Lebanon** | (al-Jumhouriya al-Lubnaniya) | | |
| | Beirut | Arabic | Lebanese pound |
| **Oman** | (Saltanat 'Uman) | | |
| | Muscat | Arabic | Rial Omani |
| **Qatar** | (Dawlet al-Qatar) | | |
| | Doha | Arabic | Riyal |
| **Saudi Arabia** | (al-Mamlaka al-' Arabiya as-Sa'udiya) | | |
| | Riyadh | Arabic | Riyal |

| COUNTRY | CAPITAL | LANGUAGE | CURRENCY |
|---|---|---|---|
| **Syria** | (al-Jamhouriya al-Arabia as-Souriya) | | |
| | Damascus | Arabic | Syrian pound |
| **United Arab Emirates** | (Ittihad al-Imarat al-Arabiyah) | | |
| | Abu Dhabi | Arabic | Dirham |
| **Yemen** | (al-Jumhurïyah al-Yamaniyah) | | |
| | Sana | Arabic | Yemeni riyal |

# PART 3

# HISTORY

# EARLY MAN 3 MILLION–3000 BC

| | |
|---|---|
| 3 million–8000 | **Palaeolithic (Old Stone Age)** |
| c. 400 000 –360 000 | Middle Pleistocene Period. Peking man in Asia, southern Europe. Makes tools, uses fire, hunts, gathers berries, grains, nuts. Practises burial |
| c. 120 000 –75 000 | Neanderthal man (*Homo sapiens neanderthalensis*) in Africa, Europe and Asia. Improves hunting skills, cares for the old |
| c. 60 000 | Neanderthal man includes flowers in burial rites (Near East) |
| c. 50 000 | Last Ice Age ends. Neanderthal man reaches Australia |
| c. 40 000–20 000 | ***Homo sapiens sapiens*** develops. Controls fire, improves tools, hunts, fishes, collects honey, fruit and nuts |
| c. 36 000 | *Homo sapiens* reaches Americas from Asia |
| c. 35 000 | Cave paintings in France and Spain |
| c. 33 000 | *Homo sapiens* dominant species; Neanderthal man declines |
| c. 28 000 | Seafarers reach New Guinea and Japan from Asian mainland |
| c. 13 500 | Northern ice sheet melts, causing flooding |
| c. 12 000 | Dogs domesticated (Near East) |
| c. 10 000 | Goats domesticated (Near East) |
| 8000–2700 | **Mesolithic (Middle Stone Age)** |
| c. 8000 | Agriculture begins (Near East) |
| c. 7500 | Sheep domesticated (Greece) |
| c. 7000 | Wheat and barley cultivated, walled settlements develop (Near East) |
| c. 6500 | Wheel developed by Sumerians |
| c. 6000 | Pottery evolved. Stilt houses built by lake dwellers, bread made, fruit and vegetables preserved by drying (Switzerland) |
| c. 5500 | Copper smelted (Persia) |
| c. 5000 | Irrigation canals and ditches built in Nile area |
| c. 4000 | Horses domesticated (Europe). Fruit cultivated, wine made (Indus Valley) |
| c. 3500 | **Bronze made** (south-west Asia). Wheeled vehicles and oar-propelled ships developed by Sumerians |
| c. 3000 | Cuneiform writing developed by Sumerians |

# MIDDLE EAST 3000–500 BC

| | |
|---|---|
| c. 2800 | **Menes of Upper Egypt first pharaoh of first dynasty** |
| c. 2700 | Gilgamesh builds walls around Uruk |
| c. 2600 | Third Egyptian dynasty; step pyramid built |
| c. 2550 | Fourth Egyptian dynasty; **Great Pyramid at Giza**, Great Sphinx |
| c. 2500 | First civilization at Troy |
| c. 2400 | Akkad dynasty in Mesopotamia |
| c. 2300 | Guti tribesmen destroy Mesopotamian empire |
| c. 2200 | Egypt fragments with dynasties in rival capitals |
| c. 2000 | Middle kingdom reunites Egypt |
| c. 1900 | Start of first Babylonian empire |
| c. 1800 | Babylon supreme: **Hammurabi's legal code** |
| c. 1500 | Hittites sack Aleppo and Babylon; establish Hittite old kingdom |
| c. 1375–1350 | Pharaoh Akhenaton attempts to introduce monotheistic religion |
| c. 1300 | **Exodus of Jews from Egypt** |
| c. 1250–1200 | Israelites conquer Palestine, replacing Canaanites |
| c. 1200 | Hittite empire overthrown by Phrygians |
| c. 1005 | King David of Judea defeats |
| 841 | Philistines, unites Israel |
| 750 | Assyrians conquer Syria |
| | Nubians conquer Egypt |
| 732–29 | Assyrians annexe Babylon and Damascus |
| 724–21 | Assyria annexes Israel |
| 708 | Empire of Medes founded |
| 669–63 | **Assyrians conquer Egypt** |
| | Second Babylonian empire established. Collapse of Assyrian empire |
| 614 | Medes sack Assur |
| 612 | Babylonians and Medes sack Nineveh |
| 610 | Babylonians annihilate Assyrian army; end of Assyrian state |
| 605 | King Nebuchadnezzar of Babylon defeats Egyptians |
| 598 | Nebuchadnezzar takes Jerusalem |
| 550 | Cyrus of Persia defeats Medes |
| 539 | Cyrus annexes Babylonia; Persian empire supreme |
| 525 | Egypt conquered by Persians |
| 521 | Darius usurps Persian throne |
| 516 | Darius campaigns against Syths; annexes Indus valley |

# ASIA 3000 BC – AD 1

| c. 3000 | Harappan culture in Indus Valley |
| 2200 | Haia dynasty in China |
| c. 1800 | Indus Valley invaded by Aryans |
| c. 1200 | Cambodia settled |
| c. 1100 | Zhou dynasty in China overthrows Shang |
| c. 770 | Nomads invade Zhou capital Hao |
| c. 720 | Warring feudal states claim independence in China |
| c. 660 | Jimmu Tenno emperor in Japan |
| 605–520 | **Lao Zi, Chinese philosopher, founder of Taoism** |
| 563–483 | **Siddhartha Gautama, the Buddha** |
| 551–479 | Confucius (Kongzi), Chinese founder of Confucianism |
| c. 510 | Persians annexe Indus Valley |
| c. 500 | Mons and Tibetan peoples enter Burma. **Magadha kingdom on Ganges** |
| c. 400 | Nana dynasty usurps Magadha kingdom |
| 330 | Viet kingdom in lower Yangtse Valley destroyed |
| 329–25 | Alexander the Great campaigns in India and conquers the Punjab |
| 321 | Mauryan dynasty in north-east India |
| 316 | Chinese destroy Au Lac kingdom |
| 305 | Alexander's general Seleucus attempts to invade India |
| c. 300 | China invaded by Huns (Hsiung-nu) |
| 273 | Ashoka becomes Mauryan emperor |
| 258 | Second kingdom of Au Lac |
| c. 250 | Korean Yaoi people in Japan |
| 232 | Ashoka dies; kingdom divided between grandsons |
| 220–10 | **Great Wall of China built to keep out Hsiung-nu** |
| 206 | Han dynasty in China as last Qin emperor dies; independent feudal states incorporated into territory |
| c. 200 | Tamils invade Ceylon |
| c. 174–60 | Yueh-Chi enter India from China |
| 160–40 | Hsiung-nu fight Han dynasty |
| 133–19 | Renewed conflict between Hsiung-nu and Han dynasty |
| 111 | Vietnam conquered by China |
| 108 | West Korea conquered by China |
| 104–2 | Hsiung-nu fail to follow up military success against Han troops |
| c. 100 | Andhra dynasty in South India |
| 58–51 | Hsiung-nu revert to nomadism |
| c. 50 | Satavhana dynasty in South India |
| c. 10 | Langkasuka kingdom in Malaysia c. |

# HELLENISTIC WORLD 2000 BC – AD 1

| | |
|---|---|
| 2000– | Bronze Age: Athens, Argos, Thebes founded |
| 1800 BC | **Minoan culture in Crete** |
| 1800–1700 | Mycenaean civilization begins |
| 1580 | Minoan culture destroyed |
| 1450–1375 | Corinth founded |
| 1350 | Mycenaean king mainland overlord |
| 1300–1200 | **Trojan war; Greece defeats Troy** |
| c. 1200 | Iron Age. North Greeks (Dorians) conquer Mycenaeans |
| 1200–1100 | Sparta founded |
| 1100–1000 | **Olympic Games founded** |
| 776 | Greeks settle Anatolia and Syria |
| 650–650 | Democratic constitution in Athens |
| 508 | Ionian Greeks rebel against Persia; suppressed |
| 499–494 | **Persians, under Darius, invade Greece; defeated at Marathon** |
| 490 | Persians invade under Xerxes; Athens burned |
| 480 | **Greeks defeat Persians at Salamis and Plataea** |
| 479 | League of Delos establishes Athenian democracy |
| 477 | |

| | |
|---|---|
| 443–29 | Athens under Pericles |
| 431–4 | **Peloponnesian War;** Sparta defeats Athens. |
| 415–13 | Athenian expedition to Syracuse |
| 408 | Rhodes founded |
| 398 | **Socrates condemned to death in Athens** |
| 387 | Sparta makes treaty with Persia |
| 385 | Plato (Socrates' pupil) founds Academy in Athens |
| 378 | Athens allies with Thebes |
| 382 | Thebes defeated by Sparta |
| 359 | Philip II becomes King of Macedon |
| 356 | Birth of Alexander the Great |
| 343 | Aristotle appointed Alexander's tutor |
| 338–36 | Philip II of Macedon defeats Athenians and Thebans, then is assassinated |
| 334–26 | **Alexander the Great conquers Persian empire; founds Alexandria** |
| 280 | Pharos of Alexandria and Colossus of Rhodes built |
| 211 | Romans sack Syracuse |
| 197 | Romans defeat Philip V of Macedon |
| 171–68 | Rome conquers Macedon |
| 148–46 | **Rome annexes Greece** |

# THE ROMAN WORLD 750 BC – AD 500

| | |
|---|---|
| **753 BC** | **City of Rome founded** |
| c. 338 | Earliest Roman coins |
| 312 | Emperor Appius Claudius completes Appian aqueduct and begins Appian Way |
| **264–41** | **First Punic War between Rome and Carthage** |
| 218–1 | Second Punic War. Hannibal defeated by Fabius Maximus in Crete |
| 215 | Roman armies in Spain |
| 172–68 | War between Rome and Macedon. Beginning of Roman world domination |
| 170 | Earliest known paved streets in Rome |
| **149–46** | **Third Punic War. The destruction of Carthage** |
| 82–79 | Dictatorship of Sulla |
| 70–19 | Virgil, Roman poet |
| 73–71 | Slaves' rebellion led by gladiator Spartacus |
| 65–8 | Horace, Roman poet |
| 60 | First Triumvirate between Julius Caesar, Pompey and Crassus |
| **59–51** | **Caesar conquers all of Gaul** |
| 49 | Caesar crosses the Rubicon, an action which begins civil war |
| 47–44 | Dictatorship of Caesar. Assassination of Caesar. |
| 46 | Julian calendar adopted; introduction of leap year |
| 43–AD 18 | Ovid, Roman poet |
| 43–36 | Second Triumvirate between Mark Antony, Octavian Caesar and Lepidus |
| 40 | **Herod appointed king of Judea** |
| 39–31 | Mark Antony allies with Cleopatra of Egypt. They are defeated by Octavian (Augustus) at Battle of Actium. Construction of Roman Pantheon begins |
| 27 | **Augustus proclaimed emperor** |
| AD 14 | Augustus succeeded by Tiberius |
| 37 | Caligula succeeds Tiberius |
| 41 | Caligula assassinated. Succeeded by Claudius |
| 43 | **Roman invasion of Britain under Claudius** |
| 54 | Claudius murdered by his wife. Succeeded by Nero |
| 60–61 | Revolt of Queen Boudicca |

# THE ROMAN WORLD 750 BC – AD 500

| Year | Event |
|---|---|
| 64 | Great fire of Rome. **First persecution of Christians** |
| 65–70 | Jewish revolt crushed. Destruction of Jerusalem |
| 69 | Year of Four Emperors; Vespasian gains throne |
| 78 | Titus proclaimed emperor |
| 79 | Eruption of Mount Vesuvius |
| 81–96 | Titus succeeded by his brother, Domitian |
| 98 | Domitian succeeded by Trajan |
| 98–117 | **Roman empire reaches its greatest geographical extent under Trajan** |
| 116 | Second Jewish revolt led by Bar Kokhba |
| 121–32 | Construction of Hadrian's Wall from Solway to Tyne |
| 161–80 | Reign of Marcus Aurelius |
| 164–80 | Plague sweeps Roman empire |
| 192–3 | Severus emperor |
| c. 190 | Galen establishes medical practices that last 1500 years |
| 257 | Goths invade Black Sea area |
| 248 | **Rome celebrates 1000th anniversary** |
| c. 250–70 | Increased persecution of Christians under Decius |
| 268 | Goths sack Athens, Corinth and Sparta |
| 270–75 | Aurelian emperors launch reconquest |
| 284 | Diocletian proclaimed emperor |
| 305–11 | Renewed persecution of Christians |
| 305 | Diocletian abdicates in the east |
| 306 | Constantine proclaimed emperor |
| 337 | Constantine converts to Christianity on deathbed |
| 363 | **Roman empire splits into West and East** |
| 375–78 | Visigoths invade Roman territory |
| 383 | Romans begin evacuation of Britain |
| 406 | Vandals invade Gaul |
| 408 | **Visigoths, under Alaric, invade Italy** |
| 409–39 | Vandals invade Spain and cross into North Africa (Carthage) |
| 410 | **Alaric captures and sacks Rome** |
| 436 | Last Roman troops leave Britain |
| 451 | Attila leads Hun invasion of Gaul |
| 455 | **Vandals sack Rome** |
| 460 | Vandals destroy Roman fleet |

# THE DARK AGES 500–1000

| | |
|---|---|
| 511 | Clovis, king of Franks, dies |
| 526 | Theodoric the Great, king of the Ostrogoths, dies |
| 527 | Justinian I, east Roman emperor |
| 535–40 | Belisarius conquers Sicily and enters Rome |
| 552 | Narses reconquers Italy |
| 558 | Chlotar, son of Clovis, reunites kingdom of Franks |
| 572 | Emperor Justin at war with Persia |
| 610 | Heraclius, east Roman emperor |
| 613 | Frankish kingdom reunited by Chlotar's grandson, Chlotar |
| 629 | Byzantines expelled from Spain by Visigoths |
| 640–42 | Byzantines defeated by Arabs |
| 687 | Pepin II, mayor of the Franks |
| 732 | **Charles Martel defeats Arabs at Poitiers** |
| 751 | Pepin the Short becomes king of Franks |
| 779 | Offa becomes Anglo-Saxon overlord in England |
| 800 | Charlemagne emperor of West |
| 828 | Egbert, king of Wessex, becomes Anglo-Saxon overlord |
| 843 | Charlemagne's empire partitioned |
| 844 | Picts and Scots united under Kenneth MacAlpine |
| 845–46 | Normans pillage Paris. Arabs pillage Rome |
| 865–74 | Vikings conquer north-east England |
| 871 | Alfred (the Great) king of Wessex |
| 880 | Treaty between Alfred and Viking leader Guthrum partitions England |
| 894–96 | Byzantium at war with Bulgars |
| 895 | Magyars migrate to Hungary |
| 896 | France recognizes dukedom of Normandy |
| 927 | Athelstan established as first king of all England |
| 962 | Otto I crowned emperor of West (Holy Roman Emperor) |
| 965 | Danish king accepts Christianity |
| 979 | Ethelred (the Unready) becomes king of England |
| 980–82 | Renewed Danish raids on southern England |
| 989 | Vladimir, great prince of Kiev, accepts Christianity |
| 991 | Danes raiding East Anglia bought off (Danegeld) |
| 1000 | Sveyn of Denmark kills Olaf of Norway. Venetians conquer Istria |

# ISLAMIC WORLD 500–1500

| | |
|---|---|
| c. 570 | Mohammed born in Mecca |
| 610 | Mohammed preaches first sermon |
| 622 | **Flight to Medina (Hegira); start of Islamic calendar** |
| 630 | Mecca submits to Mohammed |
| 632 | Mohammed dies; father-in-law Abu Bakr elected successor (caliph) |
| 636–41 | Arab expansion begins |
| 634 | Abu Bakr succeeded by Omar |
| 644 | Omar succeeded by Othman |
| 656 | Othman assassinated; succeeded by last Suni caliph, Ali |
| 651 | **Umayyad dynasty founded in Damascus** |
| 680 | Origin of Shiites, supporters of the Prophet's son-in-law, Ali |
| 694 | Umayyads take Carthage |
| 711 | Umayyads invade Spain |
| 750 | Abbasids overthrow Umayyads |
| 786 | Harun al Rashid caliph of Baghdad |
| 874 | Samanid dynasty in Samarkand |
| 962 | Samanids conquer Afghanistan |
| 969 | Fatamids from Morocco conquer Egypt |
| 999 | Ghaznevids overthrow Samanids |
| 1009 | Caliph al Hakim orders destruction of Holy Sepulchre in Jerusalem |
| c. 1020 | Origin of Druzes, a sect venerating the Fatimid caliph al-Hakim, proclaimed God incarnate in 1017 |
| 1037–39 | Seljuk revolt against Ghaznevids |
| 1071 | Seljuks take Anatolia |
| 1099 | Seljuks lose Jerusalem ⊃ Crusaders |
| 1145 | Almohades, a Berber dynasty, cross to Spain |
| 1174 | Saladin sultan of Egypt |
| 1187 | Saladin conquers Jerusalem |
| 1191 | Saladin defeated by Crusaders |
| 1212 | Almohade rule in Spain ends |
| 1236 | Almohade empire starts to fragment |
| 1258 | Mongols take Baghdad |
| 1291 | Mamluks of Egypt take Acre |
| 1356 | Ottomans cross into Europe |
| 1363 | Timur begins conquests in Asia |
| 1390 | Ottoman sultan Beyazit annexes five Turkish emirates in Anatolia |
| 1402 | Timur invades Anatolia |
| 1453 | Ottomans take Constantinople. As Istanbul, it becomes capital of Ottoman (Turkish) empire |
| 1456 | Turks besiege Belgrade; repulsed |
| 1492 | Granada, last Muslim enclave in Spain, falls. Forced conversion of Spanish Muslims to Christianity |

# GOTHIC WORLD 1000–1500

| Year | Event |
|---|---|
| 1001 | St Stephen of Hungary crowned |
| 1002 | Danish settlers in England massacred. Ethelred (the Unready) buys peace (Danegeld) |
| 1013 | **Danes invade England. Sveyn takes throne from Ethelred** |
| 1014 | Sveyn succeeded by Canute |
| 1031 | Muslim Spain fragments, with Christian kingdoms in north. Canute dies; Danish empire fragments |
| 1042 | Edward (the Confessor), king of England |
| 1054 | **Schism between Orthodox and Catholic churches final** |
| 1059–61 | Normans in southern Italy and Sicily |
| 1066 | **Battle of Hastings; William of Normandy defeats King Harold** |
| 1077 | German Emperor Henry IV does penance at Canossa |
| 1086 | **Domesday Book (census) compiled in England** |
| 1092 | Moroccan Almoravides aid Muslims in Spain |
| 1094 | Roderigo Diaz (El Cid), in service of Alfonso I of Castile, defeats Almoravides |
| 1096 | **First Crusade to take Muslim Jerusalem begins** |
| 1099 | Crusaders take Jerusalem. El Cid defeated at Cuenca |
| 1122 | Concordat of Worms, on relations between papacy and secular government, signed by papal legate and emperor Henry V |
| 1129 | Roger II of Sicily takes over mainland Norman territories |
| 1140 | Roger II of Sicily captures Pope Innocent II |
| 1146 | Almohades take Morocco from Almoravides and cross into Spain |
| 1147 | Second Crusade sets out |
| 1155 | Frederick I (Barbarossa) German emperor |
| 1163 | Lombard League formed by Italian cities Padua, Verona and Vicenza |
| 1167 | Oxford University founded |
| 1170 | **Thomas Becket, archbishop of Canterbury, murdered** |
| 1176 | Lombard League defeats Barbarossa |
| 1182 | Jews banished from France |

# GOTHIC WORLD 1000–1500

| | |
|---|---|
| 1187 | Jerusalem kingdom falls to Muslims under Saladin |
| 1190 | **Third Crusade led by Richard I (the Lionheart), Philip II of France and Barbarossa** |
| 1192 | Richard I held for ransom in Austria |
| 1199 | Richard I succeeded by John |
| 1201 | Fourth Crusade sets out |
| 1204 | Crusaders sack Constantinople; Latin empire set up |
| 1209 | King John excommunicated |
| 1212 | Almohade rule in Spain ends |
| 1215 | **John concedes charter of rights (Magna Carta)** |
| 1237 | Lombard League defeated by German Frederick II |
| 1263–65 | **Civil war in England between Henry III and barons led by Simon de Montfort** |
| 1271–96 | Marco Polo's voyage to China |
| 1290 | Jews expelled from England |
| 1337 | Edward III of England claims France; Hundred Years' War begins |
| 1346 | Edward defeats French at Battle of Crécy |
| 1346–49 | **Black Death ravages Europe** |
| 1356 | Edward, Prince of Wales (Black Prince), wins Battle of Poitiers |
| 1380 | Byzantine empire subject to Ottoman (Turkish) sultan |
| 1381 | Peasants' Revolt in England, led by Wat Tyler |
| 1415 | **Henry V of England invades France; wins Battle of Agincourt** |
| 1420 | Hussite Wars in Bohemia against Holy Roman Empire |
| 1428 | English besiege Orléans |
| 1429 | Joan of Arc raises siege of Orléans |
| 1431 | **Joan of Arc burned at stake** |
| 1434 | Medici dynasty controls Florence |
| 1436 | End of Hussite Wars in Bohemia |
| 1453 | English lose France except Calais, after battles at Bordeaux and Castillon. **Hundred Years' War ends** |
| 1455 | Civil war in England between Yorkists and Lancastrians begins (Wars of the Roses) |
| 1485 | Richard III killed at Bosworth; Henry VII succeeds |
| 1492 | Last Muslim state in Spain falls. Columbus discovers New World |
| 1498 | Vasco da Gama reaches India |

## ASIA AD 1–1500

| | |
|---|---|
| AD 9–23 | Usurpation of Han throne by Wang Man; Chinese influence in north Korea wanes |
| 40–42 | **Vietnam rebellion against China, led by Trong sisters** |
| 57 | Japan sends embassy to China |
| c. 100 | Kushan empire in Turkestan, Afghanistan and Punjab. Funan empire in Mekong Delta, Cambodia |
| 220 | Han empire falls. Replaced by Wei, Wu and Shu-Han kingdoms |
| 280 | China reunited under Wei dynasty. Jin annexes Wu kingdom |
| 308 | China divided into northern (Xiong-nu) and southern (Jin) empires |
| 320 | Gupta empire of north India founded by Chandra Gupta I |
| c. 340 | **Yamato state emerges in Japan.** Champa kingdom in central Vietnam |
| c. 425 | Funan empire in Cambodia declines |
| 470 | Gupta kingdom disintegrates as White Huns attack |
| 552 | Turks of central Asia control steppes |
| 562 | **Japanese driven out of north Korea** |
| 581 | Sui dynasty reunites China |
| 605–10 | **Grand Canal links Yangtse and Yellow rivers** |
| 612 | Harsha conquers upper India |
| 618 | Tang dynasty founded in China |
| 639 | Chinese protectorate established over central Asia |
| 645 | Japan begins to model government on Chinese lines |
| 655 | Empress Wu is virtual Tang ruler |
| 661 | China at war with Korea |
| 668 | Silla kingdom unites Korea, with China as overlord |
| 678 | Tibetans defeat Chinese armies |
| 684 | China withdraws from Korea |
| 690 | Manavamura dynasty in Ceylon |
| 705 | Empress Wu seizes Tang throne |
| 712 | Arabs invade Turkestan. Anarchy in Cambodia |
| | Arabs invade India |
| c. 750 | Arabs defeat Chinese armies in central Asia |
| 755–57 | An Lushan rebellion in China weakens Tang dynasty |
| c. 790 | **China abandons attempt to control central Asia** |
| 794 | Heian period in Japan |

# ASIA AD 1–1500

| | |
|---|---|
| c. 800 | **Khmer kingdom established in Cambodia** |
| 821 | Tibetan independence from China |
| c. 840 | Sanjaya dynasty conquers Srivijaya kingdom in Java |
| 842 | Tibetan kingdom collapses; rule passes to Buddhist clergy |
| 849 | Pyu kingdom in Burma collapses |
| 857–58 | Fujiwara clan controls Japan |
| 879–80 | Huang Chao rebellion in China |
| 892 | Korean kingdom of Koryo claims independence from China |
| c. 900 | Khmer capital Angkor founded |
| 907 | Tang dynasty collapses and is succeeded by 5 dynasties in northern Vietnam |
| 947–48 | Khitan Mongols sack Yellow River towns, establish capital at Beijing |
| 960 | Song dynasty in China founded |
| 979 | Song complete reunification of China except Mongol territory |
| 986 | Khitan Mongols defeat Song dynasty |
| 993–4 | **Delhi founded** |
| 1086 | Shenzong emperor in China. State interference leads to disorganization |
| 1115 | Jin state founded in northern China |
| 1175 | Muhammed of Ghor invades India |
| 1186–93 | Kamakura era in Japan |
| 1187 | Muhammed of Ghor conquers Punjab |
| 1206 | Islamic sultanate established in Delhi |
| 1211 | Genghis Khan invades China |
| 1271 | Kublai Khan founds Yuan dynasty in China |
| 1271–95 | Marco Polo's journey to China |
| 1274 | Kublai Khan fails to conquer Japan |
| 1279– | Yuan dynasty ruling in China |
| 1368 | Iliyas Shah founds kingdom in Bengal |
| 1355 | |
| 1363 | **Timur the Great begins conquest of Asia** |
| 1398 | Timur conquers Delhi |
| 1405 | Timur succeeded by Shah Rokh Beijing established as Chinese capital |
| 1447 | India, Persia and Afghanistan independent as Timur's empire breaks up |

# THE RENAISSANCE 1400–1600

| | |
|---|---|
| **1400** | Rise of Medici family in Florence. *Chronicles* by Jean Froissart |
| **1403** | Lorenzo Ghiberti begins work on *Gates of Paradise* for Baptistry in Florence |
| **1405** | Pisa bought by Florence; Florence gains direct access to sea |
| **1406** | Venice seizes Padua after break-up of Visconti territories |
| **1408** | Statue of David by Donatello |
| **1412** | Filippo Brunelleschi's *Rules of Perspective*. Donatello's statues of St Peter, St George and St Mark |
| **1414** | Thomas à Kempis *Imitatio Christi*. Medici become bankers to the papacy |
| **1416–18** | First Venetian–Turkish War |
| **1420** | Brunelleschi's cupola of Florence cathedral |
| **1425–30** | Second Venetian–Turkish War |
| **1429** | Joan of Arc takes Orléans from English |
| **1431** | Universities of Poitiers and Caen founded |
| **1434–64** | Cosimo de' Medici rules in Florence |
| **1436** | **Gutenberg invents moveable type for printing** |
| **1447** | University of Palermo founded |
| **1450** | Pope Nicholas V founds Vatican Library. **Florence under the Medici becomes centre of the Renaissance and Humanism** |
| | Francesco Sforza, duke of Milan |
| **1450–66** | Ghiberti completes *Gates of Paradise* at Florence Baptistry. |
| **1452** | Metal plates are used for printing |
| **1453** | Constantinople captured by Ottoman Turks |
| **1454** | Peace of Lodi between Venice and Milan |
| **1455** | Palazzo Venezia, Rome, built |
| **1456** | First Bible printed. François Villon's *Le Petit Testament* |
| **1460** | Palazzo Pitti, Florence, begun |
| **1462** | Marsilio Ficino, translator of Plato from Greek to Latin, appointed head of Platonic Academy of Florence, among Europe's chief intellectual centres |
| **1463–79** | Great Venetian–Turkish War; Venice obliged to pay annual tribute for Black Sea trade |
| **1472** | Dante Alighieri's *Divine Comedy* |

# THE RENAISSANCE 1400–1600

| | |
|---|---|
| **1477** | first printed |
| | Sandro Botticelli's *Primavera* |
| **1478** | Inquisition established in Spain |
| **1478–92** | Lorenzo de' Medici, 'The Magnificent', rules in Florence |
| **1482–84** | Venice at war with Ferrara; Venetian territory at its greatest extent |
| **1484** | *Birth of Venus* by Botticelli. |
| | Albrecht Dürer's self-portrait |
| **1486** | Pico della Mirandola, *Oration on the Dignity of Man* |
| **1489** | Venice annexes Cyprus |
| **1490** | Beginnings of ballet at Italian court |
| **1492** | Expulsion of Jews from Spain. Leonardo da Vinci draws a flying machine. Lorenzo de' Medici dies. Piero de' Medici becomes ruler of Florence |
| **1494** | French invasion begins Italian Wars. In Florence, theocracy of Girolamo. Savonarola, a Dominican friar, denounces Renaissance paganism |
| **1495** | *Holy Family with St Elizabeth and the young St John* by Andrea Mantegna. *Last Supper* by Leonardo da Vinci |
| **1497** | Expulsion of Jews from Portugal |
| **1498** | Savonarola burnt at stake |
| **1499** | French invade Italy, seize Milan |
| **1500** | Milan regained from French by Ludovico Sforza |
| **1501–4** | *David* by Michelangelo |
| **1502** | Peter Henlein constructs the 'Nuremberg Egg', the first watch |
| **1503** | *Mona Lisa* by Leonardo da Vinci |
| **1504** | Spain captures Naples |
| **1506** | St Peter's, Rome, rebuilding begun to designs by Bramante |
| **1508–11** | Villa Farnesina, Rome, by Baldassare Peruzzi |
| **1508–12** | Michelangelo paints ceiling of Sistine Chapel |
| **1508–15** | King's College Chapel, Cambridge |
| **1511** | *Adoration of the Trinity* by Albrecht Dürer |
| **1512** | Copernicus' *Commentariolus*, in which he states that the Earth and planets orbit the Sun |
| **1515–30** | Tudor palace of Hampton Court built outside London |
| **1515–16** | Statue of Moses by Michelangelo |
| **1516** | Establishment of Jewish ghetto in Venice |

# THE RENAISSANCE 1400–1600

| | |
|---|---|
| **1516** | *Orlando Furioso* by Ludovico Ariosto |
| **1517** | *Madonna of the Harpies* by Andrea del Sarto |
| **1518** | *Assunta* by Titian |
| **1519** | **Charles I of Spain elected Holy Roman Emperor Charles V.** Château of Chambord by Pierre Nepveu |
| **1522** | Beginning of Habsburg–Valois Wars in Italy |
| **1527** | **Sack of Rome by German and Spanish mercenaries.** Castiglione's *The Courtier* |
| **1528** | Founding of Capuchin Order. Palace of Fontainebleau begun by Diego de Siloe. Granada Cathedral begun |
| **1529** | Treaty of Cambrai between Emperor Charles V and Francis I of France |
| **1532** | Machiavelli's study of realpolitik. *Il Principe (The Prince)* |
| **1533** | *The Ambassadors* by Hans Holbein |
| **1534** | Statue of Hercules and Cacus, Florence, by Baccio Bandinelli. *Gargantua* by Rabelais |
| **1534–41** | *Last Judgement* by Michelangelo |
| **1536–40** | Dissolution of the monasteries in England |
| **1537** | Sansovino's façade of the Doge's Palace loggietta, Venice |
| **1538** | *The Urbino Venus* by Titian |
| **1542** | Inquisition established in Rome |
| **1545** | *Venus, Cupid, Time and Folly* by Agnolo Bronzino |
| **1545–54** | *Perseus* by Benvenuto Cellini |
| **1545–63** | **Council of Trent begins the Counter-Reformation** |
| **1546** | Michelangelo designs the dome of St Peter's |
| **1547** | Ivan the Terrible gains power in Russia. First predictions of the astrologer Nostradamus |
| **c. 1548** | Potatoes brought to Europe from South America |
| **1550** | *Lives of the Artists* by Georgio Vasari. *Odes* by Pierre Ronsard |
| **1550–51** | Villa Rotonda, Vicenza, by Andrea Palladio |
| **1553** | *Venus and Adonis* by Titian |
| **1554–67** | *Mars and Neptune* by Jacopo Sansovino |
| **1555** | Michelangelo's sculpture *Pietà* |
| **1558** | France regains Calais from England |

# THE RENAISSANCE 1400–1600

| Year | Event |
|---|---|
| 1559 | **Treaty of Cateau-Cambresis ends Habsburg–Valois and Italian Wars.** Battle of Carnival by Pieter Brueghel the Elder |
| 1560 | Uffizi Palace begun by Giorgio Vasari |
| 1561–65 | Town Hall, Antwerp, begun by Cornelius Flock |
| 1563 | Tower of Babel by Brueghel the Elder |
| 1563–86 | Escorial Palace, Spain, by Juan de Toledo and Juan de Herrera |
| 1564–87 | Life of Christ and Scenes of the Passion series begun by Tintoretto |
| 1565 | Alexander and the Family of Darius by Paolo Veronese |
| 1569–71 | Revolt of the Moriscos in Spain |
| 1570 | Abraham Ortelius' first modern atlas. Leda by Tintoretto |
| 1570–71 | Turks capture Cyprus from Venice |
| 1571 | **Battle of Lepanto.** Holy League (Pope, Venice and Spain) defeats Turks in last great galley battle |
| 1572 | Lusiads by Camoens |
| 1573 | The Feast in the House of Levi by Veronese |
| 1575 | El Greco arrives in Spain. |
| 1579 | Union of Utrecht forms Dutch republic |
| 1580 | **Philip II annexes Portugal and its empire.** Essais by Michel de Montaigne |
| 1581 | Gerusalemme Liberata by Torquato Tasso |
| 1581–85 | The Tortoise Fountain by Landini |
| 1582 | Gregorian calendar introduced |
| 1585 | Quirinale Palace, Rome, by Domenico Fontana |
| 1587 | Drake destroys Spanish fleet at Cadiz |
| 1587–91 | Rialto Bridge, Venice, built |
| 1588 | Spanish Armada launched against England |
| 1589 | Bacchus by Caravaggio |
| 1590 | First microscope built by Janssen. William Shakespeare begins to write his plays |
| 1594 | Henri of Navarre crowned Henri IV of France. Tyrone Rebellion in Ireland begins |
| 1596 | Galileo develops heat measurement |
| 1597 | Bankruptcy of Spanish Crown |
| 1600 | Giordano Bruno burned for heresy by Inquisition |

# EUROPEAN EXPLORATION 1400–1600

| | |
|---|---|
| 1402–6 | Europeans conquer three Canary Islands |
| 1418–19 | Exploration of Madeira Island |
| 1425 | West Africa assigned to Portugal |
| c. 1427– | Portuguese discover and settle the Azores |
| 1432 | |
| 1446 | Fernão Gomes discovers Cape Verde and Senegal |
| 1447 | Map of world drawn by Toscanelli |
| 1448 | Beginning of Portuguese empire in Africa. Portuguese build fort at Arguin in Mauretania |
| 1452 | **Pope allows Portuguese and Spanish to practise slavery** |
| 1455–57 | Alvise da Cadamosto explores Senegal and Gambia rivers |
| 1470–71 | João de Santavern reaches Gold Coast |
| 1472 | Lopo Goncalves crosses Equator |
| 1482 | Portuguese establish fort at Elmina, Gold Coast. Diego Cão reaches Congo River mouth |
| 1487 | Bartolomeu Diaz's voyage round Cape of Good Hope |
| 1492–1504 | **Columbus discovers New World** and makes further voyages of discovery to Central America |
| 1493–1898 | Spanish Caribbean-American empire |
| 1494 | **Treaty of Tordesillas between Spain and Portugal marking their halves of the world for exploration** |
| 1497 | John Cabot discovers Newfoundland while searching for the North-west Passage |
| 1498 | **Vasco da Gama reaches India by sea.** John Cabot's second voyage |
| 1499 | **Amerigo Vespucci's first voyage to America** |
| 1500–1 | Pedro Cabral discovers Brazil and travels to India |
| 1501–2 | Vespucci's second voyage to America |
| 1503 | Portuguese trading post of Cochin, China, established. Portuguese set up first East Africa trading post at Zanzibar |
| 1508–15 | Spanish conquer Puerto Rico and Cuba |
| 1510 | Portuguese capture Goa in India |
| 1510–11 | **Importation of slaves to the Americas begins** |

# EUROPEAN EXPLORATION 1400-1600

| | |
|---|---|
| 1511 | Portuguese capture Malacca (Malaya) |
| 1513 | Portuguese arrive in Moluccas (Spice Islands) and begin trading. Jorge Alvarez lands near Canton. Ponce de León lands Florida |
| 1515 | Portuguese capture Hormuz in the Persian Gulf |
| 1518– 1824 | Spanish Latin American empire |
| 1519 | Spanish found Panama City |
| 1519–21 | **Hernán Cortés' conquest of Mexico** |
| 1519–22 | **Ferdinand Magellan's circumnavigation** |
| 1520–22 | First Portuguese mission to Beijing |
| 1521 | Magellan claims the Philippines for Spain |
| 1521–55 | Portuguese expand into inland Brazil |
| 1521–61 | Failed Spanish attempt to colonize Florida |
| 1522 | Spanish conquer Nicaragua and found New Spain. **Spanish discover Inca empire** |
| 1524 | Verrazano explores coast of North America and enters New York Bay. |
| 1527–35 | Spanish found Guatemala City |
| 1528–36 | Conquest of Yucatan, Mexico |
| 1530– | Narvaez' Florida expedition |
| 1822 | Portuguese empire in Brazil |
| 1531 | Spanish found Guadalajara, Mexico |
| 1531–33 | **Conquest of Peru by Pizarro** |
| 1532 | Spanish found Cartagena, Colombia |
| 1534–42 | Henri Cartier discovers St Lawrence River |
| 1536 | Spanish found Buenos Aires; later destroyed by Indians |
| 1537 | Spanish found Asunción, Paraguay |
| 1538 | Spanish found Bogotá, Colombia |
| 1540–61 | Spanish conquest of Chile |
| 1541 | Hernando de Soto discovers Mississippi River. Coronado explores New Mexico, Colorado and Texas |
| 1542 | Antonio da Mota reaches Japan. Cabillo discovers California |
| 1545 | Opening of Spanish Potosi silver mines in Bolivia. Spaniard Retes finds northern New Guinea coast |
| 1546 | Mayan revolt against Spanish conquerors crushed |

# EUROPEAN EXPLORATION 1400–1600

| | |
|---|---|
| **1549–51** | Francis Xavier introduces Christianity to Japan |
| **1553** | Willoughby and Chancellor round North Cape and reach Archangel |
| **1557** | Portuguese settlement at Macao, China |
| **1565** | Portuguese found Rio de Janeiro after destroying French colony. First permanent Spanish colony in Florida after French are ousted |
| **1567** | Mandana discovers Solomon, Marshall and Ellice Islands. Spanish found Caracas, Venezuela |
| **1569** | Mercator's world map |
| **1570–71** | Spain begins colonization of the Philippines |
| **1574** | Portuguese found Luanda, Angola |
| **1578–80** | Drake's circumnavigation |
| **1578–84** | Gilbert's attempts at colonization of North America |
| **1580** | Spain annexes Portugal. Spain refounds Buenos Aires |
| **1584–90** | Raleigh's missions to colonize Roanoke Island, North Carolina |
| **1592** | Portuguese settle at Mombasa on East African coast |
| **1595** | First Dutch posts on Guinea coast. Mendana discovers Marquesas and Santa Cruz Islands |
| **1596** | Dutch set up trading posts on Sumatra. Spanish found Monterey |
| **1596–97** | Barents discovers Bear Island and Spitzbergen |

# THE AMERICAS 2000 BC – AD 1550

| | |
|---|---|
| c. 2000 BC | Maya culture in southern Mexico, Guatemala and Belize |
| c. 1200 | Olmec culture along Gulf of Mexico |
| c. 900 | Chavin culture in northern Peru |
| c. 800 | First Tiahuanaco culture in Bolivia |
| c. 400 | Olmec culture wanes |
| c. 200 | Teotihuacan culture in central Mexico |
| c. 200 | Chavin culture wanes, replaced by Mochica culture |
| c. 100 | Nazca culture in southern Peru |
| c. 30 | Olmec 'long count' dating inscriptions provide accurately calculated dates |
| AD c. 250 | **Golden age of Maya culture begins** |
| c. 350 | Teotihuacan empire at peak |
| c. 600 | Mochica culture wanes. |
| | Teotihuacan empire declines |
| c. 750 | Toltecs destroy Teotihuacan empire |
| c. 900 | Golden age of Maya culture fades |
| c. 1000 | Chimu culture in north-west Peru |
| c. 1100 | Inca culture in Peru emerges |
| c. 1200 | Toltecs conquered by Aztecs |
| c. 1370 | Chimu culture under Nancan Pinco expands into Andes |
| 1440 | Montezuma I Aztec ruler |
| 1471 | Tupa Inca ruler. Incas conquer Chimu |
| 1492 | **Columbus discovers New World** |
| 1493 | Huayna Capac Inca ruler |
| c. 1500 | Chibcha culture of Colombia destroyed. Nazca culture disappears. Aztec ruler Ahuizotl extends empire |
| 1501 | Coelho explores Brazilian coast |
| 1502 | **Montezuma II Aztec ruler** |
| 1504 | Hernán Cortés, Spanish conquistador, arrives in Cuba |
| 1509 | Aztecs defeat Spanish in Colombia |
| 1511 | Velázquez conquers Cuba |
| 1519 | Cortés begins invasion of Mexico |
| 1520 | Montezuma II killed while prisoner of Cortés |
| 1521 | Cortés takes Tenochtitlan; last Aztec ruler, Cuauhtemoc, surrenders |
| 1525 | Huayna-Capac dies; civil war |
| 1527 | Atahualpa defeats his brother Huascar in civil war. Pizarro in Panama |
| 1532 | Atahualpa defeated by Pizarro |
| 1533 | Atahualpa executed by Pizarro |
| 1535 | **Pizarro completes conquest of Inca empire** |

# THE REFORMATION

| | |
|---|---|
| **1505** | Martin Luther joins the Augustinian Order of monks |
| **1510** | Luther visits Rome |
| **1517** | **Luther's 95 theses against the sale of clerical indulgences are nailed to Wittenberg church door** |
| **1518** | Huldreich Zwingli called to be minister in Zürich |
| **1519** | **Luther questions infallibility of the Pope.** Zwingli begins Swiss Reformation |
| **1520** | Luther is declared a heretic by Pope Leo X and excommunicated but protected by Elector Frederick the Wise of Saxony. Beginnings of Anabaptist (radical Reformist) movement in Germany under Thomas Münzer |
| **1521** | **Diet of Worms bans Luther and all new doctrines.** Pope confers title 'Defender of the Faith' on Henry VIII of England |
| **1522** | Luther returns to Wittenberg; condemns fanatics and iconoclasts. Finishes translating New Testament |
| **1523** | Zwingli's programme of reform in 67 theses; Reformation adopted in Zürich |
| **1524** | **Zwingli abolishes Catholic mass in Zürich** |
| **1525** | Luther marries an ex-nun |
| **1526** | Luther's German Mass. Anabaptists settle as Moravian Brothers in Moravia |
| **1527** | Lutheranism established in Sweden. First Protestant university established in Marburg |
| **1528** | Austrian Anabaptist Balthasar Hubinier burned at the stake in Vienna. Reformation begins in Scotland |
| **1529** | Luther and Zwingli hold discussion on Eucharist at Marburg. Diet of Speyer; Lutheran-inclined states protest at Catholic domination of diet and are called 'Protestant' |
| **1530** | Schmalkaldic League formed by Protestant princes and imperial cities |
| **1531** | Zwingli killed at Battle of Kappel with Swiss Catholic reformers. |
| **1532** | Inquisition in Portugal Reformation in France |

# THE REFORMATION

| | |
|---|---|
| **1534** | First complete translation of Luther's Bible. Act of Supremacy in England. **Jesuit Order founded by Ignatius Loyola** |
| **1535** | English clergy renounce authority of Pope. Thomas More executed for loyalty to Rome and refusal to accept Henry VIII as head of English Church. Anabaptist John of Leiden tortured to death. Study of canon law forbidden in Cambridge, England |
| **1536** | Act of Parliament declares authority of Pope void in England. Reformation in Denmark and Norway. Calvin's *Instructions in Christ*. Dissolution of the monasteries begins in England, followed by Pilgrimage of Grace, an uprising against it |
| **1536–39** | Lutheranism becomes the faith of Denmark, Norway and Baltic states |
| **1537** | Pilgrimage of Grace and similar risings put down |
| **1538** | **Calvin expelled from Geneva;** settles in Strasbourg. Destruction of relics and shrines in southern England |
| **1540** | Order of Jesuits confirmed by Pope Paul III |
| **1541** | Calvin brings Reformation to Geneva. John Knox leads Calvinist Reformation in Scotland |
| **1542** | **Pope Paul III reintroduces Inquisition in Rome** |
| **1543** | First Protestant burned at the stake by Spanish Inquisition |
| **1545** | Transylvania becomes Lutheran |
| **1545–47** | First session of Council of Trent to discuss Catholic reform |
| **1546** | Death of Luther |
| **1547** | Schmalkaldic War; Charles V defeats Protestant League. *Chambre ardente* created in France for trial of heretics |
| **1549** | Only new Book of Prayer can be used in England. Agreement between Calvin and followers of Zwingli on Holy Communion |
| **1550** | Jews persecuted in Bavaria |
| **1551–52** | Second session of Council of Trent |
| **1553–58** | Catholic Restoration in England under Mary I |
| **1555** | Knox returns to Scotland from exile |

# THE REFORMATION

| | |
|---|---|
| **1555** | Peace of Augsburg; a compromise giving princes right to chose and enforce their subjects' faith. In Germany Lutheran states to enjoy equal rights with Catholics |
| **1557** | *Index of Forbidden Books* issued by Pope. First Presbyterian church founded in Scotland by Knox |
| **1558** | Lutherans at Seville and Valladolid |
| **1559** | First national synod of French Huguenot Calvinists |
| **1560** | Scottish National Church established. Beginnings of Puritanism in England |
| **1561** | First Calvinist refugees from Flanders settle in England. Edict of Orléans suspends persecution of Huguenots |
| **1562** | **Third session of Council of Trent reforms Catholic Church; Counter-Reformation begins.** 1200 French Huguenots massacred at Vassy leads to First War of Religion |
| **1563** | **Completion of Anglican Church's establishment.** Counter-Reformation begins in Bavaria |
| **1564** | Death of Calvin. Calvinist riots in the Netherlands. |
| **1566** | Regent Margaret of Palma abolishes Inquisition. Synod of Antwerp forms Calvinist Church of the Netherlands |
| **1570** | Peace of St Germain-en-Laye ends third civil war in France. Huguenots gain amnesty |
| **1571** | Reconciliation between Charles IX of France and Huguenots |
| **1572** | **St Bartholomew's Day Massacre;** 2000 Huguenots are killed in Paris on Charles IX's orders |
| **1573** | Religious tolerance in Poland |
| **1577** | Henry of Navarre recognized as head of Huguenots |
| **1579** | Catholic Reform commission founded in Austria. Protestants expelled from Bavaria |
| **1593** | Henry of Navarre becomes Catholic |
| **1594** | Edict of St Germain-en-Laye grants Huguenots freedom of worship |
| **1598** | **Edict of Nantes grants Huguenots equal political rights** |
| **1600** | Persecution of Catholics in Sweden |

# THE REFORMATION

| | |
|---|---|
| | under Charles IX. Giordano Bruno burned as a heretic |
| **1606** | Penal laws against Papists in England |
| **1609** | Catholic League of German princes formed against Protestant Union. Emperor Rudolf II permits religious freedom in Bohemia |
| **1609–14** | Expulsion of Moriscos from Spain |
| **1611** | Cardinal Pierre de Bérulle founds French Congregation of the Oratory |
| **1615** | Galileo Galilei faces Inquisition for the first time |
| **1616** | Catholic oppression intensifies in Bohemia. Copernicus declared a heretic |
| **1618** | Thirty Years' War begins after closure of Czech protestant churches by Catholic authorities |
| **1620** | Battle of White Mountain. Habsburg Counter-Reformation defeats Czech Protestants |
| **1622** | Congregatio de Propaganda Fide unites Catholic missionaries |
| **1625** | Sisters of Mercy established in Paris |
| **1628** | Ignatius Loyola canonized by Pope Gregory XV |
| **1629** | Catholic Edict. Restoration of church property in Germany which had been secularized since 1555 |
| **1632** | Galileo declared a heretic |
| **1633** | **Galileo forced by Inquisition to renounce theories of Copernicus** |
| **1640** | Cornelius Jansen's *Augustinus* published posthumously. Begins Jansenist disputes |
| **1648** | **A bull of Pope Innocent X condemns the Peace of Westphalia, which ends the Thirty Years' War** |
| **1673** | Test Act excludes Roman Catholics from both houses of English Parliament |
| **1684** | 93 Jewish families expelled from Bordeaux |
| **1685** | Louis XIV revokes Edict of Nantes and exiles French Protestants |
| **1686** | Roman Catholics readmitted to English army |
| **1759** | Jesuits banned in Portugal |
| **1764** | Jesuits banned in France |
| **1767** | Spain bans Jesuits |
| **1773** | Pope Clement XIV bans all Jesuits |

# PROTESTANT EUROPE 1600–1700

| 1600 | Protestants expelled from Austria |
|---|---|
| 1608 | Protestant states of Rhineland form Protestant Union under Christian of Anhalt and Frederick IV of the Palatinate |
| 1609 | English Baptist Church founded by John Smyth and Thomas Hewys |
| 1611 | King James Bible in England |
| 1618-19 | General synod of Calvinists at Dodrecht, Holland |
| 1618 | **War in Bohemia starts Thirty Years' War.** Protestant nobles invade Czech royal palace. |
| 1619 Aug | Diet of Bohemia elects Frederick |
| 1620 | End of Bohemian independence. Massacre of Protestants in Valtelline |
| Jul | Treaty of Ulm with Catholic League Princes of Protestant Union sign to maintain German neutrality in Bohemian War |
| 1621 | Huguenots rebel against Louis XIII |
| 1621-23 | **Palatinate War** |
| 1622 | Richelieu created cardinal. Treaty of Montpellier ends Huguenot rebellion |
| 1623 | Holy Roman Emperor Ferdinand II grants Maximilian, Duke of Bavaria, the Upper Palatinate |
| 1624-29 | **Danish War** |
| 1624-42 | Richelieu administration in France |
| 1625 Apr | Ferdinand appoints Wallenstein commander in chief. Mansfeld defeated by Wallenstein at Dessau |
| 1625-48 | Netherlands joins anti-Spanish coalition |
| 1626 | Peace of La Rochelle between Huguenots and French Crown |
| Aug | Catholic League defeats Christian IV of Denmark in Germany |
| 1627 | Wallenstein conquers Silesia. Tilly conquers Brunswick |
| May | Renewed constitution for Bohemia by Ferdinand |
| 1628 | Gustav Adolphus of Sweden enters Thirty Years' War |
| Jul | Ferdinand issues a renewed constitution for Moravia |
| 1629 Mar | Ferdinand orders the return of all lands taken over by Protestants since 1552 |
| Sep | Treaty of Altmark extricates Gustav Adolphus from war against Poland. |
| 1630 | Gustav Adolphus invades Germany |
| Aug | Wallenstein replaced by Tilly |

# PROTESTANT EUROPE 1600–1700

| | | |
|---|---|---|
| **1630–35** | | **Swedish War** |
| **1631** | Jan | Sweden signs Treaty with France |
| | May | Tilly and Catholic League destroy Magdeburg. Tilly defeated by Swedish and Saxon troops |
| **1632** | Nov | Gustav killed in Battle of Lützen |
| | Apr | Wallenstein reinstated by Ferdinand |
| **1633** | | First Baptist Church in England |
| **1634** | | Wallenstein assassinated |
| **1635** | Apr | Sweden renews French alliance with Treaty of Compiègne. France declares war on Spain |
| | Sep | Sweden signs treaty with Poland |
| **1635–48** | | Franco-Habsburg War |
| **1639** | | **Dutch destroy Spanish fleet in English Channel** |
| **1641** | | English and Scottish Protestant settlers massacred by Catholics in Ulster |
| **1642–46** | | **English Civil War** between Royalist forces of Charles I and Parliamentarians under Cromwell |
| **1642** | | Mazarin succeeds Richelieu |
| **1643** | May | Mazarin destroys Spanish army at Rocroi, Ardennes |
| | Sep | Solemn League and Covenant: Scots Covenanters (Presbyterians) |

| | |
|---|---|
| | make alliance with Parliamentarians |
| **1644** | Battle of Marston Moor: Royalists defeated. English parliament bans religious festivities at Christmas |
| **1645** | Peace talks begun between Holy Roman Empire and France |
| **1646** | Sweden takes Prague and invades Bavaria with the French |
| **1648** | **Peace of Westphalia and Münster ends Thirty Years' War.** George Fox founds Society of Friends (Quakers) in England |
| **1649** | Charles I executed |
| **1653–58** | Cromwell Lord Protector of the Commonwealth |
| **1655** | Cromwell prohibits Anglican services in England |
| **1660** | Charles II restored |
| **1667** | Calvinists acknowledged by Lutherans |
| **1678** | John Bunyan's *Pilgrim's Progress* |
| **1685** | Edict of Nantes revoked |
| **1688** | **Glorious Revolution:** William III and Mary II proclaimed joint monarchs after James II of England exiled for pro-Catholic sympathies |
| **1689** | Act of Toleration in England |

# AMERICAN COLONIZATION 1600–1700

| | |
|---|---|
| **1599–1634** | Champlain's voyages in Canada |
| **1607–9** | **English settlement of Jamestown, Virginia** |
| **1608** | Quebec founded by French |
| **1608–11** | Henry Hudson explores east coast |
| **1612** | Earliest colonization of Bermudas from Virginia. Dutch use Manhattan as fur trading centre. Tobacco planted in Virginia |
| **1613** | English colonists in Virginia destroy French settlement at Port Royal, Nova Scotia. Prevent French colonization of Maryland |
| **1614** | Dutch Fort Nassau built on Hudson River. Virginian colonists stop French from settling Maine and Nova Scotia |
| **1617** | Walter Raleigh reaches mouth of Orinoco River in South America |
| **1619** | First African slaves arrive in North America in Virginia. First representative colonial assembly in America held at Jamestown, Virginia |
| **1620** | **Pilgrim Fathers leave Plymouth in the Mayflower** and land at New Plymouth, Mass. First English settlement in New Hampshire |
| **1624** | **Dutch settle in New Amsterdam.** Virginia becomes a royal colony |
| **1626** | Salem, Mass. settled. Dutch East India Company buys Manhattan Island from the native Indian chiefs |
| **1627** | Barbados claimed for England |
| **1630** | Puritans found Massachusetts colony |
| **1630–40** | Great Migration to America of 16 000 settlers |
| **1631** | Dutch West India Company founds settlement on Delaware River |
| **1632** | English settlers in Antigua and Montserrat |
| **1633** | Dutch settle in Connecticut |
| **1635** | English colonize Connecticut |
| **1635–36** | Rhode Island settled |
| **1636** | Harvard College founded |
| **1636–37** | Pequot Indian War in New England |
| **1638–43** | New Hampshire settled |
| **1638–55** | Swedes settle on Delaware River |
| **1640–54** | Maine settled |
| **1642** | Montreal, Canada, founded |
| **1643** | New England Confederation to govern in war and Indian relations |

# AMERICAN COLONIZATION 1600–1700

| | |
|---|---|
| 649 | Puritan exiles from Virginia settle in Providence, Maryland |
| **1650** | **Wars against North American Indians begin** |
| **1654** | **First Jewish settlers arrive in New Amsterdam** |
| 1660 | Puritans settle in New Jersey |
| 1661 | English conquer New Netherlands |
| 1661–62 | Suspension of Quaker persecution |
| 1661–63 | Connecticut and Rhode Island charters |
| 1663–65 | Charters given for the Carolinas |
| 1663–69 | Massachusetts annexes Maine |
| 1664 | New Amsterdam renamed New York |
| 1668–88 | Anglo-French struggle for Hudson Bay |
| 1670 | Charleston settled by English. English Hudson Bay Company incorporated by royal charter to trade in regions of North America |
| 1672–73 | Father Marquette and Louis Joliet explore environs of Chicago and upper Mississippi |
| 1674 | Treaty of Westminster recognizes inhabitants of New York and New Sweden as British subjects |
| 1675–76 | King Philip's Indian War |
| 1676 | Nathaniel Bacon leads rebellion in Jamestown |
| 1679–82 | La Salle explores Great Lakes and reaches mouth of Mississippi. Hennepin discovers Niagara Falls |
| 1680–86 | Royal government in New Hampshire |
| 1682 | Pennsylvania founded by William Penn. La Salle claims Louisiana territory for France and takes possession of Mississippi Valley |
| 1683 | First German immigrants in North America. Penn's treaty with Indians |
| 1684 | Bermudas become Crown property |
| 1685 | First French settlers in Texas. French Huguenots emigrate to North America |
| 1686 | First French settlers in Arkansas |
| 1689 | Massacre of French settlers near Montreal by Iroquois |
| 1692 | Witchcraft trials and hangings at Salem, Mass. |
| 1693 | Kingston, Jamaica founded. Carolina divided into North and South Carolina |
| 1698 | French begin to settle in Louisiana and on upper Mississippi |

# MOGUL INDIA 1500–1858

| | |
|---|---|
| **1526** | **Babur, a descendant of Timur the Great, founds Mogul dynasty** |
| **1539** | Afghan ruler Sher Shah defeats Moguls and founds Sur dynasty |
| **1556** | Akbar, Babur's grandson, regains Punjab; consolidates empire throughout North India |
| **1564** | Akbar abolishes tax on non-Muslims (jizya); heralds new era of conciliation |
| **1573–94** | Akbar conquers Gujarat, Bihar, Bengal and Kandabar |
| **1634–48** | **Shah Jehan, Akbar's grandson, builds Taj Mahal** |
| **1669** | Aurangzeb, son of Shah Jehan, bans Hindu faith |
| **1681** | Akbar, son of Aurangzeb, rebels. Aurangzeb conquers Deccan |
| **1689** | Aurangzeb defeats Marathas |
| **1707** | Aurangzeb succeeded by Bahadur |
| **1708** | Bahadur defeats Sikhs who had threatened the empire |
| **1737** | Marathas defeat Moguls at Delhi |
| **1738–39** | Nadir Shah of Persia invades Afghanistan and sacks Delhi |
| **1756** | Over 100 British die while |

| | |
|---|---|
| | imprisoned in 'black hole' of Calcutta after ruler of Bengal region captures the city |
| **1757** | Robert Clive secures Bengal for the British after Battle of Plassey |
| **1768** | Gurkhas conquer Nepal |
| **1775–81** | Anglo-Maratha War results from alliance between Bombay government and ruler of Maratha |
| **1781** | Coote conquers Mysore |
| **1795** | British take Ceylon from Dutch |
| **1799** | Hindu royal family in Mysore |
| **1816** | Treaty with Gurkhas; Nepal in British sphere of influence |
| **1824–26** | Anglo-Burmese War ends with British acquisition of Assam |
| **1838–42** | Anglo-Afghan War ends with 16 000 British troops evacuating Kabul |
| **1843** | **Slavery in India abolished** |
| **1844** | Anglo-Sikh War after disorder in Punjab |
| **1849** | Sikh state ends as Britain annexes Punjab |
| **1858** | **Government of India passes from East India Company to Crown; Lord Canning becomes first viceroy** |

# CHINA AND JAPAN 1500–1900

| | |
|---|---|
| 1516 | Portuguese begin trade with China |
| 1523 | Europeans expelled from China |
| 1549–51 | Francis Xavier makes Christian converts in Japan |
| 1571 | Nobunaga deposes Ashikaga, shogun in Japan |
| 1582 | Nobunaga assassinated; replaced by Hideyoshi |
| 1587 | Hideyoshi bans Christian missionaries from Japan |
| 1600 | Tokugawa defeats rivals; Japanese capital moved to Edo. |
| 1603–1867 | Tokugawa shogunate in Japan |
| 1621 | Manchu under Nurbaci establish Jurchen state |
| 1623 | Persecution of Christians in Japan; English trade stops after eight seized and killed |
| 1644 | Manchu enter Beijing; establish Qing dynasty |
| 1683 | Manchu conquer Taiwan |
| 1685 | China opens ports to foreign trade |
| 1692 | Christianity tolerated in China |
| 1715 | British trading post in Canton |
| 1707–17 | China mapped |
| 1727 | China's border with Russia fixed |
| 1736 | Christianity banned in China |
| 1736–39 | Mongols at war with Chinese |
| 1751 | China invades Tibet |
| 1775 | Britain takes over India–China opium trade from Portugal |
| 1825 | Muslim rebellion in Turkestan |
| 1830 | Chinese emigration to Malaya |
| 1838–42 | **First Anglo-Chinese Opium War** |
| 1842 | China opens ports to foreign trade; cedes Hong Kong to Britain. Japan relaxes rules against foreign ships |
| 1846 | Japan refuses to allow US warships dock |
| 1850–64 | Taiping rebellion in China |
| 1857–58 | Second Opium War |
| 1868 | Last Tokugawa shogun abdicates |
| 1881 | **Political parties formed in Japan** |
| 1882 | French capture Hanoi |
| 1885 | Kuroda Kiyotaka first Japanese prime minister |
| 1894–95 | China at war with Japan over Korea; Japan takes Taiwan; Korea independent |
| 1900 | Boxer Rebellion attempts to oust foreign powers from China. Military domination begins in Japan |

# INDUSTRIAL REVOLUTION 1700–1850

| | |
|---|---|
| **1702** | Serfdom abolished in Denmark |
| **1704** | Earliest subscription library in Berlin |
| **1709** | First Copyright Act in Britain. 14 000 inhabitants of German Palatinate emigrate to North America; 100 000 Germans follow in the next hundred years. **Abraham Darby discovers method of smelting iron ore with coke** |
| **1710** | Porcelain factory at Meissen, Germany, founded |
| **1712** | Slave revolts in New York |
| **1714** | French surgeon Dominique Anel invents fine-pointed syringe for surgical purposes. D G Fahrenheit constructs mercury thermometer with temperature scale |
| **1715** | First Liverpool dock built |
| **1716** | *Diario di Roma*, first Italian newspaper, published |
| **1717** | School attendance in Prussia made compulsory |
| **1718** | First bank notes in England. Collegiate School of America transferred to new site in New Haven and renamed Yale University |
| **1720** | English speculation craze, South Sea Bubble, bursts. First collective settlement in Vermont |
| **1721** | Regular postal service between London and New England |
| **1722** | Workhouse Test Act introduced |
| **1724** | Gin drinking becomes popular in Britain. Paris Bourse opens |
| **1726** | Lloyd's List issued in London twice weekly |
| **1727** | Coffee first planted in Brazil. Quakers demand abolition of slavery |
| **1730** | Zinc smelting first practised in England |
| **1731** | English factory workers not allowed to emigrate to America |
| **1733** | John Kay patents shuttle loom |
| **1735** | Linnaeus' *Systema Naturae*, establishes principles of naming and classifying plants |
| **1736** | Manufacture of glass begins in Murano, Venice. Hard rubber, caoutchouc, comes to Britain |
| **1742** | **Cotton factories established in Birmingham and Northampton.** Anders Celsius |

# INDUSTRIAL REVOLUTION 1700–1850

| | |
|---|---|
| **1743** | invents centigrade thermometer. East Indian yarns imported into Lancashire for manufacture of finer goods |
| **1749** | Giacobbo Rodriguez Peraire invents sign language |
| **1754** | First iron-rolling mill at Farnham, Hampshire |
| **1756** | First chocolate factory in Germany. Cotton velvets first made at Bolton, Lancashire |
| **1758** | Ribbing machine invented for making ribbed stockings |
| **1760** | Josiah Wedgwood founds pottery works in Staffordshire |
| **1761** | Society of Arts, London, opens first exhibition of agricultural machines. Bridgewater Canal is first canal in Britain |
| **1762** | Cast iron converted into malleable iron in Scotland |
| **1763** | First Chambers of Commerce in New York and New Jersey |
| **1765** | Earliest use of ponies in mines. Spallanzani suggests preserving by hermetic sealing |
| **1768** | First weekly instalments of the |
| **1769** | Encyclopedia Britannica appear. James Watt patents steam engine. Richard Arkwright's waterframe, a spinning frame powered by water, is patented |
| **1770** | James Hargreaves patents spinning jenny |
| **1771** | Richard Arkwright opens first spinning mill in England |
| **1773** | Boston Tea Party; protest against tea duty in American colonies. First cast-iron bridge built at Coalbrookdale, Shropshire |
| **1775** | James Watt perfects his invention of the steam engine. Pierre-Simon Girard invents water turbine |
| **1777** | Co-operative workshop for tailors opens in Birmingham |
| **1778** | Act of Congress prohibits import of slaves into the United States |
| **1779** | Pope Pius VI begins draining Pontine Marshes. Samuel Crompton invents spinning mule |
| **1781** | Serfdom abolished in Austrian dominions |
| **1782** | Bank of America established in Philadelphia. Montgolfier brothers |

# INDUSTRIAL REVOLUTION 1700–1850

**1783** construct air balloon. James Watt invents double-acting rotary steam engine

A paddle-wheel steamboat is sailed on Saône River, France

**1784** **English ironmaster Henry Cort introduces puddling and rolling processes for manufacture of wrought iron.** Andrew Meikle, a Scottish millwright, invents threshing machine. Edmund Cartwright invents power loom

**1785** **Chemical bleaching invented. James Wall and Matthew Boulton install a steam engine with rotary motion in a cotton-spinning mill at Papplewick, Nottinghamshire**

**1786** Earliest attempts at internal gas lighting in Germany and England

**1789** **First steam-driven cotton factory in Manchester**

**1790** First steam-powered rolling mill built in England

**1793** Eli Whitney introduces the cotton gin

**1794** Abolition of slavery in French colonies

**1795** Joseph Braman invents hydraulic press

**1700** **Edward Jenner introduces vaccination against smallpox**

**1797** **England begins to export iron.** Merino sheep are introduced to Australia

**1800** Richard Trevithick constructs light-pressure steam engine. Alessandro Volta produces first electricity from a cell, the first form of battery

**1802** First practical steamship on the Clyde, Scotland. West India docks built in London

**1803** American inventor, Robert Fulton, propels a boat by steam power

**1806** Francis Beaufort designs a scale to indicate wind strength

**1807** Abolition of slave trade by Britain. Street lighting by gas in London

**1810** Techniques for canning food developed

**1811** Luddites destroy industrial machines in northern England

**1812** Philippe Girard invents machine for

# INDUSTRIAL REVOLUTION 1700–1850

| | |
|---|---|
| **1814** | spinning flax |
| **1815** | George Stephenson constructs first practical steam locomotive |
| | Humphry Davy invents miner's safety lamp. First steam warship, USS *Fulton*, built |
| **1815–16** | English economic crisis leads to large-scale emigration to North America |
| **1824** | Erie Canal, US, finished |
| **1825** | Stockton–Darlington Railway opens: first in world to carry passengers. Expansion of trade union movement in Britain |
| **1826** | Joseph Niepce produces photos on metal plates |
| **1828** | Building of Baltimore–Ohio railroad begins: first in US to carry passengers and freight |
| **1829** | First co-operative stores in US. Shillibeer's omnibus becomes part of London's public transport |
| **1830** | French tailor Barthélemy Thimmonier devises a stitching machine |
| **1833** | First British Factory Act provides a system for factory inspection. |
| **1834** | Abolition of slavery in British colonies. Cyrus Hall McCormick patents reaping machine in the US. Walter Hunt of New York constructs one of the first sewing machines. Poor Law Amendment Act: all poor to go to the workhouse. Louis Braille invents reading system for the blind |
| **1835** | Samuel Colt takes out English patent for single-barrelled pistol and rifle |
| **1837** | Electrical telegraph patented |
| **1838–48** | Chartist Movement in Britain |
| **1839** | Charles Goodyear makes commercial use of rubber possible by vulcanization |
| **1844** | Wood pulp paper invented |
| **1845** | Hydraulic crane patented by William G Armstrong. E B Bigelow constructs power looms for making carpets |
| **1846** | Britain repeals Corn Laws |
| **1847–48** | Great Irish Famine |
| **1848** | Communist Manifesto published by Marx and Engels |

# US WAR OF INDEPENDENCE

| 1765 | | Stamp Act; US colonies rebel against British taxes |
|---|---|---|
| 1773 | | **Boston Tea Party; cargo of tea thrown overboard in Boston Harbour to protest against British taxes** |
| 1775 | Apr | First skirmishes of war between Minutemen and British soldiers at Lexington |
| | Jun | British victory at Battle of Bunker's Hill |
| | Jul | **George Washington assumes control of Continental army** |
| | Nov | Montreal taken from British |
| 1776 | Jan | Thomas Paine calls for full American independence in pamphlet *Common Sense* |
| | Feb | British forces defeated near Wilmington, North Carolina |
| | Mar | Continental fleet captures New Providence in the Bahamas. British evacuate Boston. Congress authorizes privateering |
| | Jun | Declaration of American Independence drafted by Thomas Jefferson |
| | Jul | **Declaration of Independence adopted** |
| | Aug | British victory at Long Island |
| | Sep | British occupy New York |
| | Oct | Americans defeated at Lake Champlain and forced to retreat |
| | Dec | American victory at Battle of Trenton. Washington captures 1000 mercenaries |
| 1777 | Jan | American victory at Princeton |
| | Jul | La Fayette joins Washington |
| | Aug | American victories at Oriskany and Bennington |
| | Sep | British win Battle of Brandywine; La Fayette wounded |
| | Oct | Articles of Confederacy; first organizing document of the US |
| | Dec | Washington winters at Valley Forge |
| 1778 | Feb | France signs treaty of alliance with Americans |
| | Apr | British peace commission; American naval raid on Whitehaven, England |
| | Jun | British evacuate Philadelphia; stalemate at Battle of Monmouth |
| | Jul | French fleet arrives |

# US WAR OF INDEPENDENCE

| | | |
|---|---|---|
| | Jul–Aug | Franco-American attack on Newport repulsed; Americans evacuate Rhode Island |
| | Dec | British capture Savannah |
| 1779 | Feb | American victory at Vincennes |
| | Jun | Spain declares war on Britain but refuses to acknowledge American independence, fearing for her possessions |
| | Aug | Congressional peace terms approved by Congress |
| | Sep | American naval victories in North Sea |
| | Oct | Franco-American attempt to recapture Savannah fails |
| 1780 | Mar | Russia suggests a league of armed neutrality |
| | **May** | **Fall of Charleston to the British** |
| | Jul | French reinforcements land |
| | Aug | British victory at Battle of Camden |
| | Sep | West Point surrender plot by Benedict Arnold discovered |
| | Oct | American victory at Battle of King's Mountain |
| 1781 | Jan | Mutiny in Pennsylvania crushed. American victory at Cowpens |
| | **Mar** | **Articles of Confederation ratified.** Costly British victory in Battle of Guildford Courthouse British campaign in Virginia |
| | May–Aug | Congressional peace commission |
| | Jun | Yorktown campaign |
| | Aug–Oct | French naval victory in Battle of Chesapeake Bay |
| | **Oct** | **British capitulation at Yorktown** |
| 1782 | Mar | British government defeated in vote on war and forced to resign |
| | Apr | Peace talks in Paris |
| | Jul | Formal peace negotiations begin |
| | **Nov** | **Preliminary peace treaty signed** |
| | Dec | British evacuate Charleston |
| 1783 | Feb | Cessation of hostilities |
| | Apr | Congress ratifies peace treaty; 7000 loyalists sail home from New York |
| | Jun | American army disbanded |
| | **Sep** | **Treaty of Paris signed by Britain, France, Spain and the United States** |
| | Nov | British leave New York |

# FRENCH REVOLUTION 1789–99

**1789 May** Estates General meet at Versailles

**Jun** Third Estate forms National Assembly and takes Tennis Court Oath

**Jul Storming of the Bastille**

**Aug** Declaration of the Rights of Man

**Oct** Royal Family brought from Versailles to Paris; National Assembly moves to Paris

**1790 Jun** Hereditary nobility and titles abolished; Louis XVI accepts constitution

**1791 Jun** Flight to Varennes; Louis XVI's escape thwarted

**Sep** National Assembly dissolved

**Oct** Legislative Assembly elected

**1792 Apr** France declares war on Austria and Prussia (First Coalition)

**Jun** Mob attacks Tuileries Palace, Paris

**Sep** Monarchy abolished

**1793 Jan Louis XVI executed**

**Feb** War declared on Britain and Holland

**Mar** War declared on Spain

**Apr** Committee of Public Safety formed

**Jul** Robespierre elected to Committee of Public Safety

**Sep Reign of Terror begins**

**Oct** Republican calendar adopted. Execution of Marie Antoinette

**1794 Apr** Danton executed

**Jun** Festival of the Supreme Being

**Jul** Robespierre executed

**1795 Feb** Separation of Church and State

**Apr Bread riots in Paris**

**May** Revolutionary Tribunal suppressed

Napoleon appointed major-general. The Directory of five members established to rule France

**1796 Apr** Italian campaigns begin

**1797 Jul** Italian campaigns end

**Oct** Treaty of Campo Formio between France and Austria

**1798 Feb** French occupy Rome

**Apr** French invade Switzerland

**Jul** Battle of the Pyramids; France conquers Egypt

**Aug** Battle of the Nile; French navy defeated by British

**Dec** Second Coalition (Russia and Britain)

**1799 Jan** Formation of Republic of Naples

**Nov** Napoleon overthrows Directory

**Dec** Napoleon appointed First Consul

## NAPOLEONIC WARS 1800–15

**1800** Jun Battle of Marengo; France defeats Austria

**1801** Mar Spain cedes Louisiana to French
Apr Nelson destroys Danish fleet at Copenhagen

**1802** Mar Peace of Amiens between France and Britain
Aug New constitution. Napoleon Consul for life

**1803** Apr USA purchases Louisiana from France
Oct France threatens to invade England

**1804 May Napoleon proclaimed emperor**

**1805 Oct Battle of Trafalgar.** Britain defeats Franco-Spanish fleet
Dec France defeats Austria and Russia at Battle of Austerlitz; signs Treaty of Pressburg

**1806** Oct France occupies Berlin. Battle of Jena; France defeats Prussia
Nov Poland invaded

**1807** Jun French defeat Russian and Prussian forces at Friedland
Nov France occupies Portugal

**1808** Mar France invades Spain
Dec British troops land at Lisbon

**1809** Jul Battle of Wagram; France defeats Austria
Dec Napoleon divorces Josephine

**1810** Apr Napoleon marries Marie Louise of Austria

**1812** Jun Russian campaign begins
Jul Battle of Salamanca. Britain defeats France in Spain
Sept Battle of Borodino; Russians retreat. French advance to Moscow
**Oct–Dec French retreat from Russia**

**1813** Jun Battle of Vitoria; Britain defeats France in Spain
Aug Battle of Dresden; Napoleon defeats allies
Oct Battle of Leipzig; allies defeat Napoleon

**1814 Apr Napoleon abdicates; exiled to Elba**
Nov Congress of Vienna opens to redefine Europe

**1815 Mar Napoleon returns to Paris**
Jun Congress of Vienna closes. **Battle of Waterloo; Napoleon defeated.** Napoleon abdicates again; exiled to St Helena
Jul Louis XVIII returns to Paris

# POST-NAPOLEONIC EUROPE

| | |
|---|---|
| **1811–20** | Regency in Britain |
| **1815** | Congress of Vienna closes. Corn Law passed in Britain |
| Sep | Holy Alliance formed between Prussia, Austria and Russia |
| **1816** | Carl August of Saxe-Weimar grants first constitution in Germany |
| **1818** | **Allied army of occupation leaves France.** Prussia divided into 10 provinces |
| **1819** | Customs union in Germany (Zollverein) formed |
| **1820** | Revolutions in Italy, Portugal and Spain. Spain cedes Florida to USA |
| **1821** | Greek uprising against Turkey |
| May | **Death of Napoleon on St Helena** |
| **1822** | Turkish invasion of Greece. Bottle riots in Dublin. Orangemen attack viceroy |
| Oct | Congress of Verona opens, to discuss European difficulties |
| **1823** | War between France and Spain |
| **1824** | Death of Byron in Turko-Greek war at Missolonghi |
| **1825** | **World's first railway opens between Stockton and** |
| **1827** | **Darlington.** Trade unions recognized as legal in England |
| | Battle of Navarino; destruction of Turkish fleet by Britain, France and Russia |
| **1828** | Turko-Russian War. Duke of Wellington becomes British prime minister |
| **1830** | Revolutionary uprisings in Germany. Separation of Holland and Belgium. **Revolution in Paris** |
| **1831** | Electoral Reform Bill introduced into House of Commons |
| **1834** | Spanish Inquisition finally suppressed. Slavery ended in British possessions |
| **1836** | The Peoples' Charter launches first workers movement in Britain |
| **1837** | **Accession of Queen Victoria in Britain.** Liberal constitution in Spain |
| **1839** | First British Opium War with China |
| **1840** | Louis Napoleon makes an attempt to lead Bonapartist uprising against July Monarchy |
| **1847–48** | Great Irish Famine |

# POST-NAPOLEONIC EUROPE

**1848**

    **Communist Manifesto published by Marx and Engels.** Unsuccessful revolt by Germans in Schleswig-Holstein

Feb  Ferdinand II of Naples is forced to concede a constitution. In France July Monarchy overthrown. Louis-Philippe abdicates and Louis Napoleon elected president of France. Second Republic established

Feb–Mar  Rulers of Tuscany and Piedmont and the Pope forced to grant constitutions

Mar  Metternich, Austrian chancellor, dismissed and flees. Revolt in Vienna. Revolts in Venice. Berlin and Parma. Street fighting in Milan against Austrians forces Austrian troops to withdraw. Piedmont declares war on Austria. Republic of St Mark set up in Venice. Hungarian Diet adopts March Laws of autonomy

Jun  Habsburg power restored. Emperor Ferdinand of Austria abdicates. Franz Joseph becomes emperor. Second uprising in Paris. Czech revolts suppressed by Austrian troops

Jul  Piedmontese defeated at Custoza by Austrians

Sep  Croats invade Hungary

Nov  Pope Pius IX flees from Rome to Kingdom of Naples.

**1848–49**  Revolution in the Austrian Empire

**1849**  Russians intervene to help crush Hungarian Revolution. Austria retakes Venice

Mar  Piedmontese defeated by Austrians at Novara. Charles Albert of Sardinia abdicates in favour of his son, Victor Emmanuel II

Jun  Danes secure constitution from Frederick VII

Aug  End of Republic of St Mark

**1850**  Apr  Pope Pius IX returns to Rome with French military help

# EUROPEAN NATIONALISM 1840–1914

| | |
|---|---|
| **1851** | Great Exhibition in London. |
| **1852** | Cavour becomes prime minister of Piedmont |
| **1852–70** | Second emperor of France, Napoleon II |
| **1853–56** | **Crimean War** |
| **1859** | Franco-Austrian war in northern Italy. Liberation of Lombardy from Austrians |
| **1860** | **Garibaldi sails from Genoa to Sicily with I Mille and takes Sicily and Naples** |
| **1861** | King of Naples surrenders at Gaeta. Kingdom of Italy announced; excludes Rome and Venetia. Victor Emmanuel is announced king of Italy |
| **1862** | **Alexander II of Russia frees the serfs** |
| | Garibaldi captured in bid for Rome. Bismarck becomes Prussian minister-president |
| **1863–64** | Second Polish Revolution |
| **1864** | German-Danish War over Schleswig-Holstein |
| **1866** | Red Cross formed in Geneva |
| | Austro-Prussian War (or Seven |

| | |
|---|---|
| | Weeks' War). Battle of Königgratz. Prussians defeat Austrians. Italy gains Venetia by allying with Prussia against Austria |
| **1866–68** | Cretan Revolt against Turks |
| **1867** | Dual Monarchy of Austria-Hungary organized. Garibaldi's second bid for Rome fails |
| **1867–71** | North German Confederation established |
| **1870** | **Unification of Italy completed** Rome becomes Italian capital |
| **1870–71** | Franco-Prussian war. Siege of Paris |
| **1870–1914** | Third Republic in France |
| **1871** | Creation of German empire (Second Reich). **Paris Commune rising fails** |
| **1872** | League of Three Empires (Dreikaiserbund) between Germany, Austria-Hungary and Russia |
| **1873–74** | First Spanish republic declared |
| **1873–76** | Second Carlist War in Spain |
| **1874–80** | Disraeli becomes British prime minister |
| **1876** | Bulgar Revolt against the Turks |
| **1877–78** | Russo-Turkish War |
| **1878** | Serbia, Montenegro and Romania |

# EUROPEAN NATIONALISM 1840–1914

| | |
|---|---|
| **1879** | become independent with Berlin Congress. Britain gains Cyprus |
| **1881** | Alliance of Germany and Austria |
| **1882** | Tsar Alexander II of Russia murdered. Triple Alliance between Italy, Germany and Austria |
| **1885–86** | Serbian–Bulgarian War |
| **1886** | First Irish Home Rule Bill |
| **1886** | Year of Three Empires in Germany |
| **1890** | Bismarck dismissed by Emperor Wilhelm II |
| **1893–94** | Franco-Russian Alliance |
| **1894– 1906** | Dreyfus Affair in France |
| **1897** | Greco-Turkish War over Crete |
| **1899** | First Hague Peace Conference |
| **1901–5** | Separation of Church and State in France |
| **1904–5** | Russo-Japanese War |
| **1904** | Anglo-French Entente signed: 'Entente Cordiale' |
| **1905** | Kaiser's visit to Tangier precipitates First Moroccan Crisis. Norwegian–Swedish union dissolved |
| **1905–6** | Revolution in Russia |
| **1906** | Conference of Algeciras in Spain, between Germany, France |

| | |
|---|---|
| | and Britain |
| **1907** | Second Hague Peace Conference. Anglo-Russian Entente |
| **1908** | Austria annexes Bosnia and Herzegovina |
| **1910** | Portuguese Revolution |
| **1911** | Second Moroccan or Agadir Crisis |
| **1911–12** | Tripolitanian War between Turks and Italians |
| **1912–13** | First Balkan War between Balkan League and Turkey |
| **1913** | Second Balkan War, Bulgaria attacks former allies. Treaty of Bucharest |
| **1914** | **Archduke Francis Ferdinand murdered in Sarajevo** |

# US CIVIL WAR 1861–66

**1861** Apr Confederate batteries open fire on Fort Sumter. Lincoln calls for volunteers. Union naval forces begin blockade of Confederate ports and coastline

Jul **Confederate victory at first Battle of Bull Run**

Aug Missouri remains in Union after Battle of Wilson's Creek

Nov Confederate commissioners seized from British ship by Union patrol

Dec War between Union and Great Britain averted by their release

**1862** Jan **Lincoln orders general offensive**

Jan/Feb/Apr Union victories in Tennessee and Kentucky culminating in Battle of Shiloh

Mar–Jun Confederate forces pin down Union troops in Shenandoah Valley

Apr New Orleans taken by Union. Confederacy adopts conscription.

May–Jun Battle for Richmond at Seven Pines indecisive

Jun–Jul Seven Days' Battle ends with Confederate withdrawal towards Richmond

Aug **Union forces defeated in second Battle of Bull Run**

Sep Confederate invades Maryland. Drawn battle takes place near Sharpsburg. Lincoln issues preliminary proclamation on the emancipation of slaves

Dec Confederate victory at Fredericksburg. Lincoln weathers cabinet crisis

**1863** Jan Emancipation proclamation

Feb Congress establishes National Banking System. French attempt at mediation

May–Jul Union forces besiege and take Vicksburg to split Confederacy geographically

Jun West Virginia afforded statehood by the Union

Jul Union victory at Battle of Gettysburg. Anti-conscription riots in New York

Sep British and French governments deny shipbuilding facilities to Confederacy. Indecisive Battle of Chickamauga

Nov **Gettysburg war cemetery**

# US CIVIL WAR 1861-66

### 1864

**inaugurated with address by Lincoln.** Union victory at Battle of Chattanooga reinforces geographical split of Confederacy

Mar-May Union forces advance south and west

May Indecisive battles with heavy casualties in The Wilderness and at Spotsylvania

May-Sep Union advance through Georgia

Jun Battles at Chickahominy and Cold Harbour and siege of Petersburg cause heavy Confederate losses without total Union victory. Confederate naval losses. Union presidential election campaign begins

Jul Confederate advance towards Washington rebuffed

Jun-Oct Second Shenandoah Valley campaign

**Sep Atlanta falls to Union forces**

Nov Lincoln re-electe

Nov-Dec Union advance towards Savannah

Dec Union victory at Battle of Nashville Savannah falls

### 1865

Jan-Mar Union advance through North and South Carolina

Feb Hampton Roads conference fails to agree terms. Union forces capture Charleston

Mar Confederacy agrees to arm slaves for military duties

Apr Confederate forces evacuate Petersburg and Richmond. Lincoln inaugurated for second term. Confederate forces surrender at Appomattox. Lincoln assassinated

May Confederate capitulation. Reconstruction proclamation

**Dec Abolition of slavery**

### 1866

Apr Civil Rights Act grants citizenship to African Americans

# AFRICA 400–1914

| | |
|---|---|
| c. 400 AD | Kingdom of Ghana founded |
| 429–534 | Vandal kingdom in North Africa |
| 640–710 | Islamic conquests in northern Africa |
| c. 690 | Songhay empire founded in Niger |
| 968–1171 | Fatamid dynasty in Egypt |
| c. 1100– | Great Zimbabwe complex built in stone in Zimbabwe |
| 1440 | |
| c. 1200 | Rise of Kilwa Sultanate |
| 1235 | **Foundation of Mali Kingdom** |
| 1350 | Songhay empires at their height |
| c. 1400 | Shona civilization of Great Zimbabwe |
| 1402 | Ethiopian embassy to Venice |
| 1433 | **Tuaregs from the Sahara sack Timbuktu** |
| 1448 | Portuguese set up first fort at Arguin in Mauritania |
| 1497 | Vasco da Gama rounds the Cap of Good Hope |
| 1505–1821 | Funj empire in Sudan |
| 1517 | **Ottomans take Cairo** |
| 1626 | First French settle in Senegal and Madagascar |
| 1628–29 | War between Mozambique and Portugal |
| 1629 | Mozambique becomes a Portuguese protectorate |
| 1632–55 | Gondar Ethiopian empire |
| 1650 | Bambara kingdom of West Africa founded |
| 1651 | Swedes take Gold Coast from Dutch |
| 1652 | Dutch found Cape Colony |
| 1658 | French establish town of St Louis in Senegal |
| 1659–60 | War between Xhosa and Dutch settlers |
| 1660 | Rise of Bambara kingdoms in upper Niger |
| 1662–84 | English occupation of Tangier |
| 1670 | Bambara kingdoms defeat Mandingo empire |
| 1697 | French attempt to colonize West Africa under André de Brue |
| 1729 | Portuguese lose Mombasa to Arabs |
| 1779–81 | First Xhosa War between Boers and Xhosa people |
| 1790– | Rise of the Fulani in northern Nigeria |
| 1801 | |
| 1798–99 | Napoleon's campaign in Egypt |
| 1802 | Egypt formally restored to sultan |
| 1805 | British reconquer the Cape Colony |
| 1808 | **Britain and US outlaw slave trade** |
| 1816–28 | **Zulu kingdom is created** |

# AFRICA 400–1914

| | |
|---|---|
| 1820 | Egypt conquers Sudan. British settlers arrive in Cape Colony |
| 1822 | Liberia is established by freed African Americans |
| 1824–31 | First Anglo-Ashanti War |
| 1830–47 | **French conquest of Algeria** |
| 1835–37 | British defeat the Xhosa |
| 1835–37 | **Great Boer Trek from Cape Colony** |
| 1843 | Britain annexes Natal |
| 1844 | Treaty of Tangier ends French war in Morocco |
| 1846–47 | British defeat Xhosa again |
| 1849 | Livingstone's first journey in Africa |
| 1850–78 | Nine Kaffir wars in South Africa |
| 1852 | Britain recognizes the Transvaal as an independent Boer republic |
| 1854 | Britain recognizes Orange Free State. Egypt grants French engineer de Lesseps concession to build Suez canal |
| 1868 | Britain annexes Lesotho |
| 1869 | **Suez Canal opens** |
| 1879 | Anglo-Zulu War |
| c. 1880 | **'Scramble for Africa' begins** |
| 1881 | French seize Tunis |
| 1882 | British occupation of Egypt |
| 1882– 1941 | Italian African Empire |
| 1883 | Mahdist state in Sudan. Kruger becomes president of South African Republic |
| 1883–5 | Germany takes control of Namibia, Togoland, Cameroon and Tanzania. Berlin Conference on Africa. Congo recognized as Leopold of Belgium's personal territory |
| 1885 | Spanish African empire |
| 1885– 1975 | |
| 1885 | General Gordon killed at Khartoum while trying to evacuate Egyptian garrisons |
| 1896 | Battle of Adowa; Ethiopians defeat Italians |
| 1899 | British take Sudan |
| 1899– 1902 | **Anglo-Boer Wars** |
| 1904 | France proclaims a constitution for Federation of West Africa |
| 1912 | Founding of African National Congress |
| 1914–18 | First World War; campaigns in German Togoland, Cameroon and South-west Africa |

# US WESTERN EXPANSION 1800–1900

| | |
|---|---|
| 1800 | Thomas Jefferson wins presidential election |
| 1803 | Ohio becomes 17th state of the US. US secures land in the gulf of Mexico to north-west, including Louisiana and New Orleans from France (Louisiana Purchase) |
| 1811 | Indians defeated at Tippecanoe, Indiana |
| 1812 | Louisiana becomes 18th state of the US |
| 1814 | Battle of Horseshoe Bend ends Creek Indian War begun in 1812 |
| 1816 | Indiana becomes 19th state of the union |
| 1817 | Mississippi becomes 20th state of the union. |
| Nov | Beginning of Seminole Indian War, after Indians retaliate following attacks |
| 1818 | Illinois becomes 21st state |
| 1819 | Florida purchased from Spain. Alabama becomes 22nd state |
| 1820 | Maine becomes 23rd state |
| 1821 | Missouri becomes 24th state |
| 1823 | Monroe doctrine closes the American continent to further colonial settlements by European powers |
| 1824 | South Pass, Wyoming discovered, allowing passage through the Rockies |
| 1825 | Creek Indian Treaty signed, obliging Creeks to cede all territory in Georgia |
| 1828 | First railroad built for the transportation of passengers and freight |
| 1830 | **First covered wagon trek from Missouri River to Rockies** |
| 1832 | Black Hawk Indian War ends with massacre at Bad Axe River |
| 1835 | Texas declares its right to secede from Mexico |
| 1836 | American rebels massacred by Mexican forces at the Alamo. Texas wins independence and becomes a republic. Arkansas is 25th state |
| 1837 | Michigan is 26th state. First covered wagons reach California |
| 1845 | Florida becomes 27th state, Texas becomes 28th |
| 1846 | Westward migration of Mormons. |

# US WESTERN EXPANSION 1800–1900

| | |
|---|---|
| **1847** | Beginning of Mexican War. Iowa becomes 29th state |
| **1848** | Discovery of gold in California leads to first gold rush |
| | **Mexican War ends:** the US secures Texas, New Mexico, California, Utah, Nevada, Arizona, parts of Colorado and Wyoming from Mexico in return for a large indemnity. Wisconsin becomes 30th state |
| **1850** | California becomes 31st state |
| **1858** | Minnesota becomes 32nd state |
| **1859** | Oregon becomes 33rd state |
| **1860** | Abraham Lincoln elected 16th president of the US; South Carolina secedes from the Union in protest |
| **1861** | Kansas becomes 34th state. Confederate states break away from the Union |
| Apr | **Civil War begins at Fort Sumter, South Carolina** |
| **1862** | Union forces defeated at Bull Run and Fredericksburg |
| **1863** | **'Emancipation proclamation' effective from 1 Jan; all** |

| | |
|---|---|
| | **slaves in rebelling areas declared free** |
| **1863** | Arizona and Idaho become US territories. West Virginia becomes 35th state. Lincoln delivers 'Gettysburg Address', while dedicating a national cemetery |
| **1864** | Confederate army at Atlanta and occupies Savannah. Nevada becomes 36th state |
| **1865** Apr | Confederate states formally surrender at Appomattox |
| May | Abraham Lincoln assassinated. **Civil War ends** |
| **1867** | Nebraska becomes 37th state. Alaska purchased from Russia. Gold discovered in Wyoming |
| **1876** | Colorado becomes 38th state |
| **1880** | Railroad mileage now in operation in the US: 87 800 miles |
| **1889** | North Dakota, South Dakota, Montana, and Washington join the Union. Oklahoma opened to non-Indian settlement |
| **1890** | Idaho and Wyoming join the Union |
| **1896** | Utah becomes 45th state |

# AUSTRALASIA 1750–1990

| | |
|---|---|
| **1768–79** | James Cook discovers Hawaii, New Caledonia and other islands in the Pacific |
| **1770** | Cook sights and explores east coast of Australia and claims it for Britain; he calls it New South Wales |
| **1787** | **New South Wales is established as a convict colony. Britain ships convicts to Australia** |
| **1788** | English convict ship lands at Botany Bay |
| **1793** | **Arrival of first free settlers in New South Wales** |
| **1798–99** | George Bass and Matthew Flinders sail around Tasmania |
| **1800s** | Settlers, traders and slave traders settle on Pacific islands |
| **1829** | Western Australia is established as a colony |
| **1840** | Maoris sign Treaty of Waitangi, giving Britain sovereignty over New Zealand |
| **1845–72** | Settlers on North Island defeat Maoris in New Zealand Wars |
| **1851** | Australian colony of Victoria is established separate from New |
| **1852** | South Wales. Gold is discovered in New South Wales and Victoria |
| **1856** | Britain grants New Zealand a new constitution |
| | Britain grants self-government to all the colonies except Western Australia |
| **1859** | Queensland separates from New South Wales |
| **1860** | Maori uprising in New Zealand |
| **1865** | Wellington becomes capital of New Zealand |
| **1868** | Britain ends transportation of convicts |
| **1890** | New Zealand government starts programme for social reform |
| **1893** | **New Zealand becomes the first nation to grant women the vote** |
| **1898** | Germany and the US take over Spain's possessions in Micronesia |
| **early 1900s** | Germany also holds parts of Nauru, New Guinea and part of Samoa, and US controls Hawaii and the rest of Samoa. France and Britain also hold islands |
| **1901** | Australia becomes independent |

# AUSTRALASIA 1750–1990

| | |
|---|---|
| 1907 | New Zealand becomes a dominion within the British empire |
| 1914–18 | Australia and New Zealand join with Britain in World War I |
| 1927 | Australian capital transferred from Melbourne to Canberra |
| 1936–38 | New Zealand sets up a social security programme for all its citizens |
| **1939–45** | **Australia and New Zealand fight with the Allies in World War II** |
| 1945 | Australia becomes a member of the UN |
| 1946 | Nuclear testing by US starts on Bikini and Enewetak atolls and also on Johnston Island. Britain also carries out nuclear tests on Christmas Island |
| 1951 | Australia and New Zealand sign ANZUS Treaty |
| 1962 | Western Samoa becomes independent |
| 1965 | France begins nuclear tests on Tuamotu Island |
| **1967** | **Australian constitution changed to allow programmes to aid Aborigines** |
| 1968 | Nauru becomes independent |
| 1970 | Britain grants independence to Fiji, Tonga and the Solomon Islands |
| 1973 | New Guinea becomes self-governing and is renamed Papua New Guinea |
| 1975 | Papua New Guinea becomes independent |
| 1978 | Britain grants Tuvalu independence |
| 1979 | Britain's Gilbert Islands become independent and call themselves Kiribati |
| 1980 | New Hebrides ruled by Britain and France become independent and are renamed Vanuatu |
| 1985 | New Zealand bans nuclear weapons and nuclear-powered ships in its harbours |
| **1986** | **Many American Trust Territories made self-governing except Guam and Caroline Islands** |
| 1987 Oct | Fiji becomes a republic and leaves Commonwealth after coup |

# LATIN AMERICA 1800–1990

| | |
|---|---|
| **1810-26** | **Spanish–American wars of independence** |
| **1811** | Paraguay becomes independent of Spain |
| **1816** | Argentina is declared independent |
| **1818** | Chile proclaims its independence |
| **1819** | Colombia achieves independence led by Simon Bolivar, who proclaims himself president |
| **1820-21** | General José de San Martin leads Peru's independence from Spain. Costa Rica declares independence |
| **1821** Sep | Guatemala gains independence. Mexico achieves independence |
| **1822** | Brazil becomes independent of Portugal |
| **1823** | Confederation of United Provinces of Central America formed by Costa Rica, Guatemala, Honduras, Nicaragua and San Salvador |
| Dec | **US president Monroe issues Monroe Doctrine, banning European states from colonizing American republics** |
| **1824** | Bolivar leads final liberation of Peru |
| **1825** | Bolivia gains independence from |

| | |
|---|---|
| | Peru. Uruguay achieves independence from Brazil |
| **1826** | Last Spanish garrisons in Peru and Chile surrender |
| **1830** | Bolivar resigns office and dies on way to exile. Venezuela becomes independent. Ecuador gains independence |
| **1838** | Honduras achieves independence. Nicaragua becomes independent republic |
| **1849** | El Salvador becomes independent |
| **1865** | Paraguay declares war on Argentina, Brazil and Uruguay |
| **1870** | Paraguay ends war, having lost territory and over half its population |
| **1903** | Panama becomes independent, supported by the USA |
| **1966** | Guyana becomes independent |
| **1970** | Guyana becomes a republic within the Commonwealth |
| **1975** | Suriname gains independence |
| **1981** | Belize gains independence from Britain |

# WORLD WAR I

| | |
|---|---|
| **1901** | Queen Victoria dies |
| **1902** | Triple Alliance between Germany, Austria and Italy renewed for further six years |
| **1903** | Jun King Alexander and Queen Draga of Serbia murdered |
| **1904** | Apr French–British 'Entente Cordiale' established. Russo-Japanese war breaks out over Manchuria |
| **1905** | Mar Theodore Roosevelt wins US presidential election |
| **1908** | **Oct Austria annexes Bosnia and Herzegovina** |
| **1910** | Japan annexes Korea |
| **1911** | Sep Italo-Turkish Tripolitanian War begins |
| | Oct Winston Churchill appointed First Lord of the Admiralty |
| **1912** | Oct Montenegro declares war on Turkey. Bulgaria and Serbia mobilize their armies |
| | Dec Armistice is secured |
| **1913** | Feb Outbreak of second Balkan War |
| | Mar Woodrow Wilson wins US presidential election |
| **1914** | Peace treaty signed by Serbia and Turkey |

| | |
|---|---|
| **Jun** | **Archduke Ferdinand murdered at Sarajevo by Serbian nationalist** |
| Jul | Austria–Hungary with German support, declares war on Serbia. Russia mobilizes war on Serbia in support of Serbia |
| **Aug** | **Germany declares war on Russia and France. Britain enters war after Germany invades Belgium.** Russia declares war on Turkey. France and Britain declare war on Turkey. Russians invade east Prussia. Germans occupy Liège. Battles of Namur and Mons. Germans occupy Lille. Russians defeated at Tannenberg |
| Sep | Battle of Marne; Germans retreat. Russians defeated in Battle of Masurian Lakes. Russians invade Hungary |
| Oct | First Battle of Ypres; German offensive halted. Turkey attacks Russia |
| Nov | Hindenburg appointed German commander in the east |

## WORLD WAR I

**1915**

Dec Germans take Lodz in Poland
**German airships bomb British ports in East Anglia.** Turkish army attacks Suez Canal

Feb German blockade of Britain begins

Mar Battle at Neuve-Chapelle

Apr Initial landings at Gallipoli

Apr–May Second Battle of Ypres. **Germans use poison gas for first time**

May Sinking of Cunard liner *Lusitania* by German U-boat

Jun First Battle of Isonzo

Sep Battle of Loos. First Zeppelin attack on London. Czar Nicholas II takes over command of the Russian army. Dardanelles campaign begins. Anglo-French landings at Gallipoli

Oct Edith Cavell executed in Brussels

Dec Douglas Haig becomes British commander-in-chief in France. Russians forced back on Eastern front

**1916**

Jan First Zeppelin raid on Paris. Australian and New Zealand forces withdraw from Gallipoli

Feb Battles of Verdun

May Battle of Jutland; German fleet retreats, Sinn Fein Easter Rebellion in Dublin

July **Battles of Somme.** British take possession of the whole Sinai peninsula. Anzacs arrive in France. Italy declares war on Germany

Sept **British use tanks on Western Front**

Dec Lloyd George becomes British prime minister. Germany sends peace note to Allies. T E Lawrence (of Arabia) appointed British political and liaison officer to Faisal's army

**1917**

Feb Germans withdraw on Western front. Bread rationed in Britain. General Pershing arrives in Paris to head American forces. Russian Black Sea fleet mutinies at Sebastopol

Apr **US and Cuba declare war on Germany.**

Jun British royal family renounces German names and titles. German aircraft attack London

Aug China declares war on Austria and Germany

Jul Third Battle of Ypres begins

# WORLD WAR I

| Oct-Nov | Italian army defeated at Caporetto |
| Nov | British and US forces take Passchendaele to end Third Battle of Ypres. First tank battles take place at Cambrai. Revolution breaks out in Russia; Lenin appointed chief commissar |
| **Dec** | **US declares war on Hungary and Austria.** German–Russian armistice signed at Brest Litovsk |

| **1918** | |
| Jan | President Wilson issues 14 point peace plan. Meat and butter rationed in London |
| Mar | Transfer of Soviet government to Moscow. Germans bomb Paris |
| Jul | Second Battle of Marne. Ex-Tsar Nicholas of Russia and family are executed in Russia |
| Sep | Allied offensive on the Western Front opens |
| Oct | Fall of Damascus. Turkish resistance crumbles in Palestine. **Germany sues for peace.** Germany suspends submarine warfare |
| Nov | German fleet mutinies at Kiel. Republic declared in Bavaria. German republic proclaimed. **Allies at Versailles agree on peace terms for Germany signed Nov 11.** Revolution in Berlin. Kaiser Wilhelm abdicates and flees to Holland. Austria proclaims union with Germany |
| Dec | President Wilson arrives in Paris for Peace Conference at Versailles |

| **1919** | |
| Jan | Peace conference opens at Versailles. National Socialist party founded in Germany |
| Feb | First League of Nations meeting in Paris. Mussolini founds Fasci del Combattimento |
| Apr | Habsburg dynasty exiled from Austria |
| Jun | German peace treaty signed at Versailles. German fleet scuttled at Scapa Flow |
| Jul | Blockade of Germany ended |

# THE USSR 1900–92

| | |
|---|---|
| **1901** | Social Revolutionary Party founded |
| **1903–21** | Pogroms in Russia |
| **1904–05** | Russo-Japanese War; Russia loses |
| **1905–6** | Abortive Russian Revolution. General strike. Mutiny on battleship *Potemkin* |
| **1917** Mar | Revolution in Russia; Tsar abdicates |
| Nov | October Revolution'; Lenin appointed chief commissar. Trotsky commissar for foreign affairs. Counter-revolution led by Kerensky fails |
| **1917–22** | **Civil War.** Communists defeat anti-communist opponents |
| **1918** | Murder of Russian royal family |
| **1919** | Third International founded |
| **1919–21** | Russo-Polish War |
| **1922** | Stalin becomes general secretary of Communist Party |
| **1923** | **The USSR formally established** |
| **1924** Jan | Death of Lenin; power struggle between Stalin and Trotsky begins |
| **1927** | Trotsky is expelled from the Party |
| **1928–32** | First Five-Year Plan to expand the economy. Wealthy peasantry persecuted |
| **1928** | Grain shortage. Stalin orders immediate agricultural collectivism |
| **1929** | Trotsky is deported |
| **1932–33** | Famine and punishment of peasants farming smallholdings; approximately 15 million die |
| **1933–37** | Second Five-Year Plan to produce consumer goods |
| **1933–38** | **Stalin's Great Terror purge** |
| **1938–42** | Third Five-Year Plan to produce armaments |
| **1939** | Stalin-Hitler non-aggression pact. Russo-Japanese Mongolian border war. USSR invades Finland, and is expelled from the League of Nations |
| **1939–40** | Russo-Finnish War |
| **1940** | Trotsky assassinated in Mexico on Stalin's orders. Russia annexes Baltic states |
| **1941** | **Germany invades USSR, breaking 1939 pact** |
| **1942–43** | Battle of Stalingrad leads to Russian victory in 1943 |
| **1945** | Yalta conference between Roosevelt, Stalin and Churchill |
| **1946–47** | **Cold War begins** |
| **1949** | USSR tests atomic bomb |

# THE USSR 1900–92

| | |
|---|---|
| 1950 | Sino-Soviet Treaty of Alliance |
| 1953 | Death of Stalin. Khrushchev becomes Party first secretary |
| 1954 | Malenkov premier of the USSR |
| 1955 | Bulganin succeeds Malenkov |
| 1956 | Khrushchev denounces Stalin at Party Congress. Russia invades Hungary. |
| 1958 | Khrushchev succeeds as leader |
| 1960 | Sino-Soviet split begins |
| 1961 | Kennedy–Khrushchev summit |
| 1964 | Khrushchev falls from power and Brezhnev is elected as Party leader |
| 1968 | Red Army invades Czechoslovakia |
| 1969 | Sino–Soviet border conflict |
| 1970 | West German, Soviet and Polish treaties on European borders |
| 1973 | Brezhnev–Nixon summit |
| 1980 | West boycotts Olympic Games to protest against Soviet invasion of Afghanistan |
| 1982 | Brezhnev dies, replaced by Andropov |
| 1984 | Andropov dies, replaced by Chernenko |
| 1985 | Gorbachev becomes Soviet leader |
| 1986 | Accident at Chernobyl nuclear plant. **Gorbachev begins policies of perestroika (reconstruction) and glasnost (openness)** |
| 1987 | US–USSR arms reduction treaty |
| 1988 Mar | Troops impose curfew in Azerbaijan |
| May | USSR withdraws from Afghanistan |
| Jun | Gorbachev admits food shortages and other failures of the system |
| Sep | Russian army sent to Armenia |
| Oct | Latvia and Lithuania demand self-rule |
| Nov | Estonia insists on sovereignty |
| 1990 Jan | Azerbaijan erupts in violence |
| Mar | Lithuania declares independence |
| May | Yeltsin elected Russian leader |
| Jul | Yeltsin quits the Communist Party |
| 1991 | Reactionary communist coup to overthrow Gorbachev fails. **Eleven republics form Commonwealth of Independent States (CIS)** |
| 1992 | A federal treaty is signed by 15 republics |
| Feb | USAF flies food aid to Moscow |
| Apr | Western nations agree to aid package for CIS |

# THE 1930s

| | | |
|---|---|---|
| 1929 | Oct | **Wall Street Crash leads to world-wide economic depression** |
| 1930 | Mar | Gandhi begins campaign of civil disobedience in India |
| | Apr | Ras Tafari becomes Emperor Haile Selassie of Ethiopia. Amy Johnson first woman to fly solo UK–Australia |
| | Jun | Last French troops leave Rhineland |
| | Aug | First major Arab–Jewish conflict in Palestine |
| | Sep | German elections: National Socialists emerge as major political force |
| 1931 | | Japan invades Manchuria |
| 1932 | | Series of inconclusive elections in Germany |
| | Jan | Japanese occupy Shanghai |
| | May | French Prime Minister Doumer assassinated |
| 1933 | Jan | **Hitler appointed Chancellor of Germany** |
| | Feb | Parliament building (Reichstag) burned |
| | Mar | Roosevelt becomes US president. Boycott of Jewish businesses in Germany begins |
| | Jun | Roosevelt launches 'New Deal' to help US economy |
| | Aug | First Nazi concentration camps |
| | Dec | Prohibition laws repealed in USA |
| 1934 | Feb | Civil war in Austria |
| | May | Mazaryk elected Czech president |
| | Jun | 'Night of the Long Knives'; SS units used by Hitler to eliminate opposition. Hitler and Mussolini meet in Venice |
| | Jul | Nazi revolt in Austria |
| | Aug | Hitler assumes title of Führer (leader) |
| | Sep | USSR joins League of Nations |
| | Oct | Mao Zedong leads 'Long March' |
| 1935 | Apr | Dust storms hit US 'breadbasket' states. Hitler announces German rearmament, in defiance of League of Nations |
| | Oct | Italy invades Ethiopia. Haile Selassie flees to French Somaliland |
| | Dec | Chiang Kai-shek elected president of Chinese Executive |
| 1936 | Mar | Nazi troops enter Rhineland |
| | Jul | **Spanish civil war begins between Franco's Fascists and Republican forces** |

# THE 1930s

Nov General Franco's Fascist government receives recognition from Hitler and Mussolini.

Aug Olympic Games held in Berlin as showcase for Aryan supremacy. Black American Jesse Owens dominates athletics events

Oct Franco appointed chief of Spanish nation

Nov Rome–Berlin axis formed

Dec Abdication of King Edward VIII

1937 Jan Show trials in USSR, as Stalin purges political opponents

Apr Franco's army destroys town of Guernica

May Giant airship, the *Hindenburg*, explodes as it tries to land in New Jersey. Egypt joins League of Nations

Aug Japanese take Beijing

Sep Armies of Chiang Kai-shek and Mao Zedong join to combat Japanese

Nov Japanese capture Shanghai

1938 Mar Germany annexes Austria. Mexico seizes US and British oil fields

May Nazi revolt in Brazil is suppressed

**Sep Chamberlain meets Hitler at Munich Conference. Germans and British sign agreement handing the Czech Sudetenland to Germany.**

Oct Hitler invades Czechoslovakia. Panic in USA as Orson Welles broadcasts *War of the Worlds*

Nov 'Kristallnacht' pogroms throughout Germany. Japan withdraws from League of Nations

1939 Jan Atomic fission achieved

Mar Spanish Civil War ends. Franco takes control. Annihilation of Czechoslovakia

Apr Italy annexes Albania

May Spain withdraws from League of Nations

**Sep Germany invade Poland; World War II begins**

# WORLD WAR II

**1935** Hitler announces German rearmament

**1936** Germany occupies demilitarized Rhineland

**1938** German troops enter Austria, which is declared part of Germany

Aug Germany mobilizes

Sep British premier Neville Chamberlain returns from Munich with a peace accord to avoid Czech crisis

Oct German troops enter Sudeten territory in Czechoslovakia

Nov Pogroms throughout Germany

**1939 Mar Germany annihilates Czechoslovakian state and renounces naval agreement with Britain**

Apr Italy annexes Albania. Japan occupies Hainan. US renounces Japanese trade agreement. Hitler denounces non-aggression pact with Poland.

Aug Hitler-Stalin non-aggression pact

Sep Germany invades Poland. Britain and France declare war on Germany. **World War II begins.** USSR invades Poland from the east; also invades Finland

Dec Battle of River Plate; German *Graf Spee* is scuttled. Roosevelt declares US neutral

**1940** Mar Finland surrenders territory to USSR after 14-week war

Apr Germany invades Denmark and Norway. Italy declares war on France and Britain. Hitler names Hermann Goering reichs-marschall

May Germany invades Belgium, the Netherlands and Luxembourg

**May–Jun British forces evacuated from Dunkirk.** Germany occupies the Channel Islands

Jun Germans enter Paris. Marshall Pétain concludes armistice with Germany

Aug **Battle of Britain**

Sep Daytime bombing of London and SE Britain begins. Italy advances into Egypt but is forced to retreat

Oct Night-time bombing of Britain. War spreads to North Africa. Roosevelt re-elected US president

Sep–Nov Blitz on London

**1941** Feb Rommel arrives in North Africa

# WORLD WAR II

Apr British take control of Iraq

Apr–May British invade Ethiopia and Abyssinia

Jun Germany invades USSR. Blitz on Coventry, Britain. Rommel attacks Tobruk. Allies take Lebanon and Syria

Apr Greece falls to Germany

May Germans invade Crete

Aug Allies control Iran

Sep Siege of Leningrad begins

**Dec Japan bombs Pearl Harbor.** US and Britain declare war on Japan. Germany and Italy declare war on the USA. China enters war on the side of the Allies. Japan occupies Thailand, invades Philippines and Malaya and takes Hong Kong

**1942 Jan Under Hitler, Germany embarks on the 'Final Solution' – the systematic removal of Jews, gypsies, homosexuals, communists and dissidents.** Japan takes Manila

Feb Japan invades Burma and

Mar Singapore surrenders

Japan invades Dutch East Indies. British bomb Lübeck and Cologne. US bombs Tokyo

May Americans win Battle of Coral Sea

**Jun Battle of Midway Island stops Japanese eastward expansion.** Rommel takes Tobruk. Battle of El Alamein; Rommel defeated by Montgomery

Aug Battle of Guadalcanal; US raid on Japanese-occupied Solomon Islands

Sep Battle of Stalingrad begins

Sep–Oct Germany launches V2 rocket

**1943** Jan First daytime bombing of Berlin

Feb Russian victory at Stalingrad. Battle of the Atlantic; German U-boats defeated

Apr Massacre in Warsaw ghetto

Jul Allies land in Sicily. Mussolini overthrown and anti-fascist Badoglio takes over

Sep US troops invade Italian mainland. **Italian armistice signed.** American landings in Bay of Salerno

## WORLD WAR II

**1943** Oct Italy declares war on Germany. US forces regain control of islands in Pacific. Russians cross Dnieper River and retake Smolensk

Nov Russians retake Kiev. Allied 'round-the-clock bombing of Germany begins

**1944 Jun D-Day Normandy landings.** Strategic bombing of Japan begins

Jul Assassination attempt on Hitler fails

Jul–Aug British and North American troops take northern France

Aug German armies driven from Soviet Union. Paris falls to Allies

Sep Soviet armistice with Romania and Finland. Battle of Arnhem. Bulgaria declares war on Greece. Germans evacuate Greece. German frontier crossed

Oct Battle of Leyte Gulf; Japanese fleet decisively defeated. Soviet troops invade Germany. Moscow conference between Churchill and Stalin

Dec Battle of the Bulge. **Yalta Conference between Churchill, Roosevelt and**

**Stalin. President Roosevelt dies; succeeded by Truman**

**1945** Jan Soviet troops invade Poland, Austria and Hungary and enter Czechoslovakia

Jan–Feb Allies regain Burma

Feb Allies reconquer Manila

Apr Mussolini executed. Vienna liberated

Apr Hitler commits suicide

**May Germany surrenders**

May Berlin falls to Soviet troops

May–Jun Allies take possession of Borneo

June Allies regain Philippines. United Nations charter signed

**Aug US drops atomic bombs on Hiroshima and Nagasaki.** Japan formally surrenders.

**1946** Oct Nuremberg war criminal trials begin First Nazi war criminals sentenced at Nuremberg trials. Goering and 10 others sentenced to death; Hess sentenced to life imprisonment. Goering commits suicide

# AFRICA 1940–92

| | |
|---|---|
| 1941 | British take Italian East Africa |
| 1942 | Battle of El Alamein |
| 1950 | **Population Registration Act in South Africa classifies people by race** |
| 1951 | Libyan independence |
| 1952 | Eritrea comes under Ethiopian rule |
| 1952 Oct | Mau Mau-instigated violence begins. Kenyan government declares state of emergency |
| 1953 Mar | Massacre at Lari in Rift Valley turns opinion against Mau Mau |
| 1953–55 | Serious anti-French rioting in Morocco |
| 1954–62 | **Algerian War.** A nationalist revolt against French rule, ending in Algerian independence |
| 1956 Jan | Sudan gains independence |
| 1956 Mar | Morocco and Tunisia gain independence |
| 1956–7 | **Suez Crisis.** Egypt nationalizes Suez Canal, followed by invasion by Israel and Anglo-French military intervention. UN sends in peace-keeping forces. |
| 1957 | Ghana becomes first black African country to gain independence |

| | |
|---|---|
| 1958 | Guinea gains independence |
| 1960 | Kenyan state of emergency lifted. Western Sahara made a province of Spain. Benin, Cameroon, Central African Republic, Chad, Congo, Gabon, Ivory Coast, Madagascar, Mali, Mauritania, Niger, Nigeria, Senegal, Somalia, Togo, Upper Volta and Zaire gain independence |
| Mar | **Sharpeville riots in South Africa,** resulting in deaths of 67 people and widespread condemnation of South Africa |
| 1961 | UN general assembly condemns apartheid. Sierra Leone, Tanganyika and Zanzibar gain independence. South Africa leaves Commonwealth |
| 1962 | Algeria, Burundi, Rwanda and Uganda win independence |
| 1963 | Kenya gains independence. Organization of African Unity founded |
| 1964 | **Nelson Mandela and other African National Congress and Pan-African Congress leaders given life sentences.** Malawi, Tanzania and Zambia |

## AFRICA 1940–92

| | | |
|---|---|---|
| **1965** | Nov | gain independence Trade embargo placed on Rhodesia by British government. Gambia becomes independent |
| **1966** | | B J Vorster becomes president of South Africa. Botswana and Lesotho gain independence |
| **1967** | May | Inter-tribal conflict in Nigeria leads to secession of Biafra |
| **1967–70** | | Nigerian Civil War |
| **1968** | | Equatorial Guinea, Mauritius and Swaziland gain independence |
| **1969** | | Military officers led by Colonel Gaddafi overthrow king in Libya |
| **1970** | Jan | Biafran secession ends |
| **1971** | Jan | Major-General Idi Amin seizes power in Uganda |
| **1974** | | Haile Selassie, emperor of Ethiopia, is deposed. Guinea Bissau gains independence |
| **1975** | | Suez Canal reopens. Partition of Western Sahara between Morocco and Mauritania. Angola, Cape Verde, Comoros, Mozambique and São Tomé and Principe gain independence |
| **1976** | | South Africa declares Transkei an independent republic. No other state recognizes its independence. Seychelles gain independence |
| | Feb–Mar | Clashes between Moroccan and Algerian troops over Western Sahara |
| | Mar–Apr | Invasion of Uganda by dissident Ugandans and Tanzanians Djibouti gains independence |
| **1977** | **Sep** | **Death of Steve Biko in police detention in South Africa.** |
| | Nov | President Sadat visits Israel and offers peace |
| **1977–78** | | Ogaden War between Somalia and Ethiopia |
| **1978** | **May** | Killing and rioting in Zaire's Shaba province; Europeans are evacuated from the region |
| **1979** | | Black Africans in Rhodesia gain control of government, ending white-minority rule. Mauritania withdraws from Western Sahara which comes under Moroccan occupation |
| **1980** | | Zimbabwe gains independence |
| **1981** | | President Sadat of Egypt is assassinated |

## AFRICA 1940–92

| | |
|---|---|
| early 1980s | **Severe drought in Africa; Ethiopia devastated** |
| 1984 | Western countries begin airlift to relieve famine |
| 1986 | South African government declares state of emergency. US air force bombs Libya |
| 1987 | Chad defeats Libya |
| 1988 | |
| Apr–May | Sudanese refugees flee to Ethiopia, worsening famine situation |
| June | Two million black workers in South Africa strike in protest against apartheid |
| Aug | Peace talks for Angola between South Africa, Cuba and Angola; South African and Cuban troops withdraw |
| 1990 | UN cuts aid to refugees because of Ethiopia–Somalia War |
| Feb | **Nelson Mandela leaves prison** |
| May | Mandela and de Klerk begin talks |
| 1991 Mar | Severe famine in Sudan |
| May | Violent clashes in South African townships between ANC and Zulu Inkatha supporters. One million |

people in refugee camps in Ethiopia. Ethiopian Jews airlifted to Israel

| | |
|---|---|
| **Jul** | **USA and economic sanctions of South Africa** |
| Nov | Violent clashes break out in Somali capital |
| 1992 Jan | Algeria's president is forced to resign by Muslim fundamentalists and the army |
| Mar | De Klerk supported by white minority over reforms to give equal rights to blacks |
| Apr | UN air embargo on Libya takes effect |
| Jun | 39 die in Zulu Inkatha movement attack on ANC squatter camp. Algerian president Mohammed Boudiaf is assassinated after only five months in office |
| Aug | ANC calls two-day general strike |
| Oct | Renewed violence in Angola |
| Dec | US forces sent to Somalia to ensure food deliveries |

# THE COLD WAR 1945–91

| Year | | Event |
|---|---|---|
| 1945 | | USSR occupies eastern Germany |
| 1946–47 | | Cold War begins |
| 1946 | | USSR organizes Communist governments in Bulgaria and Romania |
| 1947 | | Marshall Aid Plan (US funding for West European reconstruction). Communists take control in Hungary |
| 1948 | | Communists take full control of Czechoslovakia. Communist coup in Poland. **Berlin Blockade and Airlift.** USSR helps set up North Korean people's republic |
| 1949 | | **COMECON (Council for Mutual Aid and Assistance) set up.** |
| | Apr | **North Atlantic Treaty Organization (NATO) formed** |
| | May | Federal Republic of Germany formed |
| | Aug | USSR tests atomic bomb |
| | Oct | Communist Democratic Republic of Germany formed. People's Republic of China proclaimed |
| 1950–53 | | Korean War |
| 1950 | | North Korea invades South Korea. McCarran Act in the USA calls for severe restrictions against communists. Friendship Treaty signed between US and USSR. China enters Korean War in support of North Korea |
| 1952 | Aug | 16 000 people escape from East to West Berlin |
| | Nov | US tests its first hydrogen bomb |
| 1953 | | Khrushchev becomes Communist Party first secretary |
| | Jan | McCarthy becomes chairman of US Senate Subcommittee on Investigations |
| | Aug | USSR sets off its first hydrogen bomb |
| 1954 | Sep | US and seven other nations sign Southeast Asia Collective Defense Treaty to prevent further communism spreading |
| 1955 | | Warsaw Pact signed between East European communist countries |
| 1956 | Nov | Russia invades Hungary |
| 1957 | Jun | USSR launches Sputnik 1 satellite |
| 1958 | Jan | US launches its first satellite |
| 1960 | | U2 spy plane affair as a US plane is shot down in USSR. USSR withdraws aid to China. Fidel |

# THE COLD WAR 1945–91

**1961** Castro's government in Cuba becomes openly communist

Jan US ends diplomatic relations with Cuba

Apr Bay of Pigs incident (US-sponsored invasion of Cuba fails)

Jun Kennedy–Khrushchev summit in Vienna to discuss disarmament

**Aug Berlin Wall built**

Sep US and USSR resume nuclear testing

**1962** USSR agrees to send arms to Cuba. **Cuban missile crisis** (USSR agrees not to base nuclear weapons in Cuba)

**1963** Jul Nuclear testing ban is signed by US, USSR and Great Britain

Aug US and USSR agree on 'hot line' from White House to the Kremlin

**1964–75** Vietnam War (US involved 1965–73)

**1967** Jun China explodes its first hydrogen bomb. US and USSR discuss disarmament

**1968** Warsaw Pact countries invade Czechoslovakia

**1969** US and USSR begin SALT (Strategic Arms Limitation Talks)

**1972** US president Nixon visits USSR for SALT I treaty. Nixon visits China

**1973** Brezhnev–Nixon summit

**1973–75** Helsinki Conference helps reduce East–West tension

**1977** US reveals neutron bomb

**1979** US–USSR SALT II treaty

**1979–80** Soviet troops invade Afghanistan

**1982** US and USSR START (Strategic Arms Reduction Talks) commence

**1985** Gorbachev becomes Soviet leader

**1986** Reagan–Gorbachev summit in Iceland

**1987** INF (Intermediate Nuclear Forces) Treaty

**1988** USSR withdraws from Afghanistan

**1990** East and West Germany are reunited

**1991** Jul Warsaw Pact dissolved

Dec Formation of Commonwealth of Independent States to replace USSR. Effective end of Cold War

# THE USA 1945–93

| | | |
|---|---|---|
| **1945** | Apr | Roosevelt dies; Vice-president Truman takes over |
| | **Aug** | **World War II ends after atomic bombs dropped on Hiroshima and Nagasaki, Japan** |
| **1946** | Sep | US forces enter Korea |
| | | Philippines gain independence. Grain shortage results from exports to Europe |
| **1947** | Jun | US launches Marshall Plan to pay for the reconstruction of Europe |
| **1948** | | High cost of living leads to strikes. Newfoundland votes to join Canada. Military service for men 18–25 |
| **1950** | | US intervention against communist North Korea. Vietnamese independence recognized |
| **1951** | | Massive flooding in Missouri and Kansas |
| **1952** | | US explodes world's first hydrogen bomb |
| **1954** | **May** | **Racial segregation in schools ruled unconstitutional by Supreme Court.** |
| | | Black community leaders killed. Racial segregation in public life |
| **1955** | | ruled unconstitutional Schools desegregation leads to civil unrest and use of National Guard |
| **1957–58** | | US imposes trade embargo on |
| **1959–60** | | Cuba after leader Batista ousted by Fidel Castro |
| **1960** | | US spy plane shot down by USSR |
| **1961** | | CIA-backed invasion of Cuba by exiles ends in Bay of Pigs defeat |
| **1962** | Oct | US and USSR have massive stand-off over nuclear build-up in Cuba; nuclear conflict avoided when USSR backs down |
| **1963** | Aug | Civil rights demonstration in Washington led by Martin Luther King |
| | **Nov** | **President Kennedy assassinated.** Alleged assassin, Lee Harvey Oswald, assassinated in custody. |
| **1964** | | Race riots flare. US intervention in Vietnam War begins |
| **1965–67** | | Escalation of US involvement in Vietnam includes bombing raids. Opposition to involvement grows. Civil rights movement continues |
| **1968** | | Opposition to Vietnam War grows |

# THE USA 1945–93

**Apr** **Civil rights leader Martin Luther King assassinated. Widespread rioting follows**

**Jun** Presidential candidate Robert Kennedy assassinated

**1969** Withdrawal from Vietnam begins

**Jul** Neil Armstrong becomes first man on moon

**1972** **Feb** China visited by President Nixon. Bombing in Vietnam resumes

**1973** **Ceasefire in Vietnam and evacuation of troops.** Oil crisis as Arabs ban sales to US

**1974** **Aug** **Nixon resigns as a result of Watergate scandal**

**1975** US and USSR sign treaty recognizing 1945 borders in Europe

US stops support for Nicaragua. American hostages taken in Iran

**1979**

**1980** Attempt to rescue hostages a fiasco; President Carter loses support

**1981** **Mar** Assassination attempt on President Reagan. Hostages released

**1983** Marines killed in Iran. Invasion of Grenada

**1985** Trade ban imposed on Nicaragua.

**1986** US and USSR begin arms reduction negotiations

Libyan missile attack on US frigate *Stark*, killing 37. Military strikes launched in retaliation. US troops in Bolivia. Iran-Contra scandal

**1987** Wall Street slump triggers international economic downturn.

US-USSR arms limitation agreement signed

**1988** **Jul** Iranian civil aircraft shot down, killing 290 people. Further arms treaties signed with USSR

Irangate scandal ends with imprisonment of Col. Oliver North.

**1989** US invades Panama to overthrow president Manuel Noriega

**1991** **Jan** **US leads the UN's Desert Shield operation against Iraq, after the invasion of Kuwait**

**1993** US intervenes in Somalia to break power of warlords and secure supplies of humanitarian aid

# THE MIDDLE EAST 1914–92

| | |
|---|---|
| **1916** | Arab revolt against Turks |
| **1917** | Balfour Declaration promises Zionists a national home in Palestine |
| **1919–23** | **Ottoman Empire collapses** |
| **1923** | Turkey declares a republic |
| **1925** | Rezak Khan becomes shah of Persia |
| **1926** | Lebanese republic established |
| **1932** | Saudi Arabia becomes a single kingdom. Iraq becomes independent |
| **1944** | Syria becomes independent |
| **1946** | Jordan becomes independent |
| **1948 May** | **State of Israel created** |
| **1948–49** | First Arab–Israeli War |
| **1953** | Ben-Gurion resigns and Moshe Sharet is elected as Israeli prime minister |
| **1956** | Second Arab–Israeli War; Israel occupies the Gaza Strip |
| **1958** | Military revolts end monarchy in Iraq |
| **1961** | Ben-Gurion forms a new coalition government |
| **1962–70** | Yemen Civil War; monarchy overthrown |
| **1967** | **Six-Day War.** Israel reoccupies the Gaza Strip and also the Golan Heights and West Bank. South Yemen becomes independent |
| **1969** | Yasser Arafat is elected the leader of the Palestinian Liberation Organization. Golda Meir becomes Israel's fourth prime minister |
| **1971** | Bahrain, Qatar and the United Arab Emirates gain independence |
| **1973** | Fourth Arab–Israeli war. Arab oil embargo |
| **1974** | Turkey invades and partitions Cyprus |
| **1975** | King Faisal of Saudi Arabia is murdered. **Lebanese Civil War begins** |
| **1976** | Israeli commandos free hostages at Entebbe, Uganda |
| **1977** | President Sadat of Egypt visits Israel to offer peace |
| **1978** | Begin and Sadat share Nobel Peace Prize |
| **1979** | **Iranian revolution.** Ayatollah Khomeini gains power after shah flees the country. Israeli–Egyptian Peace Treaty signed. USSR invades Afghanistan |
| **1979–81** | US-Iranian crisis over US embassy siege |

# THE MIDDLE EAST 1914–92

**1980** US-Iranian hostage rescue fiasco. Iran–Iraq War begins. Iraq invades

**1981** Sadat assassinated by fundamentalists

**1982** Israel invades Lebanon. Iran invades Iraq

**1983** 247 US marines and 58 French troops killed by a car bomb in Lebanon. Arafat is expelled from Syria

**1984** Multinational peace-keeping corps withdraws from Lebanon

**1985** Israelis leave Lebanon. Palestinian terrorist attacks on Rome and Vienna airports

**1987** Western navies begin escorting Gulf shipping

**1988** US bombs Iran oil base. Iraq attacks tankers at Iranian oil terminal. End of Iran–Iraq War after Iran accepts UN peace terms unconditionally. USSR withdraws from Afghanistan

**1990** May North and South Yemen are officially merged

Aug Iraqi forces attack Kuwait

**1991** Jan Foreign embassies pull out of Baghdad. 700,000 armed troops sent to the Gulf. Peace talks fail between US and Iraq. **Operation Desert Storm commences**

**Gulf War.** Iraq bombs Israel and Saudi Arabia

Feb **Saddam sets Kuwait oil wells ablaze. Land war begins in Gulf. Allies successfully defeat Iraqi forces**

Mar Iraqi revolt against Saddam. Kurds flee Iraq and intensify war against Saddam

Jul Lebanese army attacks "LO

Oct Arab–Israeli peace talks in Madrid

Dec Last US hostage released from Lebanon. Two Western hostages remain

**1992** Mar Death of Menachem Begin

Apr President Najibullah overthrown in Afghanistan

Jun Yitzhak Rabin wins elections in Israel and succeeds Yitzhak Shamir as prime minister

Nov Israeli tanks move into Lebanon after Hezbollah attacks on towns

Dec Israel expels 418 Palestinians

# EAST ASIA 1940–92

| | |
|---|---|
| **1941** | Japan takes Hong Kong, Thailand and Malaya |
| **1942** | Japan takes Singapore and Burma |
| **1944** | **Independent republic of Vietnam formed.** Ho Chi Minh is president |
| **1945** | **Atomic bombs dropped on Japanese cities of Hiroshima and Nagasaki; end of World War II, Japan surrenders.** Chinese Civil War begins |
| **1946** | The Philippines become independent |
| **1948** | Communists capture Manchuria. USSR sets up communist rule in North Korea. Soviet troops withdraw from North Korea |
| Jan | Burma gains independence |
| Aug | South Korea gains independence |
| **1948–60** | Malayan emergency |
| **1949** | USA withdraws troops from South Korea. **Communists control China** Chiang Kai-shek resigns as president of China and Chinese nationalists flee to Taiwan |
| Oct | Chinese People's Republic formally proclaimed |
| Dec | Indonesia becomes independent Republic of Indonesia proclaimed |
| **1950** Jun | **North Korean forces invade South Korea.** MacArthur appointed commander of UN forces in Korea |
| | **Korean War** |
| **1950–53** | Korean War |
| **1953** | Vietnamese rebels attack Laos |
| **1954** | French defeat at Dien Bien Phu. Indochina split into North and South Vietnam, Cambodia and Laos. Communists occupy Hanoi |
| **1957** Aug | Malaya given independence |
| **1963** | Malaya expanded to form Malaysia |
| **1964** | China explodes its first atomic bomb |
| **1965–75** | **Vietnam War between communist north and non-communist south** |
| **1965** | US ground troops enter Vietnam War Attempted communist coup in Indonesia. Singapore given independence |
| **1966–77** | **China's Cultural Revolution** |
| **1968** | North Vietnam launches Tet Offensive |

# EAST ASIA 1940–92

| | |
|---|---|
| **1970** | US troops enter Cambodia |
| **1971** | China joins the United Nations. |
| **1972** | US president Nixon visits China. Ferdinand Marcos declares martial law in the Philippines and assumes near dictatorial powers |
| **1973** Jan | Ceasefire and withdrawal of American forces from Vietnam War agreed |
| **1975** | **Khmer Rouge besiege Phnom Penh.** Urban inhabitants forced to do hard manual labour as part of their 're-education'. US embassy in Cambodia closes, last Americans leave. Cambodia becomes known as Kampuchea. Communist forces overrun South Vietnam. Immediate pulling out of all US troops |
| **1976** | Formal reunification of Vietnam. Death of Mao Zedong |
| **1978** | Vietnam invades Kampuchea, ends Pol Pot regime |
| **1979** | China invades Vietnam |
| **1980** | Trial of Gang of Four in China |
| **1983** | Benigno Aquino killed in the Philippines |
| **1984** Jan | Brunei given independence |

| | |
|---|---|
| **1986** | President Marcos exiled; Mrs Corazon Aquino succeeds in Philippines |
| **1987** Jan | Zhao Ziyang becomes party leader in China |
| **1988** Jun | Protests by students in Seoul. Burma imposes a curfew to stop rioting |
| Sep | Peace restored in Burma. Former dictator General Ne Win returns to power |
| **1989** Jun | Pro-democracy students killed in Tiananmen Square, Beijing, China |
| **1990** May | Aung San Suu Kyi wins elections in Burma but kept under house arrest by military regime who fail to recognize democracy movement |
| **1991** Jan | Thai army stages coup against government |
| **1992** May | Clashes between army and pro-democracy movement in Thailand. China tests biggest ever nuclear bomb |
| Jun | Fidel Ramos wins presidential elections over Corazon Aquino |
| Sep | General Le Duc Anh becomes president of Vietnam |

# EUROPE 1970–93

| | |
|---|---|
| 1972 | The 18th Olympic games held in Munich; Israeli athletes murdered by terrorists |
| 1973 | Britain, Ireland and Denmark join the EEC |
| 1974 | Revolution in Portugal led by military initiates democratic reforms |
| 1975 | Juan Carlos becomes first King of Spain for 44 years, after General Franco's death |
| 1978 | John Paul becomes first Polish Pope. Former Italian prime minister Aldo Moro murdered by terrorists |
| Nov | In Spain, right-wing army officers attempt coup |
| 1979 | Margaret Thatcher becomes first woman prime minister in Europe **Polish trade union Solidarity founded** |
| 1980 Apr | The EEC in disarray over issue of Britain's budget contributions |
| May | **President Tito of Yugoslavia dies.** London siege of Iranian embassy ends with storming by SAS |
| Aug | Solidarity gains major concessions from Polish government |
| 1981 | Major demonstrations calling for nuclear disarmament |
| Feb | Right-wing paramilitary forces attempt coup in Spain; MPs held hostage in parliament |
| May | Francois Mitterrand elected president of France. Pope John Paul wounded in assassination attempt |
| Dec | Polish reforms reversed; martial law imposed |
| 1982 Oct | A socialist government is voted into office in Spain |
| Dec | Over 20 000 women protesters camp at Greenham Common US missile site in Britain to protest against nuclear missiles |
| 1983 | First cruise missiles arrive in Western Europe |
| 1985 | Mikhail Gorbachev leader of USSR |
| 1986 | Spain and Portugal join the EEC |
| Jan | Britain and France agree to build Channel tunnel |
| Feb | Olof Palme, Swedish prime minister, murdered |
| 1987 | Mrs Thatcher wins third general election in Britain |

# EUROPE 1970–93

| | | |
|---|---|---|
| **1987** | Oct | Stockmarket crash in London triggers European recession |
| **1988** | Sep | Russian army sent to Armenia to stop unrest |
| | Oct | Latvia and Lithuania demand self-rule |
| | Nov | Estonia insists on sovereignty. Serbians rally for independence |
| | Dec | Yugoslav government collapses |
| **1990** | Jan | Yugoslavia allows new political parties. German unification treaty is ratified |
| | Oct | East and West Germany reunited |
| | Dec | Lech Walesa elected Polish president |
| **1991** | Jan | Soviet troops sent to Lithuania and Latvia |
| | Mar | Anti-communist protests in Yugoslavia |
| | Jun | Boris Yeltsin is voted president of Russia. Berlin becomes the capital of the reunited Germany. Slovenia and Croatia declare independence |
| | Aug | Yugoslav federal army and Serbian guerillas launch assault on Vukavar. Gorbachev is overthrown in a |

coup but returns to the Kremlin days later. Communist rule ends in the USSR

| | | |
|---|---|---|
| | Dec | Germany recognizes the independence of Slovenia and Croatia |
| | | **End of the USSR. Eleven republics form the Commonwealth of Independent States** |
| **1992** | | Fighting continues in the former Yugoslav republics |
| | Apr | State of emergency declared in Bosnia-Herzegovina. Mass strikes in Germany |
| | May | UN imposes sanctions on Serbia and Montenegro |
| | Jun | Vaclav Havel resigns as president of Czechoslovakia |
| | Jul | UN forces control Sarajevo airport |
| | Aug–Nov | Racist violence against immigrants in eastern Germany |
| | Aug | Serbian concentration camps shock world |
| **1993** | Jan | Czechoslovakia split into Czech Republic and Slovakia |

# 4

# SCIENCE

# ORIGIN AND SIZE

How the Universe came about is a mystery. However, many
scientists today accept the 'big bang' theory which suggests
that the Universe started with a huge explosion in which
matter was created and scattered through space. This
produced atomic particles which turned into the hydrogen
atoms that now make up 90 per cent of the Universe. The
hydrogen cloud expanded and then broke up into separate
clouds forming galaxies of stars like our own Milky Way
galaxy.

### Age and size

Research proves that the universe is still expanding. It might
do so forever or eventually collapse inwards. Astronomers
believe that the universe is 13 000 million to 20 000 million
years old.

### Measuring space

No one knows how large the universe is, but ways have been
devised to measure distance and space. For example, based
on the Earth's orbit: a light year (ly) is the distance light
travels at a speed of 299 792.458 km/s through space every
year. An astronomical unit (au) is the distance between the
Earth and the Sun. A par sec (pc) is the distance at which a
base line of 1 au in length subtends an angle of 1 second.

1 au = 149 600 000 km = 93 000 000 miles
1 ly = 9 460 500 000 000 km = 5 878 000 000 000 miles
1 pc = 30 857 200 000 000 km = 19 174 000 000 000 miles
1 ly = 63 240 au
1 pc = 206 265 au = 3.262 ly

The scale of the universe is enormous. The diagram opposite
illustrates this fact. Each of the cubes has sides 100 times
longer than the previous cube.

**1 Cube side 950 au (0.015 ly)**
Contains the entire Solar System.

**2 Cube side 1.5 ly**
This is the whole Solar System surrounded by Oort clouds of comets believed to be the original source of comets which pass through the Solar System. It surrounds the Sun at about a distance of 40 000 au (2–3 ly).

**3 Cube side 150 ly**
The Solar System and the nearer stars.

**4 Cube side 15 000 ly**
This contains the nearer spiral arms of our galaxy.

**5 Cube side 1.5 million ly**
This comprises the whole of our galaxy, Large and Small Magellanic Clouds and nearby galaxies in the Local Group.

**6 Cube side 150 million ly**
This contains the whole of the Local Group and the Pisces, Cancer and Virgo clusters of galaxies.

**7 Cube side 1.5 billion ly**
This holds all the known clusters and super clusters of galaxies and all other known objects in space. This is the limit of our current knowledge of the universe.

# GALAXIES AND STARS

## Galaxies

Galaxies are giant groups of stars, planets, gas, dust and nebulae that form 'islands' in space. Over 1000 million galaxies have been detected and some have measured from 1000 ly to 10 million ly across.

Galaxies are classified by their shape.

**1 Spiral galaxies** Our galaxy, the Milky Way, is a spiral galaxy with arms wrapped around its nucleus, or centre. It takes about 225 million years to spin round once.

**2 Barred spiral** A barred spiral has a short bar, into which most of its stars are concentrated, and arms emerging from opposite ends. Nearly 30 per cent of galaxies are spirals or barred spirals

**3 Elliptical galaxy** These galaxies do not have spiral arms. They are shaped mainly like a huge ball either spherical or very flattened like a rugby ball.

**4 Irregular** These galaxies have no particular shape and only make up 10 per cent of galaxies.

## What are stars?

Stars are beaming spheres of gas. Deep inside them heat is created when hydrogen is turned into helium. Like the Sun many stars shine continuously for thousands of millions of years before they fade.

**Celestial poles**

On Earth we have a North and a South Pole and in space there is an equivalent called the North and South Celestial Poles. The Earth's axis joins the North and South Poles and if it was extended it would point to the North and South Celestial Poles.

**North Celestial Pole**

In the diagram the North Celestial Pole is roughly marked by the star Polaris (**a**) in the constellation Ursa Minor (**1**). Polaris is only a short distance from the true pole. To find Polaris we find Ursa Major (**2**) and extend the imaginary line joining two stars known as the Pointers (**b**, **c**).

**South Celestial Pole**

No star marks the South Celestial Pole. Sigma Octantis (**e**) is the nearest visible star. To find the South Celestial Pole, find the constellation of the Southern Cross (**3**), then draw an imaginary line to meet the constellation Octans (**4**) at point **f**. Sigma Octantis is to be found between **d** and **f**.

# CONSTELLATIONS
**Northern hemisphere**

For over 2000 years stars have been divided into artificial groups called constellations. What we see today was originally suggested by the ancient Greeks who gave the stars names of characters from their mythology. No new constellations have been named since the middle of the 18th century. Astronomers recognize 88 constellations and call them by their Latin names.

| | | |
|---|---|---|
| **1** Virgo | **7** Canis Minor | **14** Draco | **22** Lyra |
| **2** Coma Berenices | **8** Gemini | **15** Hercules | **23** Cygnus |
| **3** Leo | **9** Ursa Major | **16** Ophiuchus | **24** Aquila |
| **4** Cancer | **10** Corona Borealis | **17** Orion | **25** Aries |
| **5** Canes Venatici | **11** Serpens | **18** Taurus | **26** Andromeda |
| **6** Boötes | **12** Auriga | **19** Perseus | **27** Pisces |
| | **13** Ursa Minor | **20** Cassiopeia | **28** Pegasus |
| | | **21** Cepheus | |

**Southern hemisphere**

The first people to study the stars of the southern hemisphere were the explorers of the 17th and 18th centuries. The stars of the southern skies are never visible in the northern hemisphere but they are more spectacular because this part of the world faces the centre of our galaxy. The charts below show the major constellations.

| | | | |
|---|---|---|---|
| 1 Virgo | 9 Vela | 15 Sagittarius | 23 Capricorn |
| 2 Corvus | 10 Monoceros | 16 Pavo | 24 Grus |
| 3 Libra | 11 Triangulum | 17 Octans | 25 Phoenix |
| 4 Hydra |    Australe | 18 Dorado | 26 Eridanus |
| 5 Centaurus | 12 Carina | 19 Columba | 27 Piscis |
| 6 Ophiuchus | 13 Puppis | 20 Lepus |    Austrinus |
| 7 Scorpius | 14 Canis | 21 Orion | 28 Aquarius |
| 8 Crux |    Major | 22 Tucana | 29 Cetus |

**Northern constellations**

The constellations of the northern hemisphere vary throughout the year. Watch the Plough (Ursa Major) in April and in October.

April

October

**Southern constellations**

The position of the southern constellations also varies throughout the year. Look out for the Southern Cross (Crux) in April and again in October.

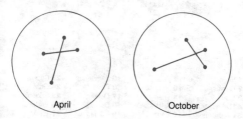

April

October

# PULSARS, BLACK HOLES, QUASARS

A star whose mass is more than 1.5 times that of the Sun will end its life as a small dense star called a pulsar. A very massive star – one with a mass more than three times that of the Sun – may collapse further to become a black hole.

**Pulsars** Neutron stars are called 'pulsars' because they give out radio waves which are received on Earth as regular, rapid pulses. The pulse rate slows down as the neutron star ages. Pulsars are detected with radio telescopes. The average diameter of a neutron star is 10 km, and so they are almost undetectable with optical telescopes.

**Black holes** are invisible and can only be detected by their effect on stars near them. Black holes warp space and time: time stops at their edges. The gravity in black holes is so great that not even light can escape from them. Anything coming close to a black hole is pulled into it and vanishes from our universe for ever. No one has yet proved that black holes definitely exist.

**Quasars** 'Quasar' is an abbreviation of 'quasistellar object', i.e. an object that appears to be a star. When seen by optical telescopes, quasars look like ordinary faint stars. When seen by radio telescopes, they are clearly not stars but distant objects that give out massive amounts of energy. The diameter of our galaxy is 1 million ly. The diameter of a typical quasar is less than 11 ly. If the diameter of our Galaxy is represented by the distance by air from London (**1**) to New York (**2**), then the diameter of the quasar would be less than the length of a Concord (**3**) flying the route.

# SOLAR SYSTEM

**Ratio of size of planet to Earth**

Pluto 1: 0.47
Neptune 1: 3.8
Uranus 1: 4

Saturn 1: 9.4

Jupiter 1: 11.2

Mars 1: 0.53
Earth 1:1
Venus 1: 0.95
Mercury 1: 0.38
Sun 1: 110

**Planetary distances**

|  | Mean distance from the Sun (in millions) | | Mean distance from Earth (in millions) | |
|---|---|---|---|---|
|  | km | mi | km | mi |
| **1** Mercury | 58 | 36 | 80.8 | 50 |
| **2** Venus | 108 | 67 | 40.4 | 25 |
| **3** Earth | 150 | 93 | – | – |
| **4** Mars | 227 | 141 | 56.8 | 35 |
| **5** Jupiter | 778 | 484 | 591 | 367 |
| **6** Saturn | 1427 | 887 | 1198 | 744 |
| **7** Uranus | 2869 | 1784 | 2585 | 1607 |
| **8** Neptune | 4497 | 2796 | 4308 | 2678 |
| **9** Pluto | 5888 | 3661 | 4297 | 2670 |

**Orbits and rotation**

All the planets in the Solar System move around the Sun. Each planet also rotates on its axis. The sidereal period calculates the time taken by a planet to orbit the Sun once. For Earth it is approximately 365 days. The diagram compares the planets' sidereal periods. Black lines show how much of a planet's orbit has been completed in a year.

| Sidereal period (years) | | | Sidereal period (days) | |
|---|---|---|---|---|
| **1** | Pluto | 247.7 | **6** Mars | 687.0 |
| **2** | Neptune | 164.8 | **7** Earth | 365.256 |
| **3** | Uranus | 84.01 | **8** Venus | 224.7 |
| **4** | Saturn | 29.46 | **9** Mercury | 88.0 |
| **5** | Jupiter | 11.86 | | |

**Planetary data**

| | Mercury | Venus | Earth |
|---|---|---|---|
| **Mean distance from Sun** | 0.39 au | 0.72 au | 1.00 au |
| **Distance at perihelion** | 0.31 au | 0.72 au | 0.98 au |
| **Distance at aphelion** | 0.47 au | 0.73 au | 1.02 au |
| **Closest distance to Earth** | 0.54 au | 0.27 au | |
| **Average orbital speed** | 47.9 km/s | 35 km/s | 29.8 km/s |
| **Rotation period** | 58.6 days | 243 days | 23 hr 56 min |
| **Sidereal period** | 88 days | 225 days | 365 days |
| **Diameter at equator** | 4878 km | 12 104 km | 12 756 km |
| **Mass (Earth's mass = 1)** | 0.06 | 0.82 | 1 |
| **Surface temperature** | 350° C (day) −170° C (night) | 480° C | 22° C |
| **Gravity (Earth's gravity = 1)** | 0.38 | 0.88 | 1 |
| **Density (density of water = 1)** | 5.5 | 5.25 | 5.517 |
| **No. of satellites** | 0 | 0 | 1 |
| **No. of known rings** | 0 | 0 | 0 |
| **Main gases in atmosphere** | no atmosphere | carbon dioxide | nitrogen, oxygen |

**Planetary data (continued)**

|  | Mars | Jupiter |
|---|---|---|
| **Mean distance from Sun** | 1.52 au | 5.20 au |
| **Distance at perihelion** | 1.38 au | 4.95 au |
| **Distance at aphelion** | 1.67 au | 5.46 au |
| **Closest distance to Earth** | 0.38 au | 3.95 au |
| **Average orbital speed** | 24.1 km/s | 13.1 km/s |
| **Rotation period** | 24 hr 37 min | 9 hr 50 min |
| **Sidereal period** | 687 days | 11.86 years |
| **Diameter at equator** | 6 795 km | 142 800 km |
| **Mass (Earth's mass = 1)** | 0.11 | 317.9 |
| **Surface temperature** | −23° C | −150° C |
| **Gravity (Earth's gravity = 1)** | 0.38 | 2.64 |
| **Density (density of water = 1)** | 3.94 | 1.33 |
| **No. of satellites known** | 2 | 16 |
| **No. of rings known** | 0 | 1 |
| **Main gases in atmosphere** | carbon dioxide | hydrogen, helium |

| Saturn | Uranus | Neptune | Pluto |
|---|---|---|---|
| 9.54 au | 19.18 au | 30.06 au | 39.36 au |
| 9.01 au | 18.28 au | 29.8 au | 29.58 au |
| 10.07 au | 20.09 au | 30.32 au | 40.14 au |
| 8.01 au | 17.28 au | 28.8 au | 28.72 au |
| 9.6 km/s | 6.8 km/s | 5.4 km/s | 4.7 km/s |
| 10 hr 14 min | 16 hr 10 min | 18 hr 26 min | 6 days 9 hr |
| 29.46 years | 84.01 years | 164.8 years | 247.7 years |
| 120 000 km | 50 800 km | 48 500 km | 5995 km |
| 95.2 | 14.6 | 17.2 | 0.002–0.003 |
| −180° C | −210° C | −220° C | −230° C |
| 1.15 | 1.17 | 1.2 | not known |
| 0.71 | 1.7 | 1.77 | not known |
| 19 | 5 | 2 | 1 |
| 1000+ | 9 | 0 | 0 |
| hydrogen, helium | hydrogen, helium, methane | hydrogen, helium, methane | methane |

## SUN, EARTH, MOON

The Earth and the Moon are about the same age, 4600 million years old, though they were formed separately. Earth has large oceans, a protective atmosphere and a surface which is active and constantly changing. The Moon is dead, a barren airless world a quarter of the size of the Earth. The Sun, thought to be 5000 million years old, is a star. It generates light and heat and its enormous gravitational pull keeps all the planets in their orbits.

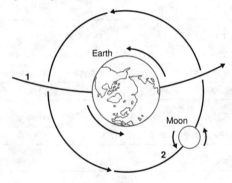

**1 The Earth's orbit around the Sun**
The Earth completes an orbit of the Sun every 365.25 days.

**2 The Moon's orbit around the Earth**
The Moon completes one orbit of the Earth every 28 days.

The Sun is a mass of glowing hydrogen gas which is so hot and compressed that hydrogen atoms fuse to make helium. This reaction generates huge amounts of energy which reach us in the forms of heat and light. The Sun's energy is shared out over the whole Earth. Its energy is more spread out in some areas and more concentrated in others.

Sunshine that reaches the Earth is more spread out at the top and bottom areas of the globe than at the centre.

At noon near the Equator the Sun is overhead. Sunlight is concentrated on a small area.

At noon near the Poles the Sun is low in the sky and its heat is spread over a large area.

## ECLIPSES

An eclipse occurs when the passage of all or part of an astronomical body moves into the shadow of another.

**A lunar eclipse** happens when the Earth is in a direct line between the Sun and the Moon. The Moon will then be in the Earth's shadow and it will be unable to receive direct sunlight. Normally only three eclipses of the Moon occur in one year.

**A solar eclipse** is different. To our eye the Sun and the Moon seem to be the same size though in reality the Sun is 400 times larger than the Moon. It is also 400 times further away from the Earth. If the Moon is in a direct line between the Sun and the Earth then the Moon appears to cover the Sun's photosphere (its visible surface). This would mean that any section of the Earth directly in the Moon's shadow would experience a total eclipse of the Sun and areas around it a partial eclipse.

**Types of eclipse**

Three types of eclipse are possible. A total eclipse (**1**) occurs when the Sun's disc is completely but briefly obscured. This can last from a split second up to a maximum of 7 minutes 31 seconds. The corona, however, can be seen. A partial eclipse (**2**) is when the Moon's disc only obscures part of the photosphere. An annular eclipse (**3**) occurs if the Moon is too far away to totally cover the Sun. A rim of light is visible around the eclipsed Sun.

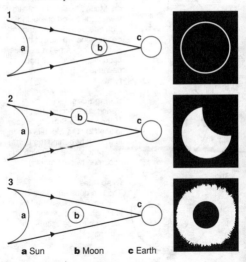

**a** Sun     **b** Moon     **c** Earth

# TIDES

A tide is the rise and fall of water throughout the Earth's oceans. Occurring every 12 hours, 26 minutes, they are created by the Moon's pull of gravity on the water and sometimes even the Sun's pull.

When the Earth is nearer to the Moon (**1**), water is pulled toward the Moon producing a high tide. A high tide happens on the opposite side of the Earth at the same time. Tides occur about every 12 hours because of the Earth's rotation.

## Spring tides

Spring tides occur when the Moon and the Sun are directly in line (**2**). The Moon is either in front of or behind the Earth. This produces a very high tide occurring twice a month.

## Neap tides

The tide does not rise as high as normal because the Moon is at right angles to the Sun (**3**). A neap tide occurs twice a month.

## PHASES OF THE MOON

The Moon only reflects sunlight, it produces no light of its own. From Earth we can see the amount of the lit half as it changes from day to day. These normal changes are known as phases of the Moon. The diagram shows how the Moon appears to us on selected nights within a month. It takes 29 days, 12 hours, 44 minutes and 3 seconds before a new moon occurs again. The phases have different names. For example a waxing moon means one that is increasingly visible, a waning moon is less visible, a gibbous moon is between half and full phase.

# ASTRONOMICAL TIME

### Units of time

Listed below are the ways of measuring time that are
artificially derived, as opposed to astronomical methods.

### Years, months, weeks

Below are some widely used names for periods of time.

| Name | Period | Name | Period |
|------|--------|------|--------|
| millennium | 1000 years | leap years | 366 days |
| half-millennium | 500 years | year | 365 days |
| century | 100 years | year | 12 months |
| half-century | 50 years | year | 52 weeks |
| decade | 10 years | month | 28–31 days |
| half-decade | 5 years | week | 7 days |

### Days, hours, minutes

Below are listed the basic subdivisions of a day and their
equivalents.

1 day = 24 hours = 11 440 minutes = 86 400 seconds
1 hour = 1/24 day = 60 minutes = 3 600 seconds
1 minute = 1/1440 day = 1/60 hour = 60 seconds
1 second = 1/86 400 day = 1/3 600 hour = 1/60 minute

### Seconds

Greater precision in measuring time has required seconds (s)
to be broken down into smaller units, using standard metric
prefixes.

| | | |
|------|------|------|
| 1 tetrasecond (Ts) | $10^{12}$ s | 31 689 years |
| 1 gigasecond (Gs) | $10^{9}$ s | 31.7 years |
| 1 megasecond (Ms) | $10^{6}$ s | 11.6 days |
| 1 kilosecond (ks) | $10^{3}$ s | 16.67 minutes |

| | | |
|---|---|---|
| 1 millisecond (ms) | $10^{-3}$ s | 0.001 seconds |
| 1 microsecond (μs) | $10^{-6}$ s | 0.000 001 |
| 1 nanosecond (ns) | $10^{-9}$ s | 0.000 000 001 |
| 1 picosecond (ps) | $10^{-12}$ s | 0.000 000 000 001 |
| 1 femtosecond (fs) | $10^{-15}$ s | 0.000 000 000 000 001 |
| 1 attosecond (as) | $10^{-18}$ s | 0.000 000 000 000 000 001 |

**Astronomical time**

Time can be measured by motion; in fact, the motion of the Earth, Sun, Moon and stars provided humans with the first means of measuring time.

**Years, months, days**

Sidereal times are calculated by the Earth's position according to fixed stars. The anomalisitc year is measured according to the Earth's orbit in relation to the perihelion (Earth's minimum distance to the Sun). Tropical times refer to the apparent passage of the Sun and the actual passage of the Moon across the Earth's Equatorial plane. The synodic month is based on the phases of the Moon. Solar time (as in a mean solar day) refers to periods of darkness and light averaged over a year.

| Time | Days | Hours | Minutes | Seconds |
|---|---|---|---|---|
| Sidereal year | 365 | 6 | 9 | 10 |
| Anomalistic year | 365 | 6 | 13 | 53 |
| Tropical year | 365 | 5 | 48 | 45 |
| Sidereal month | 27 | 7 | 43 | 11 |
| Tropical month | 27 | 7 | 43 | 5 |
| Synodic month | 29 | 12 | 44 | 3 |
| Mean solar day | 0 | 24 | 0 | 0 |
| Sidereal day | 0 | 23 | 56 | 4 |

# TIMELINE OF SPACE EXPLORATION
### USA

| | |
|---|---|
| **1958** | NASA founded. First US satellite Explorer 1 finds Van Allen radiation belts. |
| **1960** | First weather satellite: Tiros 1 |
| **1961** | First US-manned space flight (Alan Shephard). |
| **1962** | John Glenn is first American to orbit the Earth. Telstar first TV-relay satellite |
| **1963** | Quasars first identified from Mt Palomar Observatory, California. |
| **1965** | Gemini missions practice two-man flight, spacewalks and docking |
| **1966** | Surveyor (unmanned) lands on Moon. |
| **1967** | First astronauts die (in ground fire). Apollo program delayed 18 months. |
| **1968** | Apollo 8 makes first manned orbit of Moon. |
| **1969** | First men walk on Moon: Neil Armstrong, then Buzz |

Aldrin from Apollo 11 (31 July). Five more Apollo Moon landings.

| | |
|---|---|
| **1973** | First US space station: Skylab (4 missions). |
| **1975** | First international space docking: Apollo 18 and Soyuz 19. |
| **1976** | First Mars surface landing, by unmanned Viking 1. |
| **1979** | First spacecraft, Pioneer 11, visits Saturn. |
| **1981** | First space shuttle flight. |
| **1983** | First US woman in space: Sally Ride aboard shuttle *Columbia*. Pioneer 10 (launched 1972) first probe to leave Solar System. |
| **1986** | 24th space shuttle flight: *Challenger* explodes (28 Jan) killing crew of 7. Voyager 2 (launched 1977) reaches Uranus, finds 10 more moons. |
| **1988** | *Discovery* resumes space shuttle flights. |

**1989** Galileo probe taken up by shuttle *Atlantis* for Jupiter 1995 mission.

**1990** Hubble Space Telescope launched by *Discovery*; optics flawed and to be repaired on future shuttle mission.

## USSR

**1957** First satellite Sputnik 1 launched (4 Oct) to start the Space Age.

**1959** Rocket Luna 2 hits the Moon.

**1961** First manned spaceflight by Yuri Gagarin in Vostok 1: single orbit.

**1962** First dual mission (Vostok 3 and 4).

**1963** First woman in space: Valentina Tereshkova in Vostok 6.

**1965** First spacewalk: Alexei Leonov from Voskhod 6

**1966** Venera 3 (unmanned) hits Venus.

**1969** First spacewalk transfer between Soyuz 5 and 4.

**1970** First space station launched, Salyut 1, but 3 cosmonauts die on return flight.

**1975** First double docking. First photos from Venus's surface by Venera 9.

**1987** First permanently manned space station Mir sets 326-day crew duration record.

## Others

**1957** Jodrell Bank radio telescope, England.

**1961** Parkes radio telescope completed west of Sydney, Australia.

**1965** First French satellite.

**1967** First pulsar identified by Jocelyn Bell from Cambridge, England.

**1970** First Chinese and Japanese satellites.

**1975** European Space Agency (ESA) founded.

**1978** Rings of Uranus recorded.

**1986** European space probe Giotto passes through Halley's comet.

# DELIVERY ROCKETS

**1 Saturn V** Built originally to send astronauts to the Moon. A three-stage launch vehicle. It stood 111 metres high and with fuel weighed 2910 tonnes. The USA made six landings on the Moon using the Saturn rocket.

**2 Soyuz** The first Soviet Soyuz mission was launched in 1967. It was designed for a crew of three men with three sections: the orbital module, the descent module and the service module.

**3 Ariane** Ariane's main purpose is to put a satellite or space probe into space for the European Space Agency.

**4 Gemini Titan** The first manned Gemini flight took off in March 1965. It carried two astronauts.

**5 Vostok** In April 1961 this Soviet spacecraft carried the first man into space and completed one orbit of the Earth.

# MANNED SPACEFLIGHT

The space shuttle is a reusable launcher. At lift-off the
Shuttle is thrust into space by two solid-fuel booster rockets
(**1**). The used rockets then parachute away into the ocean (**2**)
from where they are recovered and then reused. The large
fuel tank is abandoned (**3**) 8 minutes into the flight. The
spacecraft goes into orbit (**4**) and delivers its load. After the
mission the shuttle begins descent (**5**) protected by hundreds
of heat-resistant tiles. It coasts back to Earth (**6**) like a glider
and lands on a runway (**7**).

See page 511 to find out more about the space shuttle's
rockets.

# SATELLITES

A satellite is a spacecraft placed into orbit with equipment for sending pictures and radio signals back to Earth.

**1 Spy satellites** generally operate in polar orbit to cover the whole Earth as it turns. They survey military movements and pick up communications between countries. The USA has a missile-warning satellite.

**2 The IUE** (International Ultraviolet Explorer) is a science research satellite. It has made thousands of discoveries and has enabled astronomers to weigh a black hole and to discover more about the Sun, stars and comets.

**3 An Earth resources satellite** is roughly the size of a family car. These satellites can cross over the whole Earth as it rotates. Images from the Landsat satellite have helped to survey areas of minerals, forest growth and disasters.

**4 Communication satellites** of which the US Comstar is one, can relay 18 000 telephone calls over the whole of the USA. It can also send dozens of television channels.

**5 Telescopic satellites** have a clear view of the universe and can transmit images of space far beyond what was previously known. They normally lie above the Earth's atmosphere.

**6 Weather satellites** can see how the clouds move and how temperatures are changing. They are used by weather forecasters to predict weather days ahead.

## SPACECRAFT

**1 The Mercury** capsule carried one space pilot. The capsule was bell-shaped to reduce the enormous heat encountered on re-entry into the atmosphere. The heat shields were made from layers of glass fibre and plastic and the astronaut's cabin was double skinned for protection.

**2 Apollo** command and service module was used for Moon-landing. It carried life-support systems, communication and navigation equipment, re-entry and landing equipment. It was manned by three astronauts and built in three sections: the lunar module (used to go to and from the surface of the Moon), the command module, and the service module and engine

**3 The Soviet Soyuz** spacecraft was built to shuttle crews backwards and forwards from established space stations. It was designed for three men. It consisted of three sections: an orbiting module, a descent module and a service module.

# HISTORIC NUMBER SYSTEMS

Different civilizations have developed their own systems for
writing numbers. Here we show numerals from eight such
systems.

|  | Roman | Arabic | Chinese | Hindu |
|---|---|---|---|---|
| 1 | I | ١ | 一 | ? |
| 2 | II | ٢ | 二 | ? |
| 3 | III | ٣ | 三 | ? |
| 4 | IV | ٤ | 四 | ? |
| 5 | V | ٥ | 五 | ? |
| 6 | VI | ٦ | 六 | ? |
| 7 | VII | ٧ | 七 | ? |
| 8 | VIII | ٨ | 八 | ? |
| 9 | IX | ٩ | 九 | ? |
| 10 | X | ١٠ | 十 | ?٠ |
| 50 | L | ٥٠ | 五十 | ?٠ |
| 100 | C | ١٠٠ | 百 | ?٠٠ |
| 500 | D | ٥٠٠ | 百五 | ?٠٠ |
| 1000 | M | ١٠٠٠ | 千 | ?٠٠٠ |

| Babylonian | Egyptian | Hebrew | Japanese |
|---|---|---|---|
| 𒁹 | \| | א | 一 |
| 𒐖 | \|\| | ב | 二 |
| 𒐗 | \|\|\| | ג | 三 |
| 𒐘 | \|\|\|\| | ד | 四 |
| 𒐙 | \|\|\|\|\| | ה | 五 |
| 𒐚 | \|\|\|\|\|\| | ו | 六 |
| 𒐛 | \|\|\|\|\|\|\| | ז | 七 |
| 𒐜 | \|\|\|\|\|\|\|\| | ח | 八 |
| 𒐝 | \|\|\|\|\|\|\|\|\| | ט | 九 |
| 𒌋 | ∩ | י | 十 |
| 𒌍 | ∩∩∩∩ | כ | 五十 |
| 𒁹𒌍 | ⌒ | ל | 百 |
| 𒐖𒌋 | ⌒⌒⌒ | ר | 五百 |
| 𒁹 | 𓆼 | א | 千 |

## Roman number system

The Roman system is a method of notation in which the capitals are modelled on ancient Roman inscriptions. The numerals are represented by seven capital letters of the alphabet:

| | |
|---|---|
| **I** | one |
| **V** | five |
| **X** | ten |
| **L** | fifty |
| **C** | one hundred |
| **D** | five hundred |
| **M** | one thousand |

These letters are the foundation of the system; they are combined in order to form all numbers. If a letter is preceded by another of lesser value (e.g. IX), the value of the combined form is the difference between the values of each letter (e.g. IX = X (10) − I (1) = 9).

To determine the value of a string of Roman numbers (letters), find the pairs in the string (those beginning with a lower value) and determine their values, then add these to the values of the other letters in the string:

**MCMXCIII** = M+CM+XC+III = 1000+900+90+3 = **1993**

A dash over a letter multiplies the value by 1000 (e.g. $\bar{V}$ = 5000).

| | | | |
|---|---|---|---|
| 1 I | 12 XII | 35 XXXV | 100 C |
| 2 II | 13 XIII | 40 XL | 200 CC |
| 3 III | 14 XIV | 10 XLV | 300 CCC |
| 4 IV or IIII | 15 XV | 50 L | 400 CD |
| 5 V | 16 XVI | 55 LV | 500 D |
| 6 VI | 17 XVII | 60 LX | 600 DC |
| 7 VII | 18 XVIII | 65 LXV | 700 DCC |
| 8 VIII | 19 XIX | 70 LXX | 800 DCCC |
| 9 IX | 20 XX | 75 LXXV | 900 CM |
| 10 X | 25 XXV | 80 LXXX | 1000 M |
| 11 XI | 30 XXX | 90 XC | 2000 MM |

# NAMES FOR NUMBERS

Many numbers have names. Some of these names are in everyday use, while others apply in more specialized areas such as music and multiple births, and for sums of money. Some names for specialized numbers have the same first part (prefix). These prefixes indicate the number to which the name refers.

### Everyday use

| | | | |
|---|---|---|---|
| $1/10$ | Tithe | 20 | Score |
| 2 | Pair, couple, brace | 50 | Half-century |
| 6 | Half a dozen | 100 | Century |
| 12 | Dozen | 144 | Gross |
| 13 | Baker's dozen | | |

### Musicians

| | | | |
|---|---|---|---|
| 1 | Soloist | 5 | Quintet |
| 2 | Duet | 6 | Sextet |
| 3 | Trio | 7 | Septet |
| 4 | Quartet | 8 | Octet |

### Multiple births

| | | | |
|---|---|---|---|
| 2 | Twins | 5 | Quintuplets (quins) |
| 3 | Triplets | 6 | Sextuplets |
| 4 | Quadruplets (quads) | | |

### Slang for money

| | | | |
|---|---|---|---|
| £25 | Pony | £500 | Monkey |
| £100 | Century | £1000 | Grand |

## Numerical prefixes

### Prefixes in numerical order

| | | | |
|---|---|---|---|
| 1/10 | Deci- | 7 | Hept-, hepta-, sept-, septi-, septem- |
| 1/2 | Semi-, nemi-, demi- | 8 | Oct-, octa-, octo- |
| 1 | Uni- | 9 | Non-, nona-, ennea- |
| 2 | Bi-, di- | 10 | Dec-, deca- |
| 3 | Tri-, ter- | 11 | Hendeca-, undec-, undeca- |
| 4 | Tetra-, tetr-, tessera-, quadri-, quadr- | 12 | Dodeca- |
| 5 | Pent-, penta-, quinqu-, quinque-, quint- | 15 | Quindeca- |
| 6 | Sex-, sexi-, hex-, hexa- | 20 | Icos-, icosa-, icosi- |

### Prefixes in alphabetical order

| | | | |
|---|---|---|---|
| Bi-, | 2 | Pent-, penta- | 5 |
| Dec-, deca- | 10 | Quadr-, quadri- | 4 |
| Deci- | 1/10 | Quindeca- | 15 |
| Demi- | 1/2 | Quinqu-, quinque- | 5 |
| Di- | 2 | Quint- | 5 |
| Dodeca- | 12 | Semi- | 1/2 |
| Ennea- | 9 | Sept-, septem-, septi- | 7 |
| Hemi- | 1/2 | Sex-, sexi- | 6 |
| Hendeca- | 11 | Ter- | 3 |
| Hept-, Hepta- | 7 | Tessera- | 4 |
| Hex-, hexa- | 6 | Tetr-, tetra- | 4 |
| Icos-, icosa-, icosi- | 20 | Tri- | 3 |
| Non-, nona- | 9 | Undec-, undeca- | 11 |
| Oct-, octa-, octo- | 8 | Uni- | 1 |

| Prefixes in order of value | Value |
|---|---|
| *Atto- | 0.000 000 000 000 000 001 |
| *Femto- | 0.000 000 000 000 001 |
| *Pico- | 0.000 000 000 001 |
| *Nano- | 0.000 000 001 |
| *Micro- | 0.000 001 |
| *Milli- | 0.001 |
| *Centi- | 0.01 |
| *Deci- | 0.1 |
| Semi-, hemi-, demi- | 0.5 |
| Uni- | 1 |
| Bi-, di- | 2 |
| Tri-, ter- | 3 |
| Tetra-, tetr-, tessera-, quadri-, quadr- | 4 |
| Pent-, penta-, quinqu-, quinque-, quint- | 5 |
| Sex-, sexi-, hex-, hexa- | 6 |
| Hept-, hepta-, sept-, septi-, septem- | 7 |
| Oct-, octa-, octo- | 8 |
| Non-, nona-, ennea- | 9 |
| Dec-, deca- | 10 |
| Hendeca-, undec-, undeca- | 11 |
| Dodeca- | 12 |
| Quindeca- | 15 |
| Icos-, icosa-, icosi- | 20 |
| Hect-, hecto- | 100 |
| *Kilo- | 1000 |
| Myria- | 10 000 |
| *Mega- | 1 000 000 |
| *Giga- | 1 000 000 000 |
| *Tera- | 1 000 000 000 000 |

*These prefixes can be uesd in the SI system of units

# MULTIPLICATION GRID

Below is a grid of numbers which gives you quick reference to multiplication tables and answers to division calculations.

## Multiplication

In order to multiply 6 by 7, for example, look down the column with 6 at the top. Continue down the column until you reach row 7. The number in the square where column 6 and row 7 meet gives the answer of 42.

## Division

To divide 63 by 9, for example, look down the column with 9 at the top until you find 63. Look along the row to find the row number. The answer is 7.

|       | Column |     |     |     |     |     |     |     |     |     |     |     |
|-------|------|-----|-----|-----|-----|-----|-----|-----|-----|-----|-----|-----|
| **Row** | **1** | **2** | **3** | **4** | **5** | **6** | **7** | **8** | **9** | **10** | **11** | **12** |
| **1** | 1 | 2 | 3 | 4 | 5 | 6 | 7 | 8 | 9 | 10 | 11 | 12 |
| **2** | 2 | 4 | 6 | 8 | 10 | 12 | 14 | 16 | 18 | 20 | 22 | 24 |
| **3** | 3 | 6 | 9 | 12 | 15 | 18 | 21 | 24 | 27 | 30 | 33 | 36 |
| **4** | 4 | 8 | 12 | 16 | 20 | 24 | 28 | 32 | 36 | 40 | 44 | 48 |
| **5** | 5 | 10 | 15 | 20 | 25 | 30 | 35 | 40 | 45 | 50 | 55 | 60 |
| **6** | 6 | 12 | 18 | 24 | 30 | 36 | 42 | 48 | 54 | 60 | 66 | 72 |
| **7** | 7 | 14 | 21 | 28 | 35 | 42 | 49 | 56 | 63 | 70 | 77 | 84 |
| **8** | 8 | 16 | 24 | 32 | 40 | 48 | 56 | 64 | 72 | 80 | 88 | 96 |
| **9** | 9 | 18 | 27 | 36 | 45 | 54 | 63 | 72 | 81 | 90 | 99 | 108 |
| **10** | 10 | 20 | 30 | 40 | 50 | 60 | 70 | 80 | 90 | 100 | 110 | 120 |
| **11** | 11 | 22 | 33 | 44 | 55 | 66 | 77 | 88 | 99 | 110 | 121 | 132 |
| **12** | 12 | 24 | 36 | 48 | 60 | 72 | 84 | 96 | 108 | 120 | 132 | 144 |

# MATHEMATICAL SYMBOLS

| | | | |
|---|---|---|---|
| $+$ | plus or positive | $\geq$ | greater than or equal to |
| $-$ | minus or negative | $\leq$ | less than or equal to |
| $\pm$ | plus or minus, positive or negative | $\gg$ | much greater than |
| $\times$ | multiplied by | $\ll$ | much less than |
| $\div$ | divided by | $\sqrt{\ }$ | square root |
| $=$ | equal to | $\infty$ | infinity |
| $\equiv$ | identically equal to | $\propto$ | proportional to |
| $\neq$ | not equal to | $\Sigma$ | sum of |
| $\not\equiv$ | not identically equal to | $\Pi$ | product of |
| $\approx$ | approximately equal to | $\Delta$ | difference |
| $\sim$ | of the order of or similar to | $\therefore$ | therefore |
| $>$ | greater than | $\angle$ | angle |
| $<$ | less than | $\parallel$ | parallel to |
| $\not>$ | not greater than | $\perp$ | perpendicular to |
| $\not<$ | not less than | $:$ | is to (ratio) |

# ARITHMETIC OPERATIONS

The four basic arithmetic operations are addition, subtraction, multiplication and division. Each part of an arithmetic operation has a specific name.

**Addition**

29   Addend
+6   Addend
35   Sum

**Subtraction**

74   Minuend
−16   Subtrahend
58   Difference

**Multiplication**

46   Multiplicand
×9   Multiplier
414   Product

**Division**

      Divisor
     3   Quotient
13 )44   Dividend
   39
    5   Remainder

**Fraction**

5/8   5   Numerator
     8   Denominator

**Simple (or vulgar) fraction**

9/7   9   Numerator
     7   Denominator

# GEOMETRY

## Angles

Angles can be measured using two different units. Both of these are divisions of a circle. Degrees are the more widely used unit of measurement but radians are also used for some types of mathematics (see opposite).

**Acute angle** This is an angle that measures more than 0° but less than 90°.

**Right angle** An angle that measures exactly 90°. The lines at right angles are perpendicular to one another.

**Obtuse angle** This is an angle of more than 90° but less than 180°.

**Straight angle** An angle that measures 180° and forms a straight line.

**Reflex angle** This angle measures more than 180° but less than 360°.

**Complimentary angles** These are two angles that add up to 90°.

**Supplementary angles** Two angles whose sum is 180°.

**Conjugate angles** Two angles whose sum is 360°.

**Angles in circles**

**Degrees (A)** A circle is divided into 360 equal parts called degrees (°). One degree is the angle at the centre of a circle which cuts off an arc that is 1/360 of the circumference. Below is a quarter of a circle divided into 90 degrees (°).

**Radians (B)** One radian is the angle between 2 radii of a circle which cuts off on the circumference an arc equal in length to the radius. 1 radian (rad) ≈ angle 57.296°. There are 2π (approximately 6.28) radians in a circle. Below is an angle of 1 radian.

**Subdivisions of circles**
60 minutes (60') = 1 degree (1°)
60 seconds (60") = 1 minute (1')
100 centirads = 1 rad
1000 millirads = 1 rad

## Polygons

A polygon is a plane figure, or a shape with three or more straight sides. Poly is the Greek word for many and gonia means angle. There are irregular and regular polygons. Regular polygons have sides which are all the same length and angles which are all the same size. Irregular polygons have sides which are different lengths and angles of different sizes. The table lists the names and number of sides of the first 10 regular polygons. On the facing page the 10 polygons are all drawn with sides of the same length.

| | | |
|---|---|---|
| **A** Triangle | **E** Heptagon | **I** Undecagon |
| **B** Square | **F** Octagon | **J** Dodecagon |
| **C** Pentagon | **G** Nonagon | |
| **D** Hexagon | **H** Decagon | |

| | Name of polygon | Number of sides | Each internal angle | Sum of internal angles |
|---|---|---|---|---|
| | Triangle | 3 | 60° | 180° |
| | Square | 4 | 90° | 360° |
| | Pentagon | 5 | 108° | 540° |
| | Hexagon | 6 | 120° | 720° |
| | Heptagon | 7 | 128.6° | 900° |
| | Octagon | 8 | 135° | 1080° |
| | Nonagon | 9 | 140° | 1260° |
| | Decagon | 10 | 144° | 1440° |
| | Undecagon | 11 | 147.3° | 1620° |
| | Dodecagon | 12 | 150° | 1800° |

### Quadrilaterals

A quadrilateral is a four-sided polygon or a four-sided plane figure.

**A square** has all the sides the same length and all the angles are right angles.

**A rectangle** has opposite sides which are the same length. All the angles are right angles

**A rhombus** has all sides of the same length but none of the angles are right angles.

**A parallelogram** has opposite sides which are parallel to each other and are of the same length.

**A trapezium** has one pair of opposite sides which are parallel.

**A kite** has adjacent sides of the same length. The diagonals intersect at right angles.

**Triangles**

Shown below are six types of triangle. The sum of the
internal angles of any flat triangle is always 180°.

 **An equilateral triangle** has all the
sides of the same length. All the
internal angles are equal.

 **An isosceles triangle** has two sides
which are of the same length and two
angles which are of equal size.

 **A scalene triangle** has all the sides of
different lengths and has all the angles
of different sizes.

**A right-angle triangle** is a triangle
which contains one right angle of 90°.

 **An obtuse-angle triangle** is a triangle
which contains one obtuse angle – an
angle over 90°.

 **An acute-angle triangle** is a triangle
which contains three acute angles.
These are each less than 90°.

### Solids

Solid shapes are three-dimensional. This means they have length, width and depth. A polyhedron is a solid shape with polygons for faces, or sides. Opening out a polyhedron gives a shape called a net.

All the faces of a regular solid are identical regular polygons of equal size. A regular polyhedron will fit into a sphere with all the vertices, or edges, touching the sphere. There are five regular solids which are shown below with their nets.

  **A tetrahedron** has four equilateral triangles for faces.

  **A cube** has six faces, each of which is a square.

 **An octahedron** has eight sides and is made from eight equilateral triangles.

**A dodecahedron** is a solid with 12 sides, each of which is a pentagon.

 **An icosahedron** has 20 sides consisting of equilateral triangles.

**Semi-regular figures** have two or more types of polygon as their faces. Like regular solids they fit into a sphere with all the vertices touching the sphere. Below are six semi-regular solids.

A **truncated octahedron** has 14 faces made of squares and hexagons

A **cuboctahedron** also has 14 faces. These consist of triangles and squares.

A **truncated cuboctahedron** has 26 faces which are made of squares, hexagons and octagons.

A **truncated icosahedron** has 32 faces which consist of pentagons and hexagons.

An **icosidodecahedron** has 32 faces made up of triangles and pentagons.

A **truncated icosidodecahedron** has 62 faces consisting of squares, hexagons and decagons.

**Geometry of area**
**Abbreviations**
**a** = length of top
**b** = length of base
**h** = perpendicular height
**r** = length of radius

$$\pi = 3.1416$$

Circle

$$\pi \times \mathbf{r}^2$$

Rectangle

$$\mathbf{b} \times \mathbf{h}$$

Parallelogram

$$\mathbf{b} \times \mathbf{h}$$

Triangle

$$\frac{1}{2} \times \mathbf{b} \times \mathbf{h}$$

Trapezium

$$\frac{(\mathbf{a} + \mathbf{b}) \times \mathbf{h}}{2}$$

## Geometry of volume

**Abbreviations**
**b** = breadth of base
**h** = perpendicular height
**i** = length of base
**r** = length of radius

$$\pi = 3.1416$$

**Cube or cuboid**

$$b \times h \times l$$

**Prism**

$$\frac{b \times h \times l}{2}$$

**Pyramid**

$$\frac{b \times h \times l}{3}$$

**Cylinder**

$$\pi \times r^2 \times l$$

**Sphere**

$$\frac{4 \times \pi \times r^3}{3}$$

**Cone**

$$\frac{\pi \times r^2 \times h}{3}$$

# UNIT SYSTEMS

## International System of Units

The International System of Units (or Système International d'Unités – SI) is the current form of the metric system that has been in use since 1960. In the UK, the SI system is used in education, science and, increasingly, in everyday life.

## Base units

There are seven base units in SI:

| Unit | Symbol | Quantity |
|------|--------|----------|
| metre | m | length/distance |
| kilogram | kg | mass |
| ampere | A | electric current |
| kelvin | K | temperature |
| candela | cd | luminosity |
| second | s (or sec) | time |
| mole | mol | amount of substance |

## Prefixes to use with SI units

Prefixes are added to each of the base units to indicate multiples and submultiples of ten:

| Submultiple/ multiple | Prefix | Symbol |
|-----------------------|--------|--------|
| $10^{-6}$ | micro- | r |
| $10^{-3}$ | milli- | m |
| $10^{-2}$ | centi- | c |
| $10^{-1}$ | deci- | d |
| $10$ | deca- | da |
| $10^2$ | hecto- | h |
| $10^3$ | kilo- | k |
| $10^6$ | mega- | M |

## Derived units

In addition, the system uses derived units. For example, velocity is given in metres per second (m/s, $ms^{-1}$). Other derived units in SI are referred to by special names: the watt (W) is a unit of power; the joule (J) is a unit of energy.

### Imperial system of units

| Length | | | | |
|---|---|---|---|---|
| | 1 inch (in or ") | | | |
| | 1 foot (ft or ') | 12 in | | |
| | 1 yard (yd) | 36 in | 3 ft | |
| | 1 fathom (fm) | 72 in | 6 ft | 2 yd |
| | 1 chain (ch) | | 66 ft | 22 yd |
| | 1 furlong | | | 220 yd |
| | 1 mile (mi) | | 5280 ft | 1760 yd |
| **Area** | 1 square inch (in²) | | | |
| | 1 square foot (ft²) | 144 in² | | |
| | 1 square yard (yd²) | | 9 ft² | |
| | 1 square chain (ch²) | | | 484 yd² |
| | 1 acre | | | 4840 yd² |
| | 1 square mile (mi²) | 640 acres | | |
| **Volume** | 1 cubic in (in³) | | | |
| | 1 fluid ounce (fl oz) | | | |
| | 1 pint (pt) | 20 fl oz | | |
| | 1 quart (qt) | 40 fl oz | 2 pt | |
| | 1 gallon (gal) | | 8 pt | 4 qt |
| | 1 cubic foot (ft³) | 1728 in³ | | |
| | 1 cubic yard (yd³) | 46 656 in³ | 27 ft³ | |
| **Weight** | 1 grain (gr) | | | |
| | 1 ounce (oz) | 437.5 gr | | |
| | 1 pound (lb) | | 16 oz | |
| | 1 stone (st) | | | 14 lb |
| | 1 ton | | 35 840 oz | 2240 lb |

# CONVERSION FORMULAE

Below are listed the multiplication/division factors for converting units of length from imperial to metric, and vice versa. For conversion formulae for area see pp. 314–15; for volume see pp. 315–18; for weight see pp. 318–19; for energy see p. 320; for speed see 321–2; and for temperature see p. 323. Note that two kinds of factors are given: quick, for an approximate conversion that can be made without a calculator; and accurate, for an exact conversion.

The diagram drawn with each conversion shows an approximate visual comparison of the two units.

## Length

| Milli-inches (mils) Micrometres (µm) | | **Quick** | **Accurate** |
|---|---|---|---|
| mils ⟶ µm | | × 25 | × 25.4 |
| µm ⟶ mils | | ÷ 25 | × 0.0394 |

| Inches (in) Millimetres (mm) | | | |
|---|---|---|---|
| in ⟶ mm | | × 25 | × 25.4 |
| mm ⟶ in | | ÷ 25 | × 0.0394 |

| Inches (in) Centimetres (cm) | | | |
|---|---|---|---|
| in ⟶ cm | | × 2.5 | × 2.54 |
| cm ⟶ in | | ÷ 2.5 | × 0.394 |

| Feet (ft) Metres (m) | | | |
|---|---|---|---|
| ft ⟶ m | | ÷ 3.3 | × 0.305 |
| m ⟶ ft | | × 3.3 | × 3.281 |

| Yards (yd) Metres (m) | | | |
|---|---|---|---|
| yd ⟶ m | | ÷ 1 | × 0.914 |
| m ⟶ yd | | × 1 | × 1.094 |

Fathoms (fm) Metres (m)

| | | Quick | Accurate |
|---|---|---|---|
| fm → m | | × 2 | × 1.83 |
| m → fm | | ÷ 2 | × 0.547 |

Chains (ch) Metres (m)

| | | | |
|---|---|---|---|
| ch → m | | × 20 | × 20.108 |
| m → ch | | ÷ 20 | × 0.0497 |

Furlongs (fur) Metres (m)

| | | | |
|---|---|---|---|
| fur → m | | × 200 | × 201.17 |
| m → fur | | ÷ 200 | × 0.005 |

Kilometres (km) Yards (yd)

| | | | |
|---|---|---|---|
| yd → km | | ÷ 1000 | × 0.00091 |
| km → yd | | × 1000 | × 1093.6 |

Miles (mi) Kilometres (km)

| | | | |
|---|---|---|---|
| mi → km | | × 1.5 | × 1.609 |
| km → mi | | ÷ 1.5 | × 0.621 |

Nautical miles (n mi) Miles (mi)

| | | | |
|---|---|---|---|
| n mi → mi | | × 1.2 | × 1.151 |
| mi → n mi | | ÷ 1.2 | × 0.869 |

Nautical miles (n mi) Kilometres (km)

| | | | |
|---|---|---|---|
| n mi → km | | × 2 | × 1.852 |
| km → n mi | | ÷ 2 | × 0.54 |

**Area**

| | | | **Quick** | **Accurate** |
|---|---|---|---|---|
| Circular mils (cmil) Square micrometres ($\mu m^2$) | | | | |
| cmil | → | $\mu m^2$ | × 500 | × 506.7 |
| $\mu m^2$ | → | cmil | ÷ 500 | × 0.002 |
| Square inches ($in^2$) Square millimetres ($mm^2$) | | | | |
| $in^2$ | → | $mm^2$ | × 650 | × 645.2 |
| $mm^2$ | → | $in^2$ | ÷ 650 | × 0.0015 |
| Square inches ($in^2$) Square centimetres ($cm^2$) | | | | |
| $in^2$ | → | $cm^2$ | × 6.5 | × 6.452 |
| $cm^2$ | → | $in^2$ | ÷ 6.5 | × 0.15 |
| Square chains ($ch^2$) Square metres ($m^2$) | | | | |
| $ch^2$ | → | $m^2$ | × 400 | × 404.686 |
| $m^2$ | → | $ch^2$ | ÷ 400 | × 0.0025 |
| Square miles ($mi^2$) Square kilometres ($km^2$) | | | | |
| $mi^2$ | → | $km^2$ | × 2.5 | × 2.590 |
| $km^2$ | → | $mi^2$ | ÷ 2.5 | × 0.386 |

| | | Quick | Accurate |
|---|---|---|---|
| Square miles (mi²) Hectares (ha) | | | |
| mi² → ha | | × 250 | × 258.999 |
| ha → mi² | | ÷ 250 | × 0.0039 |
| Hectares (ha) Acres | | | |
| ha → acre | | × 2.5 | × 2.471 |
| acre → ha | | ÷ 2.5 | × 0.405 |
| Square metres (m²) Square yards (yd²) | | | |
| m² → yd² | | × 1 | × 1.196 |
| yd² → m² | | ÷ 1 | × 0.836 |
| Square metres (m²) Square feet (ft²) | | | |
| m² → ft² | | × 11 | × 10.764 |
| ft² → m² | | ÷ 11 | × 0.093 |

## Volume

**1**
**1**

| | Quick | Accurate |
|---|---|---|
| UK gallons (gal) US fluid gallons (fl gal) | | |
| UK gal → US fl gal | × 1 | × 1.201 |
| US fl gal → UK gal | ÷ 1 | × 0.833 |

| | | | Quick | Accurate |
|---|---|---|---|---|
| **1** **1** | UK quarts (qt) US fluid quarts (fl qt) | | | |
| | UK qt ⟶ US fl qt | × 1 | × 1.201 |
| | US fl qt ⟶ UK qt | ÷ 1 | × 0.833 |
| **1** **1** | UK pints (pt) US fluid pints (fl pt) | | | |
| | UK pt ⟶ US fl pt | × 1 | × 1.201 |
| | US fl pt ⟶ UK pt | ÷ 1 | × 0.833 |
| **1** **1** | UK fluid ounces (fl oz) US fluid ounces (fl oz) | | | |
| | UK fl oz ⟶ US fl oz | × 1 | × 0.961 |
| | US fl oz ⟶ UK fl oz | ÷ 1 | × 1.041 |
| **1** **2** | UK fluid ounces (fl oz) Cubic inches (in³) | | | |
| | UK fl oz ⟶ in³ | × 2 | × 1.734 |
| | in³ ⟶ UK fl oz | ÷ 2 | × 0.577 |
| **1** **16** | Cubic inches (in³) Cubic centimetres (cm³) | | | |
| | in³ ⟶ cm³ | × 16 | × 16.387 |
| | cm³ ⟶ in³ | ÷ 16 | × 0.061 |
| **1** **28** | UK fluid ounces (fl oz) Millilitres (ml) | | | |
| | UK fl oz ⟶ ml | × 28 | × 28.413 |
| | ml ⟶ UK fl oz | ÷ 28 | × 0.035 |
| **1** **1** | UK quarts (qt) Litres (l) | | | |
| | UK qt ⟶ l | × 1 | × 1.137 |
| | l ⟶ UK qt | ÷ 1 | × 0.880 |

| | | Quick | Accurate |
|---|---|---|---|
| **1** **4.5** | UK gallons (gal) Litres (l) | | |
| | UK gal ⟶ l | × 4.5 | × 4.546 |
| | l ⟶ UK gal | ÷ 4.5 | × 0.220 |
| **1** **2** | Litres (l) UK pints (pt) | | |
| | l ⟶ UK pt | × 2 | × 1.760 |
| | UK pt ⟶ l | ÷ 2 | × 0.568 |
| **1** **35** | Cubic metres (m³) Cubic feet (ft³) | | |
| | m³ ⟶ ft³ | × 35 | × 35.315 |
| | ft³ ⟶ m³ | ÷ 35 | × 0.028 |
| **1** **1** | Cubic metres (m³) Cubic yards (yd³) | | |
| | m³ ⟶ yd³ | × 1 | × 1.308 |
| | yd³ ⟶ m³ | ÷ 1 | × 0.765 |
| **1** **220** | Cubic metres (m³) UK gallons (gal) | | |
| | m³ ⟶ UK gal | × 220 | × 219.970 |
| | UK gal ⟶ m³ | ÷ 220 | × 0.005 |
| **1** **30** | US fluid ounces (fl oz) Millilitres (ml) | | |
| | US fl oz ⟶ ml | × 30 | × 29.572 |
| | ml ⟶ US fl oz | ÷ 30 | × 0.034 |
| **1** **4** | US fluid gallons (fl gal) Litres (l) | | |
| | US fl gal ⟶ l | × 4 | × 3.785 |
| | l ⟶ US fl gal | ÷ 4 | × 0.264 |

| **1** | Litres (l) | **Quick** | **Accurate** |
|---|---|---|---|
| **2** | US fluid pints (fl pt) | | |
| | l ⟶ US fl pt | × 2 | × 2.113 |
| | US fl pt ⟶ l | ÷ 2 | × 0.473 |

| **1** | Litres (l) | | |
|---|---|---|---|
| **1** | US fluid quarts (fl qt) | | |
| | l ⟶ US fl qt | × 1 | × 1.056 |
| | US fl qt ⟶ l | ÷ 1 | × 0.947 |

| **1** | Cubic metres ($m^3$) | | |
|---|---|---|---|
| **264** | US fluid gallons (fl gal) | | |
| | $m^3$ ⟶ US fl gal | × 264 | × 264.173 |
| | US fl gal ⟶ $m^3$ | ÷ 264 | × 0.004 |

| **1** | Cubic metres ($m^3$) | | |
|---|---|---|---|
| **227** | US dry gallons (dry gal) | | |
| | $m^3$ ⟶ dry gal | × 227 | × 227.020 |
| | dry gal ⟶ $m^3$ | ÷ 227 | × 0.004 |

### Weight

The term 'weight' differs in everyday use from its scientific use. In everyday terms, we use weight to describe how much substance an object has. In science, the term 'mass' is used to describe this quantity of matter. Weight is used to describe the gravitational force on an object and is equal to its mass multiplied by the gravitational field strength. In scientific terms, mass remains constant but weight varies according to the strength of gravity. All units that follow are strictly units of mass rather than weight, apart from the pressure units $kg/cm^2$ and PSI.

| | Quick | Accurate |
|---|---|---|
| Grains (gr) Grams (g) | | |
| g ⟶ gr | × 15 | × 15.432 |
| gr ⟶ g | ÷ 15 | × 0.065 |
| Ounces (oz) Grams (g) | | |
| oz ⟶ g | × 28 | × 28.349 |
| g ⟶ oz | ÷ 28 | × 0.035 |
| Ounces troy (oz tr) Grams (g) | | |
| oz tr ⟶ g | × 31 | × 31.103 |
| g ⟶ oz tr | ÷ 31 | × 0.032 |
| Stones (st) Kilograms (kg) | | |
| st ⟶ kg | × 6 | × 6.350 |
| kg ⟶ st | ÷ 6 | × 0.157 |
| Long tons (l t) Tonnes (t) | | |
| l t ⟶ t | × 1 | × 1.016 |
| t ⟶ l t | ÷ 1 | × 0.984 |
| Kilograms (kg) Pounds (lb) | | |
| kg ⟶ lb | × 2 | × 2.205 |
| lb ⟶ kg | ÷ 2 | × 0.454 |

Kilograms per square centimetre (kg/cm$^2$)
Pounds per square inch (PSI)

| | | | |
|---|---|---|---|
| kg/cm$^2$ → PSI | | × 14 | × 14.223 |
| PSI → kg/cm$^2$ | | ÷ 14 | × 0.070 |

Tonnes (t)
Short tons (sh t)

| | | | |
|---|---|---|---|
| t → sh t | | × 1 | × 1.102 |
| sh t → t | | ÷ 1 | × 0.907 |

Ounces troy (oz tr)
Ounces (oz)

| | | | |
|---|---|---|---|
| oz tr → oz | | × 1 | × 1.097 |
| oz → oz tr | | ÷ 1 | × 0.911 |

**Energy**

Kilowatts (kW)
Horsepower (hp)

**Quick Accurate**

| | | | |
|---|---|---|---|
| kW → hp | | × 1.5 | × 1.341 |
| hp → kW | | ÷ 1.5 | × 0.746 |

Calories (cal)
Joules (J)

| | | | |
|---|---|---|---|
| cal → J | | × 4 | × 4.187 |
| J → cal | | ÷ 4 | × 0.239 |

Kilocalories (kcal)
Kilojoules (kJ)

| | | | |
|---|---|---|---|
| kcal → kJ | | × 4 | × 4.187 |
| kJ → kcal | | ÷ 4 | × 0.239 |

## Speed

| | | Quick | Accurate |
|---|---|---|---|
| **Miles per hour (mph)** | | | |
| **Kilometres per hour (km/h)** | | | |
| mph ⟶ km/h | | × 1.5 | × 1.609 |
| km/h ⟶ mph | | ÷ 1.5 | × 0.621 |
| | | | |
| **Yards per minute (ypm)** | | | |
| **Metres per minute (m/min)** | | | |
| ypm ⟶ m/min | | × 1 | × 1.094 |
| m/min ⟶ ypm | | ÷ 1 | × 0.914 |
| | | | |
| **Feet per minute (ft/min)** | | | |
| **Metres per minute (m/min)** | | | |
| ft/min ⟶ m/min | | ÷ 3 | × 0.305 |
| m/min ⟶ ft/min | | × 3 | × 3.281 |
| | | | |
| **Inches per second (in/s)** | | | |
| **Centimetres per second (cm/s)** | | | |
| in/s ⟶ cm/s | | × 2.5 | × 2.54 |
| cm/s ⟶ in/s | | ÷ 2.5 | × 0.394 |
| | | | |
| **International knots (kn)** | | | |
| **Miles per hour (mph)** | | | |
| kn ⟶ mph | | × 1 | × 1.151 |
| mph ⟶ kn | | ÷ 1 | × 0.869 |
| | | | |
| **British knots (UK kn)** | | | |
| **International knots (kn)** | | | |
| UK kn ⟶ kn | | × 1 | × 1.001 |
| kn ⟶ UK kn | | ÷ 1 | × 0.999 |

International knots (kn)
Kilometres per hour (km/h)

**Quick** **Accurate**

| | | Quick | Accurate |
|---|---|---|---|
| kn ———▶ km/h | | × 2 | × 1.852 |
| km/h ———▶ kn | | ÷ 2 | × 0.540 |

Miles per hour (mph)
Feet per second (ft/s)

| | | | |
|---|---|---|---|
| mph ———▶ ft/s | | × 1.5 | × 1.467 |
| ft/s ———▶ mph | | ÷ 1.5 | × 0.682 |

Kilometres per hour (km/h)
**Metres per second (m/s)**

| | | | |
|---|---|---|---|
| km/h ———▶ m/s | | × 3.5 | × 3.599 |
| m/s ———▶ km/h | | ÷ 3.5 | × 0.278 |

### Temperature

Below the different systems of temperature measurement are compared: Fahrenheit (°F), Celsius (°C), Réaumur (°r), Rankine (°R) and Kelvin (K). Also listed are the formulae for converting temperature measurements from one system to another. The Kelvin is the base unit of temperature in the SI system.

### Formulae

| | | |
|---|---|---|
| °F ➡ °C | (°F−32)÷1.8 | |
| °C ➡ °F | (°C×1.8)+32 | |
| °F ➡ K | (°F+459.67)÷1.8 | |
| °C ➡ K | °C+273.16 | |

| | | |
|---|---|---|
| °r ➡ K | (°r×1.25)+273.16 | |
| °R ➡ K | °R÷1.8 | |
| K ➡ °F | (K×1.8)−459.67 | |
| K ➡ °C | K−273.16 | |

| | °F | °C | °r | K | °R |
|---|---|---|---|---|---|
| a | 212 | 100 | 80 | 373.16 | 671.67 |
| b | 32 | 0 | 0 | 273.16 | 491.67 |
| c | −459.67 | −273.16 | −218.52 | 0 | 0 |

**a** boiling point of water     **c** absolute zero
**b** freezing point of water

# ENERGY

Energy is the capacity for doing work. Energy and work have particular meanings in science. A man climbing some stairs or a car moving along are examples of actions that involve energy and work. Work is done whenever a force causes movement.

There are different forms of energy. Any form of energy can be changed into any other form of energy. Below are some of the important energy forms and the ways in which energy changes can be made.

**1 Electrical energy** is provided by an electrical current which is produced by the movement of electrons from one atom to another.

**2 Chemical energy** is stored in an atom or a molecule. It is produced by chemical reactions. It is stored in fuels and in food.*

**3 Radiant energy** consists of rays, waves or particles, especially electromagnetic radiation. This includes infra-red radiation, ultraviolet radiation, X-rays, gamma rays and cosmic rays.

**4 Nuclear energy** uses the energy stored in an atom's nucleus.

**5 Mechanical energy** is the energy of things that move. It includes both kinetic and potential energy.

**6 Heat energy** is produced by the random movement of a substance's atoms. The faster the atoms move, the hotter the substance becomes.

**Examples of energy changes**

The diagram shows the energy changes in each situation, for example in a dynamo, mechanical energy is converted to electrical energy.

a Dynamo
b Friction
c Electric motor
d Electric heater
e Light bulb
f Nuclear power station
g Atomic bomb

h Hot-air balloon
i Anything red- or white-hot
j Solar heating panels
k Solar cells
l Photosynthesis
m Batteries
n Oil furnace

## Kinetic and potential energy

In scientific terms a tile (**1**) falling off a roof (**2**) and
breaking a pane of glass (**3**) below is doing work. The tile
has energy. When the tile is falling it has kinetic energy. All
moving objects have kinetic energy. Potential energy is the
energy a stationary object has because of its state or position.
The tile had potential energy because of its position above
the ground and the force of gravity could act on it and make
it move. Potential energy becomes kinetic energy when the
object moves.

### Einstein

Early this century a German scientist, Albert Einstein,
suggested that matter was a form of energy. This theory
was shown in his equation $E = mc^2$. $E$ is the amount of
energy produced, $m$ is the mass and $c$ (which is a constant)
is the speed of light in a vacuum (300 000 km/s).
Einstein's theory was proved by the development of
nuclear power stations. Nuclear power stations convert matter in
an atom directly into heat energy.
Even in efficient power stations only a tiny amount of fuel
is converted into energy. The rest remains as matter.
Einstein's theory makes it possible to calculate the huge
amount of energy that could be released if the whole of the
available mass could be converted into pure energy.

**Examples of potential energy**
1 stored in a spring
2 stored in a stretched bow
3 on top of a hill

**Examples of kinetic energy**
1 moving clockwork train
2 arrow in flight
3 downhill skier

# VOLUME, WEIGHT, MASS, DENSITY

## Volume

Volume is the amount of space occupied by an object. The volume of a hollow object can be measured by the amount of water needed to fill it. The volume of solid objects (such as cubes) can be found by suspending them in water in a measuring cylinder and observing how much the water level rises. The greater the volume of the object, the greater the change in water level. Displaced water equals the volume of the object.

## Weight

Weight is the force with which gravity pulls an object towards the ground. Weight varies with the force of gravity. Gravitational forces decrease with distance from the Earth's centre. The further away an object moves from the Earth's centre the lighter it becomes. Weight is measured using a spring balance. A lighter object will extend the spring balance less than a heavier one.

## Mass

Mass is the amount of matter an object contains. The greater an object's mass the more difficult it becomes to move. The mass of an object remains the same wherever it is. An object's mass can be measured in a beam balance to compare it with objects whose mass is known already.

## Density

Density is mass per unit volume. This means that if an object with a small volume has the same mass as an object with a large volume, the smaller object is said to have a greater density. Density is calculated by dividing the mass of an object by its volume.

The four cubes below represent 4 g each of platinum (**1**), granite (**2**), lead (**3**) and milk (**4**). The denser the material the smaller the volume for a fixed mass.

# FORCES

Forces can change an object's shape, size or the speed or direction in which it is travelling. Force is measured in newtons (N). 1 N is the amount of force needed to give a 1 kg mass an acceleration of 1 metre per second per second (1 m/s²). This means with each second that passes the mass travels 1 m/s faster than it did the previous second.

## Gravity

Gravity is the natural force pulling one object towards another. Its strength depends on the mass of the objects involved. Because the Earth is so large, objects on it are pulled towards it more than they are pulled towards each other. Earth's gravity exerts a pull of 9.8 N on a mass of 1 kg, so its weight on Earth is 9.8 N.

An apple is pulled towards the centre of the Earth. The Earth's mass is greater than the apple's mass, so its gravitational pull is stronger. An apple's mass is 0.1 kg. The pull of gravity gives the apple its weight. The weight of the apple = mass x gravity (= 0.1 x 9.8). The apple weighs 0.98 N.

## Pressure

A force acting over a small area has a greater effect than a force acting over a large area. Pressure is 'force per unit area'. It is calculated by dividing the force by the area over which it is acting. The Earth's atmosphere has weight, and therefore exerts pressure (1 m³ of air weighs about 12 N). Atmospheric pressure can be measured using a barometer. In the diagrams below 1 kg exerts ¹/₁₀₀ kg over each of the squares in diagram (**1**). In diagram (**2**) the weight is distributed over one square only. Therefore the full 1 kg of pressure is exerted on the small square.

**1** 1 kg over 1 m² has a pressure of ¹/₁₀₀ kg per cm²

**2** 1 kg over 1 cm² has a pressure of 1 kg per cm²

# MACHINES

Machines are devices that perform work. Machines overcome resistance at one point by applying a force, usually at another point. All machines depend on energy being supplied. There are six types of machine: the lever, the inclined plane, the wedge, the screw, the wheel and the pulley. Most machines, however complex, are all based in some way on these six simple machines.

## 1 Levers

A lever is a stiff rod which turns about a point called a fulcrum (**a**). This supports a load (**b**) which is moved by effort (**c**). The positions of these elements create three types of lever. The nearer the fulcrum is to the load, the less effort is needed and the machine's mechanical advantage is greater.

A

B

C

A seesaw (**A**) has a fulcrum in the centre. This is where the lever pivots.

A wheelbarrow (**B**) and a knife (**C**) have the fulcrum at one end with the load in the centre. The effort is exerted at the opposite end to the fulcrum.

Raising your arm to lift an object (**D**, **E**) has the load furthest away from the fulcrum. The effort is exerted in the centre.

## 2 Inclined plane

An inclined plane is a flat sloping surface. Much less effort is needed to move an object up an inclined plane than a vertical face.

## 3 Wedge

A wedge is a machine made of two inclined planes (**3a**). The smaller the angle formed by the wedge, the smaller the force needed for moving the load. Both the chisel (**3b**) and axe (**3c**) shown are examples of wedges.

## 4 Screw

A screw is an inclined plane which spirals around a pole (**4a**). A screw is much easier to get into a piece of wood than a nail. An archimedian screw is a cylinder with a screw inside (**4b**). It lifts river water to irrigate fields in the Middle East.

## 5 Wheel and axle

A wheel and axle is a form of lever but it is capable of moving a load further than a lever, helping to move loads overland.

## 6 Pulley

The pulley is a wheel over which a rope or belt passes (**6a**). It is a form of wheel and axle which helps to change the direction of the force. A rope is pulled while the other end raises a load. A block and tackle has two pulleys (**6b**), one attached to a fixed support while the other moves with the load.

# MOTION

Everything in the Universe is in motion. The Earth moves
around the Sun, and the Solar System is moving in its
galaxy. People and animals move around by using their
limbs, moved by muscles. Some animals, such as
earthworms, move by contracting and squeezing muscles.

### Speed

The rate of motion is called speed. It is measured by
calculating the distance moved in a certain time.

### Acceleration

Objects that are accelerating are increasing their speed. The
faster the speed of an object increases, the greater its
acceleration.

### Velocity

Velocity is the rate at which an object changes position. An
object's velocity describes its speed and the direction in
which it is moving. An object travelling at a constant speed
but moving in more than one direction has a changing
velocity.

### Laws of motion

The study of how objects move is called mechanics. Isaac
Newton (1643–1727) discovered the laws that govern this.
His three laws of motion are:
1 An object remains at rest or moves in a straight line until a
force acts upon it.
2 When a force acts on a moving object its rate of
acceleration is proportional to the force and in the direction
of the force.
3 Action and reaction are equal and opposite. This means
that the action of a force always produces a reaction in the
object.

# ELECTRICITY

Electricity involves the flow of electric charges which are either positive or negative. Electricity is about the way atoms behave. Atoms are made of subatomic particles. These are electrons which are negatively charged, protons which are positively charged and neutrons which are neutral.

## Properties of charged particles

Charged particles react to each other in specific ways.

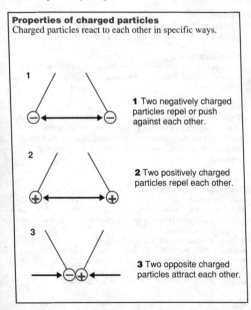

**1** Two negatively charged particles repel or push against each other.

**2** Two positively charged particles repel each other.

**3** Two opposite charged particles attract each other.

### Electrons

Electrons move around the nucleus of an atom at high speeds. When negatively charged electrons move from atom to atom, the energy released is electricity.

### Ions

Ions are atoms or groups of atoms that are electrically charged because they have lost or gained one or more electrons. An atom is usually neutral because the number of positively charged protons in the nucleus equals the number of negatively charged electrons.

An electrically neutral atom (**1**) has an equal number of electrons and protons. When an atom has an electron removed (**2**), it becomes a positive ion because it has one more proton than electrons. When an atom gains an electron, it becomes a negative ion. It has one more electron than protons.

# ELECTRIC CURRENT

An electric current is a continual flow of electrons through a conductive material, such as copper wire. This illustration represents static electricity.

## Direct current

Direct current (DC) will flow in one direction only, from the negative to the positive terminal within the electric circuit, as the electrons move between the atoms in one direction only. A good example of this is the electric current produced by a battery.

## Alternating current

Alternating current (AC) will change its direction of flow at regular intervals. The electrons move between each other in one direction and then in another very quickly. They generate energy as they move. A domestic electricity supply can convert alternating current to direct current.

# MAGNETISM

Magnetism is the name given to the invisible force which attracts some materials to each other and which acts between electric currents. Magnetism is produced by 'ferromagnetic' metals. They have tiny molecules which act like miniature magnets and are called dipoles. If a bar is unmagnetized (**1**), the dipoles form closed chains, their opposite ends (poles) attract and there are no free poles. In a magnetized bar (**2**) the chains are broken and the dipoles are aligned, producing free poles at each end of the bar.

**1**                                **2**

## Magnetic fields

A magnet is surrounded by a magnetic field which is invisible. The magnetic field is strongest at its north and south poles. Two different poles of two magnets attract each other.

Two like poles repel each other.

# ELECTROMAGNETISM

An electromagnet is a magnet which only produces magnetism because of an electric current flowing through a wire. Electromagnets are usually made from a piece of wire coiled around many times to increase the magnetic effect. The magnetic field created by the coil can be increased further by putting a magnetic material, such as an iron rod, inside the coil. The current flowing through the coil causes the iron to become temporarily magnetic.

## Creating an electromagnetic field

When an electric current is passed along a wire, a magnetic field is created around it (**1**).

**1**

When the wire is wrapped around a piece of metal, leaving the north and south poles free, the metal becomes magnetized (**2**). This is now an electromagnet. Scrap metal merchants often use large electromagnets to pick up old cars. When the electric current is turned off the magnet loses its power and a car can be dropped in another spot.

**2**

**Electromagnetic waves**

Light, radio waves, X-rays and other forms of radiant energy are transmitted through space as energy waves called electromagnetic waves. These waves have crests (**1**) and troughs (**2**), just like those formed when a stone is thrown into still water. The distance between the waves' crests is called the wavelength (**3**). It is measured in metres. The number of waves per second is called the frequency and it is measured in hertz (Hz). All electromagnetic waves travel at the speed of light. This is the frequency of an electromagnetic wave multiplied by its wavelength.

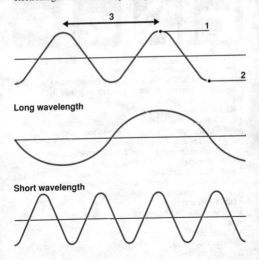

**Long wavelength**

**Short wavelength**

# ELECTROMAGNETIC SPECTRUM

Above is a diagram of the electromagnetic spectrum, showing the different forms of energy in order of frequency and wavelength. The top part of the diagram shows the frequency in hertz (Hz); the lower part measures the wavelength in metres.

## 1 Radio waves

These waves transmit television and radio signals. This section of the spectrum is divided into bands, from VLF (very low frequency) – used for time signals – to SHF (super-high frequency) – used for space and satellite communication.

## 2 Radar and microwaves

Radar bounces off objects, allowing unseen objects to be located; microwaves can cook food quickly.

## 3 Infra-red waves

These invisible waves are emitted by all objects that radiate heat.

## 4 Visible light

The spectrum of colours which we can see, from violet at the

highest frequency, through indigo, blue, green, yellow and
orange to red at the lowest frequency end. The visible
spectrum can be seen in a rainbow or with a prism. It was the
first part of the spectrum to be discovered.

### 5 Ultraviolet light

In small amounts, these waves produce vitamin D and cause
skin to tan; in larger amounts they can damage living cells.

### 6 X-rays

X-rays are capable of passing through many materials that
are opaque to light. Their most familiar use is the
photographing of internal structures of the body for medical
purposes.

### 7 Gamma rays

Emitted during the decay of some radioisotopes, these waves
can be very damaging to the body.

### 8 Cosmic rays

Caused by nuclear explosions and reactions in space, nearly
all of these waves are absorbed by the Earth's atmosphere.

# LIGHT

Light is produced by electromagnetic waves which have a particular range of frequencies and wavelengths. Each colour we see has a different wavelength, ranging from violet which is $3.9 \times 10^{-7}$ m to red which is $7.8 \times 10^{-7}$ m. White light is a combination of the various wavelengths which produce red, orange, yellow, green, blue, indigo and violet. These are the seven colours of the rainbow. They are known as the visible spectrum. Most objects, such as the Moon, rocks and plants, do not produce light. They are seen by the light that they reflect. The Sun, stars and electric lights give off their own light.

## How light travels

Light travels in a straight line. This can be seen in a simple test using a light bulb. Three cards, each with a pinhole in the same place, are set up in front of the light bulb. The light can only be seen through the holes when all three cards are in a straight line.

### Visible spectrum

A glass prism (1) splits a beam of white light (a) into seven colours in the visible spectrum (b). The second prism (2) combines the colours to give white light again (c). When it rains and the Sun is shining, the raindrops act as a giant prism splitting the sunlight into the colours of the rainbow.

### Coloured substances

When white light falls on coloured objects or surfaces, most objects absorb some wavelengths in the spectrum and reflect others. The wavelengths an object reflects give it its colour. For example, a white object reflects all the colours of the spectrum (1). A black surface absorbs all the colours (2). A red surface (3) appears red because it reflects the red wavelengths but absorbs all the others.

# LIGHT INTENSITY

Light intensity diminishes as the square of the distance
between the light source and the lit surface increases. For
example, the amount of light falling on a 1-cm square (**1**)
from a light source will spread over four squares that are
placed twice as far from the light (**2**). And the light will fall
on nine squares which are placed three times as far from the
light source (**3**).

## Mirrors

Mirrors and other shiny
surfaces change the direction
in which light rays travel by
reflecting the light.

→ **Flat**

→ **Convex**

→ **Concave**

### Flat mirror

A flat mirror produces an
image which appears to be
the same distance behind
the mirror as the original
object is in front of it. The
image is the same way up
and the same size as the
object, but it is reversed.

**Convex mirror**
A convex mirror gives a larger field of vision than a flat mirror of equal size. The image seen in a convex mirror is upright but reversed and larger than the original object.

**Concave mirror**
A concave mirror produces an image which is smaller than the original.

# LENSES

Lenses and other transparent materials change the direction in which light is travelling by bending it. This is called refraction. There are various shapes of lens which bend light in different directions.

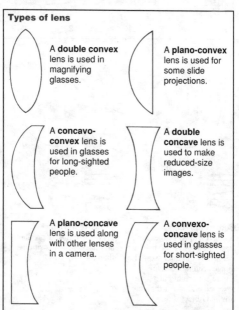

**Types of lens**

A **double convex** lens is used in magnifying glasses.

A **plano-convex** lens is used for some slide projections.

A **concavo-convex** lens is used in glasses for long-sighted people.

A **double concave** lens is used to make reduced-size images.

A **plano-concave** lens is used along with other lenses in a camera.

A **convexo-concave** lens is used in glasses for short-sighted people.

### Concave lens

A concave lens is thinner at the centre than at the edges. It bends parallel light rays outwards as they pass through the lens. A concave lens produces a reduced image which is the right way up and appears on the same side as the original object. This is a virtual image and it cannot be focused onto a screen.

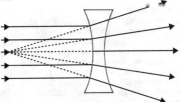

### Convex lens

A convex lens is thicker in the centre than at the edges. It bends light rays inwards to meet at a focal point behind the lens, producing a real image. The distance from the centre of the lens to the focal point is the focal length. An object which is less than one focal length from the lens becomes an enlarged image, the correct way up on the same side of the lens. If the object is moved further away a reduced inverted image is seen on the opposite side of the lens.

# SOUND

Sound travels in the form of waves in air. Sound waves can also travel through water, metal or any other material but they cannot travel through a vacuum. Sound travels at different speeds in different mediums, for example, it travels faster through water than air.

## How sound is produced

The illustration shows how sound is produced when a metal tuning fork (1) vibrates backwards and forwards. The bar's vibrations send pressure waves through the air. Our ears detect waves of certain frequencies which we hear as sound. The prongs of a tuning fork vibrate outwards, compressing air molecules nearby (2) and creating high pressure. As the fork vibrates inwards (3), the air expands, leaving an area of low pressure. Sound waves have many different frequencies, wavelengths (4) and amplitudes (5).

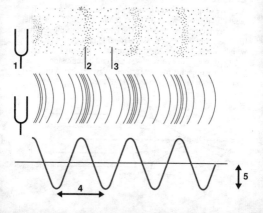

**Pitch and quality**

A sound's pitch and quality, whether it is high or low, depends on its frequency or its wavelength.

**1** Short wavelength or high frequency waves give high pitched sound.

**2** Long wavelength or low frequency waves give low pitched sound.

**3** Irregular waves give noise.

**4** Regular waves give music.

**How sound travels**

Sound travels much faster through some mediums than others. The chart below shows the effectiveness of some mediums in transmitting sound.

|   | | m/s |   | | m/s |
|---|---|---|---|---|---|
| **1** | Iron | 5200 | **4** | Water | 1500 |
| **2** | Wood | 3800 | **5** | Air | 340 |
| **3** | Brick | 3600 | | | |

# DECIBELS

The decibel (dB) is the unit used for the loudness of a sound, or its sound pressure.

### Decibel scale

The decibel scale is relative and increases in stages, beginning with the tiniest sound change that can be heard by a human being (0–1 dB). A 20 dB sound is ten times louder than a 10 dB sound and 30 dB is 100 times louder than 10 dB. A noise around the level of 120 dB or higher is likely to be damaging to human hearing. Even higher levels can cause permanent ear damage.

### Wave amplitude

One of the main properties of a sound wave is its amplitude. This is the distance between a wave crest or trough and an in-between line of balance (**1**). The greater the amount of energy transmitted in a sound wave, the greater is the wave's amplitude and the louder the sound.

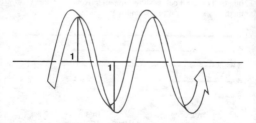

The chart shows the decibels of various sounds at certain distances and the effects on the human ear.

1 Human minimum
   0 dB
2 Soft whisper at 5 m
   30 dB
3 Inside an urban home
   50 dB
4 Light traffic at 15 m
   55 dB
5 Conversation at 1 m
   60 dB
6 Pneumatic drill at 15 m
   85 dB
7 Heavy traffic at 15 m
   90 dB
8 Loud shout at 15 m
   100 dB
9 Aeroplane taking off at
   600 m 105 dB
10 Inside full-volume disco
   117 dB
11 Aeroplane taking off at
   60 m 120 dB
12 Pain threshold for
   humans 130 dB
13 Aeroplane taking off at
   30 m 140 dB

# NUCLEAR PHYSICS

Nuclear physics is essentially the study of what occurs in the nucleus, or heart of an atom. A nucleus is approximately a thousand million millionth of a metre across. The human eye cannot see the nucleus but information about it and the particles inside it is obtained by smashing nuclei and observing the results.

## Composition of an atomic nucleus

The study of the properties of the atomic nucleus has led to many important advances in science, medicine and technology. An atomic nucleus is made up of protons and neutrons. These particles make up 99.9 per cent of the mass of all matter. The nucleus is mainly held together by a powerful force called the strong interaction or the strong nuclear force. It is this force that causes protons and neutrons to interact and bind together.

## Radioactive emissions

Most nuclei are stable and they do not break down easily. However, the nuclei of some elements, such as radium and uranium, are unstable and they are radioactive. They break apart spontaneously and release energy as radioactive emissions called alpha, beta and gamma rays. An understanding of nuclear reactions called fission, when a heavy nucleus splits in two, and fusion, when two light nuclei join together, has enabled scientists to release the tremendous energy of the nucleus for practical use.

## Nuclear fission

Nuclear fission is the production of energy from the splitting of an atom's nucleus.

**1** When the nucleus of an atom of uranium is struck by a neutron it causes fission

**2** The combined reactions produce an unstable atom.

**3** Energy in the form of heat is released by the splitting atom.

**4** Two or three additional neutrons are also produced. These new neutrons can cause further uranium nuclei to split, resulting in a continuous chain reaction.

## Nuclear fusion

Nuclear fusion is the production of energy from the joining together of atoms to form larger atoms.

**1** When two isotopes of hydrogen, deuterium (hydrogen 2) and tritium (hydrogen 3) collide, fusion takes place.

**2** The combination produces energy by the release of a neutron.

**3** It also produces a larger atom of helium.

# RADIOACTIVE ELEMENTS

Radioactive elements have atoms which tend to break down into simpler atoms and radiate energy. This process is called radioactive decay. Some elements which occur naturally have nuclei which break down, making them naturally radioactive. Other elements can be made radioactive under certain conditions in nuclear reactors.

### Well-known radioactive elements

**Uranium** is a radioactive silver-white metal and it is the main source of nuclear energy. Uranium is plentiful but it is

### Types of radiation

There are three kinds of radiation which are given out by a radioactive element. They are called after letters in the Greek alphabet: α alpha, ß beta, γ gamma. The type of radiation given out depends on the radioactive element. Some radioactive elements give off more than one type of radiation.

only found in tiny amounts in most rocks where it occurs. It is highly reactive. Uranium is used chiefly as fuel for nuclear reactors and also for making atomic bombs.

**Plutonium** is a radioactive metallic element. Almost all plutonium is produced artificially and only a very small amount occurs naturally. Plutonium is highly poisonous because it rapidly gives off radiation in the form of alpha rays. Plutonium is also extremely explosive.

**Thorium** is a naturally-occurring radioactive metal which is more abundant than uranium. It has one of the highest known melting points at 3330° C.

### 1 Alpha radiation

The emission of alpha particles. When a nucleus emits a fragment called an alpha particle it loses two protons and two neutrons. This gives it a positive electrical charge. Alpha particles are emitted with high energy but they lose it rapidly passing through matter and can be stopped by two sheets of paper.

### 2 Beta radiation

The emission of negative beta particles, which are electrons. A change of particle in the nucleus creates an electron. Some nuclei emit positive electrons, or positrons. Beta particles travel almost at the speed of light. Beta radiation is about 100 times more penetrating than alpha radiation.

### 3 Gamma radiation

Gamma rays are similar to X-rays but with shorter wave lengths. Gamma rays have no electrical charge. They move at the speed of light and can travel long distances. Gamma radiation does not change the nucleus which is left behind. It is also much more penetrating than alpha or beta radiation.

# MATTER

Matter on Earth is made up of atoms forming solids, liquids and gases.

**An element** is a single substance which cannot be broken down chemically into simpler substances. Zinc, oxygen and gold are elements. There are about 90 elements which occur naturally and about another 20 elements have been produced artificially but not all of these have been recognized.

**A compound** is made of two or more elements chemically joined to form a new substance which has different qualities from the elements which produced it. Water is a compound. It is a liquid made from two elements, hydrogen and oxygen. In a compound the proportions of the elements are always the same.

**A mixture** is made from two or more substances which have not been chemically joined. Each element can be separated without a chemical change. A mixture can have ingredients in any proportion.

## Examples of mixtures

**A solution** is a mixture of two or more substances which cannot be separated by using mechanical methods such as filtering. A solution can be a solid, a liquid or a gas but the most common are liquids. The dissolved substance spreads evenly in the substance in which it dissolves.

**A suspension** is a mixture where one substance spreads evenly through another without dissolving. It includes solids in liquids or gases, gases in liquids and liquids in gases. Suspensions containing very small particles are called colloids.

**An emulsion** is a liquid which is evenly spread through another liquid. Droplets of one liquid are evenly spread in the other but in time the two separate. This can be delayed by adding emulsifying agents. Paints and cosmetic lotions are examples of emulsions.

# SOLIDS, LIQUIDS AND GASES

### Solid

A solid takes up a specific amount of space. Its molecules cannot move around freely, although they are not completely still. A solid will not alter its shape unless it is forced to do so.

### Liquid

A liquid also occupies a specific amount of space but, unlike a solid, it can alter its shape easily. A liquid will take the shape of any container into which it is poured. The molecules in a liquid can move around, but only in a limited way.

### Gas

A gas does not have a specific shape or size. Its molecules can move around completely freely so a gas will spread out to fill a container. If the gas is not restricted it will continue to expand.

## ATOMS AND MOLECULES

An atom is a minute unit of matter. Everything around us is made of atoms. Each element is made up of one particular type of atom.

Atoms are the smallest units that can take part in a chemical reaction to produce a chemical change. They do not vary much in size but they do vary in weight. Atoms are so small that more than 10 billion make up the tiniest object that can be seen through a microscope.

### Atomic structure

Atoms contain even smaller units called subatomic particles. Scientists have found more than 200 of these. Some exist for only a tiny fraction of a second. Others are stable and do not break down easily. Protons, neutrons and electrons are stable particles. Different chemical elements have different numbers of protons, neutrons and electrons.

### Proton

The proton is part of the nucleus (the central core) of an atom. An element is identified by the number of protons in the atom. This is called the atomic number. If an atom gains or loses a proton, it becomes an atom of a different element. A proton has a positive electrical charge of one unit. It has a mass of $1.6726 \times 10^{-27}$ kg.

**1** Proton
**2** Neutron
**3** Electron

### Neutron

A neutron is also part of the nucleus. The number of neutrons in an atom can vary without the element changing identity. Forms of an element with different numbers of neutrons in the nucleus are called an element's isotopes. A neutron is electrically neutral as it carries no charge. It has a mass of $1.6748 \times 10^{-27}$ kg.

### Electron

Electrons move around the nucleus of an atom at high speed. The arrangement of electrons in an atom determines the element's chemical behaviour. An electron has a negative charge of 1 unit. Atoms are electrically neutral as they have the same number of electrons as protons. An electron has a mass of $9.1096 \times 10^{-31}$ kg.

### Molecules

Two or more atoms joined together form a molecule. The atoms may come from the same element or from different elements. Molecules that contain atoms from two or more elements make up a compound. When a molecule is broken down it splits into the atoms of the elements from which it was made. Molecules can be made of two atoms or thousands of atoms. For example an oxygen molecule only has two atoms but a rubber molecule has between 13 000 and 65 000 atoms.

**1** Oxygen molecule: 2 atoms
**2** Water molecule: 3 atoms
**3** Rubber molecule: 13 000–65 000 atoms

# PERIODIC TABLE

Calcium, gold and hydrogen are chemical elements which are examples of basic chemical substances. They cannot be broken down into simpler forms. This gives each element distinctive properties. The Periodic Table gives information about all the 103 known elements. (Elements 104 to 109 have been produced artificially but have not been officially named.)

| 1 H | | | | | | | | |
|------|------|------|------|------|------|------|------|------|
| 3 Li | 4 Be | | | | | | | |
| 11 Na | 12 Mg | | | | | | | |
| 19 K | 20 Ca | 21 Sc | 22 Ti | 23 V | 24 Cr | 25 Mn | 26 Fe | 27 Co |
| 37 Rb | 38 Sr | 39 Y | 40 Zr | 41 Nb | 42 Mo | 43 Tc | 44 Ru | 45 Rh |
| 55 Cs | 56 Ba | 57-71 - | 72 Hf | 73 Ta | 74 W | 75 Re | 76 Os | 77 Ir |
| 87 Fr | 88 Ra | 89-103 - | | | | | | |

| 57 La | 58 Ce | 59 Pr | 60 Nd | 61 Pm | 62 Sm | 63 Eu |
|------|------|------|------|------|------|------|
| 89 Ac | 90 Th | 91 Pa | 92 U | 93 Np | 94 Pu | 95 Am |

It was devised in 1869 by the Russian chemist Dmitri Mendeleyev. The table groups elements into seven lines or periods. As we read from left to right the elements become less metallic. The elements in each vertical group have similar chemical properties. Further information about the elements is given on pages 364–73.

| | | | | | | | | | | | | | | | | | 2 He |
|---|---|---|---|---|---|---|---|---|---|---|---|---|---|---|---|---|---|
| | | | | | | | | | | | | 5 B | 6 C | 7 N | 8 O | 9 F | 10 Ne |
| | | | | | | | | | | | | 13 Al | 14 Si | 15 P | 16 S | 17 Cl | 18 Ar |
| 28 Ni | 29 Cu | 30 Zn | 31 Ga | 32 Ge | 33 As | 34 Se | 35 Br | 36 Kr |
| 46 Pd | 47 Ag | 48 Cd | 49 In | 50 Sn | 51 Sb | 52 Te | 53 I | 54 Xe |
| 78 Pt | 79 Au | 80 Hg | 81 Tl | 82 Pb | 83 Bi | 84 Po | 85 At | 86 Rn |

| 64 Gd | 65 Tb | 66 Dy | 67 Ho | 68 Er | 69 Tm | 70 Yb | 71 Lu |
|---|---|---|---|---|---|---|---|
| 96 Cm | 97 Bk | 98 Cf | 99 Es | 100 Fm | 101 Md | 102 No | 103 Lr |

# CHEMICAL ELEMENTS

Chemical element; symbol; atomic number (relative atomic mass); origin of name; date of discovery.

Actinium; Ac; 89 (227.027 8); from the Greek *aktis*, ray; 1899

Aluminium; Al; 13 (26.98); from the Latin *alum*, an ore; 1827

Americium; Am; 95 (243); after America; 1944

Antimony; Sb; 51 (121.75); origin unknown; Latin *stibium*, antimony; before 1500

Argon; Ar; 18 (39.948); from Greek *argos*, inactive; 1894

Arsenic; As; 33 (74.9216); from Greek *arsenikon*, yellow ore containing arsenic; 1250

Astatine; At; 85 (210); from Greek *astatos*, unstable; 1940

Barium; Ba; 56 (137.33); from Greek *barys*, heavy; 1808

Berkelium; Bk; 97 (247); after Berkeley, California; 1950

Beryllium; Be; 4 (9.012 18); from Greek *beryllos*, beryl; 1798

Bismuth; Bi; 83 (208.980); from the German *wismut;* 1753

Boron; B; 5 (10.81); from Arabic *burak*, borax; 1808

Bromine; Br; 35 (79.904); Greek *bromos,* unpleasant smell; 1826

Cadmium; Cd; 48 (112.41); after Cadmus, founder of Thebes; 1817

Caesium; Cs; 55 (132.905); from Latin *caesius*, bluish-grey; 1860

Calcium; Ca; 20 (40.08); from Latin *calx*, lime; 1808

Californium; Cf; 98 (251); after California; 1950

Carbon; C; 6 (12.011); from Latin *carbo*, charcoal; prehistoric

Cerium; Ce; 58 (140.12); after the asteroid Ceres; 1803

Chlorine; Cl; 17 (35.453); from Greek *khloros*, green; 1797

Chromium; Cr; 24 (51.996); from Greek *khroma*, colour; 1797

Cobalt; Co; 27 (58.933 2); from German *kobold*, goblin; 1735

Copper; Cu; 29 (63.546); from Latin *cuprum*, Cyprus metal; prehistoric

Curium; Cm; 96 (247); after Marie and Pierre Curie; 1944

Dysprosium; Dy; 66 (162.50); from Greek *dysprositos*, hard to get at; 1896

Einsteinium; Es; 99 (254); after Albert Einstein; 1952

Erbium; Er; 68 (167.26); after Ytterby, a Swedish town; 1843

Europium; Eu; 63 (151.96); after Europe; 1896

Fermium; Fm; 100 (257); after physicist Enrico Fermi; 1952

Fluorine; F; 9 (18.998 4); from the mineral fluorspar; 1771

Francium; Fr; 87 (223); after France; 1939

Gadolinium; Gd; 64 (157.25); after chemist, Gadolin; 1880

Gallium; Ga; 31 (69.72); from Latin *Gallia*, France; 1875

Germanium; Ge; 32 (72.59); from Latin *Germania*, Germany; 1886

Gold; Au; 79 (196.967); Old English gold; Latin, *aurum;* prehistoric

Hafnium; Hf; 72 (178.49); from Latin *Hafnia*, Copenhagen; 1923

Helium; He; 2 (4.002 60); from Greek *helios*, Sun; 1895

Holmium; Ho; 67 (164.930); from Latin *Holmia*, Stockholm; 1878

Hydrogen; H; 1 (1.007 9); from Greek *hydor*, water; *genes*, producing; 1766

Indium; In; 49 (114.82); from indigo line in its spectrum; 1863

Iodine; I; 53 (126.905); from Greek *iodes*, violet; 1811

Iridium; Ir; 77 (192.22); from Latin and Greek *iris*, rainbow; 1803

Iron; Fe; 26 (55.847); Old English *iren*; Latin *ferrum;* prehistoric

Krypton; Kr; 36 (83.8); from Greek *kryptos*, hidden; 1898

Lanthanum; La; 57 (138.906); Greek *lanthanein*, to lie unseen; 1839

Lawrencium; Lr; 103 (260); after physicist Ernest Lawrence; 1961

Lead; Pb; 82 (207.2); Old English *lead*; Latin *plumbum*; prehistoric

Lithium; Li; 3 (6.941); from Greek *lithos*, stone; 1817

Lutetium; Lu; 71 (174.97); after *Lutetia*, old name for Paris; 1907

Magnesium; Mg; 12 (24.305); after Magnesia, in Thessaly; 1808

Manganese; Mn; 25 (54.938); alteration of Latin *magnesia*; 1774

Mendelevium; Md; 101 (258); after chemist Mendeleyev; 1955

Mercury; Hg; 80 (200.59); after planet; Latin *hydrargynum*; prehistoric

Molybdenum; Mo; 42 (95.94); from Greek *molybdos*, lead; 1778

Neodymium; Nd; 60 (144.24); Greek *neo*, new; *didymos*, twin; 1885

Neon; Ne; 10 (20.179); from Greek *neo*, new; 1898

Neptunium; Np; 93 (237.048); after planet Neptune; 1940

Nickel; Ni; 28 (58.69); from German *kupfernickel*, devil's copper; 1751

Niobium; Nb; 41 (92.9064); after Niobe in Greek myth; 1801

Nitrogen; N; 7 (14.006 7); from nitre, saltpetre; Greek *genes*, producing; 1772

Nobelium; No; 102 (259); after Alfred Nobel; 1958

Osmium; Os; 76 (190.2); from Greek *osme*, smell; 1903

Oxygen; O; 8 (15.999 4); from Greek *oxys*, acid; *genes*, producing; 1774

Palladium; Pd; 46 (106.42); after asteroid Pallas; 1803

Phosphorus; P; 15 (30.973 8); from Greek *phosphorus*, light-bearing; 1669

Platinum; Pt; 78 (195.08); from Spanish *plata*, silver; 1735

Plutonium; Pu; 94 (244); after planet Pluto; 1940

Polonium; Po; 84 (209); from Latin *Polonia*, Poland; 1898

Potassium; K; 19 (39.098 3); after potash; Latin *kalium*, alkali; 1807

Praseodymium; Pr; 59 (140.908); Greek *prasios*, green; *didymos*, twin; 1885

Promethium; Pm; 61 (145); after Prometheus in Greek myth; 1945

Protactinium; Pa; 91 (231.036); from Greek *protos*, first; *actinium;* 1917

Radium; Ra; 88 (226.025); from Latin *radius*, ray; 1898

Radon; Rn; 86 (222); from radium; 1900

Rhenium; Re; 75 (186.207); from Latin *Rhenus*, Rhine; 1925

Rhodium; Rh; 45 (102.906); from Greek *rhodon*, rose; 1803–4

Rubidium; Rb; 37 (85.467 8); from Latin *rubidus*, ruby; 1861

Ruthenium; Ru; 44 (101.07); from Latin *Ruthenia*, Russia; 1844

Samarium; Sm; 62 (150.36); after mineral samerskite; 1879

Scandium; Sc; 21 (44.955 9); from Latin *Scandia*, Scandinavia; 1879

Selenium; Se; 34 (78.96); from Greek *selene*, moon; 1817

Silicon; Si; 14 (28.085 5); from Latin *silex*, flint; 1823

Silver; Ag; 47 (107.868); Old English *siolfor*; Latin *argentum;* prehistoric

Sodium; Na; 11 (22.989 8); from soda; Latin *natrium;* 1807

Strontium; Sr; 38 (87.62); after Strontian, a Scottish village; 1808

Sulphur; S; 16 (32.06); from Latin *sulfur;* prehistoric

Tantalum; Ta; 73 (180.948); after Tantalos in Greek myth; 1802

Technetium; Tc; 43 (97); from Greek *tekhnetos*, artificial; 1937

Tellurium; Te; 52 (127.60); from Latin *tellus*, earth; 1782

Terbium; Tb; 65 (158.925); after Ytterby, town in Sweden; 1843

Thallium; Tl; 81 (204.383); from Greek *thallos*, green shoot; 1861

Thorium; Th; 90 (232.038); after Thor, Norse god of thunder; 1828

Thulium; Tm; 69 (168.934); from Latin *Thule*, Northland; 1879

Tin; Sn; 50 (118.71): Old English *tin*; Latin *stannum*; prehistoric

Titanium; Ti; 22 (47.88); after Titans in Greek myth; 1791

Tungsten; W; 74 (183.85); Swedish *tung sten*, heavy stone; 1781

Uranium; U; 92 (238.029); after planet Uranus; 1789

Vanadium; V; 23 (50.9415); after Vanadis, Norse goddess; 1801

## Chemical elements by symbol

| | | | | | |
|---|---|---|---|---|---|
| Ac | Actinium | Cf | Californium | H | Hydrogen |
| Ag | Silver | Cl | Chlorine | He | Helium |
| Al | Aluminium | Cm | Curium | Hf | Hafnium |
| Am | Americium | Co | Cobalt | Hg | Mercury |
| Ar | Argon | Cr | Chromium | Ho | Holmium |
| As | Arsenic | Cs | Caesium | I | Iodine |
| At | Astatine | Cu | Copper | In | Indium |
| Au | Gold | Dy | Dysprosium | Ir | Iridium |
| B | Boron | Er | Erbium | K | Potassium |
| Ba | Barium | Es | Einsteinium | Kr | Krypton |
| Be | Beryllium | Eu | Europium | La | Lanthanum |
| Bi | Bismuth | F | Fluorine | Li | Lithium |
| Bk | Berkelium | Fe | Iron | Lr | Lawrencium |
| Br | Bromine | Fm | Fermium | Lu | Lutetium |
| C | Carbon | Fr | Francium | Md | Mendelevium |
| Ca | Calcium | Ga | Gallium | Mg | Magnesium |
| Cd | Cadmium | Gd | Gadolinium | Mn | Manganese |
| Ce | Cerium | Ge | Germanium | Mo | Molybdenum |

Xenon; Xe; 54 (131.29); from Greek *xenos*, strange; 1898

Ytterbium; Yb; 70 (173.04); after Ytterby, town in Sweden; 1907

Yttrium; Y; 39 (88.905 9); after Ytterby, town in Sweden; 1828

Zinc; Zn; 30 (65.39); from German *zink*; 1800

Zirconium; Zr; 40 (91.334); from German *zirkon*, and originally Persian *zargun*, golden; 1789

| | | | | | |
|---|---|---|---|---|---|
| N | Nitrogen | Pu | Plutonium | Te | Tellurium |
| Na | Sodium | Ra | Radium | Th | Thorium |
| Nb | Niobium | Rb | Rubidium | Ti | Titanium |
| Nd | Neodymium | Re | Rhenium | Tl | Thallium |
| Ne | Neon | Rh | Rhodium | Tm | Thulium |
| Ni | Nickel | Rn | Radon | U | Uranium |
| No | Nobelium | Ru | Ruthenium | V | Vanadium |
| Np | Neptunium | S | Sulphur | W | Tungsten |
| O | Oxygen | Sb | Antimony | Xe | Xenon |
| Os | Osmium | Sc | Scandium | Y | Yttrium |
| P | Phosphorus | Se | Selenium | Yb | Ytterbium |
| Pa | Protactinium | Si | Silicon | Zn | Zinc |
| Pb | Lead | Sm | Samarium | Zr | Zirconium |
| Pd | Palladium | Sn | Tin | | |
| Pm | Promethium | Sr | Strontium | | |
| Po | Polonium | Ta | Tantalum | | |
| Pr | Praseodymium | Tb | Terbium | | |
| Pt | Platinum | Tc | Technetium | | |

# GROUPING THE ELEMENTS

The Periodic Table (see pages 362–3) is a way of ordering and comparing chemical elements. It gives information about all known chemical elements.

### Periods

Each element is shown by its symbol (**1**) in the table. The elements are arranged in seven rows called periods (**2**). They are read from left to right and show a progression from metals to non-metals. Hydrogen does not clearly belong to any of the classes.

Elements are arranged in the periods according to their atomic number, from 1 to 103. This appears in the top left corner of each box (**3**). The number states how many protons (**4**) are in the element's nucleus (**5**). Protons are positively charged particles in an atom's centre.

### Groups

Each column in the table is a group, read vertically. It contains elements with similar properties. There are eight major groups of elements arranged according to how many electrons (6), negatively charged particles, are in the outer shell of the atom (7). Elements have between 1 and 8 electrons in the outer shell. Elements in each group behave similarly.

### Alkali metals (1)

Lithium, sodium, potassium, rubidium, caesium and francium are the elements in Group 1 of the Periodic Table. Alkali metals are so reactive that they are stored in oil to protect them from oxygen and water vapour in the air. Their melting and boiling points are low for metals, they float in water and they can be cut with a knife. They react with water to form alkaline solutions

### Alkaline-earth metals (2)

The elements in Group 2 are beryllium, magnesium, calcium, strontium, barium and radium. These elements are

1

2

greyish-white in colour. They are all malleable although varying in hardness. The alkaline-earth metals have a pair of electrons on the outermost shell which can be removed from their atoms relatively easily to form positive ions. This gives them their particular chemical quality. They are not as reactive as the alkali metals.

### Halogens (3)

Halogens are the elements in Group 7. They are fluorine, chlorine, bromine, iodine and astatine. They are so reactive they never occur free in nature. Instead, they are found combined with metals in salts such as sodium chloride. This has led to them being called halogens, or salt-formers. Halogens occur in compounds with negative ions. Astatine is the other element in the group that does not occur in nature .

### Noble gases (4)

Group 8 contains very unreactive elements. This group includes helium, neon, argon, krypton, xenon and radon. They are all colourless gases at room temperature, with low melting and boiling points. They all exist as separate single atoms. Until 1962 no compounds of the noble gases were known and chemists thought they were completely unreactive, calling them inert gases.

### Carbon (5)

Carbon is an important element. It is a nonmetallic element and forms only 0.2 per cent of the Earth's crust. Carbon is found naturally both in pure forms and in combination with other elements. Carbon occurs naturally in three forms: diamond, graphite and charcoal. In diamond the carbon atoms are arranged regularly in a framework. Each atom is surrounded by four others producing a strong crystal structure and making diamond the hardest substance known. In graphite each atom is surrounded by three others. This produces a layer pattern, and makes graphite soft. Charcoal has a non-regular structure.

Carbon is a unique element because of the huge number and variety of its compounds. Carbon is the basis of organic chemistry and all living systems. The extensive and varied chemistry of carbon results from its ability to form single, double and triple bonds with itself and other elements.

**Transition elements (6)**

The elements (highlighted) in this part of the table are called transition metals. Each element differs from its neighbour in another numbered period by the number of electrons (**a**) in its next to outer electron shell (**b**).

**Lanthanide and actinide series (7)**

The two bottom rows of the table are lanthanides and actinides. They are shown separately because their properties are so similar that they only cover two elements on the main table. Lanthanides are rare metallic elements. Actinides are chemically similar to them. Uranium is an actinide.

## CHEMICAL SYMBOLS

A chemical symbol is a letter or a pair of letters which stands for a chemical element. The symbols are used in chemical equations and formulae. A chemical formula is a group of symbols used to describe different molecules.

| | Atoms joined together | Formula | Name |
|---|---|---|---|
| | 2 oxygen atoms | $O_2$ | oxygen |
| | 2 hydrogen atoms + 1 oxygen atom | $H_2O$ | water |
| | 1 carbon atom + 2 oxygen atoms | $CO_2$ | carbon dioxide |
| | 1 carbon atom + 4 hydrogen atoms | $CH_4$ | methane |
| | 3 oxygen atoms | $O_3$ | ozone |
| | 6 carbon atoms + 12 hydrogen atoms + 6 oxygen atoms | $C_6H_{12}O_6$ | glucose |
| | 9 carbon atoms + 8 hydrogen atoms + 4 oxygen atoms | $C_9H_8O_4$ | aspirin |

# CHEMICAL REACTIONS

In a chemical reaction molecules in a substance gain or lose atoms or they are rearranged. Four main types of chemical reaction occur:

**A combination reaction (1)**
This occurs when two or more substances combine to form a compound.

**Decomposition (2)** This occurs when a chemical compound breaks up forming simpler substances.

**Replacement (3)** This occurs when a compound loses one or more elements but gains other elements to replace them.

**Double decomposition (4)** This is when two decomposing compounds exchange atoms to form two new compounds.

## Common chemical reactions

**Combustion** This is a rapid burning that occurs when oxygen combines quickly with another substance. **Corrosion** This happens on metal surfaces which react to air, chemicals or moisture. **Destructive distillation** Decomposing substances in a closed container. **Digestion** In animals this involves the breakdown of food by protein catalysts called enzymes. **Dissociation** This is the break-up of a compound's molecules into simpler ingredients which may be recombined. **Electrolysis** Occurs when an electric current passed through a liquid breaks up its parts. **Fermentation** A change to organic substances caused by enzymes. **Oxidation** This occurs when a substance loses electrons. These are gained by another substance, which undergoes **reduction**. The two reactions occur together (**redox** reaction).

# BIOCHEMICAL CYCLES

The Earth's resources are constantly being used and reused.
Biochemical changes recycle some of the key elements
required by living things.

### The oxygen cycle

The oxygen cycle is a vital part of life on Earth. All living
things need oxygen to live and breathe.

1 Oxygen is in the air.

2 The oxygen is breathed in by animals.

3 It is breathed out as carbon dioxide which is a carbon–
oxygen compound.

4 The carbon dioxide is absorbed by plants which combine it
with water to make food.

5 Plants release the surplus oxygen into the air.

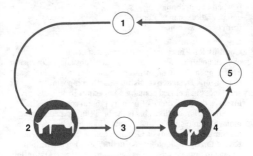

### The carbon cycle

Carbon compounds make up the living tissues of all plants and animals. The carbon cycle is the circulation of carbon between living organisms and their surroundings. It describes the processes which increase and decrease the amount of carbon dioxide in the environment.

1 Carbon dioxide is in the air.
2 It is breathed in, or absorbed by plants.
3 Animals eat the plants.
4 Carbon dioxide is breathed out as waste by plants and animals.
5 Dead plants and animals are broken down by bacteria.
6 Bacteria convert the carbon compounds to carbon dioxide and the cycle starts again.
7 The remains of living organisms which have been dead a long time and microscopic organisms form fossil fuels. When burnt, carbon dioxide enters the atmosphere.
8 Volcanoes release carbon dioxide into the air.

## The nitrogen cycle

All plants and animals need nitrogen, present in proteins and nucleic acids. Most living things, however, cannot use nitrogen directly from the atmosphere.

1 Nitrogen in the air.

2 Nitrogen in the atmosphere is trapped by some plant roots.

3 Plants use nitrogen for making proteins.

4 Animals eat plant proteins.

5 The proteins in dead organisms and in body wastes are converted to ammonia by bacteria and fungi.

6 Other bacteria convert the ammonia to nitrates.

7 Artificial nitrates added to soil as fertilizer. When too much is added, water supplies become polluted with nitrates.

8 Plants absorb the nitrates.

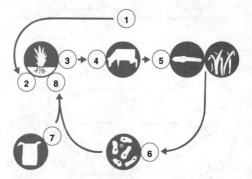

### The sulphur cycle

Sulphur is an important part of almost every protein.

**1** Sulphates, or sulphur–oxygen compounds, are absorbed by plant roots.

**2** The oxygen in the sulphates is replaced by hydrogen in a plant process making amino acids.

**3** Animals eat the plants

**4** In dead animals and plants the amino acids which contain sulphur are broken down by decomposer micro-organisms to obtain hydrogen sulphide.

**5** Bacteria extract sulphur from sulphides.

**6** Other bacteria combine sulphur with oxygen to produce sulphates.

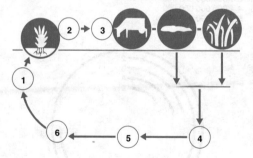

## EVOLUTION

The clock below marks key events in the Earth's history.
They appear as if on a 12-hour clock which represents
millions of years. The Earth (**1**) formed 4.6 billion years ago
which is 12 hours ago. The first life on Earth (**2**) began 3.5
billion years ago in the form of single-cell organisms. Plants
and animals (**3, 4**) appeared 1 billion years ago. Most fossils
(**5**) were formed from 590 million years ago. On the next
page are first appearances of animal and plant life on Earth
in millions of years, which occurred in the last two hours.

**Years ago**

**1** 4 600 000 000 000
**2** 3 500 000 000 000
**3** 1 000 000 000 000
**4** 1 000 000 000 000
**5**   590 000 000 000

### First appearance of life forms

The creatures today evolved from earlier species and some appeared in their present forms earlier than others. Crustaceans were among the first animals. They appeared nearly 650 million years before humans. Midway between their first appearance and that of humans, the insects developed their characteristics 000 million years ago.

**First appearances
(millions of years ago)**

| | | |
|---|---|---|
| 1 | Crustaceans | 650 |
| 2 | Fishes | 510 |
| 3 | Land plants | 420 |
| 4 | Insects | 380 |
| 5 | Seed plants | 360 |
| 6 | Amphibians | 360 |
| 7 | Reptiles | 340 |
| 8 | Mammals | 213 |
| 9 | Birds | 150 |
| 10 | Flowering plants | 140 |
| 11 | Man | 2 |

# AGE OF DINOSAURS 248–65 million years ago
## Triassic (248–213)

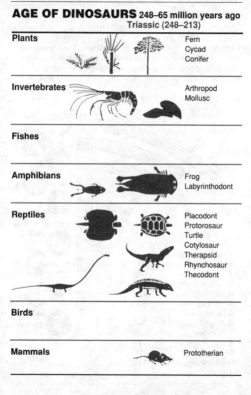

**Plants**
Fern
Cycad
Conifer

**Invertebrates**
Arthropod
Mollusc

**Fishes**

**Amphibians**
Frog
Labyrinthodont

**Reptiles**
Placodont
Protorosaur
Turtle
Cotylosaur
Therapsid
Rhynchosaur
Thecodont

**Birds**

**Mammals**
Prototherian

| Jurassic (213–144) | Cretaceous (144–65) |
|---|---|
| Conifer<br>Cycad<br>Ginkgo | Flowering plant |
| Tentaculate<br>Arthropod<br>Mollusc | Molluscs<br>Arthropod<br>Echinoderm |
| Bony fish<br>Chondrichthyan | Chondrichthyan<br>Sarcopterygian |
| Salamander | Frog |
| Plesiosaur<br>Ichthyosaur<br>Pterosaur<br>Crocodilian | Turtles<br>Plesiosaur<br>Eosuchian<br>Mosasaur<br>Crocodilian<br>Pterosaur |
| *Archaeopteryx* | *Ichthyornis*<br>*Hesperornis* |
| Prototherian | Insectivore |

# DINOSAURS

There were two main groups of dinosaurs. The Ornithischians had a hip joint similar to that of a bird. The Saurischian dinosaurs had hips similar to those of a lizard.

### Saurischian dinosaurs

Two main groups developed.
1 **Theropods** were flesh-eating, two-legged creatures. The *Tyrannosaurus* was typical of these creatures.
2 **Sanropods** had four legs and were mainly plant-eaters. The *Diplodocus* is the most familiar of this group.

**Ornithischian dinosaurs**
There are four suborders.
**1 Stegosaurs** were giant lizards with spiky tails and large bony plates on their backs.
**2 Ceratopsians** were horned dinosaurs. The *Triceratops* had three horns, as its name suggests.
**3 Ornithopods** were fast-moving, ostrich-like creatures. The *Dromicelomimus* was possibly the fastest of all the dinosaurs.
**4 Ankylosaurs** were large heavy creatures with protective plates covering their bodies.

# CELLS

Living things are made of cells. Animal cells (**1**) and plant cells (**2**) share some characteristics of cells, although, in any plant or animal, the cells are specially developed to do certain jobs. All cells contain the following elements:

**Cytoplasm** (**a**) a transparent jelly-like substance, in which the chemical reactions of life occur.

**Cell membrane** (**b**) a skin around a cell which allows the entry and exit of materials.

**Nucleus** (**c**) the cell's control centre, containing hereditary material (chromosomes). Plant cells have additional features. These are:

**Cell wall** (**d**) outside the membrane, this gives the cell rigidity and shape. It is made of cellulose, a non living substance.

**Plastids** (**e**) units involved in making and storing food.

**Vacuoles** (**f**) large fluid-filled cavities containing sap. Many plant cells have one large vacuole.

3

— a

— c

— f

4

— a

— c

— e

— d

1 Simple animal cell
2 Simple plant cell
3 Single cell *Euglena*
4 Bacteria cell
5 Specialized animal cell
  (nerve cell)

5

— a

— c

# CELL REPRODUCTION

The cell nucleus contains chromosomes, which transmit hereditary characteristics. They consist largely of protein and DNA (deoxyribonucleic acid). For cells to pass on chromosomes they must reproduce. They do this by one of two methods: mitosis or meiosis. In mitosis the chromosomes duplicate themselves to give two identical cells (skin grows like this). In meiosis, the chromosomes split into two gametes, each containing half the chromosomes. Gametes from different cells can combine to give a new cell (this is the basis of sexual reproduction).

A simple cell with the nucleus (**1**) containing chromosomes (**2**)

## DNA

**1** DNA groups are assembled in spiral form (**a**). Each strand (**b**, **c**) of the spiral ribbon is linked to its partner with cross-strands (**d**) by 'bases' called cytosine (**C**), thymine (**T**), guanine (**G**) and adenine (**A**). The order of these bases gives the genetic code.

**2** When chromosomes begin to duplicate, the DNA ladder unzips.

**3** Each side gains a new matching side made from chemicals within the cell.

**4** Two independent DNA spirals are now formed.

**DNA**

# GENES AND GENETICS

### Sex determination

A baby's sex depends on the chromosomes it receives from each parent. Each of its mother's cells includes a pair of X-shaped sex chromosomes. Each of the father's cells includes a pair made of an X and a Y-shaped sex chromosome. The baby inherits one sex chromosome from each parent. If it inherits two Xs it will be a girl. If it inherits an X and a Y it will be a boy. Here are various ways in which (**a**) the mother and (**b**) the father can pass on sex cells to create (**c**) a female or (**d**) a male.

**Inherited traits**

A child inherits certain character traits from its parents as well as similarities in physical appearance, such as the same colour eyes or hair. These are coded in genes, which are units carried on chromosomes. Each type of gene occurs in a pair and we inherit one gene from each parent in each pair. In the inherited pair of genes, the dominant gene will overpower the weaker, or recessive, gene. The diagram below shows the gene for brown eyes dominating the gene for blue eyes in four out of five cases.

**a** Brown eye gene
**b** Blue eye gene

■ Brown eyes
□ Blue eyes

# LIFE FORMS

## The five kingdoms

All living things are divided, or classified, into five major groups called kingdoms. The plant and the animal kingdoms are the two best-known ones. Fungi are another kingdom. They are plant-like but they do not make their own food like plants. Protists and monera make up two more kingdoms. Most protists are one-celled organisms such as amoebae. However, a few exceptions, such as seaweeds, are multicellular. Monera are bacteria and blue-green algae.

## Numbers of species

Not all the species of living things have yet been identified, but of those that are known it is estimated that there are more than 1.2 million species of animal, about 300 000 species of plant and more than 100 000 species of other living things.

**Classification systems**

All living organisms are classified, or divided into groups of organisms. The system is based on a series of levels with the five kingdoms at the top and more than a million species at the bottom. Each kingdom is divided and subdivided so that organisms with similar features are classified together at each level. The dogrose *Rosa canina,* for example, is a species in the *Rosa* genus. It is part of the Rosaceae family, which belongs to the Rosales order. This order is in the Dicotyledon class, which is in turn a member of the division known as Angiospermophyta, one of the 10 main divisions in the plant kingdom (see over).

Plant kingdom

Division:
Angiospermophyta

Class:
Dicotyledon

Order:
Rosales

Family:
Rosaceae

Genus:
*Rosa*

Species:
*Rosa canina*

# PLANT KINGDOM

Apart from the traditional groupings (shown opposite), botanists also divide plants into groups determined by plant structure. The simplest group in this system consists of the algae and one-celled organisms (**1**). This is now recognized as the monera kingdom. These plants do not have any phloem or xylem which, in other plants, provide a network to carry water or food from one part of the plant to another.

The other major group (**2**), the plant kingdom, includes plants that have phloem and xylem to carry water, mineral salts and food between the roots, stem and leaves. This group is called the tracheophytes.

Tracheophytes are further divided into two groups: plants such as clubmosses, ferns and horsetails (**3**) which do not flower and do not form seeds, and plants that bear seeds (**4**).

There are two sorts of seed-bearing plants. Conifers and cycads are one. They belong to the gymnosperm family (**5**) which have seeds and cones. The others are angiosperms (**6**), flowering plants and trees that bear seeds protected in an ovary.

**Plant Classification**
**Traditional groupings of the plant kingdom**

Plant kingdom

- Bryophytes — Liverworts
- Psilophyta — Mosses
- Clubmosses — Hornworts
- Horsetails
- Ferns
- Cycads
- Ginkgoes
- Ephedra
- Conifers
- Angiosperms / Flowering plants — Dicots / Monocots

◇ Plant kingdom
○ Division
□ Class

# PLANT CHARACTERISTICS

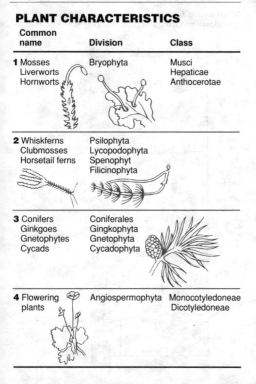

| Common name | Division | Class |
|---|---|---|
| **1** Mosses<br>Liverworts<br>Hornworts | Bryophyta | Musci<br>Hepaticae<br>Anthocerotae |
| **2** Whiskferns<br>Clubmosses<br>Horsetail ferns | Psilophyta<br>Lycopodophyta<br>Spenophyt<br>Filicinophyta | |
| **3** Conifers<br>Ginkgoes<br>Gnetophytes<br>Cycads | Coniferales<br>Gingkophyta<br>Gnetophyta<br>Cycadophyta | |
| **4** Flowering plants | Angiospermophyta | Monocotyledoneae<br>Dicotyledoneae |

| Vascular tissue | Structure | Habitat |
| --- | --- | --- |
| Absent | Multicellular; no true roots, stems or leaves | Moist areas on land |
| Present | Multicellular; true roots, stems and leaves | Moist areas on land |
| Present | Multicellular; true roots, stems and leaves | Land |
| Present | Multicellular; true roots, stems and leaves | Land |

# STRUCTURE AND FUNCTION

**Breathing and feeding**

Plants as well as animals breathe. Taking in oxygen from the air is called respiration. It releases energy from sugars that a plant stores and carbon dioxide is given out. Plants also absorb carbon dioxide which, together with sunlight, helps them to make food, by a process known as photosynthesis.

## A flowering plant

**1** The roots keep the plant firmly in the soil.

**2** The root hairs absorb water and minerals from the soil which the plant needs for growth and to stay healthy.

**3** The stem carries the water and minerals to the leaves. Food made in the leaves is carried to the rest of the plant. The stem supports the leaves and flowers. It holds them in the air and light.

**4** The leaves use sunlight to convert water and carbon dioxide into food.

**5** The flowers are the plant's reproductive structure.

### Parts of a leaf

1 Dicotyledon leaf
2 Petiole, or leaf stalk
3 Midrib
4 Vein
5 Leaf blade margin

### Inside a leaf

A cross section of a leaf magnified many times would show the following parts:

1 The epidermis.

2 A leaf cell.

3 A chloroplast, containing chlorophyll, a green pigment that helps plants use light energy to make food from water, minerals and carbon dioxide and giving out oxygen as waste.

4 A stoma is a pore in the leaf. Stomata let out water vapour and waste oxygen. They let in carbon dioxide and oxygen.

5 A vein carrying water and minerals in and food out of the leaf.

# PLANT REPRODUCTION
## Asexual reproduction

In spring the buds of plants called herbaceous perennials (which do not die in winter, but lie dormant until spring) sprout and produce new shoots. The shoots formed by buds on the side of the plant often grow roots. By the end of the summer these have become independent of the parent plant. In this way, new plants are produced from buds without pollination or fertilization being necessary. This is a form of asexual reproduction. Flowering plants can reproduce themselves in a number of ways, including runners and rhizomes.

### Runners
Strawberry plants send out long slender stems called runners. The tip of each runner grows roots and shoots. The runner eventually withers and the new plant becomes independent of the parent.

### Rhizomes
Rhizomes are swollen stems of iris and some grasses which grow horizontally under the ground. Side buds produce roots and continue the rhizome's growth each year. A bud at the rhizome's tip grows upwards, producing stems and flowers.

## Sexual reproduction

A flower is a plant's reproductive structure. Flowers have stamens (**1**), or male reproductive organs. These have (**a**) anthers and (**b**) filaments, which produce pollen grains containing male sex cells. The pistil (**2**) is the female reproductive organ consisting of the ovary (**c**), the style (**d**) and the stigma (**e**). Here, pollen from another flower is received and pollination takes place. The male sex cells join the female one and the flower begins to produce seeds. Some flowers are self-pollinating.

## Seed dispersal

When flowering is over and the seeds are mature, the ovary or the individual seeds fall from the plant and scatter. The wind spreads poppy seeds (**1**) by shaking the dry ovary which has slits. It also spreads clematis seeds (**2**) which have feathers, dandelion seeds with parachutes (**3**) and winged sycamore seeds (**4**). Some seeds are carried by birds as they drop berries (**5**) in flight or eat and excrete the seeds. Animals also do this and sometimes seeds are carried in their fur, attached by the seeds' hooks or barbs (**6**).

# FEATURES OF FRUITS AND FLOWERS
## Fruits

A fruit is a flowering plant's ovary, holding seeds. The wall of a mature fruit has three layers collectively called the pericarp. There is an outer layer called the exocarp, a mesocarp, the middle layer, and an inner layer, or endocarp.

a seed

1. A tomato is a berry, a simple fruit with a fleshy pericarp.
2. Pomes are fleshy fruits with paperlike cores, like apples.
3. Drupes such as plums are fleshy with a thin skin and a stone or pip.
4. Aggregate fruits are those like raspberries.
5. Simple fruits with a dry pericarp include pea pods.
6. Hazelnuts are single-seeded fruits with a hard pericarp.

## Flower forms

Flowers can be grouped together on stems in a variety of ways:

1 Spike (racemose spike)
2 Raceme (simple raceme)
3 Panicle
4 Cyme
5 Spadix (fleshy spike)
6 Umbel (simple umbel)
7 Capitulum
8 Composite head (discoid flower head)
9 Hollow flower head
10 Bostryx (helicoid cyme)
11 Cincinnus(scorploid cyme, curled cyme)

# SIMPLE LIFE FORMS

## Monera

Monera are primitive one-celled organisms. They are
bacteria (**1**) and blue-green algae (**2**). Some make their own
food by photosynthesis, like plants, in chloroplasts. Others
take in particles from around them. Monera do not have a
nucleus or organelles, structures found in other cells.

## Protists

Protists form another kingdom of one-celled organisms such
as amoeba (**3**), euglena (**4**), paramecium (**5**) and diatoms
(**6**).They have a well-defined nucleus and organelles.
Paramecium have hair-like threads which enable them to
move. Euglenas make food using sunlight  and they move by
beating  a long whip-like part backwards and forwards.
Amoebae eat by wrapping themselves around food and then
absorbing it through the outer cell membrane.

### Fungi

Fungi are organisms which lack chlorophyll. Fungi cannot make their own food, like most other plants, so they absorb food from their surroundings. Some of the most common fungi are moulds (**7**), mushrooms (**8**) and mildews. Yeasts (**9**) are also called fungi. They are too small to be seen without a microscope. Bread moulds are fungi which can be seen. Like many fungi they form thread-like cells called hyphae which grow beneath the surface of the material on which the fungi are feeding. Most fungi produce spores which are simpler than the seeds of a plant but which enable fungi to reproduce. Lichens (**10**) are fungi living in a mutual relationship with algae.

# THE ANIMAL KINGDOM

There are more than one million different kinds of animal in the animal kingdom. The animal kingdom is divided into smaller groups of animals with similar features, just as plants are classified (see page 393). If we look at the lion, *Panthera leo*, it is one of several species in the genus *Panthera*. This genus is one of several in the family Felidae.

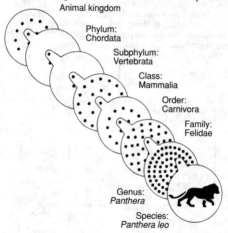

Animal kingdom

Phylum: Chordata

Subphylum: Vertebrata

Class: Mammalia

Order: Carnivora

Family: Felidae

Genus: *Panthera*

Species: *Panthera leo*

This family is in the order Carnivora, and carnivores belong to the class Mammalia. This class belongs with several others in the subphylum Vertebrata, of the phylum Chordata. This phylum is one of the many phyla in the animal kingdom. A phylum is equivalent to a plant division.

# ANIMAL CLASSIFICATION

| | |
|---|---|
| **1** | Porifera (sponges) |
| **2** | Coelenterata (coelenterates) |
| **3** | Platyhelminthes (flatworms) |
| **4** | Nematoda (roundworms) |
| **5** | Annelida (true worms) |
| **6** | Mollusca (molluscs) |
| **7** | Arthropoda (arthropods) |
| **7a** | Chilopods (centipedes) |
| **7b** | Diplopods (millepedes) |
| **7c** | Crustacea (crustaceans) |
| **7d** | Insecta (insects) |
| **7e** | Arachnida (spiders) |
| **8** | Echinodermata (echinoderms) |
| **9** | Chordata (chordates) |
| **9a** | Cephalochordate (amphioxus) |
| **9b** | Vertebra (vertebrates) |
| **9c** | Urochordata (sea squirts) |
| **9bi** | Agnatha (jawless fish) |
| **9bii** | Chondrichthyes (cartilaginous fish) |
| **9biii** | Osteichthyes (bony fish) |
| **9biv** | Amphibia (amphibians) |
| **9bv** | Reptilia (reptiles) |
| **9bvi** | Aves (birds) |
| **9bvii** | Mammalia (mammals) |

# INVERTEBRATE CHARACTERISTICS

| Class<br>Common name | | Locomotion | Number of<br>body openings |
|---|---|---|---|
| **Porifera**<br>Sponges |  | None | One |
| **Coelenterata**<br>Coelenterates | | Mostly sessile<br>free floating | One |
| **Platyhelminthes**<br>Flatworms | | Muscles;<br>cilia | One |
| **Nematoda**<br>Roundworms | | Muscles | Two |
| **Annelida**<br>Segmented worms | | Muscles | Two |
| **Mollusca**<br>Molluscs | | Muscles | Two |

Invertebrates are animals with no backbones.

| Nervous system | Digestive system | Circulatory system |
| --- | --- | --- |
| None | None | None |
| | | |
| Present | Present | None |
| | | |
| Present | Present | None |
| | | |
| Present | Present | None |
| | | |
| Present | Present | None |
| | | |
| Present | Present | Present |

# ARTHROPOD CHARACTERISTICS

| Class and common names | External appearance | Body sections |
| --- | --- | --- |
| **1 Chilopoda** Centipedes |  | Head and body segments |
| **2 Diplopoda** Millepedes |  | Head and body segments |
| **3 Crustacea** Crabs, lobsters, water fleas |  | Cephalothorax and abdomen |
| **4 Insecta** Grasshoppers, butterflies, fleas | | Head, thorax and abdomen |
| **5 Arachnida** Scorpions, ticks, spiders | | Cephalothorax and abdomen |

| Antennae | Mouth parts | Number of walking legs | Gas exchange |
|---|---|---|---|
| 1 pair | Mandibles | 1 pair per segment | Tracheae |
| 1 pair | Mandibles | 2 pairs per segment | Tracheae |
| 2 pairs | Mandibles | 5 pairs in most forms | Gills |
| 1 pair | Mandibles | 3 pairs | Tracheae |
| None | First pair of legs adapted to hold prey | 4 pairs | Tracheae, lungs |

# **VERTEBRATE CHARACTERISTICS**

| Class | Examples | External | Integument appearance |
|-------|----------|----------|----------------------|
| **1** Agnatha | Jawless fish (lampreys, hagfish) | | Slimy skin |
| **2** Chondr-ichthyes | Cartilaginous fish (sharks, rays) | | Scales |
| **3** Osteich-thyes | Bony fish (cod, perch) | | Scales and slimy skin |
| **4** Amphibia | Amphibians (frogs, salamanders) | | Slimy skin most forms |
| **5** Reptilia | Reptiles (lizards, crocodiles, turtles) | | Dry, scaly |
| **6** Aves | Birds | | Feathers, scales on legs |
| **7** Mammalia | Mammals | | Hair |

| Body temperature | Limb structure | Gas exchange | Fertilization |
|---|---|---|---|
| Cold-blooded | No paired limbs | Gills | External |
| Cold-blooded | 2 pairs of fins | Gills | Internal |
| Cold-blooded | 2 pairs of fins | Gills | External |
| Cold-blooded | 2 pairs of legs, no claws | Gills; lungs | External |
| Cold-blooded | 2 pairs of legs, claws | Lungs | Internal |
| Warm-blooded | 1 pair of wings, 1 pair of legs, claws | Lungs | Internal |
| Warm-blooded | 2 pairs of legs, claws in most forms | Lungs | Internal |

# FISH

Fish are divided into two main groups – jawless and jawed fish. The jawed fish are divided into bony or cartilaginous fish according to the skeleton.

## Jawless fish

Jawless fish belong to the class Agnatha. They include lamprey and hagfish and they are the most primitive fish and vertebrates. They lack jaws, paired fins, air bladder and scales. Lampreys have a sucker-like mouth and a toothed tongue. Hagfish have a slit mouth with sharp teeth. They both have a skeleton of cartilage.

## Cartilaginous fish

This is the class Chondrichthyes, which consists of fish with a skeleton of tough gristly cartilage instead of bone. Sharks, rays and chimaeras belong to this class. All the fish have jaws and have tiny tooth-like scales and paired fins, but no swim bladder. They live mainly in saltwater.

## Bony fish

The class Osteichthyes includes all fish with bony skeletons. The fish all have scales or bony plates and swim bladders. Bony fish divide into two groups. Modern bony fish (ray-finned) such as tuna, cod, catfish and herring have skeletons mainly of bone. They form the larger group. Primitive bony fish include coelacanth and lungfish which have skeletons of bone and cartilage. They are related to fish that lived millions of years ago.

## Classification of fish

| | | |
|---|---|---|
| A | Jawless | |
| B | With jaws | |
| B1 | Cartilaginous | |
| B2 | Bony | |
| B1a | Sharks | |
| B1b | Chimaera | |

| | | |
|---|---|---|
| B2a | Primitive fish | |
| B2b | Ray-finned | |
| | 1 | Coelacanths |
| | 2 | Lungfish |
| | 3 | Sturgeon |
| | 4 | Perch |

# CLASSIFICATION OF FISH

# AMPHIBIANS

Amphibians include frogs, newts and toads. They are cold-blooded vertebrates which are mainly scaleless and spend most of their time on land. Most lay eggs in water.

## Caecilians

Caecilians are limbless, worm-like amphibians. They have rings around their bodies and some have scales. Caecilians burrow into the forest floor and river beds of tropical countries. The largest Caecilians are 1.5 m long.

## Tailed amphibians

Tailed amphibians are also called Caudata. They include salamanders and newts. They have four legs and a long body and tail. Most tailed amphibians start life as swimming larvae with feathery gills. As they grow older, they lose their gills and leave the water, with the exception of the axolotl and the olm, which keep their gills and remain in water.

## Frogs and toads

Frogs and toads are tailless amphibians and form the order Anura. They have long hind legs and the majority are strong swimmers. Most frogs and toads start as swimming limbless tadpoles with feathery gills. As they grow they develop limbs and lose their gills.

---

### Amphibian characteristics
- Metamorphosis from larvae to adult in most amphibians
- Skeleton mostly bone
- Heart has three chambers
- Mouth connects with two nostrils
- Four limbs
- Lungs, gills or skin used for breathing
- Skin moist and scaleless
- Fertilization inside or outside the body

---

## Frogs

1 Eardrum usually visible
2 Skin smooth and damp – shed regularly. Absorbs oxygen from both air and water
3 Pulls eyes into head to close
4 Some secrete poison through skin to deter or ... predators
5 Tailless
6 Hind legs usually long – leaps rather than walks or hops
7 Slim-waisted body
8 Hind feet usually webbed

## Toads

1 Skin may cover the eardrum
2 Skin dryish, warty and shed regularly. Absorbs water and oxygen
3 Pulls eyes into head to close
4 Parotid glands secrete poison as defence against predators
5 Tailless
6 Hind legs short – hops, walks or runs
7 Body short and squat
8 Hind feet usually webbed

## Salamanders and newts

1 No ears
2 Skin smooth and warty – shed regularly. Absorbs water and oxygen
3 Eyelids do not move
4 Skin secretes poison
5 Long, often flattened tail
6 Limbs short; lost limbs regrow. Females have no rear limbs
7 Long, often thin body
8 Has toes without claws

# REPTILES

Reptiles are a class of land animals with dry-skinned, scaly bodies. They are cold-blooded vertebrates and include lizards, crocodiles and tortoises.

## Turtles and tortoises

This order is called Chelonia. Turtles and tortoises are four-legged toothless reptiles which have a protective shell. Tortoises are land-dwelling and turtles live either in salt or fresh water. Most tortoises eat plants but some turtles are carnivores. The leatherback turtle is the largest animal in this group. It is about 2.5 m long.

## Lizards and snakes

This order is called Squamata. The lizards usually have four legs but snakes have none. They have jaws which allow them to swallow large prey whole. The largest snake is the python, which can be 10 m long. The Komodo dragon is the largest lizard (3 m long and weighing 140 kg).

**Crocodiles and alligators**

Crocodiles and alligators belong to the order Crocodilia.
They have long tails, short legs and long jaws with sharp
teeth giving them an elongated head. The largest reptile and
the largest of the crocodilians is the estuarine crocodile
which may be more than 7 m long.

**Tuatara**

Tuatara are lizard-like creatures with a beaked upper jaw and
a scaly crest along the back. They are the sole survivors of
the Sphenodontida order of reptiles. They only
live on islands off New Zealand. Tuatara are about 60 cm
long, although the females are smaller.

---

**Reptile characteristics**
- Skin dry and leathery
- Skeleton mostly bone
- Heart has four chambers
- Lungs for breathing
- Eggs are fertilized inside the body
- Eggs covered with waterproof shell
- Embryo protected by four membranes
- No metamorphosis

# BIRDS

Birds make up the Aves class, one of the eight classes of vertebrates. Birds are the only animals with feathers. All birds hatch from eggs and have wings. Most birds can fly.

**Parts of a bird**

1 Bill
2 Throat
3 Ear coverts
4 Claws
5 Tarsus
6 Secondary feathers
7 Primary feathers
8 Tail coverts
9 Tail feathers
10 Rump
11 Scapular feathers
12 Alula
13 Nape
14 Crown

**Feather types**

a Coverts – roost feathers
b Primary or flight feathers
c Down feathers
d Filoplumes

**Bird orders**
1 Struthioniformes (ostriches)
2 Rheiformes (rheas)
3 Casuariiformes (cassowaries)
4 Apterygiformes (kiwis)
5 Gaviiformes (divers)
6 Podicipediformes (grebes)
7 Sphenisciformes (penguins)
8 Procellariiformes (albatross, petrels)
9 Pelecaniformes (cormorants, pelicans, gannets)

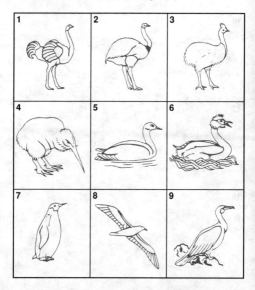

**10** Ciconiiformes (storks, herons)
**11** Anseriformes (ducks)
**12** Falconiformes (hawks, eagles, vultures)
**13** Galliformes (game birds)
**14** Gruiformes (rails, cranes)
**15** Charadriiformes (gulls, waders, terns, plovers)
**16** Pteroclidiformes (sand grouse)
**17** Columbiformes (pigeons)
**18** Psittaciformes (parrots, cockatoos)

**19** Cuculiformes (cuckoos)
**20** Strigiformes (owls)
**21** Caprimulgiformes (nightjars)
**22** Apodiformes (swifts, hummingbirds)
**23** Coliiformes (mousebirds)
**24** Trogoniformes (trogons)
**25** Coraciiformes (kingfishers, hornbills, hoopoes, toucans)
**26** Piciformes (woodpeckers)
**27** Passeriformes (thrushes, sparrows, perching birds; 60% of all birds are in this order)

# MAMMALS

The class Mammalia is one of the eight classes of vertebrates. All mammals are warm-blooded, they have hair and the mothers suckle the young.

### Monotremes

Monotremes are primitive animals. They lay eggs and have a horny beak. Only the young have teeth. This order consists of the duck-billed platypus from Australia and echnidas from Australia and New Guinea.

### Marsupials

Marsupials give birth to poorly developed young which continue to grow attached to the mother's nipples in a pouch. The order includes the Australian bandicoots, koalas, kangaroos and wombats, and the American opossums.

### Placental mammals

Placental mammals, or Eutheria, are mammals whose young develop in the mother's body nourished by an organ called the placenta. The order includes primates, rodents and grazing animals. The largest mammal is the blue whale.

**Mammal groups**

Most mammals eat plants but some eat meat or insects.

### Herbivores
Herbivores are the largest group of mammals. Their teeth and other parts are adapted to eat only plants.

### Carnivores
Carnivores are mammals that eat the flesh of other animals. Many are fast-moving animals which catch and hold their prey. They have claws and large canine teeth which rip flesh, eating chunks whole.

### Omnivores
Omnivores eat both plants and meat.

### Insectivores
Insectivores are small mammals that eat insects. Their teeth are adapted to crush the hard outer coating of insects to extract the soft body and juices. Insectivores mainly have pointed snouts.

### Frugivores
Frugivores only eat fruit from trees and their bodies are adapted to life in the treetops.

# MAMMAL CLASSIFICATION

**Subclass**
1 Prototheria (monotremes)
2 Theria

**Infraclass**
3 Metatheria (marsupials)
4 Eutheria (placentals)

**Eutherian orders**
a Chiroptera (bats)
b Edentata (sloths, armadillos, anteaters)
c Insectivora (moles, shrews)
d Pholidota (pangolins)

**e** Primates (monkeys, apes)
**f** Rodentia (rats, mice)
**g** Lagomorpha (rabbits, hares)
**h** Cetacea (dolphins, whales)
**i** Carnivora (cats, wolves)
**j** Tubulidentata (aardvarks)
**k** Hyracoidea (hyrax)

**l** Proboscidea (elephants)
**m** Sirenia (sea cows)
**n** Perissodactyla (tapirs, horses, rhinoceroses)
**o** Artiodactyla (pigs, cattle, camels)
**p** Dermoptera (flying lemurs)

# ANIMAL LIFE SPANS

The natural life span of each species varies. Humans (**M**) live an average 70 to 80 years, while mice (**B**) seldom live more than three years.

**A** Mayfly (adult stage) 1 day
**B** Mouse 2–3 years
**C** Trout 5–10 years
**D** Sheep 10–15 years
**E** Cat 13–17 years
**F** Rattlesnake 18 years
**G** Lion 25 years
**H** Horse 30 years
**I** Albatross 33 years
**J** Hippopotamus 40 years
**K** Ostrich 50 years
**L** African elephant 60 years
**M** Human 70–80 years (oldest 120 years)
**N** Tortoise 80+ year (oldest 152+ years)

# ANIMAL HEIGHTS AND DEPTHS

Animals and plants survive in conditions most favourable to their needs. Some species can live at high altitudes (**1**), while others thrive thousands of metres below sea level (**2**).

**1 Highest altitudes at which animals have been observed**

**a** Bird: Roppell's vulture 11 280 m

**b** Amphibian: toad 8000 m

**c** Arthropod: spider 6700 m

**d** Flowering plant: 6400 m

**e** Mammal: yak 6100 m

**f** Reptile: lizard 5500 m

**2 Lowest levels**

**g** Reptile: marine iguana 10 m

**h** Bird: emperor penguin 265 m

**i** Plant-like organism: blue-green algae 400 m

**j** Mammal: sperm whale 2250 m

**k** Arthropod: shrimp 10 900 m

**l** Fish: flatfish 10 900 m

1=1000 m

# ECOLOGY

The environment in which a particular animal or plant exists is called its habitat. In an untouched habitat, each organism is adapted to cope with the characteristics of the environment and its neighbours (either predators or prey). Within each habitat, organisms are linked to each other in various ways. Ecology is the study of these relationships.

## Food web

A food web consists of interlinking food chains in a single habitat, in this case a wood. Arrows show the flow of food energy.

1 Owl
2 Mouse
3 Acorns
4 Fox
5 Rabbit
6 Grass
7 Bacteria, decomposing organic matter, then used by plants

### Food chain

A food chain consists of consumers and consumed. In this food chain, arrows show the flow of food energy along a chain consisting mainly of marine plants and animals.

1 Algae (food producers)
2 Animal plankton (primary consumers)
3 Herring (secondary consumers)
4 Cod (tertiary consumers)
5 People (quaternary consumers)

### Food pyramid

A food pyramid consists of a broad base of food-producing plants supporting successively higher stages of consumers. Each stage provides food for a smaller weight of animals than from the stage above. The pyramid's apex consists of the top predator. The following example is of a food pyramid in 2.5 sq km of East African grassland, but does not take into account small mammals.

1 6.6 million kg of plants
2 55 000 kg of large consumers (e.g. wildebeest, antelope)
3 187 kg of secondary consumers (e.g. lions, hyena, wild dog)

# THE MAJOR BIOMES

Most animals live in specific areas of the world because they have precise ecological requirements. The Earth can be divided into regions, or biomes, which are determined by the main types of vegetation growing there.

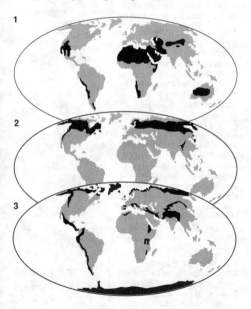

**1 Deserts** Deserts are dry areas of the world which receive very little rainfall and where dry winds blow across the land. Deserts can be hot or cold. They are found in North and South America, Africa, Asia and Australia. Some deserts have vast areas of sand whilst others are covered in bare rocks. Plants may grow there. Animals that live in deserts include lizards, scorpions, rattlesnakes, roadrunner birds and camels.

**2 Coniferous forest** Cold snowy forests cover vast tracts of land in northern areas near the Arctic. Here summers are cool and short and the winters are severe. Evergreen conifers such as spruces, pines, firs, and larches grow here. Ermine, beavers, grizzly bears and wolves live in the coniferous forests. In Russia, Siberian tigers and brown bears also live in the forests.

**3 Arctic, tundra and mountain** The tundra lies between the coniferous forests and the Arctic. It is a flat and featureless plain where virtually the only vegetation is mosses and lichen. The polar regions are covered with snow and ice. Few animals and plants live here. Polar-type climates are also found at high altitudes. The Andes and the Himalayan mountains have a polar climate above a certain level. Animals living in these cold areas are musk oxen, penguins, polar bears, whales, seals, and yaks and llamas in the mountains.

# MAJOR BIOMES (continued)

4

5

6

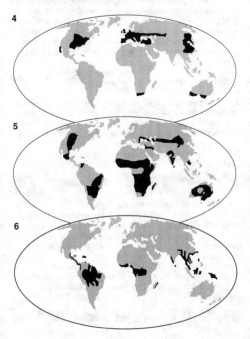

**4 Deciduous forest** Deciduous forests are found in the temperate parts of the world where the temperatures are cool to warm, such as Europe, eastern North America and eastern Asia. These areas all receive adequate rainfall. Vegetation includes evergreen trees, fruit trees, hardwoods, eucalyptus, maple, oak and birch. Animals of the deciduous forests are deer, bears, owls and bats.

**5 Grasslands** There are grasslands throughout the world, in North and South America, Africa and Australia. These areas are mainly flat, with trees and bushes providing food and shelter for the animals. The animals include a wide variety of herbivores. Some grasslands have many predators and carrion-eating animals.
Giraffes, lions, antelopes, bison, coyote and rabbits are animals of the grasslands.

**6 Tropical rainforest** Tropical rainforests are found around the tropics. They are the richest biomes with the greatest variety of plants and animals. The rainforests are hot humid places which receive plenty of sunshine. Plants grow quickly and densely. Few large animals live in the rainforests, but there are many smaller ones such as jaguars, tapirs, monkeys, birds and insects.

## BODY SYSTEMS

An organ is a group of tissues working together to carry out a major activity in the body, for example the heart or the liver. Groups of organs form organ systems. Some organs play a part in more than one system. Here we show 10 major systems. Later pages describe their parts in detail.

**1 Skeletal system** Bones and joints, the scaffolding or framework of the body.
**2 Muscular system** Muscles, elastic fibres that move limbs and drive blood around the body.

**3 Skin, nails and hair** The skin, a barrier that protects the body and helps control its temperature.

**4 Nervous system** Brain, spinal cord and nerves, the body's control centre and communication system, including the five senses.

**5 Respiratory system** The breathing organs, nose, windpipe, lungs, etc., which take in oxygen and remove carbon dioxide waste.

**6 Circulatory system** Blood vessels, heart and lymphatic system, supplying cells, removing waste, and helping fight disease.

**7 Digestive system** Mouth, alimentary canal and glands, including the liver, that break down food for use inside the body.

**8 Urinary system** Kidneys, bladder and tubes that remove body waste as urine.

**9 Endocrine system** Glands producing hormones that regulate a number of body functions.

**10a Female reproductive system** Organs for producing eggs and babies.

**10b Male reproductive system** Organs for producing and releasing sperm.

# SKELETAL SYSTEM

## Bone and cartilage

Bone is the hard, strong substance that forms the skeleton.
Bones develop from soft connective tissue which is replaced
by cartilage, the white springy substance also known as
gristle, which becomes bone.

## Bone structure

Bone is mainly calcium and phosphorus but one-third is
living matter. This is chiefly the fibrous protein collagen.
Bone has two types of tissue. In a long bone, hard dense
compact tissue (**1**) forms the outside. A light, spongy
honeycomb, or cancellous tissue (**2**) is in each bulging end.
Marrow (**3**) is soft tissue contained in a cavity inside bones.
Red marrow is involved with the manufacture of blood cells.
Yellow marrow fills adult bones and contains fat cells.

## How bone is made

Bones are not dry, dead material; one-third of them is living
tissue with a constant turnover of cells carrying out the jobs
of maintenance and repair. Bones are serviced by blood
vessels, nerves and lymph vessels (transporting body fluids)
which run through a labyrinth of tiny canals. Special cells
(osteoblasts) carry out repair work on bones, while others
(osteoclasts) dissolve and break down damaged bones so that
they can be repaired.

## What bone does

Bone forms an inner framework for the body. It stores
calcium, phosphorus, fat and other substances. Bone also
manufactures blood cells, and helps remove some harmful
substances from blood.

### Cartilage structure

Cartilage is formed of the hard protein collagen and the elastic protein elastin.

### What cartilage does

Cartilage forms the skeleton in unborn babies. In an adult, cartilage gives shape to the nose and outer ears, keeps large airways open, links ribs and buffers joints.

### Joints

Joints are where two or more bones meet. A joint can be fixed or movable. Fixed joints help to protect abutting bones from damage caused by blows. Movable joints let bones move smoothly against one another. Many joints are held in place by bands of flexible tissue called ligaments, and buffered by smooth cartilage and fluid.

### Types of joint

Joints vary greatly in complexity and range of movement, from a simple junction between two bones, as between skull bones, to the intricacy of, for example, the elbow.

The four principal types are:
1. Hinge joint (e.g. elbow)
2. Slicing joint (e.g. wrist)
3. Saddle joint (e.g. finger)
4. Ball and socket joint (e.g. hip)

**Principal bones**

Identified are the most important human bones. Common names are also given.

1. Cranium (skull)
2. Mandible (jawbone)
3. Clavicle (collarbone)
4. Scapula (shoulder blade)
5. Sternum (breastbone)
6. Ribs
7. Humerus
8. Vertebrae (spine or backbone)
9. Radius
10. Ulna
11. Carpals (wrist bones)
12. Metacarpals
13. Phalanges (finger and toe bones)
14. Pelvis or pelvic girdle
15. Femur (thighbone)
16. Patella (kneecap)
17. Tibia (shinbone)
18. Fibula
19. Tarsals
20. Metatarsals

### Teeth

Teeth are hard bone-like projections set in sockets in the jaws. Teeth bite and chew food into smaller pieces as a first stage in food digestion.

### Structure

Each tooth has a visible crown (**1**) rising from one or more roots (**2**) hidden by the gums and embedded in the jaw. The crown has a very hard, smooth, shiny outer layer of enamel (**3**). The root is covered by bone-hard cementum (**4**). Inside the tooth, hard yellow dentine (**5**) surrounds soft pulp (**6**) that contains nerves and blood vessels.

**Molar**　　　　　**Incisor**

### Types of teeth

Adults have four types of teeth.

**Incisors** Sharp, chisel-like cutting teeth, with one root.

**Canines** Pointed biting teeth, with one root.

**Premolars** Square grinding and crushing teeth, with two small projections called cusps, and one or two roots.

**Molars** Like premolars but larger, with up to five cusps and three roots.

### Primary teeth

These teeth are also called deciduous or milk teeth. By about the age of two most children have gained 20 teeth (10 upper, 10 lower): 8 incisors, 4 canines and 8 molars. Appearing in stages, usually between the age of 6 and 30 months, these teeth are usually lost from age 7–12 years to be replaced by permanent teeth.

### Permanent teeth

An adult has 32 permanent or adult teeth (16 upper, 16 lower): 8 incisors, 4 canines, 8 premolars and 12 molars.

**Comparison of upper teeth in a child and an adult**

**Child**
1 Incisors
2 Canines
3 Molars

**Adult**
1 Incisors
2 Canines
3 Premolars
4 Molars

# MUSCLES

Muscles are tough elastic tissues made of cells called muscle fibres. The body's more than 600 muscles account for 40 per cent of its weight. Muscles work limbs, lungs and other parts of the body, and largely give it bulk and shape. They come in three main types. Skeletal muscles hold the bones of the skeleton together, they give the body shape and make it move. They make up a large part of the arms, legs, abdomen, chest and face. Smooth muscles are found in various organs. They control body processes such as digestion and are found in the stomach wall, intestines, blood vessels and bladder. Cardiac muscle is found in the heart.

## How muscles work

Muscles pull but cannot push. This means to and fro movements need muscles that work in pairs with opposite effects. Bending and straightening the arm involves biceps (**a**) and triceps (**b**) muscles.

**1** When the biceps contract the triceps relax and the arm bends.

**2** When the triceps contract the biceps relax and the arm straightens.

**Principal muscles**
The right side of the body shown from the front (**1**) and the back (**2**).

a Sternomastoid
b Trapezius
c Deltoid
d Pectoralis major
e Biceps
f Triceps
g Latissimus dorsi
h External oblique
i Gluteus maximus
j Vastus externus
k Biceps femoris
l Rectus femoris
m Gastrocnemius
n Tibialis anterior

# SKIN, NAILS, HAIR

### Skin

Skin is the largest body organ. Peeled off, an average man's skin occupies about 1.9 sq m (20 sq ft).

### Structure

Skin has an outer layer, the epidermis, an inner layer, the dermis, and subcutaneous tissue.

**1 Epidermis** The base of the epidermis produces new cells and the pigment melanin. The amount of melanin determines skin and hair colour. The epidermis surface contains old dying cells of the horny protein keratin, which also forms hair and nails.

**2 Dermis** The dermis contains elastic fibres that give skin tensile strength. The dermis also has blood vessels (**a**), nerve endings (**b**), sweat glands (**c**), and hair follicles (**d**), bag-like structures from which grow hair shafts (**e**). Each hair has an erector muscle (**f**), and a sebaceous gland (**g**) releasing oily sebum.

**3 Subcutaneous tissue** This lies below the dermis. It is mainly connective tissue supporting organs and filling space around them, fat (**h**) and blood vessels.

### What skin does

Skin provides a flexible, waterproof barrier that keeps in body fluids and keeps out bacteria and harmful rays from the Sun. Nerve endings in the skin sense heat, cold, pain, and pressure. Sweat glands and tiny blood vessels in skin help to control body temperature. Subcutaneous tissue buffers the body's internal structures against blows.

### Nails

Nails form before birth. Certain epidermal cells in toes and fingers divide (**1**) and the upper cells accumulate hard keratin to produce a nail plate (**2**). This plate grows out of the nail groove (**3**) and over the skin, forming a fingernail or toenail.

### Hair

Hair forms before birth. First, part of the epidermis grows thicker (**a**). Then it invades the dermis (**b**) and forms a projection called a papilla (**c**). Its multiplying cells produce a hair (**d**) which accumulates the hard protein keratin as it grows up and away from its supply of nourishment. Other cells in the papilla form a keratinized root sheath (**e**) which produces a sebaceous gland (**f**).

# NERVOUS SYSTEM
**The brain**

**Structure**

**Structure**

The cross-section (left) shows the five layers that guard the brain and help to shape it. Scalp (**1**), with hair, fat and other tissue. Cranium (**2**), the part of the skull housing the brain. Its inner network of bony struts and dome-like shape give this structure its strength. Dura mater (**3**), the tough membrane embracing the brain. Arachnoid (**4**), the elastic 'skin' enclosing the so-called subarachnoid space. Pia mater (**5**), a thin 'skin' that clings closely to the brain's irregular surface.

**Functions**

In this illustration of the left side of a human brain, the numbered areas are involved with the following functions: (**1**) Movement of body parts, (**2**) Speech, (**3**) Receiving body sensations, (**4**) Hearing, (**5**) Sight.

### The senses

### Ears

Ears contain structures that enable us to hear and keep our balance. The human ear is sensitive to sounds ranging in loudness from 10 to 140 decibels (10 million million times as loud as 10), and ranging in pitch from 20 to 20,000 hertz (cycles per second). The distance between both ears helps the brain to locate the source of sound.

**How we hear** Sound waves that have been gathered by the ear pass through the auditory canal (**1**). The sound waves cause the eardrum (**2**) to vibrate. Vibrations from the eardrum are passed on and strengthened by the three ossicles: the stapes (stirrup, **3a**), the incus (anvil, **3b**) and the malleus (hammer, **3c**). The oval window (**4**) now vibrates. Vibrations pass into the fluid in the cochlea (**5**) where they are detected by special cells. Information is sent via the auditory nerve (**6**) to the brain.

### Eyes

Our eyes work by sensing the light that objects give off or reflect. Eyes look like two balls of jelly, each about 2.5 cm (1 in) across, set in sockets in the skull on each side of the nose. Nerves inside the eyes send signals to the brain, providing information on shape, size, colour and distance. The overlapping areas of vision of each eye help us to assess distance. Eyelids and eyelashes protect eyes from dust and injury.

### Parts of an eye

**1** Cornea: transparent tissue at front of eye
**2** Iris: coloured disc, controls size of pupil
**3** Pupil: hole through which light enters eye
**4** Lens: focuses light onto retina
**5** Retina: light-sensitive nerve cells
**6** Optic nerve: transmits information to brain

**How we see** Inside the eye, light rays from an object are bent by the cornea (**a**), lens (**b**), aqueous humour (**c**), which is fluid-like, and vitreous humour (**d**), which is jelly-like. These liquids help to bend the light so that the rays come to a focus on the retina (**e**) and produce an image. (The focused image is upside down, but the brain 'sees' it the right way up.)

1 Light rays from a distant object are bent relatively slightly inside the eye. Its lens (**b**) has gently curved sides.
2 Light rays from a nearby object must be bent more sharply to bring them into focus. The lens (**b**) grows shorter and fatter, with strongly curved sides.

**Sense of smell**

Our sense of smell is less keen than a dog's, yet some people can identify 10 000 odours, all based on combinations of just seven. We smell substances whose molecules are breathed into the roof of each nasal cavity (**1**) and dissolved on a patch of olfactory membrane (**2**) armed with 100 million smell receptor cells equipped with tiny sensitive 'hairs'. Scent molecules react with these to stimulate nerve impulses in the receptor cells. Olfactory nerves transmit these signals to olfactory bulbs (**3**) then via olfactory tracts (**4**) to the front part of the cerebrum (**5**) of the brain.

## Sense of touch

Touch is the sense that allows us to know we have made contact with an object. We learn shape, texture and hardness from the sense of touch. Through touch, feelings of warmth, cold, pain and pressure are experienced. Free nerve endings in the tissue give the sense of pain.

There are several types of touch organs in the skin. One kind is found near hairs, another in hairless areas of skin. Yet another type is found in deeper tissues. We feel something when an object comes in contact with the sense organs and presses them out of shape or touches a nearby hair. Nerves then carry impulses to the brain which let us know what has happened.

### Sense of taste

The organs of taste (the taste buds) are found on the tongue. Food is chewed and moistened with saliva, which carries tiny particles of the food to the taste buds. Taste buds in different areas of the tongue register the different flavours of food. At the same time, the olfactory system is stimulated, and the information from both tongue and nose combines to give the sensation the brain perceives as taste.

Areas of the tongue register different flavours: (**a**) bitter, (**b**) sour, (**c**) salty, (**d**) sweet.

**Skin sensitivity** Some parts of the body are more sensitive to touch than others. This is because the end organs for touch are not scattered evenly over the body. Instead they are arranged in clusters. Feeling is greatest where there is a large number of end organs. The tip of the tongue, the lips and fingertips are the areas most sensitive to touch. The area where sensitivity to touch is poorest is the back of the shoulders.

**Skin structure**

Specialized nerve endings in the skin send signals that the brain identifies as touch, pain, pressure, heat and cold.

1  Free nerve endings (pain)
2  Merkel's discs (touch)
3  Meissner's corpuscles (touch)
4  Beaded nerve net (pain)
5  Krause's end bulbs (cold)
6  Ruffini corpuscles (heat)
7  Pacinian corpuscles (pressure, stretching and vibration)
8  Hair organs (touch)
9  Hair
10  Epidermis
11  Dermis
12  Subcutaneous fat (fatty layer)
13  Nerve fibre

# RESPIRATORY SYSTEM

### How we breathe

Lungs are operated by the diaphragm (a muscular sheet below the lungs) and by muscles that move ribs up and out.

**Breathing in** Ribs move up and out (**1**) and the diaphragm moves down (**2**). This expands the chest cavity and draws air into the lungs.

**Breathing out** Ribs move down and in (**3**) and the diaphragm moves up (**4**). This contracts the chest cavity and forces air out of the lungs.

# CIRCULATORY SYSTEM
## Blood

Blood is a complex fluid that brings body tissues the food and oxygen they need to grow and live. It also helps remove waste products. Some substances in blood help fight disease.

## Substances in blood

The four main ingredients of blood are plasma, red blood cells, white blood cells and platelets.

## What they do

Plasma is a straw-coloured fluid that contains the other three constituents, along with foods, proteins and waste. White blood cells or leucocytes (**1**), are big, rounded blood cells with variously shaped nuclei; special kinds of leucocytes attack harmful bacteria, viruses and other foreign bodies. Red blood cells or erythrocytes (**2**), are the next largest cells in blood. They contain haemoglobin, the red substance that gives fresh blood its colour. Red blood cells take oxygen from the lungs to body tissues. They also play a part in absorbing carbon dioxide waste from body tissues and taking it to the lungs. Platelets (**3**) are tiny discs that seal tears or cuts in damaged blood vessels. They also produce substances that make blood clot. Clotting stops an injured person bleeding to death.

### Arteries and veins

These are the largest blood vessels. Arteries (**1**) are large tubes carrying high-pressure blood away from the heart. They have thick, muscular walls. Arteries branch into countless tiny tubes called arterioles. Veins (**2**) are large tubes that return low-pressure blood to the heart. Veins have thinner walls than arteries. Veins are supplied by tiny blood vessels called venules. The tiniest blood vessels are capillaries. Capillaries (**3**) link arterioles and venules.

The heart's pumping action forces blood out through arteries into arterioles and capillaries. Foods in the blood pass out through capillaries' walls to nourish surrounding tissues. Wastes pass in through the walls, and oxygen enters capillaries next to the lungs. From capillaries, blood flows back to the heart through the venules and veins. Muscles near veins keep this blood on the move, and valves in big veins stop blood sinking back down in the legs and feet.

---

**Blood facts and figures**

- An adult man is likely to have 5 litres (1 gallon) of blood.
- About 55 per cent of blood is plasma.
- About 90 per cent of plasma is water.
- A healthy adult has about 20 000 billion red blood cells.
- Blood contains over 500 times more red cells and 25 times more platelets than white cells.
- Red blood cells live about 17 weeks.
- The body destroys about 120 million old red blood cells every minute.

**Important arteries**
1 Carotid to head
2 Subclavian to arm
3 Aorta supplying all but lungs
4 Pulmonary to lungs
5 Brachial in arm
6 Hepatic to liver
7 Gastric to stomach
8 Renal to kidney
9 Iliac to thigh
10 Femoral in thigh
11 Tibial in leg

**Important veins**
12 Jugular from head
13 Subclavian from arm
14 Pulmonary from lung
15 Superior and inferior vena cava from all but lungs
16 Brachial in arm
17 Renal from kidney
18 Hepatic from liver
19 Iliac from thigh
20 Femoral in thigh

### The heart

The heart is a muscular pump which drives blood around the body. Its nonstop action supplies oxygen and nutrients to body cells, and removes their waste products.

a From body
b To lungs
c From lungs
d To body
e Ventricle
f Atrium

## Structure

The heart is a fist-sized hollow muscle with a broad top and pointed base. It lies roughly in the middle of the chest. A wall called a septum (**1**) divides the right side (**A**) from the left side (**B**). Each side has an inlet, outlet and two chambers; atrium and ventricle. Valves (**2**) control the blood flow in and out.

## How it works

The heart works as two pumps. As the heart relaxes, blood flows into both atria. As the atria contract, blood flows through valves into the ventricles. Lastly, the ventricles contract, forcing blood out of the heart.

Deoxygenated blood from the body flows via the superior vena cava and inferior vena cava (**3**) into the right atrium (**4**) and right ventricle (**5**) then out through the pulmonary artery (**6**) to the lungs.

Oxygenated blood from the lungs flows via the pulmonary vein (**7**) into the left atrium (**8**) and left ventricle (**9**) then out through the aorta (**10**) to the body.

Each complete contraction produces one heartbeat. Nerve signals to the heart keep heartbeats regular. But heartbeats speed up during exercise as the heart pumps faster and harder to satisfy the body's extra needs for blood and oxygen.

## Lymphatic system

A body-wide network of vessels that traps fluid escaped from blood vessels, and returns it to the blood supply. This stops tissues swelling. The system also absorbs harmful bacteria and other dangerous substances.

## Spleen

This organ plays a part in circulation and combating infection. It manufactures some of the blood formed in the body before birth, and contains cells that kill old or injured blood cells and destroy bacteria and parasites. It also produces antibodies – proteins that attack viruses and other agents of infection.

# DIGESTIVE SYSTEM
## Structures and processes

Digestion happens in the alimentary canal, a tube 9 m (30 ft) long with different parts. Waves of movement in its walls force food along. Food entering the mouth (**a**) is swallowed by the pharynx (**b**), then passes through the gullet or oesophagus (**c**) to the stomach (**d**). This muscular bag churns food and dissolves some by releasing gastric juices. The gall bladder (**e**) and pancreas (**f**) release digestive juices in the duodenum (**g**), the first part of the small intestine (**h**). Most digested food enters the blood through tiny finger-like projections in the small intestine's walls. The large intestine (**i**) absorbs water and forms faeces, solid wastes expelled from the anus (**j**).

## Where digestion happens

Different foods chiefly undergo digestion in specific parts of the digestive system.
**1 Carbohydrates** Mouth, oesophagus, stomach, small intestine.
**2 Proteins** Stomach and small intestine.
**3 Fats** Small intestine.
**4 Water (not a food)** Absorbed in the large intestine.

**Parts of the digestive system**

## The mouth

The mouth takes in food and starts the process of digestion. Lips (**a**) help us drink and bring food inside the mouth. Teeth (**b**) break food into smaller pieces. Salivary glands (**c**) produce saliva that moistens and softens food and begins digesting starches. The bony hard palate (**d**) and the soft palate (**e**) stop food entering and blocking the airway through the nose and upper throat or pharynx. The tongue (**f**) helps to form each mouthful into a ball or bolus, then moves it back into the throat for swallowing.

**The mouth**

# URINARY SYSTEM

## Kidneys

Kidneys are a pair of organs for filtering impurities from blood, and prevent poisons fatally accumulating in the body.

### Structure

Kidneys are two bean-shaped objects behind the stomach, one on each side of the spine. Together, kidneys add up to the same size as the heart. Each kidney has three layers. From the outside in, these layers are the cortex (**1**), medulla (**2**) and pelvis (**3**). The cortex and medulla contain tiny blood filtration units called nephrons (**4**). (A single kidney has more than a million nephrons.) Urine, the waste product of filtration, collects in the kidney's pelvis.

### How they work

Blood for processing enters the medulla from the renal artery (**5**). Inside the medulla and cortex, the artery splits into tiny coiled blood vessels. Each coiled vessel is called a glomerulus (**8**). Almost completely surrounding this lies a pinhead-sized sac called Bowman's capsule (**9**). Pressure forces water and dissolved chemicals from the blood in the glomerulus into the Bowman's capsule. The filtered liquid then continues through a tubule (**10**) surrounded by capillaries (**11**). These tiny blood vessels reabsorb into the blood most of the water and such useful chemicals as amino acids. The treated blood then leaves the kidney via the renal vein (**6**). Meanwhile, wastes remaining in the convoluted tubule flow on via a collecting tubule to the kidney's pelvis. These wastes now form urine, an amber liquid largely made of water, uric acid, urea and inorganic salts. From the kidney's pelvis, urine leaves the kidney through a tube known as the ureter (**7**). From there it passes into the bladder (**12**) where it is stored until it is released.

One pair of kidneys can process 190 litres (42 gallons) of blood a day. Their urine output drops in sleep or during perspiration, and rises after someone has been drinking more liquid than usual.

# ENDOCRINE SYSTEM

Endocrine glands release into the blood hormones ('chemical messengers') that reach target glands and organs to control growth, reproduction and the daily processes of living.

**1** Hypothalamus releases hormones especially from the pituitary gland
**2** Pituitary releases several hormones; one controls water reabsorbed into blood by kidneys, another is a growth hormone
**3** Thyroid controls rates of growth in young and in adults controls rate of chemical activity
**4** Parathyroid releases calcium from bones to blood

**5** Adrenal glands produce several hormones including cortisone to accelerate conversion of proteins to glucose and adrenaline
**6** Pancreas (contains some endocrine cells) secretes digestive juices and insulin
**7** Ovaries in females produce several hormones called oestrogens
**8** Testicles in males produce testosterone

# EXOCRINE SYSTEM

Exocrine glands produce substances released via ducts to other organs or the surface of the skin. Here are some major types and their products.

1 Lacrimal glands (tears)
2 Salivary glands (saliva)
3 Mucus glands (mucus)
4 Sweat glands of skin (sweat)
5 Sebaceous glands of skin (sebum, oily substances which keep skin supple)

6 Mammary glands in women (milk)
7 Liver (bile)
8 Pancreas (digestive juices)
9 Prostate in men (seminal fluid)

# REPRODUCTIVE SYSTEM

### Male

A man's sex organs produce the minute tadpole-shaped sex
cells called sperm. A sperm that fertilizes an egg produces
an embryo that develops into a baby.

### Structures and functions

Sperm are produced in two testes (**1**), endocrine glands
which hang in a pouch, the scrotum. Sperm cells develop in
the epididymis (highly coiled tubes in the testes) then travel
via two vas deferens tubes (**2**) to the prostate gland (**3**),
where seminal fluid is added from seminal vesicles (**4**).
Sperm then enter the urethra (**5**) and escape through the
penis (**6**).

## Female

A woman's reproductive system produces eggs and babies and provides these with nourishment.

## Structures

The vagina (**1**) is a muscular tube opening between the rectum and urethra. A narrow neck, the cervix (**2**), leads to the womb or uterus (**3**), a hollow, muscular organ as big as a pear. Fallopian tubes (**4**) connect the uterus to the ovaries (**5**), where the eggs are produced. Breasts (**6**) are milk-producing glands.

# MENSTRUATION

Menstruation is a woman's monthly 'period', when the vagina discharges blood and mucus. This happens as part of the 28-day menstrual cycle of egg production controlled by a hormone feedback system run by the hypothalamus (**1**) and pituitary (**2**) in the brain.

**From day 1** Follicle-stimulating hormone or FSH (**3**) helps a new egg form in an egg follicle (**4**), which is a fluid-filled cavity in the ovary.

**From day 4** The follicle produces the hormone oestrogen (**5**), promoting growth of the uterus (**6**) and breasts (**7**), releasing luteinizing hormone or LH (**8**) which stimulates ovulation (and conversion of the ruptured follicle), and blocking FSH output.

**From day 12** LH bursts the follicle, releasing an egg or ovum (**9**) and transforming the follicle into a solid body, the corpus luteum (**10**), yielding oestrogen and the hormone progesterone (**11**).

**From day 14** Progesterone stimulates thickening of the uterus wall and increased blood supply in preparation for the uterus receiving a fertilized egg. If fertilization fails to occur, the corpus luteum shrinks, LH, oestrogen and progesterone output fall, the uterus lining breaks up and its bloody fragments escape in the monthly discharge.

# CONCEPTION

A new life starts when a sperm fertilizes an egg. During sexual intercourse, a man's penis releases millions of sperm into a woman's vagina (**1**).

Lashed along by their tails, the microscopic sperm wriggle through the cervix (**2**), a narrow neck, into the womb or uterus (**3**).

Fewer than 3000 sperm probably survive to continue on into the two Fallopian tubes (**4**). If the woman has recently ovulated (released an egg or ovum from an ovary (**5**)) some sperm may find an egg (**6**) already in a tube. If egg release has not occurred, the sperm can survive up to three days until an egg arrives.

**Fertilization**

Fertilization occurs when sperm meet an egg as it passes down the oviduct. Hugely magnified, a tadpole-like sperm (**1**) fertilizes an egg or ovum (**2**) much larger than itself. The sperm's head, or nucleus will stick to the ovum and fuse with the ovum nucleus. The ovum then gains a hardened wall to keep out other sperm.

An ovum can live for between 12 and 24 hours once it has been released, but sperm can live inside a female for 3–4 days. Each month there are therefore 3–4 days when fertilization can occur.

From puberty to old age, men's testes produce 10–30 billion sperm a month. Women are born with perhaps 350 000 immature eggs. Between puberty and menopause, at least one egg matures in an ovary each month and is released for possible fertilization. Only some 375 eggs mature throughout a lifetime.

# DEVELOPMENT OF A BABY

These line drawings show how an embryo becomes a fetus within the mother's uterus (womb), and they also show how the mother's body adapts and changes both for gestation and for the events of birth and nursing.

## The embryo

At conception, the fertilized egg comprises one single cell, known as a zygote. Following cell division, the zygote becomes a small bundle of cells that then implants in the lining of the uterus (womb), creating a placenta (a union of cells between mother and child) at the junction. From that time until week 8 of pregnancy, the developing child is technically described as an embryo.

| 0 | 8 | 16 | 24 |

**The fetus**

Well before week 8 of gestation, the developing child is
protected from damage and pressure by a surrounding
membranous sac filled with amniotic fluid. Its nutrition is
supplied through the placenta via an umbilical cord.

By week 8, the human embryo is less than 2 cm in length
and has arms, legs, eyes and eyelids.

From week 8 to the time of birth is a period of sustained
growth for the fetus; the length of the fetus increases some
20 times during that period, and the weight increases by
around 1700 times.The embryo cells divide rapidly and have
special functions, becoming muscles, bones and organs. The
later stages of an embryo when all the organs are present is
called the fetus.

A few weeks before the birth the embryo lies head down in
the uterus with the head just above the cervix.

28      32      36      40

# METHODS OF CONTRACEPTION

The following list gives types of contraceptive most commonly used by both male and female.

**Condom (1)** Also known as a sheath, rubber or French letter, this is worn by the man over his erect penis and prevents sperm from entering the vagina. It also protects against sexually-transmitted diseases. A condom for use by women also exists.

**Contraceptive pill (2)** Taken by the woman, this contains the hormones oestrogen and progesterone, or just progesterone, and acts by preventing ovulation (ripening and release of an egg by an ovary). There are often side effects, and so the pill should be taken under medical supervision. A male pill is currently being developed.

**Diaphragm (3)** A rubber cap that is inserted by the woman to fit across her cervix, acting as a barrier to sperm. It should be used in conjunction with a spermicide cream or gel. Similar, but not as widely used in the US, is the cervical cap.

**IUD (4)** (intrauterine device) Also known as the coil or loop. This small plastic device is inserted in the uterus by a physician and left in place for several years. It helps to prevent conception by interfering with the implantation of fertilized eggs.

**Female sterilization** This involves cutting, tying or removing all or part of the Fallopian tubes so that eggs cannot pass from the ovaries to the uterus and sperm cannot reach the egg. A hysterectomy (complete removal of the uterus) is not generally recommended for the purposes of birth control.

**Injectables** These are based on hormones similar to the contraceptive pill but are given by injection every few weeks. There are often many side effects.

**Mucus method** This requires recognition of natural changes in the nature of cervical mucus during a woman's menstrual cycle, in order to recognize 'safe' days. It is not one of the more reliable methods.

**Postcoital methods** These include a 'morning after' pill, consisting of large doses of synthetic oestrogen to be taken within 72 hours of intercourse; insertion of an IUD up to 5 days after intercourse; and menstrual extraction.

**Rhythm method** The calendar method requires that a couple avoid intercourse during those days of the menstrual cycle when a woman is most likely to conceive. The temperature method requires checking the small rise in temperature that a woman has when ovulation occurs. Both methods are unreliable on the whole, particularly if menstruation is not regular.

**Spermicides** These chemical products are inserted into the woman's vagina before intercourse and either kill sperm or create a barrier. They come as creams, jellies, foaming tablets or pessaries, and should be used in conjunction with a diaphragm or condom.

**Sponge** The spermicide-impregnated sponge is inserted in the vagina prior to intercourse and left in place for 6 hours.

**Vasectomy** This simple surgical procedure involves the cutting and tying of both the tubes that connect the testes and the urethra so that semen ejected no longer contains sperm. It is not effective immediately, and rarely reversible.

**Withdrawal** This is the oldest method of birth control, by which the male takes his penis out of the vagina just prior to ejaculation. It is not considered a reliable method.

# NUTRITION AND HEALTH
## Health

Health is a state of physical, mental and social well-being.
Good health is the absence of disease, a balanced outlook on
life and all the parts of the body working properly together.
Knowledge of the human body is necessary to achieve good
health. Good nutrition, exercise, rest, sleep, cleanliness and
medical and dental care help to maintain health.

**Health guidelines**

### Cleanliness
Keeping clean helps to control the growth of bacteria
and other germs which can cause diseases. Daily
washing keeps the body free from dirt and also prevents
skin infections. Hair should also be washed regularly.
Dental care is also necessary each day and prevents tooth
decay and disease.

### Exercise
Exercise keeps the body fit and healthy. Vigorous
exercise strengthens muscles and improves the
circulatory and respiratory systems. Physical fitness
benefits physical and mental health.

### Rest and sleep
Rest helps to overcome tiredness and restores energy to
the body. Everyone needs rest and sleep but the amount
required varies from person to person.

## Nutrition

Good food is essential for health and survival. A poor intake of food, poor absorption or use of nutrients by the body results in malnutrition. Over-eating leads to obesity. Good nutrition is the proper amount of food each day.

Food provides certain chemical substances needed for good health. These are nutrients. They perform one or more of three functions:

1 provide materials for building, repairing or maintaining body tissues;
2 help to regulate body processes;
3 serve as fuel to provide energy.

### Medical care

Regular check-ups by a doctor and a dentist are important for safeguarding health. Doctors recommend that people call them at the first sign of illness. It is equally important to prevent disease, which can be done by immunization.

### Balanced diet

A balanced diet helps to provide all the substances needed by the body for healthy growth and development. These substances are called nutrients and they are classified into five main groups: proteins, vitamins, minerals, carbohydrates and fats. Water is also essential for life. A balanced diet consists of a wide variety of foods such as fresh fruit and vegetables, meat, fish, cereals, dairy products and eggs.

**Nutrients in food**

Foods give us proteins, carbohydrates, fats, vitamins and minerals.

**1 Proteins** build and repair body cells. Meat, fish, eggs, milk, beans, grains and nuts are rich in proteins.

**2 Carbohydrates** provide energy for rapid use. They include sugars in fruits, sugar cane and sugar beet; starches in potatoes, bread, cereals such as wheat, rice, maize, oats and barley, and vegetables.

**3 Fats** are concentrated stores of energy, found in butter, margarine, edible oils, meat, eggs, etc.

**4 Vitamins** in tiny quantities help regulate chemical processes inside the body. Different vitamins occur in fats and oils, fresh fruits and vegetables, liver, kidney, cereals, eggs and yeast.

**5 Minerals** are necessary for the chemical activities of the body and for the construction of tissues. Minerals of certain kinds abound in milk, cheese, fish and some green vegetables.

**Food intake**

The diagrams compare average daily calorie consumption of different foods per person in two regions. In the Western world people eat more food of more kinds than they do in the non-Western world.

## American–European food consumption

| | | |
|---|---|---|
| **Breakfast 1000 calories** | cereals, milk, sugar, juice coffee, fried foods, toast, marmalade | |
| **Snacks 400 calories** | tea, coffee, milk, sugar, biscuits | |
| **Lunch 1000 calories** | soup, main dish, salad, bread, butter, dessert, coffee, milk, sugar, wine or beer | |
| **Dinner 1100 calories** | main dish, salad, bread, butter, dessert, coffee, sugar, milk, wine or beer | |

**3500 calories average daily intake**

## Asian–African food consumption

| | | |
|---|---|---|
| **Breakfast, lunch and dinner 2000 calories** | rice, milk, pulses, vegetables, very little meat or fish | |

## TRANSPORT

| Date | Invention | Inventor |
|------|-----------|----------|
| c. 3480 BC | wheel | Sumerian civilization |
| AD 1770 | steam tricycle | Nicolas Cugnot |
| 1783 | full-size hot-air balloon | Jacques & Joseph Montgolfier |
| 1797 | parachute | Jacques Garnerin |
| 1804 | steam railway locomotive | Richard Trevithick |
| 1826 | car (gas-powered) | Samuel Brown |
| 1839 | bicycle | Kirkpatrick MacMillan |
| 1843 | railway (underground) | Charles Pearson |
| 1844 | propeller ship | Isambard Kingdom Brunel |
| 1845 | pneumatic tyre | Robert Thomson |
| 1852 | airship (nonrigid) | Henri Giffard |
| 1852 | lift | Elisha Otis |
| 1853 | glider | Sir George Cayley |
| 1866 | cable car | W. Ritter |
| 1876 | carburettor | Gottlieb Daimler |
| 1879 | electric railway | Ernst von Siemens |
| 1885 | motorcycle | Gottlieb Daimler |
| 1886 | aeroplane (steam-powered) | Clement Adler |
| 1892 | escalator | Jesse Reno |
| 1897 | turbine-propelled ship | Charles Parsons |
| 1900 | airship (rigid) | Ferdinand von Zeppelin |

| | | |
|---|---|---|
| 1902 | disc brakes | Frederick Lanchester |
| 1903 | aeroplane | Orville & Wilbur Wright |
| 1907 | helicopter | Louis & Jacques Breguet |
| 1926 | rocket | Robert H. Goddard |
| 1936 | contra-rotating helicopter rotors | Heinrich Focke |
| 1940 | first serviceable helicopter | Igor Sikorsky |
| 1954 | swing-wing aeroplane | Grumman Co. |
| 1959 | hovercraft | Sir Christopher Cockerell |
| 1981 | space shuttle | NASA |

## MEDICAL

| Date | Invention | Inventor |
|---|---|---|
| c. 1280 | spectacles | not known |
| 1540 | artificial limb | Ambroise Paré |
| 1630 | obstetric forceps | Peter Chemberlen |
| 1714 | mercury thermometer | Gabriel Fahrenheit |
| 1775 | bifocal lenses | Benjamin Franklin |
| 1792 | ambulance | Jean Dominique Larrey |
| 1796 | vaccination | Edward Jenner |
| 1816 | stethoscope | Théophile Laënnec |
| 1817 | dental plate | Anthony Plantson |
| 1827 | endoscope | Pierre Segalas |
| 1835 | hypodermic syringe | Charles Pravaz |
| 1846 | anaesthetics | William Morton |
| 1863 | barbiturates | Adolf von Bayer |

| 1865 | antiseptics | Joseph Lister |
| 1887 | contact lenses | Adolf Frick |
| 1895 | X-ray | Wilhelm Röntgen |
| 1899 | aspirin (medical use) | Heinrich Dresser |
| 1903 | electrocardiograph | Willem Einthoven |
| 1928 | antibiotics (penicillin) | Alexander Fleming |
| 1955 | contraceptive pill | Gregor Pincus |
| 1956 | pacemaker | Wilson Greatbach |
| 1966 | artificial blood | Clark & Gollan |
| 1967 | heart transplant | Christiaan Barnard |
| 1979 | ultrasound scan | Ian Donald |

## COMMUNICATIONS

| Date | Invention | Inventor |
| --- | --- | --- |
| c. 3500 BC | writing | Sumerian civilization |
| c. 1300 BC | parchment | Egyptian civilization |
| AD 105 | paper | China |
| c. 1455 | printing press | Johannes Gutenberg |
| 1565 | pencil | Konrad Gessner |
| 1774 | electrical telegraphy | Georges Lesage |
| 1787 | mechanical telegraphy | M. Lammond |
| 1826 | photography (metal) | Joseph Niepce |
| 1834 | braille | Louis Braille |
| 1835 | photography (paper) | William Fox Talbot |
| 1837 | telegraph code | Samuel Morse |
| 1868 | typewriter | Christopher Sholes |
| 1876 | telephone | Alexander Graham Bell |
| 1876 | microphone | Alexander Graham Bell |
| 1877 | gramophone | Thomas Edison |

| Date | Invention | Inventor |
|------|-----------|----------|
| 1884 | fountain pen | Lewis Waterman |
| 1895 | cinema | Auguste & Louis Lumière |
| 1898 | tape recorder | Valdemar Poulsen |
| 1900 | loudspeaker | Horace Short |
| 1902 | facsimile machine | Arthur Korn |
| 1906 | radio telegraphy | David Hughes |
| 1925 | television | John Logie Baird |
| 1938 | ballpoint pen | Laszlo & Georg Biro |
| 1948 | long-play record | Peter Goldmark |
| 1956 | video recorder | Ampex Co. |
| 1978 | compact disc | Philips (NL) |

## MILITARY

| Date | Invention | Inventor |
|------|-----------|----------|
| c. 200 BC | cannon | Archimedes |
| AD 950 | gun powder | Chinese |
| 1232 | missile rocket | Mongolians |
| c. 1300 | gun | not known |
| 1718 | machine gun | James Puckle |
| 1776 | submarine | David Bushnell |
| 1835 | revolver | Samuel Colt |
| 1862 | rapid-fire gun | R. Gatlin |
| 1916 | tank | Ernest Swinton |
| 1922 | radar | A. Taylor & L. Young |
| 1943 | air-to-air missile | Herbert Wagner |
| 1945 | atomic bomb | O. Frisch, N. Bohr & R. Peierls |

## DOMESTIC

| Date | Invention | Inventor |
| --- | --- | --- |
| c. 2500 BC | soap | Sumerian civilization |
| 1589 | flush toilet | Sir John Harington |
| 1679 | pressure cooker | Denis Papin |
| 1784 | gas lighting | Jean-Pierre Minkhales |
| 1810 | food canning | Nicolas Appert |
| 1816 | fire extinguisher | George Manby |
| 1826 | safety match | John Walker |
| 1830 | lawnmower | Edward Budding |
| 1849 | safety pin | Walter Hunt |
| 1851 | sewing machine | Isaac Singer |
| 1858 | burglar alarm | Edwin Holmes |
| 1860 | linoleum | Frederick Walton |
| 1862 | refrigerator | James Harrison |
| 1876 | carpet-sweeper | Melville Bissell |
| 1879 | electric light | Thomas Edison |
| 1882 | electric iron | Henry Seeley |
| 1883 | electric blanket | not known |
| 1889 | dishwasher | Mrs W. Cochran |
| 1889 | electric oven | Bernina Hotel, Switzerland |
| 1893 | zip fastener | Whitcombe Judson |
| 1901 | safety razor | King Camp Gillette |
| 1901 | vacuum cleaner | Hubert Booth |
| 1907 | washing machine | Hurley Machine Co. |
| 1926 | aerosols | E. Rotheim |
| 1927 | toaster | Charles Strite |
| 1929 | frozen foods | Clarence Birdseye |
| 1938 | fluorescent light | General Electric Co. |
| 1947 | microwave oven | P. Spencer |

| 1955 | nonstick pan | Mark Grégoir |
| 1971 | food processor | Pierre Verdon |

## SCIENCE

| Date | Invention | Inventor |
| --- | --- | --- |
| c. 1590 | microscope | Zacharias Janssen |
| 1644 | barometer | Evangelista Torricelli |
| 1650 | air pump | Otto von Guericke |
| 1654 | slide rule | Robert Bissaker |
| 1657 | pendulum clock | Christiaan Huygens |
| 1698 | steam pump | Thomas Savery |
| 1762 | chronometer | John Harrison |
| 1800 | electric battery | Alessandro Volta |
| 1814 | spectroscope | Joseph von Frauenhofer |
| 1824 | electromagnet | William Sturgeon |
| 1831 | electric generator | Michael Faraday |
| 1834 | galvanometer | André Ampere |
| 1851 | heat pump | Lord Kelvin |
| 1855 | bunsen burner | Peter Desdega |
| 1870 | plastics (celluloid) | John Wesley Hyatt |
| 1870 | electric motor (DC) | Zenobe Gramme |
| 1888 | electric motor (AC) | Nikola Tesla |
| 1908 | gyrocompass | Elmer Sperry |
| 1911 | superconductivity | Heika Onnes |
| 1933 | electron microscope | M. Knoll & E. Ruska |
| 1935 | radar | Robert Watson-Watt |
| 1939 | vulcanized rubber | Charles Goodyear |
| 1942 | nuclear reactor | Enrico Fermi |
| 1960 | laser | Theodore Maiman |

## ELECTRONICS AND COMPUTING

| Date | Invention | Inventor |
|------|-----------|----------|
| 1623 | adding machine | Wilhelm Schickard |
| 1822 | 'analytical engine' | Charles Babbage |
| 1890 | punched card machine | Herman Hollerith |
| 1948 | electronic computer | Frederick Williams |
| 1948 | transistor | W. Shockley, J. Bardeen & W. Brattain |
| 1958 | integrated circuit | Jack Kilby |
| 1960 | mini computer | Digital Corporation |
| 1965 | word processor | IBM |
| 1970 | floppy disk | IBM |
| 1972 | microprocessor | Intel Corporation |
| 1973 | microcomputer | Trong Truong |
| 1981 | superchip | Hewlett-Packard |
| 1985 | transputer | Inmos Ltd. |

## ENGINEERING AND CONSTRUCTION

| Date | Invention | Inventor |
|------|-----------|----------|
| c. 6000 BC | bricks | Jericho |
| c. 4000 BC | saw | Egyptian civilization |
| c. 3700 BC | bronze | Sumerian civilization |
| c. 1500 BC | lathe | Greek civilization |

| | | |
|---|---|---|
| c. AD 100 | concrete | Roman civilization |
| c. 900 | windmill | Persia |
| 983 | canal lock | Chiao Wei-Yo |
| 1738 | iron rails | Whitehaven Colliery, UK |
| 1752 | lightning conductor | Benjamin Franklin |
| 1764 | spinning jenny | James Hargreaves |
| 1769 | spinning frame | Richard Arkwright |
| 1779 | spinning mule | Samuel Crompton |
| 1824 | Portland cement | Joseph Aspdin |
| 1860 | steel production | Henry Bessemer |
| 1861 | pneumatic drill | Germain Sommelier |
| 1867 | dynamite | Alfred Nobel |
| 1883 | skyscraper | William Jenney |
| 1892 | reinforced concrete | François Hennebique |
| 1895 | electric drill | Wilhelm Fein |
| 1912 | stainless steel | Harold Brearley |

## ENGINES

| Date | Invention | Inventor |
|---|---|---|
| 1712 | piston steam engine | Thomas Newcomen |
| 1769 | steam engine (condenser model) | James Watt |
| 1884 | steam turbine | Charles Parsons |
| 1885 | internal-combustion engine | Gottlieb Daimler |
| 1885 | petrol engine | Karl Benz |
| 1892 | diesel engine | Rudolf Diesel |
| 1937 | jet engine | Frank Whittle |
| 1959 | rotary engine | Felix Wankel |

# MOVING: ON WATER

## Floating

The arrows indicate relative values of weight and upthrust.
**1** A raft floats because, overall, it is less dense than water. It settles at a point where its weight equals the upthrust produced by displaced water.
**2** A raft sinks when its laden weight exceeds upthrust.
**3** The boat's weight equals upthrust. It rides high in the water because overall it is much less dense than water.

## Hydrofoil

A hydrofoil boat uses an aerofoil-shaped device, the hydrofoil (**1**), to provide lift. At low speeds (**2**) lift from the hydrofoil is small. At higher speeds (**3**) increased lift raises the hull out of the water. With reduced friction between the hull and the water, higher speeds can now be attained.

**Aeroplane aerofoil** see page 506

### Submarine

**Diving (1)** Water is pumped into ballast tanks, and **(2)** air is expelled. The submarine's density is greater than that of the surrounding water and it sinks.

**Neutral buoyancy (3)** The submarine levels off when its overall density is the same as that of the surrounding water. **Rising (4)** Compressed air is pumped into the ballast tanks, expelling the water. The submarine's density becomes less than that of the seawater and it rises to the surface.

### Hovercraft

This floats on a cushion of compressed air. There is no contact between the craft and the ground and therefore no friction to overcome.

**1** A fan (**a**) sucks in air (**b**) and compresses it.

**2** The air is forced down and along (**c**) and a flexible rubberized skirt (**d**) keeps the cushion of air trapped.

**3** Propellers (**e**) draw in air (**f**) for forward propulsion.

**4** Air flow (**g**) is directed by a rudder (**h**) for steering.

### Sailing boat

A simple yacht has two triangular sails – the jib (**a**) and the mainsail (**b**). A rudder (**c**) steers the boat in the required direction. A boat can make progress into the wind by tacking (following a zigzag course).

**1 Sailing before the wind** Forward thrust (**d**) is in the same direction as the wind.

**2 Sailing with the wind on the quarter** Forward thrust (**d**) is provided by the wind acting on the sail (**e**). A sideways thrust (**f**) is resisted by the boat's keel, which stops the boat shifting sideways.

**3 Sailing across the wind** The wind acting on the sail (**e**) provides the forward thrust (**d**). Sideways thrust (**f**) is resisted by the keel and the crew leaning out away from the sail.

**4 Sailing into the wind** The two sails act as one large aerofoil with a slot in the centre. The slot channels air over both sails, producing a powerful force (**g**) which is split into forward thrust (**d**), and a sideways thrust, resisted by the keel and the crew leaning out away from the sail.

# MOVING: ON LAND
### Bicycle

**1 Propulsive force** This is transmitted from the cyclist's legs via pedals (**a**) and a crank (**b**) through a chain (**c**) to a rear wheel sprocket (**d**). The crank rotates at low speed with high force, while the sprocket and rear wheel rotate at a higher speed with lower force.

**2 Derailleur gears** These comprise several sprockets of different sizes (**e**) plus a gear change mechanism (**f**), which transfers the chain from one sprocket to the next. To ride on the level or downhill, a small sprocket is selected, so that one turn of the crank produces many turns of the wheel. To climb a hill, a large sprocket is selected so that the rear wheel turns slowly but with greater force.

### Internal-combustion engines

Engines are machines that convert heat energy into
mechanical energy to produce force or motion. As
their name implies, internal combustion engines burn
fuel within the engine.

### Piston engines

These are usually fuelled by petrol or by diesel oil.

**The petrol engine** A mixture of petrol vapour and air
is drawn into a cylinder (**1**), compressed (**2**) and then
ignited by a spark (**3**). As the petrol vapour/air
mixture ignites, the burnt gases expand and move a
piston within the cylinder. The piston is attached to a
crankshaft, which provides rotational power.

The three main types of petrol engine are the four-
stroke, the two-stroke and the Wankel rotary engine.

**The four-stroke engine** The piston (**a**) is connected to the crankshaft (**b**) via a big end (**c**). There are four piston strokes per cycle:

**1 Induction stroke** The inlet valve (**d**) opens and the piston moves down inside the cylinder, drawing in the petrol/air mixture (**e**).

**2 Compression stroke** The piston rises, compressing the petrol/air mixture. The inlet and exhaust valves are closed.

**3 Power stroke** A spark plug ignites the fuel (**f**) and the burning gases expand, forcing the piston down.

**4 Exhaust stroke** As the piston rises, burnt gases escape through an exhaust valve (**g**).

**The two-stroke engine** Less efficient than the four-stroke engine but cheaper and lighter. Valves are replaced by ports which are opened and closed by the piston as it moves. Two-stroke engines deliver a power stroke for every turn of the crankshaft. A four-stroke engine only does so for every other turn.

**1** The piston (**a**) is at the top of the cylinder and the petrol/air mixture is compressed. The exhaust port (**b**) and inlet port (**c**) are closed. When the spark ignites the compressed mixture (**d**), the piston is driven down on its power stroke.

**2** The piston (**a**) is near the bottom of the power stroke, burnt gases have escaped through the outlet port (**b**) and petrol/air is admitted through the inlet port (**c**).

**Wankel rotary engine** Developed by the German engineer
Felix Wankel in 1956, it has a triangular piston which
rotates inside an oval combustion chamber. The power
output is directly rotational, rather than via a crankshaft. It
has a four-stage cycle similar to a four-stroke engine:
**1 Induction stage of cycle** Inlet (**a**) admits a petrol/air
mixture into chamber (**b**).
**2 Compression** The revolving piston (**c**) compresses the
petrol/air mixture.
**3 Power** A spark plug ignites (**d**) the compressed petrol/air
mixture and the gases expand, keeping the piston turning.
**4 Exhaust** Burnt gases escape through the exhaust port (**e**).

**The diesel engine**

This uses diesel oil as a fuel, which is sprayed into the
cylinder as a liquid. It does not require an electrical ignition
system as the oil/air mixture is ignited by pressure alone.
In a diesel engine the air is drawn into the cylinder first (**1**)
and is compressed (**2**) to a much greater degree than in the
petrol engine. Because of this, the air in the diesel engine
heats up and when a small amount of diesel oil is injected, it
ignites spontaneously (**3**).

**Jet and rocket engines** see pages 509–11

### Steam engines

A steam engine converts heat energy stored in steam into usable power. In the first engines, water was heated in a furnace and converted to steam. The steam expanded into a cylinder, forcing the piston up. A spray of water was then injected. This changed the steam back to water. The steam no longer held up the piston and it dropped down ready for the cycle to start again.

### Double-acting steam engine

Many improvements were made. This engine was developed by James Watt and was used widely during the Industrial Revolution.

**1** Steam (**a**) enters the steam chest (**b**) through an inlet.
**2** Steam enters the upper piston cylinder (**c**) through an open valve (**d**). The piston is forced down. Steam in the lower cylinder (**e**) is pushed out of the valve into the exhaust (**f**).

**3** As the axle (**g**) revolves the piston starts to be forced up. More steam enters the steam chest.

**4** As the piston rises, the lower valve opens (**h**). Steam enters the lower piston cylinder, continuing to push up the piston. Steam from the upper cylinder enters the exhaust.

## Types of train
### Steam locomotive

Largely superseded by diesel and electric trains, steam locomotives burn fuel, usually coal, in a firebox (**1**). Hot gases (**2**) are drawn through tubes in a boiler (**3**), turning water to steam. A regulator (**4**) controls the delivery of steam to a cylinder (**5**). Expanding and condensing steam pushes a piston (**6**) back and forth. This drives the wheels (**7**) via a connecting rod (**8**) and a coupling rod (**9**). Exhaust steam and boiler smoke escape through the chimney (**10**).

**Diesel locomotive**

The most common type, a diesel-electric locomotive is an electric locomotive that carries diesel engines as its power source. The power of the diesel engine (**1**) is transmitted to an electric generator (**2**). This drives traction motors (**3**) mounted on axles which drive the wheels (**4**).

**Electric locomotive**

Electric trains take their power from an external supply. On electrified main-line railways, this is usually from overhead wires (**1**) via a spring-loaded arm (**2**). The high-voltage overhead current is reduced by a transformer (**3**) and fed to a motor (**4**) which, through a system of connecting rods (**5**), drives a number of wheels (**6**). On suburban and underground trains (not shown) electricity is usually obtained from an electrified third rail.

## Motor car

### 1 Steering

The steering wheel (**a**) and steering column (**b**) rotate gears in a pinion (**c**) which moves a rack (**d**) to the left or right. This in turn connects to a steering arm (**e**) that turns the axle (**f**) of each front wheel.

### 2 Transmission

The gearbox (**a**) and differential (**b**) convert engine revs to useful wheel revs. The clutch (**c**) disengages the gearbox from the engine (**d**), enabling gear changing. This shows a rear-wheel drive car. In front-wheel drive, the engine powers the front wheels.

### 3 Suspension

This cushions vertical movement of the wheels, enabling a smooth ride. The front suspension consists of shock absorber (**a**) and coil spring (**b**) attached to the chassis via a wishbone support (**c**). Rear suspension comprises leaf springs (**d**) and shock absorbers (**e**).

# MOVING: IN THE AIR
## Hot-air balloons

**1** In an ascending balloon, the air inside is heated by a burner (**a**). It expands and becomes less dense and some air escapes (**b**). The weight of the balloon becomes less than the air it displaces, so the balloon with its basket (**c**) rises.

**2** In a descending balloon, the air inside cools, contracts and becomes denser. Some air enters (**d**). The weight of the balloon becomes more than the air it displaces, so the balloon descends.

Arrow sizes show relative sizes of forces

⬆ Upthrust ⬇ Weight

## Airships

Early designs were filled with the highly flammable gas hydrogen. Nowadays, nonflammable helium is used. A modern nonrigid airship is powered by backward-directed engines (**1**) which can swivel to manoeuvre the airship during takeoff and landing. It is steered by a rudder (**2**) and passengers are carried in a car (**3**). The bulk of the airship is filled with the light gas helium (**4**), and two air-filled compartments called ballonets (**5**) control the airship's weight. Ascent in the airship is achieved by releasing air from the ballonets. Descent is achieved by pumping air into the ballonets.

**Gliders**

A glider is a fixed-wing aeroplane which is unpowered while in flight. Gliders soar upward on air that is rising faster than the glider's rate of descent. Features such as thermals (**1**), rising currents of hot air, and upcurrents (**2**) found on the windward side of ridges, enable a glider to stay aloft for long periods.

**Parachute**

When a parachutist jumps from the aeroplane he free falls (**1**) until the canopy opens (**2**). Upward forces called lift, and air resistance called drag, counteract the weight of the parachutist, slowing the rate of descent (**3**). Deceleration continues to a low constant speed of descent (**4**).

**Kite**

A kite needs wind to fly. The pulling force (**1**) on the kite string deflects the wind (**2**) downwards. This provides an uplift (**3**) equal and opposite to the string's pulling force.

### Aeroplanes

Aeroplanes fly because they are powered and their wings generate lift to hold them in the sky.

An aeroplane's engine produces thrust which moves the aeroplane through the air (**1**), causing the wings to generate lift (**2**). These two forces overcome drag (**3**) and the aircraft's weight (**4**).

### Lift

An aeroplane's wing in cross-section is called an aerofoil (**1**). Airflow (**2**) is faster over the wing than underneath it. The resulting low pressure zone above (**3**) and high pressure zone below (**4**) generate lift (**5**).

To manoeuvre an aeroplane it is necessary to control three types of movement: pitch (**1**), yaw (**2**) and roll (**3**).

**Types of movement**

Pitch is controlled by elevators (**a**) on the rear of the horizontal tail. Yaw is controlled by the rudder (**b**), a flap on the vertical tail fin. Roll is controlled by ailerons (**c**) on the outer trailing edges of the wings. When banking (turning) the rudder and ailerons are used together.

**Controlling movement**

**1** When diving, elevators are down. **2** When climbing, elevators are up. **3** When banking left, the left aileron is up, the right aileron down, and the rudder turned left. **4** When banking right, the right aileron is up, the left aileron down, and the rudder turned right.

**Helicopters**

Revolving rotor blades (**a**) have an aerofoil cross section (**b**) and act like a plane's wings to create lift (**c**). The tail rotor (**d**) helps maintain stability in flight.

**1** At rest the blades sag down.
**2** On takeoff the blades are raised.
**3** To move forward the blades are tilted forward.
**4** To move sideways the blades are tilted sideways.
**5** To stop or go backwards the blades are tilted back.

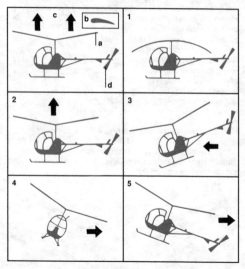

**Jet and rocket engines**

Jet and rocket engines depend on Newton's Third Law of Motion: every action has an equal and opposite reaction. A rocket or jet aircraft is thrust forward by the force of hot gases spurting from the back of the engine. Jet engines get oxygen for combustion from the air around them. Rockets carry their own compressed air or oxygen supply and so can go outside the Earth's atmosphere.

**Jet engines**

Thrust is generated by a jet of exhaust gas discharged from a nozzle at the rear of the engine.

Four types of jet engine are shown here. All rely on air being sucked in (**a**), compressed (**b**) and ignited with fuel (**c**), then burnt gases being blown out of the back (**d**) to provide the forward thrust.

**Key**

| | |
|---|---|
| **a** Air sucked in | **e** Compressor |
| **b** Air compressed | **f** Turbine |
| **c** Air/fuel mixture ignited | **g** Fans |
| **d** Gases expelled | **h** Bypass |
| | **i** Propellor |

**1** In the ramjet, used by high-speed military aircraft, flight speed is sufficient to suck in and compress air.

**2** In turbojet engines, air is compressed by a compressor (**e**) which is rotated by a turbine (**f**) powered by the jet of exhaust gases.

3 Modern turbofan engines, such as those used in subsonic jumbo jets, also have a compressor (**e**) and turbine (**f**). They differ from turbojet engines in that they have fans (**g**) at the front, and some compressed air travels through a bypass (**h**) and joins directly with the exhaust gases. This increases thrust and fuel economy.

4 In more traditional turboprop engines, the turbine (**f**) drives not only the compressor (**e**) but also a propeller (**i**) which provides most of the forward thrust.

For key see page 509

**3**

**4**

## Rocket engines

There are two types of rocket engine: those which burn solid fuel and those which burn liquid fuel.

1 Solid-fuel rocket engines. These burn fuel in a combustion chamber (**a**) that has an open end. The igniting fuel provides its own oxygen. As the fuel burns it produces gas which forces its way out of the open end of the rocket (**b**) as it expands, propelling the rocket forward. Once ignited, solid-fuel rocket engines cannot be shut off. They are used mainly as

**Rocket engines**

**1**

boosters which can be jettisoned from the space rocket's main engine.

**2** Liquid-fuel rocket engines. Rockets which burn liquid fuel carry a separate oxygen supply. Liquid hydrogen (**a**) is often used as fuel, and is fed into a combustion chamber (**b**) where it is ignited with liquid oxygen (**c**). The gas produced thrusts the rocket along (**d**). Speed of ignition is controllable, and liquid-fuel engines are used as space rocket main engines.

## Space shuttle

The space shuttle has five major rocket engines. There are two large solid-fuel boosters (**1**) either side of the orbiter (**2**) and three liquid-fuel main engines (**3**) attached at the rear of the orbiter. The huge external tank (**4**) contains liquid nitrogen and liquid oxygen for the main engines. These five engines only take the shuttle into space. Smaller liquid-fuel engines are used to manoeuvre it in space.

# ELECTRICAL DEVICES

### Electric generators

These are used for large-scale production of electrical energy. They work by electromagnetic induction. Coils of wire (**1**) are mounted so they can be spun around in a magnetic field (**2**) between magnets (**3**, **4**). This means the magnetic field points one way through the coils, then the other way. The changing magnetic field produces a current around the coil. This type of generator is called an alternator because the increase and decrease of the magnetic field produces an alternating current (AC). A direct current (DC), where the current always flows in the same direction, has the coil connected to a commutator (**5**) which makes the current flow continuously in one direction as illustrated below.

In power stations, the energy from burning coal, oil, gas or from a nuclear reaction is used to make steam. The steam drives a turbine to produce mechanical energy to turn the generator coils.

**Turbines** see page 515

**Conventional power station**

Coal (**1**) is delivered by conveyor belt to a boiler (**2**) where it is ground to a powder and ignited. Some power stations use gas or oil as an alternative fuel. Water inside pipes is heated to produce steam (**3**) which, under pressure, drives a steam turbine (**4**). This in turn powers an alternator (**5**) which delivers electricity to powerlines (**6**).

Used steam from the turbine (**4**) passes to a condenser (**7**). The condensed steam is recycled back to the boiler (**2**). Water used to cool the steam is sent to a cooling tower (**8**) and then recycled back to the condenser.

The flue gases (**9**) from the boiler (**2**) are passed through a dust extractor before release through tall chimneys (**10**).

A typical power station generates 60 000 kilowatts at 11 000 volts, enough to power a town of about 200 000 inhabitants. Coal is a dirty fuel which releases large amounts of sulphur and other pollutants into the air when it is burned, leading to acid rain. Most power plants which burn fossil fuels use pollution control equipment to limit the release of pollution into the air. Cleaner ways of making electricity are provided by hydroelectric or geothermal power plants.

### Nuclear power

This is generated by a nuclear reactor which converts nuclear (atomic) energy into thermal energy. A pressurized water reactor (PWR) is shown. In the reactor core (**1**) are fuel rods (**2**) containing uranium. When bombarded with neutrons (particles in an atom's nucleus), uranium atoms split, or undergo fission and in so doing emit more neutrons, so starting a chain reaction which must be controlled. The breakdown products of uranium collide with water molecules in the reactor, and give off heat. This is the power source.

Control rods (**3**), when lowered over the fuel rods, slow down or stop the fission process. Water (**4**), superheated by the fission process and under pressure, passes to the steam generator (**5**) where it boils unpressurized water to steam. This superheated steam is then recycled via a pump (**6**) back to the reactor core. Steam from the steam generator powers a steam turbine (**7**) which in turn drives an electrical generator (**8**). Water from the turbines is cooled in a condenser (**9**) and recycled through the steam generator (**5**). The entire reactor is surrounded by a concrete shield (**10**) to prevent radiation leaking out.

**Neutrons** see nuclear fission page 355

**Hydroelectric power**

Hydroelectric stations generate power using water turbines. Water in a reservoir (**1**) is held back by a dam (**2**) and enters an inlet (**3**) where it is directed to a turbine (**4**). The water strikes the turbine blades (**5**), rotating a drive shaft (**6**) which powers an electric generator (**7**). The water, having lost much of its energy, flows into the turbine's centre and leaves through an outlet pipe (**8**).

**Wind power**

The wind turbine has large aerofoil rotor blades (**1**) up to 50 m (160 ft) long to catch the wind. As the blades turn, a gearbox (**2**) ensures the drive shaft (**3**) rotates at high speed for efficient operation of the electric generator (**4**). Wind sensors (**5**) detect speed and direction of air movement and control the pitch, speed, and direction of the rotor blades so that power output is optimized.

### Electric motor

A very versatile power source. Electric current is fed to the stator coil (**1**), an electromagnet. Current is also fed to the brushes (**2**) in close contact with a commutator (**3**). This in turn is connected to a coil (**4**) in the rotor (**5**). The interaction between the rotor and stator magnetic fields produces a spinning movement to provide rotational power to drive other machinery. The motor shown is of a universal type, which can be powered by AC or DC supply.

### Electric light bulb

This consists of a hollow glass bulb (**1**) with a coil of tungsten wire inside called the filament (**2**). The filament is very thin and long so resistance to the current is great and heat and light output is high. The bulb is filled with inert gas (**3**). The base of the bulb has screw thread fittings (**4**) to keep it in place and a foot contact (**5**) which allows electric current to flow through the filament.

**Electric circuit symbols**

| Name | | Symbol |
|---|---|---|
| Battery | | |
| Bulb | | |
| Connecting wire | | |
| Off switch | Circuit broken | |
| On switch | Circuit made | |
| Ammeter | Measures amount of current in amps flowing in a circuit | (A) |
| Voltmeter | Measures potential difference in volts | (V) |

# MECHANICAL DEVICES

**Pumps**

Pumps use pressure differences to move fluids or gases.

**Simple water pump**

As used in a water pistol.

**1 Pumping out** When water molecules (**a**) are compressed by a moving piston (**b**) they will move to where they are at lower pressure; in this case the nozzle (**c**), where water emerges as a jet.

**2 Sucking in** When the moving piston (**b**) reduces pressure on the water molecules (**a**), more water will be drawn in from a region of higher pressure (**c**).

**Bicycle pump**

**1 Sucking air in** As the pump handle (**a**) is pulled out, air enters through a small hole at the top and moves past a collapsed flexible washer (**b**) and fills the barrel (**c**).

**2 Pumping air out** As the pump handle (**a**) is pushed in, the flexible washer (**b**) forms a seal, and air is forced out under pressure through the valve (**d**) into the tyre.

## Presses
### Hydraulic press
This transfers force via pressure in a liquid. If a 1 kg force is applied to the master cylinder (**1**) with an area of 10 sq cm, a pressure of 0.1 kg per sq cm is raised throughout the fluid system (**2**). A 4 kg load on a slave cylinder (**3**) can be moved providing the cylinder area is 40 sq cm or above.

### Car jack
In a hydraulic car jack, working the hand pump (**1**) draws oil from a reservoir (**2**) and delivers it under pressure to the cylinder (**3**) which raises the lifting piston (**4**). Valves (**5**) ensure that oil travels in one direction only. A release valve (**6**) lowers the lifting piston.

**Guns**

The common components are a barrel and a carriage.

**1 Muzzle loading** Common until the 19th century.

**a** A charge of gunpowder is rammed down the barrel, followed sometimes by a wad, and then the cannonball.

**b** A flame is applied to a touchhole which ignites the powder, propelling the ball out of the barrel.

**2 Breech loading** 19th–20th century.

**a** The breech is opened and loaded with a combined cartridge case and shell.

**b** The propellant explosive is detonated and the shell discharged through a rifled barrel.

**3 Recoilless gun** 20th century.

The gun is of light construction since recoil-absorbing features are not required. The barrel is open at both ends. The gases from the exploding propellant dissipate in a cleared area behind the gun (**a**).

# DEVICES USING LIGHT

## Optical telescope

A telescope gives a close-up view of a distant object. Most telescopes use lenses, or lenses and mirrors, to produce a real image inside the telescope tube.

### Refracting telescope

In a simple astronomical telescope, the convex objective lens (**1**) bends incoming light rays (**2**), producing an image (**3**) which is upside down, viewed through the eyepiece lens. Adding another convex lens (**4**) gives an upright image.

### Reflecting telescope

This uses a curved mirror of large diameter. Large mirrors can be made more accurately than large lenses, and are used for higher magnification telescopes. Light entering (**1**) is reflected from the concave primary mirror (**2**) onto a convex secondary mirror (**3**). This reflects light onto two flat mirrors (**4**) which form a real image (**5**) viewed through the eyepiece lens (**6**) at the side of the telescope.

## Spectacles

**1 Short-sighted person** The light rays (**a**) from a distant object pass through the eye lens (**b**) and form a focused image (**c**) in front of the retina (**d**). This is corrected using concave (diverging) lenses (**e**) to focus rays precisely on the retina.

**2 Long-sighted person** Light rays (**a**) pass through the lens (**b**) and form an image (**c**) behind the retina (**d**). Convex (converging) lenses (**e**) correct this.

## Binoculars

These are essentially two refracting telescopes joined together for use with both eyes, giving a 3-D effect.
Light (**1**) passes through the objective lens (**2**), forming an inverted and reversed image. Two prisms (**3**) correct the image before viewing through the eyepiece lenses (**4**).

**Microscope**

This works on the same principle as a refracting telescope but with the object very close to the objective lenses, giving a highly magnified view.

A mirror (**1**) reflects light rays (**2**) through a condenser (**3**) which concentrates them. The rays pass through and illuminate the object (**4**). Objective lenses (**5**) form an image which is further enlarged through the eyepiece lenses (**6**). Focusing is achieved by moving the objective lenses nearer to or further away from the object.

See also page 348 for further information

### Camera

A camera is essentially a light-proof box containing a convex lens system which focuses an image onto photographic film at the back of the camera. The single-lens reflex (SLR) camera uses a single set of lenses for both viewing and photographing. Other types of camera have separate sets of lenses for the two functions.

### Viewing

Light rays (**1**) pass through the open diaphragm (**2**) and are focused by a convex lens system (**3**) onto a mirror (**4**). This reflects the light onto a focusing screen (**5**) where the image is formed. The inverted and reversed image is corrected by a five-sided prism arrangement (**6**) and then viewed through the viewfinder eyepiece (**7**).

### Taking a photograph

When the shutter release is pressed, the mirror (**4**) flips up and the shutter (**8**) moves across, allowing light rays to reach the photographic film behind it.

The amount of light reaching the film is controlled by the size of the aperture in the diaphragm and the length of time the shutter is open.

Focusing is achieved by moving the lens system nearer to or further away from the film.

### Photographic film

**Composition** Black-and-white photographic film consists of a flexible base of cellulose triacetate (**1**), a light-sensitive emulsion of silver salts (**2**) and a protective gelatin layer (**3**). Colour films use different emulsions sensitive to red, blue and green light.

**Developing** After exposure to light, the film is developed in a chemical solution (**1**). This reduces the silver salts to black metallic silver. The more light originally reaching the film, the deeper the blackening. The developed film, or photographic negative, is then washed (**2**) to stop the development process. Fixing (**3**) dissolves away unreduced silver salts. Washing (**4**) stops any further chemical reaction, and the negative is then dried (**5**).

The negative and printing paper are held together in a frame. Light is passed through the negative to the paper underneath. This exposes the paper forming a latent image which becomes visible after development and chemical treatment to create a print, or photograph.

# COMMUNICATION DEVICES

## Radio

Radio is the communication of sound by the transmission of electromagnetic waves in the frequency range 3 kHz to 40 000 MHz (wavelength of 1 cm to over 1 km).

**Radio transmission**  **Radio reception**

Sound waves are produced by a source (**1**), converted into an electrically equivalent signal by a microphone (**2**), and then imposed on a carrier wave by a modulator (**3**). The resulting signal is then amplified (**4**) and transmitted by an antenna (**5**).

At a receiver, an aerial (**6**) picks up the signal, which is captured by a tuned circuit (**7**). The signal is then demodulated (**8**) to remove the carrier wave and the resulting signal amplified (**9**) and passed to a loudspeaker (**10**) where the electrical signal is reconverted to sound waves.

**Television**

**1** In a live broadcast a TV camera (**a**) converts the image into electrically equivalent signals representing the three primary colours. A microphone (**b**) converts sound into an electrical signal. Sound and picture signals are synchronized in a transmitter (**c**) and transmitted through an antenna (**d**).

**2** At a receiver, the aerial (**a**) picks up the transmission, relays it to a tuned circuit (**b**) in the television, and a decoder (**c**) reconverts the signals into sound and primary colour signals. In the picture tube (**d**) three electron guns (**e**) – red, blue and green – scan rapidly across the screen (**f**). Each dot lights up and fades in turn to produce 625 lines of dots in 1/25 second. The viewer sees a continously illuminated screen, rather than moving dots of colour and this gives a complete picture.

## Telephone

In the telephone's mouthpiece (**1**) a carbon microphone (**2**) converts sound waves into a fluctuating electrical current. This passes through wires (**3**) to the earpiece (**4**) of the receiver. The fluctuating current affects a magnetic coil (**5**) which in turn moves a diaphragm (**6**) acting as a loudspeaker to produce audible sounds. The telephone operates as a complete electrical circuit with a power source (**7**).

## Compact disc

A compact disc is a plastic-coated metal disc (**1**) which has about 5 km of playing track (**2**) on its underside. CDs play by means of a light beam from a low-powered laser which reads microscopic pits and flat areas on the playing track. The pits and flats form a digital code which is interpreted by the CD player, and then amplified and fed to loudspeakers.

### Record player

This is a device that replays sounds using the vibration of a stylus in the groove of a disc. As the stylus moves along the groove it is vibrated by the inner and outer walls which provide separate stereo channels. The vibrations travel to a magnet which induces electrical signals in fixed coils. The separate stereo signals are then sent to the amplifier and loudspeakers.

### Tape recorder

Reel-to-reel tapes have largely been replaced by cassette tapes, certainly for domestic use.

**1 Recording** Sound is picked up by a microphone (**a**), converted into an electrical signal, mixed with a steady tone, and fed to an amplifier (**b**). The combined signal is passed to the coil of a recording head (**c**). This produces a varying magnetic field that aligns particles in a magnetic tape (**d**).

**2 Playback** The tape (**a**) passes over the playback head (**b**) and the tape's magnetic field induces a current in the head's coil. The current is sent to an amplifier (**c**) and then to a loudspeaker (**d**) to reproduce the original recorded sounds.

### Video recorder

This works on the same principle as a tape recorder, but because picture and sound information are recorded together, bigger tapes and faster tape speeds are required. In recording, picture and sound are picked up from the signal from a TV aerial (1), the picture recorded onto the tape by the record/playback head (2) and the sound by another head (3). Picture signals are recorded as a series of sloping tracks (4) and sound signals (5) along one edge.

As with a tape recorder, playback is essentially the reverse of recording. When the play button is pressed, stored signals on the magnetic tape produce electrical signals in the record/playback heads. These feed the recorded picture and sound signals to the television set.

### Fax

Fax is short for Facsimile Transmission. A fax machine (1) is rather like a long-distance photocopier. It scans a document or picture (2) and converts it into signals which can be transmitted through a telephone line (3). A second fax machine (4) converts the signals back to a copy of the original.

**Modem**

This is short for MODulator/DEModulator. It allows computers to send data to, or receive data from, a telephone line. A computer (**1**) sends a digital signal (**2**) to a modem (**3**) which converts it to an analog signal (**4**). This is transmitted through a telephone line (**5**) to a second modem (**6**) which reconverts the signal to digital (**7**) for a receiving computer (**8**).

**Radar**

Radar is short for RAdio Detection And Ranging. Radar has many applications. Air-traffic controllers depend on it to find the positions of aircraft. A radar aerial (**1**) acts as both transmitter and receiver. Radio waves are transmitted (**2**) and reflected back (**3**) from a within-range aircraft. Time taken for return gives distance, and direction of return gives bearing. A second radar aerial (**4**) transmits radio waves (**5**) to a transponder (**6**) on the aircraft. This sends back information (**7**) giving the aircraft's height and identity. Information from the two aerials is combined and displayed on a radar screen.

# COMPUTERS

## Computer components

A computer is an electronic information processing machine. Information is fed in, or input, processed by the computer, and fed out again, or output. Recent massive advances in computer speed, power and reliability are largely due to silicon technology. The computer's complex circuitry is miniaturized inside silicon chips, wafer-thin silicon crystals with electronic circuits etched onto them (**1**). Within these circuits (**2**) are microscopic switches (**3**) which turn electric currents on and off. The resulting series of electrical pulses (bits) form the messages the computer uses to carry out instructions coded in computer programs.

## Types of computer

Computers are classified according to size, speed and capacity.

**Microcomputers** (personal computers)

These are small computers based on a single microprocessor chip. Most can only be used by one person at a time.

**Wordprocessors**

These are small computers designed specifically to handle words. They cannot do as much as microcomputers.

**Minicomputers**

These are about the size of a filing cabinet. They can handle a number of tasks at once.

**Mainframe computers**

These are large, powerful and require special air-conditioned rooms. They can handle hundreds of users at a time.

**Supercomputers**

These are used in research laboratories. They are very fast with large memories.

### Hardware

The hardware comprises the parts of a computer system that you can touch and handle. There are normally four components:

**a** input devices (to get information into the computer)

**b** a central processing unit (CPU), with its processor(s) and memory

**c** a backing store of memory

**d** output devices (to get information out of the computer)

A typical microcomputer set-up comprises:

1 A keyboard as the input device.

2 The computer itself with a CPU, backing store of memory, and a visual display unit (VDU) similar to a television screen.

3 A printer as the output device.

**Input devices**

These include:

**1 Keyboard** This is similar to a QWERTY typewriter keyboard. It is used for entering words, numbers and instructions.

**2 'Mouse'** A ball mounted in a box with sensors detecting its movement. Moving the mouse moves a pointer on the VDU screen. A button on the mouse activates the pointer to trigger commands.

**3 Joystick** Used particularly in computer games for moving parts or the whole of the VDU screen display. The joystick has a button to trigger commands.

**4 Light pen** Used with VDUs to draw or highlight items on the screen.

**5 Microphone** Used for inputting sounds.

**6 Scanner** An optical device, rather like a photocopier, which copies an image and displays it on the VDU.

**7 A bar code reader** In library use, similar to a light pen. In supermarket use, a sensitive panel in the counter. It is used to read bar code information.

**The central processing unit (CPU)**
This controls the step-by-step running of the computer by sending electrical signals to various parts of the system. It contains two types of memory. RAM (random-access memory) is a temporary memory which can be altered. Anything stored in RAM is lost when the computer is switched off. ROM (read-only memory) is a permanent memory store. ROM can be read from, but not altered.

**Storage devices**
Storage capacity is measured in kB (one thousand bytes) or MB (one million bytes). Computer information can be stored in a variety of ways:
**1** Temporarily in the RAM of the computer (64 kB – 10 MB), or more permanently

**2** On a cassette tape (less than 250 kB)
**3** On a floppy disk (0.25–2 MB) inserted in a disk drive.
**4** On a hard disk (10–80 MB).
**5** On a reel-to-reel magnetic tape (10–80 MB).
**6** On a CD-ROM, a compact disk (500–1000 MB) inserted in a disk drive.

**Output devices**

The visual display unit (VDU) can be regarded as an output device. It can be monochrome (usually black and white) or colour. It can be low resolution (few dots per sq cm) or high resolution (many dots per sq cm).

Printers produce output onto paper – what is called hard copy. All the following can print text and graphics (pictures):

**Dot matrix printers** These are cheap and fast, with relatively low print quality. They print characters from a series of dots by pins punching against a carbon ribbon.

**Inkjet printers** These are moderately costly, low-speed printers with reasonable print quality. They squirt ink through a fine nozzle to form characters.

**Laser printers** These have a higher cost and are moderately fast with reasonable to high print quality. They are similar in principle to a photocopier, but they use a laser beam to cause the powdered ink to stick to the paper.

### Software

This refers to all the instructions held in the computer which enable the hardware to do a useful job. Software is made up of programs. These are a series of step-by-step instructions which tell the computer what to do. Word-processing programs handle written text, spreadsheet programs handle tables of data and database programs handle information in a filing system arrangement. Programs can be written in a variety of computer languages such as BASIC, COBOL or PASCAL.

# CONSTRUCTION

## Roads

After soil excavation and provision of suitable drainage, the road surface is constructed. The following applies to a main road such as a motorway or bypass.

**1 Granular sub-base** Normally laid on compacted earth and consisting of rolled aggregate 30–60 cm thick.

**2 Lower road base** A 25 cm base layer of concrete to provide strength and bind to the sub-base.

**3 Upper road base** A 6.5 cm layer of rolled macadam (tar and stones).

**4 Wearing surface** A 3.5 cm top layer of rolled asphalt (bitumen). This gives a smooth, flexible road surface.

**5 Concrete haunch** This finishes off and supports the edge of the road surface.

**6 Hard shoulder** A thinner section of road surface which provides a breakdown lane.

**Building construction**

**1 Wattle and daub** Wattle and daub is a construction method of building walls in which vertical wooden stakes, or wattles, are woven with horizontal twigs and branches, then daubed, or plastered, with mud or clay. It is one of the oldest methods of making weather-proof structures. This method was used as fill-in for medieval timber-frame structures in Europe.

**2 Timber-frame** Timber is used as a frame for buildings, especially houses. A heavy timber sill is constructed on the foundation and on top of this are nailed floor joists. The frame of the house is built upwards. The frame was traditionally filled by wattle and daub or bricks. In modern timber-framed houses, the walls are covered in plywood, to which a surface cladding is added.

**3 Stone** Stone is an important building material. It is used for foundations, walls, supports of piers and bridges, finishing and decorating structures. Stone can be cut into blocks or slabs of definite, regular shape and size. Stone is a durable building material which is expected to last at least 100 years.

**4 Concrete** Concrete is fireproof and watertight. It is comparatively easy and cheap to make. When it is first mixed concrete can be moulded into almost any shape. It quickly hardens to form an extremely strong material. Concrete can be strengthened by adding metal rods or cables. It is used for frames, walls, floors, roofs and roads.

**5 Brick** Bricks are rectangular building blocks made of clay, shale or other materials. Bricks are strong, hard, resistant to fire and damage from the weather. They are uniform in shape and size and they are fired, or baked in an oven. Mortar is used to hold bricks together.

### Bridges

The majority of bridges are held up by at least two supports set in the ground, called abutments. Supports in the middle of a bridge are called piers, The distance between two supports is called a span.

**1 Single girder** Girder bridges include many road bridges. They are made of single beams, called girders, whose ends rest on piers or abutments. These bridges are used to cross most areas. A span length can reach up to 300 m. The Jesse J. Jones Bridge in Houston, Texas has a main span of 230 m.

**2 Arch bridges** These are structures in which each span forms an arch. It is one of the oldest types of bridge. The majority of arch bridges have short spans and are made of stone or wood. Long-span bridges are made of concrete or steel as is the Sydney Harbour bridge, Australia. This has a main span of 503 m.

**3 Drawbridges** These have a road crossing them which is moved to provide clearance for large ships to pass. There are three types of drawbridge: a bascule bridge (**a**) which tilts upwards to open; a lift bridge (**b**) which rises up between two towers at each end; and a swing bridge (**c**) which swings sideways to let ships pass.

**4 Truss girder** Truss bridges are supported by a framework called trusses. The parts of the trusses are arranged in triangles. A truss is lighter than a girder. These bridges are built over canyons, rivers and other areas. Many have spans of 300 m. Most modern bridges have roads on top of the trusses.

**5 Cantilever** Two individual beams called cantilevers extend from opposite banks of a river and are joined together above the water by a beam. The Forth Rail Bridge in Scotland has two main spans of 520 m.

**6 Suspension bridge** The road, or deck, of the bridge hangs from steel cables that are supported by two high towers. Suspension bridges are used to span long distances. The Golden Gate Bridge has a main span of 1280 m.

**7 Cable-stayed** These bridges are similar to suspension bridges but the cables which support the road are connected to the towers. The Second Hooghly Bridge, India is an example of a cable-stayed bridge.

# 5

# THE ARTS

# 25 000–5000 BC

25 000 BC Use of fire, stone tools and weapons
20 000 BC Improved stone, wood and bone tools and weapons
10 000 BC Delicate stone tools, sickles, handsaws, needles, fishing
lines and hooks, boats, canoes, nets and traps

ARCHITECTURE

| 20 000 BC | | AD 1 | |
|---|---|---|---|

Neolithic 7000–1500 BC

**8000–6000 BC** Catal Hüyük, Turkey

PAINTING AND SCULPTURE

**30 000–25 000 BC** Venus of Willendorf
**15 000–10 000 BC** Cave paintings, Lascaux, France
**15 000–10 000 BC** Clay relief of bison, Le Tuc d'Audobert, France
**15 000–10 000 BC** Relief horses, Cap Blanc, France
**15 000–10 000 BC** Carving of bison with turned head, La Madeleine, France
**8000–3000 BC** Hunting scene, El Cerro, Spain
**6150 BC** Painting of landscape with volcano, Catal Hüyük, Turkey
**5900 BC** Sculpture of seated goddess, Catal Hüyük, Turkey

# 5000 BC – AD 1

3200 BC Early farmers and cultivators
2500 BC Ur of the Chaldees, a Sumerian city, flourishing
1500 BC Assyrian empire develops
336 BC Alexander the Great becomes king of Macedon

ARCHITECTURE

Sumerian 3500–2500 BC
Egyptian 3500 BC–AD 480
Minoan 3000–1100 BC
Babylonian 1900–1750 BC
Mycenaean 1500–1100 BC
Assyrian 1000–612 BC
Etruscan 750–c. 200 BC
Greek c. 600–300 BC
Hellenistic 300–30 BC
Roman 300 BC–AD 395

**3000s BC** White Temple, Uruk
**2650 BC** First pyramid for King Zhoser, Saqqarah, Egypt
**2600–2500 BC** Pyramids, Giza, Egypt
**2500 BC** Stonehenge, England
**2000 BC** 'Ur-Nammu's Ziggurat, Ur
**1500 BC** Knossos, Crete, Greece
**1300 BC** Lion Gate, Mycenae
**742–706 BC** Palace of Sargon II, Khorsabad, Iraq
**575 BC** Ishtar Gate, Babylon
**518–460 BC** Persepolis, Iran
**447–436 BC** Parthenon, Athens, Greece
**300 BC** Tomb of the Reliefs, Cerveteri, Italy
**20 BC** Pont du Gard, France

## PAINTING AND SCULPTURE

**3000 BC** Murals, Egypt
**2500–2000 BC** Statuette of dancer, Mohenjo-Daro, Pakistan
**2530 BC** Great Sphinx, Giza, Egypt
**2113–2096 BC** Stele of Ur, Ur
**1712 BC** Lion Hunt, Mesopotamia
**1500 BC** Cretan figures cast in bronze, Crete
**1500 BC** Bull fresco, Knossos, Crete
**1365 BC** Bust of Nefertiti, Egypt
**850 BC** Reliefs from the city of Nimrod, Iraq
**525 BC** Frieze showing battle of gods and giants, Delphi, Greece
**500 BC** Apollo, Veii, Italy
**480 BC** Tomb of the Diver (banqueting scenes), Paestum, Italy
**450 BC** Discobolus by Myron
**190 BC** Winged Victory of Samothrace
**100 BC** *Venus de Milo*, Melos
**60–50 BC** Dionysiac frieze, Villa of the Mysteries, Pompeii, Italy

## MUSIC

**2200 BC** Egyptian harp
**2000 BC** Lute known in Mesopotamia
**800 BC** Assyrian music
**657 BC** First music school established in Sparta
**408 BC** Choir forms part of *Orestes* by Euripides

## THEATRE

**458 BC** *The Oresteia* by Aeschylus
**441 BC** *Antigone* by Sophocles

**413 BC** *Electra* by Sophocles
**411 BC** *Lysistrata* by Aristophanes
**166 BC** *The Girl from Andros* by Terence

LITERATURE

**2345 BC** Earliest pyramid texts
**2000 BC** The Gilgamesh epic, Sumer
**800 BC** Phoenician alphabet
**800 BC** *The Illiad* and *The Odyssey* by Homer
**590 BC** Poetry by Sappho of Lesbos
**500 BC** Aesop's fables
**55 BC** *De Oratore* by Cicero
**30 BC** *The Aeneid* by Virgil

# AD 1–800

**64** Great fire of Rome
**79** Eruption of Vesuvius, destruction of Pompeii and Herculaneum
**267** Goths sweep across Asia Minor
**610** Prophet Mohammed begins conversion of Arabs to Islam
**711** Muslim invasion of Córdoba, Seville and Toledo
**771** Charlemagne becomes sole ruler of the Franks

ARCHITECTURE

Roman 300 BC – AD 365
Early Christian AD 33–500
Byzantine 330–1453
**BRITAIN**
Anglo-Saxon c. 650–1100
**FRANCE**
Carolingian 750–900

**72–80** Colosseum, Rome, Italy
**118–28** Pantheon, Rome, Italy
**200** Teotihuacán, Mexico
**212–16** Baths of Caracalla, Rome, Italy
**306–16** Porta Nigra, Trier, Germany (**a**)
**432–40** Nave of Santa Maria Maggiore, Rome
**532–7** Hagia Sophia, Istanbul, Turkey (**b**)
**540–8** San Vitale, Ravenna, Italy
**691** Dome of the Rock, Jerusalem

a         b

## PAINTING AND SCULPTURE

**1–10** Painting from villa at Boscotrecase, Italy
**63–9** Paintings from the House of the Vettii, Pompeii, Italy
**113** Trajan's Column, Rome, Italy
**161–80** Bronze equestrian statue of Marcus Aurelius, Rome
**203** Carvings on the Arch of Septimus Severus, Rome
**312–15** Carvings on the Arch of Constantine, Rome
**422–32** Doors of Santa Sabina, Rome
**500** Painting of St Peter at the Monastery of St Catherine, Mount Sinai
**700** Lindisfarne Gospels, England

## MUSIC

**390** 'Allelujah' hymns established in Christian Church
**c. 500** Bone flutes and skin drums in Peru
**580** Harps of six and 12 strings played in Europe
**700–800** Wind organ introduced in western Europe
**790–815** Church organs introduced to Europe from Constantinople

## THEATRE

**c. 25–65** Seneca the Younger writes nine tragedies based on Greek myth
**197** *Apologeticus* by Tertullian
**c. 290** Roman theatre in Verona
**c. 300** Records of the earliest religious plays
**304** The actor Genesius is martyred during a performance in Rome

## LITERATURE

**9** *Metamorphoses* by Ovid
**48–130** New Testament Gospels
**77** *Natural History* compiled by Pliny the Elder
**98–128** Satires by Juvenal
**105–115** *Parallel Lives* by Plutarch
**117** *Annals* by Tacitus
**730** *Beowulf*, Anglo-Saxon poem

## 800–1200

**800** Coronation of Charlemagne as Holy Roman Emperor
**1066** Norman conquest of Britain

### ARCHITECTURE

Byzantine 330–1453
**BRITAIN**
Anglo Saxon c. 650–1100
Norman 1045–1180
Early English 1175–1250
Gothic 1175–1630
**FRANCE**
Carolingian 750–900
Cistercian 1098–1270
Romanesque c. 800–1200
Gothic 1140–1534
Rayonnant 1194–1400
**GERMANY**
Ottonian 900–1024
**SPAIN**
Mudejar 1110–1500

**1063** San Marco, Venice, Italy
**1079–93** Winchester Cathedral, England
**1093–1133** Durham Cathedral, England
**1150** Wooden stave church, Borgund, Norway
**1194–1220** Chartres Cathedral, France

### PAINTING AND SCULPTURE

**1066–77** Bayeux Tapestry, France
**1090–1100** Bronze doors of Santa Zeno, Verona, Italy
**1140** *Life of Moses*, St Denis, Paris, France
**1150–60** Winchester Bible, England
**1156** Decoration on the royal portal, Chartres Cathedral, France
**1178** *Descent from the Cross* by Antelami, Parma Cathedral, Italy
**1135** *Three Prophets* by Niccolò, Ferrara Cathedral, Italy

### MUSIC

**950** Book of Songs, by Abu'l Farad
**1175** The Minnesinger create a tradition of German songs inspired by
the troubadors

**THEATRE**
**900–1000** Miracle plays popular in England

**LITERATURE**
**821** *Life of Charlemagne* (*Vita Caroli Magni*) by Einhard
**891** *The Anglo-Saxon Chronicle* begun
**c 1100** *Chanson de Roland*
**1180** *Legend of the Holy Grail* by Chrétien de Troyes
**1196** *Igor Song* written in Russia

# 1200–1400
**1288** Ottoman Empire founded
**1347** Black Death

**ARCHITECTURE**

| 1200 | | | | 1400 |
|------|--|--|--|------|
| | | | | |

Byzantine 330–1453
**BRITAIN**
Early English 1175–1250
Gothic 1175–1630
**FRANCE**
Cistercian 1098–1270
Gothic 1140–1534
Rayonnant 1194–1400
**SPAIN**
Mudejar 1110–1500

**1220–58** Salisbury Cathedral, England
**1299–1301** Palazzo Vecchio, Florence, Italy
**1309** Ducal Palace, Venice, Italy
**1316–64** Palace of the Popes, Avignon, France
**1351–1412** Cloisters of Gloucester Cathedral, England
**1391** Court of the Lions, Alhambra, Granada, Spain

**PAINTING AND SCULPTURE**
**1210–15** Decoration on the south portal, Chartres Cathedral, France
**1225–55** Decoration on the west front, Wells Cathedral, England
**1265** Pulpit, Siena Cathedral, Italy
**1304** Fresco cycle by Giotto, Padua, Italy
**1325–8** *Book of Hours* by Jeanne d'Evreux
**1360–80** *Madonna della Rosa* by Pisano
**1380** *Nativity* by Giusto de' Menabuoi, Padua

### MUSIC

**1200–1300** Carmina Burana, songs collected
**c. 1250** 'Sumer is icumen in', English song
**c. 1300** The madrigal emerges in Italy
**1388** The recorder (end-blown flute) is first mentioned

### THEATRE

**1320** *Ten Virgin Play* performed at Eisenach, Germany
**1367–70** *Piers Plowman* by William Langland

### LITERATURE

**1205** *Nibelungenlied*, Germany
**1270** *Summa Theologica* by Thomas Aquinas
**1307** *The Divine Comedy* (*Divina Commedia*) by Dante Alighieri
**1351** *The Decameron* by Giovanni Boccaccio
**1366** *Canzoniere* by Petrarch
**1387** *The Canterbury Tales* by Geoffrey Chaucer

# 1400–1550

**1415** Battle of Agincourt
**c. 1455** Gutenberg's Bible printed
**1492** Columbus discovers San Salvador
**1527** Sack of Rome

### ARCHITECTURE

Byzantine 330–1453
**BRITAIN**
Gothic 1175–1630
Tudor 1485–1558
**FRANCE**
Gothic 1140–1534
**SPAIN**
Mudejar 1110–1500
Plateresque 1480–1552
**ITALY**
Renaissance 1420–1600
Mannerism 1530–1600

**1419** Foundling Hospital by Brunelleschi, Florence, Italy
**1458** Palazzo Pitti, Florence, begun
**1503–19** Henry VII's Chapel, Westminster Abbey, London, England
**1520** Hampton Court Palace, London, begun

## PAINTING AND SCULPTURE

**1425–52** *Gates of Paradise* by Ghiberti, Florence
**1428** *Annunciation* by Fra Angelico
**1434** *Arnolfini Marriage* by Jan van Eyck
**1435** *David* by Donatello
**1475** *Martyrdom of St Sebastian* by Antonio Pollaiuolo
**1495–7** *The Last Supper* by Leonardo da Vinci
**1498–1500** *Pietà* by Michelangelo, St Peter's Basilica, Vatican City
**1501–4** *David* by Michelangelo
**1503** *Mona Lisa* by Leonardo da Vinci
**1536–41** *Last Judgement* fresco by Michelangelo, Sistine Chapel
**1554** *Perseus* by Cellini

## MUSIC AND OPERA

**1523** Keyboard music printed in Italy with right- and left-hand staves
**1537** Music conservatories founded for boys in Naples, and for girls in Venice

## THEATRE AND BALLET

**1400–1500** Morality plays develop in France
**1490** Ballet develops at Italian courts
**1465–1519** *Mankind* and *Everyman* performed in England
**1516** *Orlando Furioso* by Ludovico Ariosto

## LITERATURE

**1424** *La Belle Dame Sans Merci* by Alain Chartier
**1435** *Della Pittura* (*On Painting*) by Leon Battista Alberti
**1444** *Eurialus and Lucretia* by Aeneas Silvius Piccolomini
**1450** Vatican Library founded
**1469** *William Tell* legend written
**1470** *Le Morte d'Arthur* by Sir Thomas Malory
**1492** *La Cárcel de amor* (*The Prison of Love*) by Diego de San Pedro
**1503** 'The Thrissill and the Rois' by William Dunbar
**1516** *Utopia* by Sir Thomas More
**1521** Bible translation begun by Martin Luther
**1528** *Il libro del cortegiano* by Baldassare Castiglione
**1534** *Gargantua* by François Rabelais
**1544** *The Heptamaron* by Mergeurite of Navarre

# 1550–1650

**1558** Coronation of Elizabeth I of England
**1618** Thirty Years' War begins
**1620** Pilgrim Fathers set sail from Plymouth for the New World
**1643** Reign of Louis XIV begins

## ARCHITECTURE

**BRITAIN**
Tudor 1485–1558
Elizabethan 1558–1603
Jacobean 1603–25
Classical-Baroque 1619–1724
**FRANCE**
Louis XIV 1643–1715
**ITALY**
Renaissance 1420–1600
Mannerism 1520–1600
Early Baroque 1585–1625
High Baroque 1625–75
**NORTH AMERICA**
English Colonial 1607–1700
Dutch Colonial 1614–64

**1555–60** Cathedral of St Basil, Moscow, Russia (**a**)
**1567** Villa Rotonda, near Vicenza, Italy, by Andrea Palladio

a

b

**1588–91** Dome of St Peter, Rome, Italy (**b**)
**1562–82** The Escorial Palace, Spain, by Juan Bautista de Toledo and Juan de Herrera
**1587–91** The Rialto Bridge, Venice
**1619–22** The Banqueting House, London, by Inigo Jones

## PAINTING AND SCULPTURE
**1554** *Venus* and *Adonis* by Titian
**1554–67** *Mars* and *Neptune* by Sansovino
**1565** *The Peasant Wedding* by Brueghel the Elder
**1591–4** *The Last Supper* by Tintoretto
**1597–1601** *The Life of St Matthew* by Caravaggio
**1586** *The Burial of Count Orgaz* by El Greco
**1622–5** Medici cycle by Rubens
**1625** *Apollo and Daphne* by Bernini
**1642** *The Night Watch* by Rembrandt

## MUSIC AND OPERA
**1571** Five-part Mass by Palestrina
**1575** *Cantiones sacrae* by William Byrd and Thomas Tallis
**1580** First mention of 'Greensleeves'
**1607** *L'Orfeo* by Monteverdi
**1627** *Dafne* by Heinrich Schütz
**1642** *L'incoronazione di Poppea* by Monteverdi

## THEATRE AND BALLET
**1590** *Tamburlaine the Great* by Christopher Marlowe
**1581** *Ballet Comique de la Reine* (the earliest ballet with music) by Baltasar de Beaujoyeux
**1600–1** *Hamlet* by William Shakespeare
**1621** *Andromeda* by Lope de Vega
**1637** *Le Cid* by Corneille
**c. 1643** Illustre Théâtre founded in Paris by Molière

## LITERATURE
**1578** *Sonets pour Hélène* by Pierre de Ronsard
**1580** *Essais* by Michel de Montaigne
**1581** *Jerusalem Delivered* (*Gerusalemme Liberata*) by Torquato Tasso
**1590–96** *The Faerie Queene* by Edmund Spenser
**1605** *Don Quixote* part I by Miguel de Cervantes
**1633** Poems by John Donne, published posthumously
**1638** *Lycidas* by John Milton

## 1650–1750

**1666** Great Fire of London
**1672–1725** Peter the Great of Russia

### ARCHITECTURE

**BRITAIN**
Classical–Baroque 1619–1724
William and Mary 1689–1702
Queen Anne 1702–14
Georgian 1714–1820
Palladian 1715–70
**FRANCE**
Louis XIV 1643–1715
**GERMANY**
Rococo 1720–60
**ITALY**
High Baroque 1625–75
**NORTH AMERICA**
English Colonial 1607–1700
Dutch Colonial 1614–64
Georgian 1714–76

a

**1661–1756** Palais de Versaille by Louis le Vau (**a**)
**1675–1710** St Paul's Cathedral, London by Christopher Wren
**1705–24** Blenheim Palace, Oxfordshire, by Vanbrugh and Hawksmoor
**1723–5** The Spanish Steps, Rome by Francesco de Sanctis

## PAINTING AND SCULPTURE

**1654** *Bathsheba* by Rembrandt van Rijn
**1656** Las Meninas by Velázquez
**1665–68** *The Lacemaker* by Jan Vermeer
**1715** *Mezzetin* by Antoine Watteau
**1725** *Four Views of Venice* by Antonio Canaletto
**1740** *The Triumph of Venus* by François Boucher

## MUSIC AND OPERA

**1689** *Dido and Aeneas* by Henry Purcell
**1724** *Julius Caesar (Giulio Cesare)* by George Frederick Handel
**1725** *The Four Seasons* by Antonio Vivaldi
**1727** *St Matthew Passion* by J.S. Bach
**1729** *The Beggar's Opera* by John Gay
**1737** *Castor et Pollux* by Jean-Philippe Rameau
**1742** *Messiah* by George Frederick Handel

## THEATRE AND BALLET

**1666** *Le Misanthrope* by Molière
**1667** *Andromaque* by Jean Baptiste Racine
**1670** *All For Love* by John Dryden
**1713** School of Dance established at the Paris Opera
**1738** Imperial Ballet School founded In St Petersburg

## LITERATURE

**1660** Samuel Pepys begins his *Diary*
**1667–74** *Paradise Lost* by John Milton
**1668–94** *Fables* by La Fontaine
**1678** *La Princesse de Clèves* by Comtesse de La Fayette
**1699** *Télémaque* by Fénelon
**1719** *Robinson Crusoe* by Daniel Defoe
**1726** *Gulliver's Travels* by Jonathan Swift
**1748** *Clarissa* by Samuel Richardson
**1749** *Tom Jones* by Henry Fielding

## 1750–1800
**1776** American Declaration of Independence
**1789** French Revolution begins

### ARCHITECTURE

| 1750 | | | | | 1800 |
|------|--|--|--|--|------|

**BRITAIN**
Georgian 1714–1820
Neoclassical 1750–1840
Gothic Revival 1750–1900s
**FRANCE**
Late Renaissance 1715–1830
Louis XV 1715–74
Neoclassical 1750–1870
**GERMANY**
Rococo 1720–60
Neoclassical 1750–1830
Greek Revival 1788–1830
**ITALY**
Neoclassical 1750–1870

**1748–77** Strawbery Hill, Twickenham, England, by Horace Walpole
**1757–90** Panthéon, Paris, by Jacques-Germain Soufflot
**1767–75** Royal Crescent, Bath, by John Wood the Younger
**1776-78** Teatro della Scala, Milan by Giuseppe Piermarini
**1789–93** Brandenburg Gate, Berlin, by Carl Langhans

### PAINTING AND SCULPTURE
**1751** *Exhibition of a Rhinoceros at Venice* by Pietro Longhi
**1755** *Madame de Pompadour* by Maurice-Quentin de La Tour
**1767** *The Swing* by Jean Fragonard
**1773** Self-portrait by Joshua Reynolds
**1784** *The Oath of the Horatii* by Jacques-Louis David
**1800** *Maja Unclothed* by Francisco Goya

### MUSIC AND OPERA
**1762** *Orfeo ed Eurydice* by Christoph Willibald von Gluck
**1786** *The Marriage of Figaro* by Wolfgang Amadeus Mozart
**1787** *Eine kleine Nachtmusik* by Mozart
**1798** *The Creation* by Franz Joseph Haydn

### THEATRE AND BALLET
**1776** Bolshoi Ballet founded in Moscow
**1784** *Le Mariage de Figaro* by Caron de Beaumarchais

**LITERATURE**
**1759** *Candide* by Voltaire
**1759–67** *Tristram Shandy* by Laurence Sterne
**1761** *Julie, ou la Nouvelle Héloïse* by Jean-Jacques Rousseau
**1766** *The Vicar of Wakefield* by Oliver Goldsmith
**1774** *The Sorrows of Young Werther* by Johann Wolfgang von Goethe
**1776–88** *Decline and Fall of the Roman Empire* by Edward Gibbon
**1782** *Les Liaisons dangereuses* by Choderlos de Laclos
**1786** *Poems, chiefly in the Scottish dialect* by Robert Burns
**1798** *Lyrical Ballads* by Wordsworth and Coleridge

# 1800–1850
**1804** Napoleon becomes Emperor of France
**1837** Accession of Queen Victoria of the United Kingdom

**ARCHITECTURE**

**BRITAIN**
Georgian 1714–1820
Gothic Revival c. 1750–1900
Neoclassical 1750–1840
Greek Revival c. 1819–40
Regency 1811–30
Victorian 1837–1901
**FRANCE**
Late Renaissance 1715–1830
Neoclassical 1750–1870
(First) Empire 1800–30
Neo-Renaissance 1830–48
High Neo-Renaissance 1848–70
**GERMANY**
Neoclassical 1750–1830s
Greek Revival 1788–1830s
Gothic Revival c. 1824–80s
Biedermeier c. 1815–48
**ITALY**
Neoclassical 1750–1870
**UNITED STATES**
Post-Colonial c. 1790–1815
Greek Revival 1798–1860
Gothic Revival c. 1825–70

**ARCHITECTURE**
**1806–15** The Admiralty, Leningrad, by Andreyan Zakharov
**1806–35** L'Arc de Triomphe, Paris, by Jean Chalgrin
**1823–47** The British Museum, London, by Robert Smirke
**1825** Buckingham Palace, London, by John Nash
**1836–41** Law Courts, Lyons, by Louis Baltard
**1840–64** Houses of Parliament, London, by Charles Barry

**PAINTING**
**1819** *The Raft of the Medusa* by Théodore Géricault
**1821** *The Haywain* by John Constable
**1821** Bust of Goethe by Christian Rauch
**1830** *Liberty Leading the People* by Eugène Delacroix
**1833-6** *La Marseillaise* by François Rude

**MUSIC AND OPERA**
**1800** Symphony No.1 in C Major by Ludwig van Beethoven
**1805** *Fidelio* by Beethoven
**1808** Symphony No.5 in C Minor by Beethoven
**1816** *The Barber of Seville* by Gioacchino Rossini
**1819** *'The Trout' Quintet* by Franz Schubert
**1830** *Symphonie Fantastique* by Hector Berlioz
**1843** *The Flying Dutchman* by Richard Wagner

**THEATRE AND BALLET**
**1804** *Wilhelm Tell* by Johann von Schiller
**1808** *Faust* part I by Johann Wolfgang von Goethe
**1836** T*he Government Inspector* by Nikolai Gogol
**1842** *Giselle* first staged in London

**LITERATURE**
**1812–15** Fairy tales by Jacob and Wilhelm Grimm
**1813** *Pride and Prejudice* by Jane Austen
**1819–24** *Don Juan* by Lord Byron
**1818** *Frankenstein* by Mary Shelley
**1826** *Last of the Mohicans* by James Fenimore Cooper
**1830** *Le Rouge et le noir* by Stendhal
**1831** *Notre Dame de Paris* by Victor Hugo
**1835–72** Fairy tales by Hans Christian Andersen
**1837–8** *Oliver Twist* by Charles Dickens
**1842** *Dead Souls* by Nikolai Gogol
**1844–5** *The Three Musketeers* by Alexandre Dumas
**1847** *Wuthering Heights* by Emily Brontë

# 1850–1900

**1859–61** Unification of Italy
**1861** Outbreak of American Civil War

## ARCHITECTURE

**BRITAIN**
Gothic Revival c. 1750–1900
Victorian 1830–1900
**FRANCE**
High Neo-Renaissance 1848–70
Beaux Arts 1865–1913
Art Nouveau 1880s–1914
**GERMANY**
Gothic Revival c. 1824–80s
**ITALY**
Neoclassical 1750–1870
**NORTH AMERICA**
Greek Revival 1798–1860
Gothic Revival c. 1825–70s
Italianate 1850–85
Beaux Arts 1865–1913
Chicago School c. 1871–93
Classical 1890–1943

**1861–74** L'Opéra, Paris, by Charles Garnier
**1865–71** St Pancras Station Hotel, London, by George Gilbert Scott
**1864–72** Albert Memorial, London, by George Gilbert Scott
**1865** The Capitol, Washington DC, completed by Thomas U. Walter
**1882–1930** Sagrada Familia, Barcelona by Antonio Gaudí
**1887–9** Eiffel Tower, Paris, by Gustave Eiffel
**1897–1909** School of Art, Glasgow, by Charles Rennie Mackintosh

## PAINTING AND SCULPTURE

**1852–4** *Ophelia* by John Millais
**1856** *Madame Moitessier* by Jean Auguste Ingres
**1859** *The Angelus* by François Millet
**1863** *Le Déjeuner sur l'Herbe* by Édouard Manet
**1871** *The Dying Centaur* by William Rimmer
**1872** *Impression: Sunrise* by Claude Monet

**1875–7** *Age of Bronze* by Auguste Rodin
**1881** *Petite Danseuse de quatorze ans* by Edgar Degas
**1889** *Self-portrait with Severed Ear* by Vincent Van Gogh
**1893** *The Scream* by Edvard Munch

## MUSIC AND OPERA

**1853** *La traviata* by Giuseppe Verdi
**1861** Piano Concerto No 1 in D Minor by Brahms
**1867** *By the Beautiful Blue Danube*, waltz by Johann Strauss
**1876** *Der Ring des Nibelungen* by Richard Wagner
**1888** *Scheherazade* by Nikolai Rimsky-Korsokov
**1894** *L'après-midi d'un faune* by Claude Debussy
**1896** *La Bohème* by Giacomo Puccini

## THEATRE AND BALLET

**1860** Imperial Russian Ballet of St Petersburg (Kirov Ballet)
**1867** *Peer Gynt* by Henrik Ibsen
**1870** *Coppélia* by Léo Delibes
**1877** *Swan Lake* by Peter Tchaikovsky
**1890** *Hedda Gabler* by Henrik Ibsen
**1891** *The Nutcracker* by Peter Tchaikovsky
**1894** *Arms and the Man* by George Bernard Shaw
**1895** *The Importance of Being Earnest* by Oscar Wilde
**1895** *The Seagull* by Anton Chekhov

## LITERATURE

**1857** *Madame Bovary* by Gustave Flaubert
**1857** *Les Fleurs du mal* by Charles Baudelaire
**1858** *The Song of Hiawatha* by Henry W. Longfellow
**1862** *Les Misérables* by Victor Hugo
**1863–9** *War and Peace* by Leo Tolstoy
**1866** *Crime and Punishment* by Fyodor Dostoevsky
**1871** *Middlemarch* by George Eliot
**1881** *Portrait of a Lady* by Henry James
**1885** *Germinal* by Émile Zola
**1891** *Tess of the D'Urbervilles* by Thomas Hardy

# 1900–1945

**1914–18** World War I
**1917** Russian Revolution
**1939–45** World War II

## ARCHITECTURE

International Modern 1930–
**BRITAIN**
Art Deco 1925–35
**FRANCE**
Art Nouveau 1880s–1914
**GERMANY**
Expressionism 1905–33
Bauhaus 1919–37
**ITALY**
Fascist 1922–43
**NORTH AMERICA**
Beaux Arts 1865–1913
Classical 1890–1943

**1905–6** La Samaritaine department store, Paris, by Frantz Jourdain
**1909–10** Robie House, Chicago, by Frank Lloyd Wright
**1909–11** St Jude's, Hampstead Garden Suburb, London, by Edward Lutyens
**1909–23** Stockholm City Hall by Ragnar Østberg
**1923–5** Tribune Tower, Chicago, by Raymond Hood
**1925–6** Bauhaus School of Art, Dessau, by Walter Gropius
**1929–31** Empire State Building, New York, by Shreve, Lamb and Harmon
**1936** Impington Village College, Cambridge, by Gropius and Fry

## PAINTING AND SCULPTURE

**1901** *Madeleine I* by Henri Matisse
**1906–7** *Les Desmoiselles d'Avignon* by Pablo Picasso
**1908** *Nu Rouge* by Marc Chagall
**1909** *The Kiss* by Gustav Klimt
**1913** *Unique Forms of Continuity in Space* by Umberto Boccioni
**1917** *Seated Girl* by Amedeo Modigliani
**1921** *Composition in Red, Yellow and Blue* by Piet Mondrian
**1929** *Reclining Figure* by Henry Moore
**1931** *The Persistence of Memory* by Salvador Dalí
**1933** *The Human Condition* by René Magritte
**1937** *Guernica* by Picasso

**MUSIC AND OPERA**
**1901** Piano Concerto No. 2 in C Minor by Sergey Rachmaninoff
**1904** *Madama Butterfly* by Giacomo Puccini
**1907** March 'Pomp and Circumstance' by Edward Elgar
**1909–10** Symphony No. 9 in D Major by Gustav Mahler
**1911** *Der Rosenkavalier* by Richard Strauss
**1922** *Façade* by William Walton
**1924** *The Cunning Little Vixen* by Leos Janácek
**1935** *Porgy and Bess* by George Gershwin
**1936** *Music for Strings, Percussion and Celeste* by Béla Bartók
**1942** *Lincoln Portrait* by Aaron Copland

**THEATRE AND BALLET**
**1904** *The Cherry Orchard* by Anton Chekhov
**1910** *The Firebird* by Igor Stravinsky
**1913** *The Rite of Spring* by Stravinsky
**1921** *Six Characters in Search of an Author* by Luigi Pirandello
**1928** *Boléro* by Maurice Ravel
**1925** *Hay Fever* by Noël Coward
**1938** *Romeo and Juliet* by Sergei Prokofiev
**1941** *Mother Courage and her Children* by Bertolt Brecht

**LITERATURE**
**1901** *Buddenbrooks* by Thomas Mann
**1908** *A Room with a View* by E.M. Forster
**1913–27** *À la recherche du temps perdu* by Marcel Proust
**1922** *The Waste Land* by T.S. Eliot
**1922** *Ulysses* by James Joyce
**1925** *The Trial* by Franz Kafka
**1927** *To the Lighthouse* by Virginia Woolf
**1928** *Lady Chatterley's Lover* by D.H. Lawrence
**1930** *Collected Poems* by Robert Frost
**1932** *Brave New World* by Aldous Huxley
**1933** *La Condition humaine* by André Malraux
**1940** *For Whom the Bell Tolls* by Ernest Hemingway
**1942** *L'Étranger* by Albert Camus

# 1945–1990s

1950–3 Korean War
1954-75 Vietnam War

## ARCHITECTURE

| 1945 | | | | 1990s |
|---|---|---|---|---|

International Modern 1930–
Brutalism 1950–80
Post Modernism 1980s–
High Tech 1980–

**1946-60** Guggenheim Museum, New York, by Frank Lloyd Wright
**1948-50** Termini Station, Rome, by Eugénio Montuori
**1950-52** Town Hall Säynätsälo, Finland, by Alvar Aalto
**1977** Centre George Pompidou, Paris, by Rogers and Piano
**1977–8** East Building, National Gallery, Washington DC, by I.M. Pei
**1980** Portland Building, Portland, Oregon, USA, by Michael Graves

## PAINTING AND SCULPTURE

**1947** *Man Pointing* by Alberto Giacometti
**1948** *Number One* by Jackson Pollock
**1953** *Figure with Meat* by Francis Bacon
**1958** *Four Darks on Red* by Mark Rothko
**1962** *Marilyn Monroe* by Andy Warhol
**1963** *Whaam!* by Roy Lichtenstein

## MUSIC AND OPERA

**1945** *Peter Grimes* by Benjamin Britten
**1954** *Moses und Aron* by Arnold Schoenberg
**1955** *A Midsummer Marriage* by Michael Tippett
**1957** *Dialogues des Carmélites* by Francis Poulenc
**1971** Mass by Leonard Bernstein
**1971** Symphony No. 15 in A Major by Dmitri Shostakovich
**1980** *Satyagraha* by Philip Glass
**1981** *Nixon in China* by John Adams

## THEATRE AND BALLET

**1946** *The Iceman Cometh* by Eugene O'Neill
**1947** *A Streetcar Named Desire* by Tennessee Williams
**1949** *Death of a Salesman* by Arthur Miller
**1954** *Waiting for Godot* by Samuel Beckett
**1956** *Look Back in Anger* by John Osborne
**1960** *The Birthday Party* by Harold Pinter
**1962** *Improvisations* by Aaron Copland
**1982** *The Real Thing* by Tom Stoppard
**1983** *The Right Stuff* by Sam Shepherd

LITERATURE
**1954** *Lord of the Flies* by William Golding
**1955** *Lolita* by Vladimir Nabokov
**1957** *On the Road* by Jack Kerouac
**1962** *One Day in the Life of Ivan Denisovich* by Alexander Solzhenitsyn
**1965** *Ariel* by Sylvia Plath
**1967** *One Hundred Years of Solitude* by Gabriel García Márquez
**1988** *The Satanic Verses* by Salman Rushdie

# WESTERN STYLES AND ART MOVEMENTS

35 000 BC– AD 1

Prehistoric Art 35 000–1500 BC
Egyptian Art 3500 BC–AD 480
Sumerian 3500–2500 BC
Babylonian 1900–750 BC
Hittite 1600–1150 BC
Assyrian 1000–612 BC
Ancient Persia 539–330 BC
Minoan 2800–1400 BC
Mycenaean 1500–1100 BC
Greece 900–30 BC
Etruscan 750–200 BC
Roman 509 BC–AD 476

AD 1–1700

Early Christian AD 33–500
Byzantine 330–1453
Islamic Art c. 600–1630
Celtic Art 600–800
Carolingian Period 750–900
Ottonian Period 900–1024
Romanesque Art 1100–1250
Gothic Art 1140–1500
Renaissance 1420–1600
Mannerism 1530–1600
Baroque 1585–1675
Dutch painting 1650–1675

## 1700–1900

Rococo 1720–60
Neoclassicism 1748–1815
Romanticism 1790–1860
Realism 1830–70
Arts & Crafts Movement 1860–1900
Impressionism 1869–1900
Post-Impressionism 1879–1900
Pre-Raphaelites 1848–60
Symbolism 1886–1914
Art Nouveau 1880–1910

## 1900–2000

Fauvism 1899–1908
Expressionism 1905–14 (**a**)
Bauhaus 1919–37
Cubism 1908–20
Futurism 1909–14
Dada 1915–24 (**b**)
Surrealism 1924–39
Social Realism 1930s
American Realism 1930–48
Abstract Art 1940s–60
Pop Art 1950s–60s
Op Art 1960s
Colour Field Painting 1955–67
Photorealism 1960s–70s

a

b

# POPULAR CULTURE

### The cinema

**1850s** Thaumatrope (spinning disc) creates illusion of movement. Zoetrope (revolving disc) involves images on the inside of a disc appearing to move when seen through a slit.

**1869** Celluloid replaces glass plates as a way of storing photographic images.

**1872** Eadweard Muybridge records movement of animals and humans with sequences of still photographs.

**1877–9** Praxihoscope projects sequential pictures onto a screen.

**1878–95** Marey explores photographic techniques of recording movement.

**1888** William Friese-Green patents a movie camera.

**1889** Edison invents 35 mm film.

**1890–4** Edison demonstrates kinetograph camera and kinetoscope (personal viewer of picture sequence).

**1895** The Lumière brothers project moving images in public performances.

**1896** Pathé combines recording discs in synchronization with film projection. Vitascope device used to project images onto a screen.

**1902** Georges Méliès annotated movie *A Trip to the Moon* (*Le Voyage dans la Lune*).

**1903** First Western, *The Great Train Robbers.*

**1906** Kinemacolor (earliest colour film) patented.

**1908–11** Emile Cohl explores film animation.

**1911** Camera records Antarctica Polar expedition.

**1912** Eugene Lauste designs system for recording sound on film.

**1914–18** Newsreel coverage of World War I.

**1915** D.W. Griffith directs *The Birth of a Nation* and introduces the techniques of flashback and fade-out.

**1916** D.W. Griffith pioneers camera close-ups in *Intolerance.*

**1919** *The Cabinet of Doctor Caligari* uses expressionist art techniques. United Artists Corporation formed.

**1922** *Nosferatu* – an early vampire film by F.W. Murnau.

**1923** Phonofilm technique produces first sound film.

**1924** Kinescope television picture tube patented.

**1925** *The Gold Rush* by Charlie Chaplin, a full-length comedy featuring the famous tramp. *Battleship Potemkin* by Sergei Eisenstein, shows significant advances in film editing.

**1926** *Napoleon* by Abel Gance makes use of the wide screen.
**1927** *The Jazz Singer*, the first major talking film.
**1928** John Logie Baird transmits television pictures across the Atlantic. *Steamboat Willie* – Walt Disney's first Mickey Mouse cartoon. Fox Films develops synchronized sound and motion film.
**1932** Technicolor process developed.
**1936** *Triumph of the Will* by Leni Riefenstahl. Cinema used for propaganda.
**1939** *Gone With The Wind* starring Clarke Gable and Vivien Leigh.
**1941** Colour television invented by Peter Carl Goldmark. *Citizen Kane*, Orson Welles' first film, gains immediate critical acclaim.
**1952** Cinerama (wide screen projections) films produced.
**1953** Cinemascope (wide screen projections) films produced. 3D films (three-dimensional projections viewed through coloured spectacles) produced.
**1956** Video recorder patented by American Ampex Corporation.
**1976–7** Films commercially available on video for home viewing.
**1977** *Star Wars* by George Lucas. Exemplary use of special effects to create a sci-fi fantasy.
**1980** Video cameras produced commercially by Japanese Sony Corporation for personal use.

## Popular music

**1884** Emile Berliner records 'The Lord's Prayer' on cylinder.
**1888** First popular artist recording made by pianist Joset Hoffman for Edison.
**1892** First million-selling song on sheet music, 'After the Ball'.
**1903** Caruso makes first million-selling record, 'On with the Motley'.
**1911** Archibald Joyce forms first British big band.
**1914** W.C. Handy records 'St. Louis Blues'. Irving Berlin's first musical, 'Watch Your Step', produced in New York.
**1917** First jazz recording, 'Darktown Strutters' Ball', by Original Dixieland Jazz Band.
**1920** 'Dardanella' by Ben Selvin's orchestra – the first million-selling dance record. First blues vocal record by a black artist – 'Crazy Blues' by Mamie Smith.
**1923** Fiddlin' John Carson makes first country music recordings.
**1924** First country music million-selling record – Vernon Dalhart's 'The Prisoner's Song'.
**1927** Al Jolson stars in first talking film, a musical film – *The Jazz Singer*.

**1928** Al Jolson has first million-seller with 'Sonny Boy'. Jimmie Rodgers becomes first major country music star with 'Blue Yodel'.
**1930** Mills Brothers' 'Tiger Rag' – first black vocal group million-seller.
**1935** First production of Gershwin's *Porgy and Bess* in New York.
**1937** First million-seller by female group – Andrews Sisters' 'Bei mir bist du schön'. Bing Crosby's first million-seller – 'Sweet Leilani'. Tommy Dorsey's first million-seller – swing arrangement of 'Marie'. George Gershwin dies in California.
**1938** Ella Fitzgerald's first million-seller – 'A Tisket, A Tasket'. Benny Goodman plays first-ever jazz concert at Carnegie Hall, New York.
**1939** Lale Anderson records 'Lily Marlene', biggest hit of World War II. Glenn Miller records his signature tune, 'In The Mood'.
**1940** *Billboard* publishes first US singles chart.
**1942** Bing Crosby's 'White Christmas' – biggest-selling single ever.
**1943** Frank Sinatra's first million-seller – 'All Or Nothing At All'.
**1944** Glenn Miller disappears in plane over English Channel. Louis Jordan's first million-seller – 'Is You Is or Is You ain't my Baby'.
**1946** Ink Spots sell a million of both 'To Each His Own' and 'The Gypsy'. Al Jolson's 'The Jolson Story' is first million-selling album.
**1947** Frankie Laine's first million-seller – 'That's My Desire'.
**1948** Nat 'King' Cole's first million-seller – 'Nature Boy'. Fat's Domino's first million-seller – 'The Fat Man'. Bluesman John Lee Hooker finds fame with 'Boogie Children' and 'I'm In The Mood'. Jazz guitarist Lonnie Johnson sells a million of 'Tomorrow Night'.
**1949** Gene Autrey records 'Rudolph the Red-Nosed Reindeer' – second all-time biggest Christmas hit. Hank Williams' first million-seller – 'Lovesick Blues'.
**1950** Roy Brown has early rhythm and blues million-seller with 'Hard Luck Blues'. Zitherist Anton Karas' instrumental million–seller, 'The Third Man'.
**1951** Johnie Ray has double-sided million-seller with 'Cry/Little White Cloud That Cried'. Vera Lynn is first UK artist to top US singles chart, with 'Auf Wiedersehen'. *NME* introduces first UK singles chart – Al Martino's 'Here In My Heart' at No. 1.
**1953** Trumpeter Eddie Calvert's million-seller 'Oh Mein Papa'. Orioles has first 'doo-wop' million-seller with 'Crying In The Chapel'.
**1954** Chuck Berry perfects individual performing style.
**1955** 'Rock Around the Clock' – Bill Haley and the Comets – No. 1 worldwide.
**1956** Elvis records for RCA, and begins his amazing career.
**1957** Jerry Lee Louis storms onto the pop scene with 'Whole Lotta

Shakin' Goin' On'.
**1958** Cliff Richard begins his pop career with 'Move It' – No. 2 in UK.
**1960** Motown records first million-seller by the Miracles – 'Shop Around'.
**1961** Chubby Checker sparks 'twist fever' across the country.
**1962** Bob Dylan signs to CBS records and releases his debut LP.
**1963** 'Love Me Do' – The Beatles first release, begins worldwide Beatlemania. In USA, they take 20 singles to No. 1 in *Billboard* chart, while in UK's *NME* chart they have 17 chart-toppers.
**1964** The Rolling Stones have the first of eight UK No. 1s and hit the US top 40 for the first time.
**1965** James Brown achieves international success with his US top-ten million-seller, 'Papa's got a Brand New Bag'.
**1966** Simon and Garfunkel's first US No. 1 – 'The Sound of Silence'.
**1967** Jimi Hendrix first appears in world's pop charts.
**1968** The Doors' biggest hit – 'Hello I Love You' – goes to No. 1 in US and No. 15 in UK.
**1969** Woodstock Rock Festival attended by 400 000 people; Isle of Wight Festival takes place in UK. Led Zeppelin release their first two best-selling LPs.
**1970** Three Dog Night go to No. 1 with Randy Norman's song 'Mama Told Me (Not To Come)'.
**1971** T-Rex's first UK No 1s – 'Hot Love' and 'Get It On'.
**1972** Chuck Berry reaches No. 1 in UK and US with 'My Ding-A-Ling'. David Bowie begins a string of hits, after a three-year gap since his most successful early single, 'Space Oddity'.
**1973** Elton John has his first US No. 1 – 'Crocodile Rock'.
**1974** Queen begin a hugely successful career with their first UK single, 'Seven Seas of Rhye'.
**1975** The Bee Gees become prime movers in the roots of the disco explosion with the release of 'Jive Talkin'. David Bowie re-releases 'Space Oddity' and hits UK No. 1 spot.
**1976** Sex Pistols release 'Anarchy in the UK'.
**1977** 16 August, Elvis dies after over 100 hits and 17 chart-toppers in US and UK.
**1978** Blondie begin success in UK, hitting No. 2 spot with 'Denis'.
**1979** Pink Floyd's only UK No. 1 – 'Another Brick in the Wall'. Police have UK No. 1 with 'Message in a Bottle'. Sugarhill Gang take 'Rapper's Delight' to No. 3 in UK chart.
**1980** John Lennon killed in New York. After his death he has three No. 1s and one No. 2 in the UK. Abba's last UK No. 1 – 'Super Trouper'.

**1981** Duran Duran begin pop success with 'Planet Earth'. Michael Jackson's first solo No. 1 in the UK – 'One Day in Your Life'.
**1982** Culture Club's first UK No. 1 'Do You Really Want to Hurt Me'.
**1983** Michael Jackson has three US No. 1s from his album 'Thriller'.
**1984** Prince achieves worldwide fame with his film 'Purple Rain'.
**1985** Live Aid concert in aid of the starving in Africa. Madonna's first UK No. 1 – 'Into the Groove'.
**1986** CBS releases a five-LP boxed set, 'Bruce Springsteen Live'. George Michael's second UK No. 1 – 'A Different Corner'.
**1987** Whitney Houston's UK No.1 – 'I Wanna Dance with Somebody'. Pet Shop Boys' third UK No. 1 – 'Always On My Mind'.
**1988** U2's first UK No. 1, 'Desire', after a string of top-ten hits. The

# NON-WESTERN ARTS

Major periods of artistic activity are given with examples.

## Central and South America

| Olmec | 1200–100 BC | Giant stone statues |
|---|---|---|
| Teotihuaca | 100 BC – AD 750 | Wall paintings at Teotihuaca |
| Maya | 100–1542 | Limestone ziggurats; Tula sculpture |
| Inca | 1100–1530s | Architecture; metalwork; pottery |
| Aztec | 1325–1521 | Gold sculpture |

## India

| Indus | c.3000–1500 BC | Copper and bronzework; fertility figures |
|---|---|---|
| Vedic | 1500–600 BC | Ajanta cave carvings |
| Mauryan | 322–185 BC | Stone carving |
| Gupta | c. AD 320–750 | Buddhist iconography; Gandhara School of Art |
| Mughal | 1526–1750 | Miniatures; red forts; tombs |

## Africa

| Pharaonic | 3000–2000 BC | Pyramids |
|---|---|---|
| Nok | 200 BC | Ironwork; terracotta |
| Shona | 1000s–1800s | Architecture |
| Dogon | 1400s | Wood carving |
| Yoruba | 1500s | Masks |
| Ife | 1500s–1800s | Bronzework |
| Ashanti | 1600s | Bronzework; gold weights |

Hollies hit the UK No. 1 spot with a re-issue of their 1969 No. 3 hit, 'He Ain't Heavy, He's My Brother'.

**1989** 'Do They Know It's Christmas' is Christmas No. 1 for the second time for Band Aid II. Previously No. 1 in 1984 for Band Aid.

**1990** After 20 years, Elton John achieves his first solo UK No. 1 with 'Sacrifice'. Cliff Richard's third UK Christmas No. 1 – 'Saviour's Day'. Madonna's seventh No. 1 in the UK – 'Vogue'. Kylie Minogue's third No. 1. Of her first ten releases, none charted lower than No. 4 in the UK.

**1991** Bryan Adams holds No. 1 in UK for 16 weeks with 'Everything I Do (I Do It For You)' – a UK record.

**1992** Freddie Mercury of Queen dies of Aids. Madonna releases her book *Sex* worldwide.

## China

| | | |
|---|---|---|
| Yangshao | 2000–1500 BC | Black and red fired pottery |
| Shang | 1766–1028 BC | Cast bronzework |
| Qin | 256–206 BC | Terracotta army |
| Han | 206 BC – AD 220 | Bronze; jade; monuments |
| Tang | 618–907 | Landscape painting; Yueh stoneware |
| Song | 960–1278 | Landscape painting; celadon stoneware |
| Ming | 1368–1644 | Porcelain |
| Qing | 1644–1912 | Lacquerwork; porcelain |

## Japan

| | | |
|---|---|---|
| Jomon | 10 500–250 BC | Pottery |
| Yayoi | c. 100 BC | Bronzework; pottery |
| Kofun | c. AD 400 | 'Key-hole' tombs |
| Heian | c. 900 | Kana script |
| Ashikaga | 1300s | Noh drama; ink painting |
| Edo | 1800s | Colour-prints; miniature sculptures; lacquerwork; Shino ware |

## Southeast Asia

| | | |
|---|---|---|
| Dong Son | 300s BC – AD 1 | Bronzework |
| Sailendra | 600–1100 | Architecture |
| Khmer | 802–1431 | Architecture (Angkor Wat) |
| Pagan | 849–1287 | Architecture (Ananda Temple) |

# CLASSICAL ARCHITECTURE
Features of the front of a temple

**1 Tympanum** The triangular space within a pediment
**2 Acroterion** A pedestal on the apex or sides of a pediment
  supporting a statue or ornamental figure
**3 Pediment** A low pitched triangular gable above a façade
**4 Entablature** The upper part of an order of architecture, comprising
  the cornice, frieze and architrave
**5 Cornice** The upper and protruding part of an entablature
**6 Frieze** The middle section of an entablature, an ornamental band,
  either abstract, botanical or figurative
**7 Architrave** The lowest of the three divisions of an entablature

## Columns

### Column structure

1 **Abacus** Flat area at the top of a capital, dividing a column from its entablature
2 **Echinus** A type of moulding
3 **Annulet** A decorative moulded ring or band used in Greek, Romanesque and Gothic architecture
4 **Capital** The architectural feature at the top of a column
5 **Astragal** Classical moulded band atop a column shaft
6 **Torus** Convex moulding at column base
7 **Scotia** Concave moulding at column base
8 **Dado** Central part of pedestal between the base and cornice
9 **Plinth** Base of column pedestal
10 **Pedestal** The supporting part of a column

### Classical orders

1 **Doric** No base, a heavy, fluted shaft, and a capital composed of an ovolo moulding under a square abacus
2 **Ionic** The capital is carved to resemble a scroll
3 **Corinthian** The capital is ornately carved to resemble acanthus leaves

# CHURCHES
## Parts of a church 1

**1 Aisle** The side corridors of the main church. The north aisle is on the left when facing the altar, and the south aisle is on the right

**2 Almonry** A special room used for the distribution of alms

**3 Ambulatory** The continuation of the aisle around the choir and behind the altar

**4 Chancel** The area containing the choir and the altar, originally reserved for the clergy

**5a Chapel** A small area set aside for private worship

**5b Chantry Chapel** An endowed chapel in which prayers could be said for the soul of a benefactor

**5c Lady Chapel** Set at the east end and dedicated to the Virgin Mary

**6 Chapterhouse** The administrative centre

**7 Choir** The area between the nave and the altar, for use by the choir and clergy

**8 Cloister** The covered walkway around a courtyard

**9 Crossing** The central area between the nave, the chancel and the transept

**10 Crypt** The area under the main church

**11 Presbytery** The area around the main altar

**12 Sacristy** or **Vestry** A room for storing the priests' vestments and sacred vessels. Often also used for meetings, Sunday School, etc

**13 Sanctuary** The most sacred part of the chancel, used in the past to provide fugitives from the law with immunity from arrest

**14 Nave** The main area of the church used by the congregation. It usually has aisles on either side

**15 Slype** A passageway from cloister to transept or chapterhouse

**16 Transept** The two areas on either side of the crossing, which form part of the cross-shaped plan of the church

**Vestry** *see* **Sacristy**

**Parts of a church 2**

1 **Bartizan** A small turret projecting from a wall, parapet or tower

2 **Bellcote** A bell tower on a roof

3 **Bell gable** A bell tower mounted on the end of a wall

4a **Buttress** A masonry support against a wall

4b **Flying Buttress** A support which is arched so that the brace is away from the wall

5 **Clerestory** A row of windows in the upper part of a wall above the roof of an aisle

6 **Finial** An ornament on top of buildings

7 **Flèche** A small wooden spire

8 **Galilee** An enclosed porch at the west end of the church

9 **Gargoyle** A spout carrying water from the roof, usually decorated with a grotesque figure or head

10 **Lancet** A tall and pointed window

11 **Louvre** A window opening, in church towers, covered with overlapping boards

12 **Narthex** A porch at the west end of a church, that is usually at right angles to the nave

13 **Pinnacle** A small stone spire on top of buttresses, parapets or roofs

14 **Porch** An entrance that is covered

15 **Rose Window** A circular window

16 **Spire** A tall, pointed structure, most commonly found on a tower

## Parts of a church 3

**1 Altar** The table at the east end of the church from which acts of worship are conducted. It is divided from the choir by rails

**2 Brasses** Engraved brass plates attached to tombs. They usually depict the deceased

**3 Canopy** A small protective hood usually placed over a pulpit or tomb

**4 Choir screen** The partition, usually of wood, between the choir stalls and the nave of the church

**5 Credence** A small table or shelf on which is placed the bread and wine used for the communion service

**6 Easter Sepulchre** A recess in the north chancel to hold the effigy of the risen Christ used during Easter celebrations

**7 Font** A large raised fixed basin containing holy water used for baptisms

**8 Funeral** A wooden painted shield, or hatchment, bearing the arms of deceased member of the local gentry

**9 Lectern** A desk or stand designed to hold a bible or large service book

**10 Misericord** A ledge, often decorated or carved, projecting from the underside of a hinged seat, built to support a standing person

**11 Pew** Wooden seating for the congregation

**12 Piscina** A stone basin with a drain placed near the altar and used for washing the sacred vessels

**13 Pulpit** An elevated platform, often approached by a flight of steps, from which the congregation is addressed

**14 Reredos** A decorated screen behind the altar

**15 Rood** A cross or crucifix placed in the east part of the nave and in front of the choir stalls

**16 Roodscreen** The support to the rood, often in elaborately carved wood or stone

**17 Screen** A parclose screen is one around an altar or shrine

**18 Sedilia** Seats for the clergy, often recessed into the wall

**19 Squint** A small slit in the wall or pier to enable members of the congregation (originally lepers in a separate room) to have sight of the altar

**20 Stall** Another name for a pew

**21 Stoup** Basin of holy water near the church entrance

# VISUAL ARTS GLOSSARY
## Painting

**abstract** Refers to artworks which do not depict objects from nature but rely on pure form for effect

**alla prima** To execute an oil painting in a single sitting

**aquatint** An etching technique using tonal areas

**bleeding** Where colours merge into each other while wet; the term applies mostly to watercolours

**bloom** Clouding which affects varnish on a picture if left exposed to cold and damp

**calvary** The depiction of the Crucifixion of Christ

**cartoon** A full-sized preparatory drawing on paper for a painting or mural

**charcoal** Made from charred wood, charcoal is among the oldest drawing materials. It is frequently used in making preparatory sketches

**chiaroscuro** The distribution of light and shade in an image. From two Italian words meaning clear and obscure

**collage** A technique in which pictures are built up of a variety of materials like paper, fabrics, found objects, etc. It is a method favoured by surrealists

**composition** The arrangement of the elements in a picture to achieve overall harmony. There are many theories about how to achieve this, but no reliable rules

**craquelure** The cracks in old varnish or paint

**diptych** An alterpiece made of two panels

**encaustic** An ancient painting technique in which colours are applied by hot beeswax and pressed in with a heated iron

**fête champêtre/fête galante** Paintings with a strong theme of escapism in a rural setting – in vogue in 18th-century France

**figurative** Applies to works of art which depict people, places or scenes, rather than abstract designs

**foreshortening** A technique for rendering linear perspective especially in figures, to give the impression that some part is 'closer' to the viewer than the rest

**fresco** Painting onto a freshly-plastered wall. It can be done while the plaster is wet or dry. The best-known example is Michelangelo's Sistine Chapel ceiling

**frieze** A decorative band running around the top of a wall or building

**frottage** A method of laying paper on a textured surface and rubbing it with charcoal or crayons, as in brass-rubbing

**glaze** Painting a layer of transparent colour over other colours which have already dried

**golden mean** A geometrical rule laid down by the Roman architect Vitruvius for ensuring harmonious composition. It states that the division of a line or two-dimensional figure should be such that the proportion of the smaller to the greater is the same as that of the greater to the sum of the two

**gouache** Opaque water colours

**grisaille** Paintings done entirely in shades of grey, which consequently have a sculptural feel to them

**grotesque** A decorative style making use of animals, foliage and human forms

**hard edge** A technique used mostly in abstract painting, in which the elements making up the image are clearly defined

**illumination** Primarily a medieval art form, involving the elaborate decoration of manuscripts with patterns, miniature paintings, gold leaf and even precious stones

**impasto** Heavily applied oil paints which show brush or palette-knife marks

**miniatures** Small paintings, usually portraits, made for putting in lockets or carrying around. The best examples are British, from the 16th and 17th centuries

**minimal art** Abstract painting or sculpture which uses simple geometric shapes and primary colours

**monochrome** Work done using different shades of a single colour, as opposed to polychrome (involving many colours)

**montage** Rather like collage, only involving the use of bits of other pictures, such as photos or drawings

**murals** Paintings done on walls. Frescoes are a kind of mural

**op art** A style of abstract art which exploits optical illusions, especially those conveying movement

**pastoral** An idealized depiction of rural life

**paysage** A depiction of the countryside, a rural landscape

**pentimento** Traces of a painting which show through a later image painted on top

**perspective** The technique of rendering the impression of three-dimensional space on a two-dimensional surface. It involves the use of one or two vanishing points

**pietà** A depiction of the Virgin Mary mourning over the body of Christ

**pointillism** A technique in which forms are made up of many closely spaced dots of colour

**sfumato** A very smooth gradation of tone, giving a hazy effect

**sgraffito** A decorative technique in which the top layer of glaze or pigment is scratched away to reveal the colour beneath

**silhouette** A picture showing a head or figure in profile, often cut from black paper

**still life** A depiction of a group of inanimate objects like a bowl of fruit

**stipple** Applying small spots of colour with the tip of a brush

**tempera** Pigment mixed with some substance such as egg yolk, to give a very permanent paint

**tint** A colour

**tondo** A circular painting or relief

**tone** The shade or value of a particular colour

**triptych** An altarpiece made of three panels

**trompe l'oeil** A style of painting which tries to convey objects so realistically that they are mistaken as genuine. From the French, meaning 'deceiving the eye'

**underpainting** The first layer of a picture, which indicates the general design and main areas of light and shade. It must be low in oil content, to allow later layers to dry without cracking

**vignette** A picture, usually small and decorative, the edges of which fade away softly rather than end in a border or frame

**wash** A coat of diluted water colour applied to a background

**watercolour** Generally, any water-soluble paint

## Sculpture and pottery terms

**alabaster** Substance used for sculpting that resembles marble

**anaglyph** A sculpture or carving in low relief

**armature** A framework to support clay or other modelling material

**atlas, telamon** A supporting column decoratively carved as a male statue

**banker** The name given to a sculptor's workbench

**basaltware** Black pottery that is unglazed

**bas-relief, basso rilievo, low relief** A type of sculpture in which the form projects slightly, but is not separate from, the background

**biscuit, bisque** Pottery that is unglazed

**bone china** Porcelain made of clay mixed with bone ash

**calvary** A sculpture of the Crucifixion of Christ

**cameo** A small portrait in low relief, with the projecting form in a different colour from the background

**cameoware** Pottery with a coloured background and raised designs in white

**caryatid** A supporting column decoratively carved as a female statue

**celadon ware** Pottery coloured with a pale grey-green glaze

**chryselephantine** A statue either made of or overlaid with ivory and gold

*cire perdue*, **lost-wax process** A method by which bronze is cast using a mould formed around a wax pattern, which is then melted and drained away

**corbeil** A decorative carving resembling a basket of fruit or flowers

**crackle ware** Pottery exhibiting a network of fine cracks in the glaze

**diaglyph** A decorative carving with the design cut into it

**faience** Fine pottery named after Faenza, Italy, decorated with a colourful glaze

**gesso** Plaster of Paris or gypsum mix used to prepare a painting surface or as a base for low-relief sculpture

**intaglio** A method of carving in which a design is cut into the material

**ironstone** Pottery that is hard and white

**jasper ware** Design of stoneware pottery invented by Josiah Wedgwood, in which a raised white design contrasts with a coloured (usually blue) background

**maiolica, majolica** Pottery that is brightly decorated in 16th-century Italian style

**mantle** A clay mould formed around a wax model, which is then melted and drained away

**maquette, bozzetto** A practice model made before a sculpture

**mobile** A sculpture suspended in midair which has balanced parts that move when pushed or blown

**nankeen** Pottery, originally imported from Nanking, with a Chinese-style blue and white design

**Parian ware** White porcelain of fine texture that resembles marble

**pietà** A sculpture showing the Virgin Mary mourning over the body of Christ

**putto, amorino** A sculpture of a small boy, cherub or Cupid

**relief, relievo** A type of sculpture in which the form half projects, but is not separate, from the background

**restrike** Re-use of a sculptor's mould sometime after it was first used

**stabile** A stationary, hanging abstract construction

**stoneware** Pottery fired at a high temperature and glazed with salt

**terracotta** Pottery made of a mix of clay and fine sand that is unglazed

## MUSICAL NOTATION

# COMPARATIVE PITCHES OF INSTRUMENTS

## Woodwind

1 Piccolo
2 Flutes
3 Clarinet
4 Oboes
5 Cor anglais
6 Bass clarinet
7 Bassoons
8 Contrabassoon

## Brass

9 French horns
10 Trumpets
11 Tenor trombones
12 Tuba

## Percussion

13 Timpani

**Strings**
14 Harp
15 1st violins
16 2nd violins
17 Violas

18 Cellos
19 Double basses
20 Piano

# ORCHESTRAL FAMILIES
## Woodwind
1 Piccolo
2 Flutes
3 Oboes
4 Cor anglais
5 Clarinets
6 Bass clarinet
7 Bassoons
8 Contrabassoon

## Brass
9 Horns
10 Trumpets
11 Trombones
12 Tuba

## Percussion
13 Tam-tam
14 Cymbals
15 Xylophone
16 Glockenspiel
17 Tubular bells
18 Side drum
19 Bass drum
20 Timpani

## Strings
21 Harp
22 1st violins
23 2nd violins
24 Violas
25 Cellos
26 Double basses

# GROUPS OF MUSICIANS

The names given to groups made up of specific numbers of musicians are listed below. These groups include either vocalists or instrumentalists, or a combination of both. The instruments used depend on the musical piece being performed.

**1** Soloist
**2** Duet
**3** Trio
**4** Quartet
**5** Quintet
**6** Sextet
**7** Septet
**8** Octet

# BALLET MOVEMENTS

**1** The Five Basic Positions

**2 Fouetté** (A whipped movement)
Step executed on point, the working
leg whipped out to the side and in to
the knee with a slight circular
movement. Frequently combined
with turns as *fouetté en tournant* to
which it gives momentum

**3 Attitude** A pose on one leg with
the corresponding arm open to the
side or back, the other leg extended
back at 90° with the knee bent,
corresponding arm raised above
the head

**4 Pirouette** A turn on one foot
propelled by a swing of the arm

**5 Arabesque** A pose as though
poised for flight, supported on one
leg, the other extended backwards
and the arms disposed
harmoniously, usually with the
greatest reach

**6 Grande jeté** A leap from one
foot to the other

**7 Pas de deux** A sequence,
walking or dancing, for two
people

**8 Cabriole** A leap with one leg
outstretched, the other leg
beating against it

# 6

# THE BRITISH ISLES

## LOCATION AND PARTS

**Location of major islands**

**1 North** 58° 40' 24" N:
Easter Head, Dunnet Head,
Scotland
**2 East** 1° 46' 20" E:
Lowestoft Ness, Lowestoft,
Suffolk
**3 South** 49° 57' 33" N:
Lizard Point, Cornwall
**4 West** 10° 32' W: Great
Blasket Island, Co. Kerry,
Republic of Ireland

**The Parts**

**1 The British Isles**

A geographical term used to
describe the United Kingdom
of Great Britain and Northern
Ireland, the Republic of
Ireland, the Isle of Man and
the Channel Islands.
Area: 314 798 sq km.

**2 Ireland**

The second largest island in the
British Isles, politically divided
between Northern Ireland and
the Republic of Ireland.
Area: 84 434 sq km.

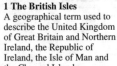

## Great Britain

The geographical and political name of the biggest island of the British Isles group. It does not include offshore islands such as the Isle of Wight, Anglesey or Shetland.

### The United Kingdom (UK)

A political term used to describe the union of England, Scotland and Northern Ireland and their offshore islands.

**1 England** The geographical and political name of the southern part of Great Britain which is governed by English law. Area: 130 441 sq km.

**2 Scotland** The northern part of Great Britain, governed by Scottish law. Area: 78 775 sq km.

**3 Wales** The Principality of Wales is politically part of England, though geographically distinct. Area: 20 768 sq km.

**4 Northern Ireland** Part of the UK consisting of six counties in the north-eastern part of Ireland. Area: 14 120 sq km.

# UNITED KINGDOM

Red Green

Blue Yellow

**England**

**Scotland**

**Wales**

**Northern Ireland**

The national flag is the Union Flag, known as the Union Jack. It symbolizes the union of England, Scotland and Ireland, being a combination of the crosses of St George, St Andrew and St Patrick. The nations of England and Wales united in 1536. Scotland was united with England in 1707, having shared its king since 1603. Northern Ireland was federated to Great Britain in 1921. Direct rule dates from 1974.

**Flag** The Cross of St George.
**Emblem** The double rose, with red outer and white inner petals. It dates from the Wars of the Roses. When Lancastrian King Henry VII married Elizabeth of York he united the warring parties. This was symbolized by joining the two flowers.

**Patron Saint** A Roman Christian who visited Britain and was martyred for his faith. His remains were taken to Lydda where, according to legend, Perseus rescued Andromeda and slayed a seamonster, the origin of St George as a dragon-slayer. He became patron saint around 1160.

**Flag** The Cross of St Andrew, patron saint of Scotland. The cross represents the crucifix on which St Andrew was martyred.
**Emblem** The thistle.
**Patron Saint** Andrew was an Apostle, the brother of Simon Peter. Martyred around AD 65, his relics were taken to Constantinople, and later to St Andrews. He was adopted as Scotland's patron saint around AD 740.

**Flag** A red dragon on a green and white field.
**Emblem** The leek. Tradition has it that Welsh soldiers wore leeks during the Battle of Poitiers.
**Patron Saint** St David lived in the 6th century AD. St David's Cathedral is on the site of his original monastery. The patron of Wales from an early date, David was only canonized in 1180. Pope Calixtus declared that two pilgrimages to St David's were equal in merit to a single one to Rome.

**Flag** A red cross on a white field, with a white six-pointed star enclosing a red hand. Above the star a yellow crown. The points of the star represent the six counties.
**Emblem** The shamrock. According to legend, St Patrick used the shamrock's three leaves to teach the Holy Trinity.

**Patron Saint** Originally Magonus Succetus Patricius, Patrick was a Roman who was called in a dream to go and convert the Irish to Christianity and was the most successful missionary of the time. He died around AD 460.

# CROWN DEPENDENCIES

Crown dependencies are territories which are associated
with the UK but not part of it. They have independent
legislative bodies, legal and administrative systems.

### The Isle of Man (Ellan Vannin)

**Capital** Douglas
**Population** 69 280
**Flag** Three white and gold
legs armed, conjoined on a
red background.

### The Channel Islands

**Jersey**

**Capital** St Helier
**Population** 80 212
**Flag** A red diagonal cross on
a white background.

**Guernsey**

**Capital** St Peter Port
**Population** 54 380
**Flag** Gold cross imposed on
a red cross on a white field.

---

**Other inhabited islands**

| | |
|---|---|
| Alderney | Herm |
| Sark | Brechau |
| Little Sark | |

---

**Uninhabited islands**

| | |
|---|---|
| Jethou | Burhou |
| Lithou | The Casquets |
| Ortach | Les Minquiers |

 Red          Gold

# BRITISH DEPENDENT TERRITORIES

British dependent territories are the colonial holdings which represent the last of the British empire.

1 Anguilla
2 Bermuda
3 British Antarctic Territory
4 British Indian Ocean Territory
5 British Virgin Islands
6 Cayman Islands
7 Falkland Islands
8 Gibraltar
9 Hong Kong
10 Montserrat
11 Pitcairn Island
12 St Helena, Ascension Island, Tristan da Cunha
13 South Georgia
14 Turks and Caicos Islands

## **POPULATION**

### 1991 estimates (000s)

| | | | |
|---|---|---|---|
| **1** England | 46 382 | **3** Wales | 2 812 |
| **2** Scotland | 4 962 | **4** N. Ireland | 1 583 |
| | | UK | 55 739 |

### Densities (people per sq km)

| | | | |
|---|---|---|---|
| **1** England | 360 | **3** N. Ireland | 112 |
| **2** Wales | 140 | **4** Scotland | 60 |
| | | UK | 228 |

**High population**
over 200 per sq km

**Low population**
under 5 per sq km

### **Regional population**

Densities (people per sq km)

| | | | |
|---|---|---|---|
| **1** Greater London | 4 230 | **6** West Yorkshire | 990 |
| **2** West Midlands urban area | 2 840 | **7** South Yorkshire | 810 |
| **3** Merseyside | 2 140 | **8** Outer London area | 610 |
| **4** Tyne and Wear | 2 030 | **9** Remainder of North-west | 430 |
| **5** Greater Manchester | 1 940 | **10** Outer South-east area | 300 |

## CITIES

## Cities of the United Kingdom

### Scotland

1 Aberdeen
2 Dundee
3 Edinburgh
4 Elgin
5 Glasgow
6 Perth

### England

7 Bath
8 Birmingham
9 Bradford
10 Bristol
11 Cambridge
12 Canterbury
13 Carlisle
14 Chester
15 Chichester
16 Coventry
17 Derby
18 Durham
19 Ely
20 Exeter
21 Gloucester
22 Hereford
23 Kingston upon Hull
24 Lancaster
25 Leeds
26 Leicester
27 Lichfield
28 Lincoln
29 Liverpool
30 London
31 Manchester
32 Newcastle upon Tyne
33 Norwich
34 Nottingham
35 Oxford
36 Peterborough
37 Plymouth
38 Portsmouth
39 Ripon
40 Rochester upon Medway
41 St Albans
42 Salford
43 Salisbury
44 Sheffield
45 Southampton
46 Stoke-on-Trent
47 Sunderland
48 Truro
49 Wakefield
50 Wells
51 Westminster
52 Winchester
53 Worcester
54 York

### Wales

55 Bangor
56 Cardiff
57 Swansea

### Northern Ireland

58 Belfast
59 Londonderry

---

**Britain's 10 largest urban areas (000s)**

Indicated on map by ⊙

| | | | |
|---|---|---|---|
| 7 567 | Greater London (**30**) | 776 | Warrington (**60**) |
| 2 339 | Birmingham urban area (**8**) | 755 | Glasgow (**5**) |
| 2 320 | Greater Manchester (**31**) | 748 | Liverpool (**29**) |
| 1 467 | Leeds urban area (**25**) | 635 | Sheffield (**44**) |
| | | 594 | Nottingham (**34**) |
| | | 517 | Bristol (**10**) |

# REGIONS (1993)
## The Counties and Shires of England

1 Avon
2 Bedfordshire
3 Berkshire
4 Buckinghamshire
5 Cambridgeshire
6 Cheshire
7 Cleveland
8 Cornwall
9 Cumbria
10 Derbyshire
11 Devon
12 Dorset
13 Durham
14 East Sussex
15 Essex
16 Gloucestershire
17 Greater London
18 Greater Manchester
19 Hampshire
20 Hereford and Worcester
21 Hertfordshire
22 Humberside
23 Isle of Wight
24 Kent
25 Lancashire
26 Leicestershire
27 Lincolnshire

28 Merseyside
29 Norfolk
30 Northamptonshire
31 Northumberland
32 North Yorkshire
33 Nottinghamshire

34 Oxfordshire
35 Shropshire
36 Somerset
37 South Yorkshire
38 Staffordshire
39 Suffolk
40 Surrey
41 Tyne and Wear
42 Warwickshire
43 West Midlands
44 West Sussex
45 West Yorkshire
46 Wiltshire

### Regions of Scotland

1 Borders
2 Central
3 Dumfries and Galloway
4 Fife
5 Grampian
6 Highland
7 Lothian
8 Orkney
9 Shetland
10 Strathclyde
11 Tayside
12 Western Isles

### The Counties of Wales

1 Clwyd
2 Dyfed
3 Gwent
4 Gwynedd
5 Mid Glamorgan
6 Powys
7 South Glamorgan
8 West Glamorgan

### The Counties of Northern Ireland

1 Armagh
2 Antrim
3 Down
4 Fermanagh
5 Londonderry
6 Tyrone

## ISLANDS

The UK has over 2000 islands, the majority are less than 1 sq km in area and uninhabited

### The 10 largest islands of England

| | | | | | |
|---|---|---|---|---|---|
| **1** | Isle of Wight | 381 sq km | **6** | Canvey | 18 sq km |
| **2** | Sheppey | 94 sq km | **7** | Mersea | 18 sq km |
| **3** | Hayling | 27 sq km | **8** | Walney | 13 sq km |
| **4** | Foulness | 26 sq km | **9** | Isle of Grain | 13 sq km |
| **5** | Portsea | 24 sq km | **10** | Wallasea | 11 sq km |

### The 10 largest islands of Scotland

| | | | | | |
|---|---|---|---|---|---|
| **11** | Lewis with Harris | 2225 sq km | **16** | Mainland, Orkney | 536 sq km |
| **12** | Skye | 1666 sq km | **17** | Arran | 435 sq km |
| **13** | Mainland, Shetland | 967 sq km | **18** | Jura | 370 sq km |
| **14** | Mull | 899 sq km | **19** | North Uist | 351 sq km |
| **15** | Islay | 615 sq km | **20** | South Uist | 332 sq km |

### The five largest islands of Wales

| | | | | | |
|---|---|---|---|---|---|
| **21** | Anglesey | 714 sq km | **24** | Ramsey | 2.5 sq km |
| **22** | Holy Island | 39 sq km | **25** | Caldey | 2 sq km |
| **23** | Skomer | 3 sq km | | | |

### The principal island of Northern Ireland

| | | |
|---|---|---|
| **26** | Rathlin | 14 sq km |

### Other islands

| | | | |
|---|---|---|---|
| **27** | Benbecula | **33** | Muck |
| **28** | Eigg | **34** | Rhum |
| **29** | Farne | **35** | Thorney |
| **30** | Holy Island (Northumbria) | **36** | Fair Isle |
| **31** | Isle of May | **37** | Yell, Shetland |
| **32** | Lundy | | |

# MOUNTAINS AND MOORS

## Highlands, moorlands and downs

| | | | |
|---|---|---|---|
| **A** | Antrim Hills | **L** | Grampian Mountains |
| **B** | Berkshire Downs | **M** | Hampshire Downs |
| **C** | Berwyn Mountains | **N** | Mountains of Mourne |
| **D** | Cairngorm Mountains | **O** | North Downs |
| **E** | Cambrian Mountains | **P** | North-west Highlands |
| **F** | Cheviot Hills | **Q** | North Yorkshire Moors |
| **G** | Chiltern Hills | **R** | Pennines |
| **H** | Cotswold Hills | **S** | Sperrin Mountains |
| **I** | Cumbrian Mountains | **T** | South Downs |
| **J** | Dartmoor | **U** | Southern Uplands |
| **K** | Exmoor | **V** | Yorkshire Wolds |

## The UK's highest peaks

| Scotland | height (m) |
|---|---|
| **1** Ben Nevis (Grampian) | 1 343 |
| **2** Ben Macdui (Cairngorm) | 1 310 |
| **3** Braeriach (Cairngorm) | 1 294 |
| **4** Cairn Toul (Cairngorm) | 1 294 |
| **5** Cairn Gorm (Cairngorm) | 1 244 |
| **6** Aonach Beag (Grampian) | 1 237 |
| **7** Cairn Mor Dearg (Grampian) | 1 222 |
| **Wales** | |
| **8** Snowdon (Cambrian) | 1 085 |
| **9** Carnedd Llewelyn (Cambrian) | 1 062 |
| **10** Carnedd Dafydd (Cambrian) | 1 044 |
| **England** | |
| **11** Scafell Pike (Cumbrian) | 978 |
| **12** Sca Fell (Cumbrian) | 963 |
| **13** Helvellyn (Cumbrian) | 950 |
| **Northern Ireland** | |
| **14** Slieve Donard (Mourne) | 852 |
| **15** Slieve Commedagh (Mourne) | 767 |

# RIVERS AND LAKES

## The UK's longest rivers

### England length (km)

| | | | | | |
|---|---|---|---|---|---|
| **1** Thames | 346 | | **6** Avon | 137 |
| **2** Trent | 297 | | **7** Tees | 127 |
| **3** Aire | 259 | | **8** Tyne | 118 |
| **4** Ouse | 230 | | **9** Eden | 111 |
| **5** Nene | 161 | | **10** Wear | 104 |

### Scotland

| | | | | | |
|---|---|---|---|---|---|
| **11** Tay | 188 | | **14** Tweed | 155 |
| **12** Clyde | 158 | | **15** Dee | 137 |
| **13** Spey | 157 | | | |

### Wales

| | | | | | |
|---|---|---|---|---|---|
| **16** Severn | 354 | | **18** Dee | 112 |
| **17** Wye | 215 | | **19** Towy | 106 |

### Northern Ireland

| | |
|---|---|
| **20** Bann | 122 |

## The UK's biggest lakes

### England area (sq km)

| | | | | | |
|---|---|---|---|---|---|
| **A** Windermere | 15 | | **C** Bassenthwaite Water | 5 |
| **B** Ullswater | 9 | | | |

### Scotland

| | | | | | |
|---|---|---|---|---|---|
| **D** Loch Lomond | 71 | | **F** Loch Awe | 39 |
| **E** Loch Ness | 57 | | | |

### Wales

| | | | | | |
|---|---|---|---|---|---|
| **G** Lake Vyrnwy | 8 | | **H** Bala Lake | 4 |

### Northern Ireland

| | | | | | |
|---|---|---|---|---|---|
| **I** Lough Neagh | 382 | | **J** Lower Lough Erne | 105 |

## The UK's deepest lakes

### England depth (m)

| | | | | | |
|---|---|---|---|---|---|
| **K** Windermere | 66 | | **M** Bassenthwaite Water | 21 |
| **L** Ullswater | 62 | | | |

### Scotland

| | | | | | |
|---|---|---|---|---|---|
| **N** Loch Morar | 309 | | **P** Loch Lomond | 189 |
| **O** Loch Ness | 228 | | | |

### Wales

| | | | | | |
|---|---|---|---|---|---|
| **Q** Bala Lake | 38 | | **R** Lake Vyrnwy | 36 |

### Northern Ireland

| | | | | | |
|---|---|---|---|---|---|
| **S** Lower Lough Erne | 68 | | **T** Lough Neagh | 31 |

E,O — 13
N — 15
D,P — 11
— 12
F — 14
9 — 8
20 — 10
I,T — 7
J,S — 3
C,M — 2
B,L — 18
A,K — 5
H,Q — 4
— 1
G,R —
19 —
17 —
16  6

## TEMPERATURE
January temperature

Isotherms are lines on a map which link the places experiencing the same temperature. This map shows typical isotherms for January. The one opposite shows those for July.

**Coldest places in the UK**

**1 Coldest ever** Braemar, Scotland, −27.2 °C (10 January 1982)

**2 Coldest annual mean** Braemar, Scotland, 6.34 °C

**3 Least sunshine** Westminster, England had no sunshine at all throughout December 1890

July temperature

**Hottest places in the UK**
1 **Hottest ever** Cheltenham, England, 37.1 °C (3 August 1990)
2 **Hottest annual mean** Penzance, England and Isles of Scilly, 11.5 °C
3 **Most sunshine** Falmouth, England had 382 hours of sunshine out of a possible 488 in June 1925

# RAINFALL

Atmospheric pressure (measured in millibars) largely determines rainfall; the lower the pressure, the higher the rainfall.

Over 2500 mm
1000 –2500 mm
0 –1000 mm

**Wettest places in the UK**
1 **Most rain in a day** 279 mm (11 inches) at Martinstown, England, 18 July 1955
2 **Most rain in a year** Sprinkling Tarn, England, 6527 mm (257 inches) in 1954
3 **Most rainfall, average** Styhead, England, 4 391 mm (173 inches) per year

January pressure

July pressure

1006

1006
1008

1008
1010

1010
1012

1014

1014
1016

1016
1018

1012
1012

1014
1014

1016
1016

**Driest places in the UK**
1 **Longest drought** Mile End, London, 73 days in 1893
2 **Lowest rainfall in one year** Margate, England, 236 mm (9.29 inches) in 1921
3 **Lowest average rainfall** St Osyth, England, 513mm (20.2 inches) per year

# PROTECTED NATURAL AREAS

**National parks of England and Wales**

**The National Parks (NPS)**

These are designated to protect scenic or environmentally important areas. The public has some right of access.

**Areas of Outstanding Natural Beauty (AONB)**

Created under the same legislation as the NP. The public has no right of access.

**National Scenic Areas of Scotland (NSAS)**

National Scenic Areas are the Scottish equivalent to AONBs.

**National parks**

1 Brecon Beacons 1 344 sq km
2 Dartmoor 945 sq km
3 Exmoor 686 sq km
4 Lake District 2280 sq km
5 Northumberland 1031 sq km
6 North Yorkshire Moors
 1433 sq km
7 Peak District
 1433 sq km
8 Pembrokeshire Coast
 583 sq km
9 Snowdonia
 2171 sq km
10 Yorkshire Dales
 1762 sq km
11 The Broads
 287 sq km
12 New Forest
 130 sq km

| England | Scotland | England | Scotland |
|---|---|---|---|
| | | Henry II 1154-1189 | William 1165-1214 |
| | Malcom II 1005-1034 | Richard I 1189-1199 | |
| | Duncan I 1034-1040 | John 1199-1216 | |
| Edward the Confessor 1043-1066 | Macbeth 1040-1057 | | |
| | Lulach 1057-1058 | | Alexander II 1214-1249 |
| Harold II 1066 | | | |
| William the Conqueror 1066-1087 | Malcom III 1058-1093 | Henry III 1216-1272 | |
| William II 1087-1100 | Duncan II 1094 | | |
| | Donald Ban 1094-1007 | | |
| | Edgar 1097-1107 | | Alexander III 1249-1286 |
| Henry I 1100-1135 | Alexander 1107-1124 | | |
| | | Edward I 1272-1307 | Margaret 1286-1290 |
| | David I 1124-1153 | | John Balliol 1292-1296 |
| Stephen 1135-1154 | | | |
| | | Edward II 1307-1327 | Robert Bruce 1306-1329 |
| Henry II 1154-1189 | Malcolm IV 1153-1165 | | |

1000
1100
1200
1300

Henry VII
1485-1509

James IV
1488-1513

1500

Edward III
1327-1377

David II
1329-1371

Henry VIII
1509-1547

James V
1513-1513

Robert II
1371-1390

Edward VI
1547-1553
Lady Jane
Grey 1553
Mary I
1553-1558

Mary
1542-1567

Richard II
1377-1399

Robert III
1390-1406

Elizabeth I
1558-1603

1400

James VI
(I of England)
1567-1625

Henry IV
1399-1413
Henry V
1413-1422

James I
1406-1437

Henry VI
1422-1461

James II
1437-1460

James
I and VI of
Scotland
1603-1625

Edward IV
1461-1483

James III
1460-1488

Charles I
1625-1649

Edward V
1483
Richard III
1483-1485
Henry VII
1485-1509

James IV
1488-1513

1600

Charles II
1660-1685

James II
1685-1689
William (III) &
Mary (II)
1689-1694
William III
1694-1702
Anne
1702-1714

George I
1714-1727

1700

George II
1727-1760

George III
1760-1820

1800

George IV
1820-1830

William IV
1830-1837

Victoria
1837-1901

Edward VII
1901-1910

1900

George V
1910-1936

Edward VIII
1936

Geroge VI
1936-1952

Elizabeth II
1952-

2000

# BRITISH PRIME MINISTERS

| Term | Prime Minister | Party |
|------|----------------|-------|
| 1721 - 1742 | Sir Robert Walpole | Whig |
| 1742 - 1743 | Earl of Wilmington | Whig |
| 1743 - 1754 | Henry Pelham | Whig |
| 1754 - 1756 | Duke of Newcastle | Whig |
| 1756 - 1757 | Duke of Devonshire | Whig |
| 1757 - 1762 | Duke of Newcastle | Whig |
| 1762 - 1763 | Earl of Bute | Tory |
| 1763 - 1765 | George Grenville | Whig |
| 1765 - 1768 | Marquis of Rockingham | Whig |
| 1766 - 1768 | Earl of Chatham | Whig |
| 1768 - 1770 | Duke of Grafton | Whig |
| 1770 - 1782 | Lord North | Tory |
| 1782 | Marquis of Rockingham | Whig |
| 1782 - 1782 | Earl of Shelburne | Whig |
| 1783 | Duke of Portland | Coalition |
| 1783 - 1801 | William Pitt | Tory |
| 1801 - 1804 | Henry Addington | Tory |
| 1804 - 1806 | William Pitt | Tory |
| 1806 - 1807 | Lord Grenville | Whig |
| 1807 - 1809 | Duke of Portland | Tory |
| 1809 - 1812 | Spencer Perceval | Tory |
| 1812 - 1827 | Earl of Liverpool | Tory |
| 1822 | George Canning | Tory |
| 1827 - 1827 | Viscount Goderich | Tory |
| 1828 - 1830 | Duke of Wellington | Tory |
| 1830 - 1834 | Earl Grey | Whig |
| 1834 | Viscount Melbourne | Whig |
| 1834 - 1835 | Sir Robert Peel | Tory |
| 1835 - 1841 | Viscount Melbourne | Whig |
| 1841 - 1846 | Sir Robert Peel | Tory |
| 1846 - 1852 | Lord John Russell | Whig |
| 1852 | Earl of Derby | Tory |
| 1852 - 1855 | Earl of Aberdeen | Peelite |
| 1855 - 1858 | Viscount Palmerston | Liberal |
| 1858 - 1859 | Earl of Derby | Conservative |
| 1859 - 1865 | Viscount Palmerston | Liberal |
| 1865 - 1866 | Earl Russell | Liberal |
| 1866 - 1868 | Earl of Derby | Conservative |

| | | |
|---|---|---|
| 1868 | Benjamin Disraeli | Conservative |
| 1868 - 1874 | William Gladstone | Liberal |
| 1874 - 1880 | Benjamin Disraeli | Conservative |
| 1880 - 1885 | William Gladstone | Liberal |
| 1885 - 1886 | Marquis of Salisbury | Conservative |
| 1886 | William Gladstone | Liberal |
| 1886 - 1892 | Marquis of Salisbury | Conservative |
| 1892 - 1894 | William Gladstone | Liberal |
| 1894 - 1895 | Earl of Rosebery | Liberal |
| 1895 - 1902 | Marquis of Salisbury | Conservative |
| 1902 - 1905 | Arthur Balfour | Conservative |
| 1905 - 1908 | Sir Henry Campbell-Bannerman | Liberal |
| 1908 - 1915 | Herbert Asquith | Liberal |
| 1915 - 1916 | Herbert Asquith | Coalition |
| 1916 - 1922 | David Lloyd-George | Coalition |
| 1922 - 1923 | Andrew Bonar Law | Conservative |
| 1923 - 1924 | Stanley Baldwin | Conservative |
| 1924 | James Ramsay MacDonald | Labour |
| 1924 - 1929 | Stanley Baldwin | Conservative |
| 1929 - 1931 | James Ramsay MacDonald | Labour |
| 1931 - 1935 | James Ramsay MacDonald | Coalition |
| 1935 - 1937 | Stanley Baldwin | Coalition |
| 1937 - 1940 | Neville Chamberlain | Coalition |
| 1940 - 1945 | Winston Churchill | Coalition |
| 1945 | Winston Churchill | Conservative |
| 1945 - 1951 | Clement Attlee | Labour |
| 1951 - 1955 | Sir Winston Churchill | Conservative |
| 1955 - 1957 | Sir Anthony Eden | Conservative |
| 1957 - 1963 | Harold Macmillan | Conservative |
| 1963 - 1964 | Sir Alec Douglas-Home | Conservative |
| 1964 - 1970 | Harold Wilson | Labour |
| 1970 - 1974 | Edward Heath | Conservative |
| 1974 - 1976 | Harold Wilson | Labour |
| 1976 - 1979 | James Callaghan | Labour |
| 1979 - 1990 | Margaret Thatcher | Conservative |
| 1990 - | John Major | Conservative |

# REPUBLIC OF IRELAND (EIRE)

**Area** 70 282 sq km  **People per sq km** 53
**Population** 3.5 million

The Irish tricolour of three vertical stripes came into use around 1848, and symbolizes Catholics (green) and Protestants (orange) unified in peace (white).

Ireland's national emblem is the shamrock, and the patron saint is St Patrick. For details, see the section on Northern Ireland.

## Provinces and counties

**Ulster**
1 Donegal
2 Cavan
3 Monaghan

**Munster**
4 Clare
5 Cork
6 Kerry
7 Limerick
8 Tipperary
9 Waterford

**Leinster**
10 Carlow
11 Dublin
12 Kildare
13 Kilkenny
14 Laois
15 Longford
16 Louth
17 Meath
18 Offaly
19 Westmeath
20 Wexford
21 Wicklow

**Connacht**
22 Galway
23 Leitrim
24 Mayo
25 Roscommon
26 Sligo

**Major cities (with population)**

| | | |
|---|---|---|
| **A** | Dublin | 502 000 |
| **B** | Cork | 133 000 |

**Longest rivers (km)**

| | | |
|---|---|---|
| **1** | Shannon | 393 |
| **2** | Barrow | 191 |
| **3** | Suir | 138 |
| **4** | Erne | 116 |
| **5** | Boyne | 113 |

**Principal lakes (sq km)**

| | | |
|---|---|---|
| **6** | Lough Corrib | 176 |
| **7** | Lough Ree | 145 |
| **8** | Lough Derg | 96 |
| **9** | Lough Conn | 93 |
| **10** | Lough Mask | 83 |

**Ireland's highest mountains (m)**

| | | |
|---|---|---|
| **11** | Carrauntual | 1 041 |
| **12** | Beenkeragh | 1 010 |
| **13** | Caher | 975 |
| **14** | Ridge of the Reeks | 975 |
| **15** | Brandon | 953 |

**Principal islands (sq km)**

| | | |
|---|---|---|
| **16** | Achill Island | 147 |
| **17** | Valentia Island | 33 |
| **18** | Inishmore | 31 |
| **19** | Clare Island | 20 |

Highlands

# COLLINS GEM

Other Gem titles that may interest you include:

**Gem Wine**
An A-Z guide to the wines of the world featuring over 1800 wine terms, all clearly explained   **£3.50**

**Gem Calorie Counter**
New revised edition, with additional nutritional information for thousands of branded foods   **£2.99**

**Gem Ready Reference**
A unique compilation of information from the world of measures, with quick reference conversion tables and helpful illustrations   **£2.99**

**Gem Quotations**
Featuring over 4000 entries, this is an ideal reference source for anyone searching for a quotable quote   **£3.50**

**Gem Babies Names**
A fascinating guide to over 2000 names, explaining their origins, meaning and evolution   **£2.99**

# COLLINS GEM

## Bestselling Collins Gem titles include:

*Gem English Dictionary* (£3.50)

*Gem Calorie Counter* (£2.99)

*Gem Thesaurus* (£2.99)

*Gem French Dictionary* (£3.50)

*Gem German Dictionary* (£3.50)

*Gem Basic Facts Mathematics* (£2.99)

*Gem Birds* (£3.50)

*Gem Babies' Names* (£3.50)

*Gem Card Games* (£3.50)

*Gem Atlas of the World* (£3.50)